T.S. ELIOT AND EARLY MODERN LITERATURE

T.S. Eliot and Early Modern Literature

STEVEN MATTHEWS

OXFORD

UNIVERSITY PRESS

OXFORD
UNIVERSITY PRESS

Great Clarendon Street, Oxford, OX2 6DP,
United Kingdom

Oxford University Press is a department of the University of Oxford.
It furthers the University's objective of excellence in research, scholarship,
and education by publishing worldwide. Oxford is a registered trade mark of
Oxford University Press in the UK and in certain other countries

First Edition published in 2013

Impression: 2

British Library Cataloguing in Publication Data
Data available

ISBN 978–0–19–957477–3

Printed in Great Britain by
MPG Printgroup

Acknowledgements

I am grateful to the following, for various conversations across a number of years which have inflected the ideas in this book: Helen Farish, Matthew Feldman, Katherine Firth, Nancy K. Gish, Hugh Haughton, Alan Marshall, Gail Marshall, Nigel Messenger, Catherine Morley, Fiona Sampson, Ashley Taggart, John Whale.

Library staff at the following libraries have been extremely helpful: Bodleian Library, University of Oxford; Brotherton Library, University of Leeds; Houghton Library, University of Harvard; King's College, University of Cambridge.

I am grateful to the British Academy, for a travel grant which enabled the visit to Harvard. Oxford Brookes University supported the completion of the book with a period of study leave.

Andrew McNeillie was a wonderfully enthusiastic encourager of the project at the outset; more recently I have benefited from the support and insight of Jacqueline Baker at Oxford University Press. The editorial work of Richard Mason has been invaluable to this book.

The book has also been improved considerably from careful and generous reading by Elleke Boehmer, Alex Goody, and Tiffany Stern.

Some portions of Chapter Two originally appeared as pages in 'Calculated Indifference: T.S. Eliot's Debt to J.M. Robertson', *American Modernism: Cultural Transactions*, edited by Catherine Morley and Alex Goody (Cambridge Scholars, 2009).

This book is dedicated to Elleke, and to those Skying boys, Thomas and Sam.

Steven Matthews
June 2012

Contents

Contents

Note to the Reader

Across this book the designation of that earlier literary period, with which Eliot's work is perceived to be in dialogue, can be confusing. Eliot used the term 'Elizabethan', in a lecture course in 1918–9 as elsewhere, to designate a period of literature produced roughly between 1565 and 1625—in other words from the Elizabethan through the Jacobean age. In doing so, he was to an extent following contemporary critical practice. Elsewhere again, however, he called the same period the 'Renaissance', deploying a term now considered appropriate only for Italian literature and artworks of a slightly earlier period. This same time was also called, by some critics contemporary with Eliot, 'The Age of Shakespeare'.

This book will use the designation 'Early Modern', according to recent scholarly practice, broadly to cover the period of Eliot's fascination. It reserves 'Elizabethan' and 'Renaissance' only for relevant titles and quotations from sources relevant to Eliot, or from his own work.

Where possible, this book cites editions of Early Modern poetry, prose, and drama that the bibliographical sources given in the text prove to be the ones Eliot owned, or with which he was familiar. In a few cases it has been impossible to identify those editions, and, as indicated, quotation is, in those cases, given from standard current texts. This means that readers will experience the important Early Modern sources for Eliot in a mixture of old spelling and standardized modern English versions. Since this book aims to provide the early twentieth-century context for Eliot's understanding of what the Early Modern period could be made to mean, only rarely does it allude to more recent scholarship and criticism of Early Modern works.

Abbreviations Used in References to Works by Eliot

CPP   *The Complete Poems and Plays of T.S. Eliot*, London: Faber, 1969; 1978 edition

FLA   *For Lancelot Andrewes*, London: Faber, 1928; 1970 edition

IMH   *Inventions of the March Hare: Poems 1909–1917*, edited by Christopher Ricks, London: Faber, 1996

LI   *The Letters of T.S. Eliot, Volume I, 1898–1922, Revised Edition*, edited by Valerie Eliot and Hugh Haughton, London: Faber, 2009

LII   *The Letters of T.S. Eliot, Volume II, 1923–1925*, edited by Valerie Eliot and Hugh Haughton, London: Faber, 2009

OPP   *On Poetry and Poets*, London: Faber, 1957

SE   *Selected Essays*, London: Faber, 1934; 1972 edition

SW   *The Sacred Wood: Essays on Poetry and Criticism*, London: Faber, 1928; 1997 edition

TCC   *To Criticize the Critic and other writings*, London: Faber, 1965; 1988 edition

UPUC *The Use of Poetry and the Use of Criticism*, London: Faber, 1933; 1967 edition

VMP   *The Varieties of Metaphysical Poetry*, edited and introduced by Ronald Schuchard, London: Faber, 1993

WLFT *The Waste Land: a facsimile and transcript*, edited by Valerie Eliot, London: Faber, 1971

Introduction

In a radio talk of December 1957, in which he presented and introduced readings of some of his favourite Early Modern poems in English, T.S. Eliot reminisced about his first encounter with the poem read out at the end of the broadcast. He recalled that, aged eleven or twelve, he had undergone frequent visits to a dentist, in order to have his teeth straightened. He therefore gained, in unfortunate circumstances, ample opportunity to read *The Collected Works of Edgar Allan Poe*, a set of which stood in the waiting room. One of Poe's Tales, in particular, grabbed his interest, not just for its content, but for the enigmatic epigraph at its head:

> Stay for me there! I shall not fail
> To meet thee in that hollow vale.

Eliot recalled that his young self was restless, until he had tracked down and read the full poem from which Poe had derived these lines: Bishop Henry King's plaintive elegy for his wife who had died in 1624, 'The Exequy'. Eliot also asserted, in this talk, that 'I get as keen a thrill today from that poem as did the boy who read it so many years ago.' Obviously in celebration of the prospect of a new-found marital happiness (for he would remarry shortly), Eliot talked about King's exceptional lyric not only as a 'love poem', but also as a poem about 'conjugal love at its highest'. It is, though, a love sadly 'matured and enriched by the experience of married happiness and of its loss'.[1]

King's poem stands for Eliot, therefore, as a moving example of an achieved, and as yet un-shadowed love. It is a love of a kind that drew Eliot across his life, and which dictated his choice of other of his favoured texts, such as Shakespeare's *Antony and Cleopatra*, or Dryden's variant upon the story, *All for Love*.[2] The combination of intense emotion, and of loss through death, is, as this study shows, one that often grounds Eliot's fascination with particular works from earlier literature. More immediately, King's couplet stands both in ironic commentary upon, and in summary encapsulation of, the story to which Poe set it as epigraph, 'The Assignation'. This is the tale of a frustrated love, between the beautiful young Marchesa di

---

[1] The script for Eliot's broadcast on 18 December 1957 is held at the BBC Written Archives Centre, Caversham, file 48114. Peter Ackroyd gives a brief, unspecific account of this incident, relating it to the way Eliot, early on, is already attuned to poetry, in *T.S. Eliot* (London: Abacus, 1985, 27).

[2] In a letter to the Shakespeare critic G. Wilson Knight, of 30 December 1930, Eliot admired the 'gradual development' of the love between Antony and Cleopatra, compared to Coriolanus's sudden 'conversion' to emotion. In particular he imagined the way love becomes 'the real thing', in Cleopatra's dying words, 'Husband! I come!' Brotherton Library, Leeds. MS 20c Knight 2(K).

Mentoni, who is married to a much older husband, and a Stranger with whom, the reader is left to surmise, she has had an illegitimate child. Through her neglect or desperation, the Marchesa allows the child to slip from her arms through an open upper window in her palace, into one of Venice's main canals. This is the incident with which the story opens; the watchful Stranger saves the drowning child, and later takes the tale's narrator to his elaborately decorated apartment to recount something of his love, to explain his presence near the canal at that moment. Then, on learning that the Marchesa has committed suicide during the night, the Stranger poisons himself in front of the narrator. The Stranger's last words repeat the epigraph's King couplet, while he slips into unconsciousness in order to join his lover, as King had imagined, in death.

Poe's 'The Assignation' is freighted with motifs that will recur in Eliot's poetry. The narrator's first glimpse of the Marchesa comes as she is posed 'alone' upon marble steps overlooking the canal, into which her child has fallen:

> Her hair, not as yet more than half loosened for the night from its ball-room array, clustered, amid a shower of diamonds, round and round her classical head, in curls like those of the young hyacinth.

Poe's image is close to the 'hyacinth hair' of the girl in his youthful poem 'To Helen'. But the Tale's scene anticipates Eliot's 'La Figlia Che Piange', with its similarly posed young woman grieving over a lost love—a woman whose hair is particularly an object of the speaker's gaze. This woman is surrounded by, and carries, flowers.[3] Like 'The Assignation', 'La Figlia Che Piange' also is spoken by a commentator on the trials of its watched-over lovers. Then, of course, such imagery is, in turn, also a precursor to the 'hyacinth girl' of *The Waste Land*. This connection between Poe's story and *The Waste Land* continues, as, when Poe's narrator arrives at the Stranger's apartment, he is overwhelmed by the profusion of styles for the many art objects with which he is greeted:

> Little attention had been paid to the *decora* of what is technically called *keeping*, or to the proprieties of nationality. The eye wandered from object to object, and rested upon none—neither the *grotesques* of the Greek painters, nor the sculptures of the best Italian days, nor the huge carvings of untutored Egypt.[4]

Such visual wandering amidst '*decora*' opens Part II of *The Waste Land*, with its room containing paintings of scenes from classical mythology, and its descriptions in various references to *Antony and Cleopatra*.

---

[3] Eliot seems drawn to similar passages in earlier literature, even when they indicate misunderstanding on the part of original speakers. He quotes a passage about a woman's hair from John Fletcher's *The Faithful Shepherdess* (1609?) in 'Ben Jonson' (1919). These lines are part of a catalogue of the title character's physical virtues: 'Hair woven in many a curious warp/Able in endless error to enfold/The wandering soul.' (*SE*, 156) The original lines, however, display the delusion of their speaker, Thenot, since Clorin, indeed, remains faithful to her (dead) lover (*Select Plays of Beaumont and Fletcher*, Introduction by G.P. Baker, London: Dent, 1907, 262). See also the lines addressed by David to the approaching Bersabe, who 'brings my longings tangled in her hair', from Peele's *The Love of David for Fair Bersabe*, in 'Seneca in Elizabethan Translation' (1927) (*SE*, 88).

[4] *The Complete Tales and Poems of Edgar Allan Poe* (Harmondsworth: Penguin, 1965), 294, 297.

At the moment of his death, Poe's Stranger in *his* apartment becomes, in a conceit which Eliot will draw on again and again in his references to Early Modern writing such as King's, almost interchangeable with his art objects. For Poe's narrator finds words from another of Eliot's favourite Early Modern works, George Chapman's tragic play *Bussy d'Ambois*, quivering 'instinctively' on his lips, as he contemplates the Stranger standing before a portrait he has had painted of the Marchesa. Poe's speaker gives two lines from the speech made by Chapman's hero very close to death, and transposes the pronouns to fit the tale ('he is up', 'he will stand'). I will give an extended version of the speech which includes these lines, as they play such an important role in Eliot's critical thinking, and poetic understanding, across his career:

> The equall thought I beare of life and death,
> Shall make me faint on no one side; I am up
> Here like a Roman statue, I will stand
> Till death hath made me marble. O my fame
> Live in despight of murther! take thy wings
> And haste thee where the gray-ey'd morn perfumes
> Her rosie chariot with Sabaean spices!
> Fly, where the evening from th'Iberean vales,
> Takes on her swarthy shoulders *Heccate*
> Crown'd with a grove of oakes! flie where men feele
> The burning axletree: and those that suffer
> Beneath the chariot of the Snowy Beare:
> And tell them all that D'Ambois now is hasting
> To the eternall dwellers.... (V.3.138–51)[5]

Bussy holds both life and death together in his mind as he approaches his end, an antithesis repeated in much of Eliot's mature writing ('Death is life and life is death', as Sweeney quirkily puts it in *Sweeney Agonistes* [*CPP*, 125]). Bussy imagines himself morphing into a statue, rather than suffering physical death, as a way of rebutting 'murder'. But his is to be a Roman statue, validated by noble history. Bussy imagines his fame living on beyond his life, in a similar demand to that

---

[5] In the 'Conclusion' to *The Use of Poetry and the Use of Criticism* (1933), Eliot recommends Frederick S. Boas's edition of Chapman's *Bussy d'Ambois and the Revenge* as the best edition. These lines appear in this version in that edition (Boston: D.C. Heath, 1905, 137). Eliot references the lines in that 'Conclusion', whilst noting the 'personal saturation value' for him of the Bussy example. (*UPUC*, 147, 149). That 'value' is amply demonstrated by Eliot's reference to Bussy's speech across his critical work. The passage is cited many times, from *The Varieties of Metaphysical Poetry* (1926) to 'The Sources of Chapman' (1927), 'Thinking in Verse' (1930) and 'John Dryden II' (1931). This 'Conclusion' is significant for noting that the version of *Bussy d'Ambois* with which Eliot had originally been working was 'inaccurate', particularly in its reference in the lines quoted in 'Reflections on Contemporary Poetry', to a 'cunning axletree'. The inaccurate text was the Mermaid *The Plays of George Chapman*, edited by William Lyon Phelps (New York: Charles Scribner's Sons, 1895)—the volume registered in the Bodleian inventory of Eliot's library. Frederick S. Boas's edition contains the more accurate 'burning axletree'. Eliot's comfort with 'cunning axletree' in his early citations of Chapman's passage, however, fits once again with *his* contemporary poetry writing: 'History has many cunning passages', as Gerontion puts it (*CPP*, 38). 'Burning axletree' appears, as Milton cites Chapman, in 'On the Morning of Christ's Nativity', which Grierson included in *Metaphysical Lyrics and Poems of the Seventeenth Century* (Oxford: Clarendon Press, 1921, 98).

made by Shakespeare's Othello near his end. Othello's is a demand that Eliot in 1919, and again in 1927, would compare to Bussy's, and which has key significance for the poet's developed theological and ontological thought, which uniquely combines a secular reading of alienated selfhood with a complex grounding in Early Modern religious writings (*SE*, 39, 137–8). In these words also, Bussy projects his fame and his speech across the world; he scatters his personality abroad, in a manner that looks forward to the final gestures of the speaker of Eliot's 'Gerontion' (1920), gestures that integrate the historical and theological resonances of the poem.

Yet, even at this desperate tragic moment, as all editors of the play have remarked (and as Eliot would have been aware), Chapman, through Bussy, is translating and adapting lines from a Latin play by Seneca, *Hercules Oetaeus*.[6] Bussy's final full speech is therefore allusively authorized by an earlier text in which the stoic attitude of the play's hero similarly enables him to resist the nearness and finality of death. The 'Roman' nature of the statue, which Bussy sees himself becoming, subliminally signals that the source of Bussy's final words lies elsewhere than with himself. This interplay between present freshness and immediacy in poetry, and the dependency of such moments upon earlier versions of the words presented, goes to the heart of Eliot's poetic from the outset. It is an interplay that will provide the major subject of this study of Eliot's particular recourse to Early Modern literary sources. Eliot was repeatedly drawn to speeches from Chapman's *Bussy* plays, and particularly to this final speech. He referred to it in his poetry and prose from 1917, in a reference in *Burnt Norton* of 1935, and into the late work. Poe's inclusion of Chapman's lines in his fraught tale of doomed love, first read by Eliot as a boy, raises, therefore, pivotal issues within Eliot's poetics. Relations between life and death, life and posterity, love and its loss, and, relevantly here, between art and artifice, often find their identification for him in his reflections on, and appropriations of, Early Modern materials. He also, as this book will trace, recurrently adverts to the ways in which tragic heroes, at the moment before death, come to narrate themselves from a perspective outside the established accents of their own consciousness.[7]

Whatever the potent imagery, and allusive charge, that Poe's 'The Assignation' set in motion within the young Eliot's mind at that time, however, the tone of the story affects much of his later work. The chill of the 'hollow vale' of death, signalled by the King epigraph, is matched by the 'mysteriousness' and ghostliness in life of the Marchesa, and of the heroic young man, her lover. The fact that the lover's 'form' 'hath risen before me!', as the narrator tells us at the start of the story, 'again in fancy' instigates his 'recounting' of the lovers' fate. It is the

---

[6] Frederick S. Boas, in his edition of *Bussy d'Ambois and the Revenge*, references the allusion in his Note to this speech (163); his Introduction sees Bussy as, for Chapman, 'the classical Hercules born anew' (xxx).

[7] Eliot's fascination here is correlative to that of W.B. Yeats. In his summary 'A General Introduction to my Work' (1937), Yeats noted that astonishing 'mingling', 'perfection in personality, the perfection of its surrender' experienced by Shakespeare's tragic heroes and heroines at the moment of their deaths, in *Essays and Introductions* (London: Macmillan, 1989 edition, 255).

haunted nature of the tale, the sense that it represents a destruction of something that is inherently, yet horrifically, human in its tragedy of frustration and loss, which remains. It is this hauntedness that presumably made it, and its allusions, so resonant for Eliot across his life. As with Bussy's speech, Eliot referred to Henry King's poem at several key moments in his career, before the December 1957 broadcast. In preparation for that broadcast, he says, he had re-read his own 1921 essay on 'The Metaphysical Poets'; the essay quotes a passage from King's 'Exequy', beginning with the couplet excerpted by Poe. Eliot there calls King's poem as one of the 'finest' of its age, and notes the 'effect of terror' in the quoted passage, a 'terror' similar to that in the writing of one of King's 'admirers', Poe (*SE*, 283–4).[8] Eliot's 'The Hollow Men', the short lyric sequence first published in its complete form in 1925, then presents a deathly realm correlative to King's 'hollow vale'.[9]

Eliot's reading of 'terror' into King's conceit that each pulse-beat brings him closer to the grave, and therefore to his dead wife, dramatizes the effect that this type of poetry, operating under the shadow of death, definitively had upon him. As we will discover across this study, Eliot strayed into some dazzled over-reading in his reaction to such writing, as comparison to its original textual context makes clear. In this instance, 'terror' seems remote from the controlled, and worked-through, nature of King's self-presentation:

> But heark! My Pulse like a soft Drum
> Beats my approach, tells *Thee* I come;
> And slow howere my marches be,
> I shall at last sit down by *Thee*.
>
> The thought of this bids mee go on,
> And wait my dissolution
> With hope and comfort.[10]

Eliot's selective quotation from 'The Exequy', in 'The Metaphysical Poets', omits the last three of these lines. His attribution of a Poe-like 'terror' to King's poem, across his own career, shows how Eliot's absorption of such writings is never a neutral one. The King poem is partly reinflected for him by the tenor of Poe's story. Rather, as we shall see, and often through the ways Eliot repeatedly returns to certain Early Modern texts, and to specific moments within them, that absorption displays a more earnest, and often unspoken, reason for the original interest and engagement. And that interest could vary dramatically within a short space of time within Eliot's writing. For example, an 'Exequy' by Eliot appears amongst the manuscripts relating to *The Waste Land*, from the same period as the essay on

---

[8] The essay also quotes from the sequel to Chapman's tragedy cited by Poe, *The Revenge of Bussy d'Ambois*, a further concatenation of these key texts in Eliot's critical thinking and his imagination.

[9] Alternatively, Eliot would compare Poe to King's main precursor, John Donne, as late as 'Poe and Valéry', 1948 (*TCC*, 40).

[10] Henry King, 'The Exequy', in Herbert J.C. Grierson, ed., *Metaphysical Lyrics and Poems of the Seventeenth Century*, 206. This is the book Eliot was reviewing in 'The Metaphysical Poets'.

'The Metaphysical Poets' (*WLFT*, 100–1). The speaker of Eliot's 'Exequy' narrates a largely calm rendition of dying, however, one that omits the original's further subject of 'mature' love, married or otherwise.

Eliot's restless search, as an eleven or twelve-year-old, to discover and absorb the full poems or plays behind the fragments excerpted in other texts, sets in train a typical method that will figure in his own poetry and drama. His concern to uncover the original texts cited exhibits an immediate responsiveness to certain literary tonalities. Eliot is also alert to the complex interweavings and inter-layerings of literary presences across history. His discovery, through 'The Assignation', of an Early Modern world of love and its loss, is typical of the way, across his life, he was drawn to the sixteenth and seventeenth centuries, and how such worlds were precursors of many of the literary modes and modalities to which, by inclination, he was drawn. 'The Assignation', for Poe's lovers, is both the clandestine meeting they seek to arrange at dawn (a meeting thwarted by the poisonings), and an assignation with death. The two are one and the same. Yet, in creating that tragedy between two worlds, Poe's tale manifests the ways in which former texts (King, Chapman) are made to live also in the changed circumstances of later writing, as they will throughout Eliot's own determinedly modern poetry. Poe also demonstrates the ways that any new work of literature forms an 'intersection', in which several voices, past and present, meet and speak together in a new context and paradigm.

This book will present a history of Eliot's engagements with Early Modern writing across the length of his career as a writer. The book will review the allusive, but also the often subliminal, presence of Early Modern writers within the development of Eliot's own poetry and, later, within his drama, which further draws upon the welter of his reading in these earlier sources. It will map the oscillations in Eliot's relationship as a critic of, and his repeated returns to, the various Early Modern plays and poems that meant most to him. These are the texts he heralded as his touchstones, in his earliest critical writing, in late commentary, such as that offered in the 1957 BBC broadcast, and in his last critical study, on the Anglican metaphysical poet, *George Herbert* (1962). Crucially, this book will also establish the context for Eliot's consistent and creative engagement with Early Modern sources, through recovery of the original critical editions and commentaries with which he was familiar, as evidenced, for instance, by his reference to them in his essays. That context will nuance the origins of the importance of Eliot's engagement with Early Modern writing for later poets and readers, and for literary culture in the English-speaking world. The remainder of this Introduction will review the crucial origins of Eliot's fascination with those Early Modern sources, an interest which (such was the quality of that fascination) in its turn created broader cultural readjustments with regard to the relation of the Early Modern to the modern world.

Eliot was assiduous, near the end of his life, in pointing out, in the face of what had by then seemed to be a popular belief, that he did not 'invent' the Early Modern period for the modern age, nor establish the accepted canon of its texts. Such, however, has been the continuing belief of academic criticism. We continue to find writers such as Richard Halpern, for instance, claiming that 'T.S. Eliot established the protocols of twentieth-century Shakespeare criticism.'[11] John Stubbs's 'Afterword' to his much-lauded 2006 biography, *Donne*, reminds us that that Early Modern poet's influence continues to extend beyond literary historians and English students. Indeed, Donne's work has been implicated in the shaping of the age that we live in (Stubbs cites as example J. Robert Oppenheimer's thoughts about Donne's relevance as hymn-writer, at the moment of witnessing the first test of the nuclear bomb). Yet Stubbs also reminds us that it was Eliot who was 'the figurehead of a...movement which reaffirmed Donne as one of the greatest of all English poets'.[12] Gary Taylor, in his substantial edition of the works of the dramatist and prose writer Thomas Middleton, claims that 'Eliot wrote the single most influential essay on Middleton', and that 'he put Middleton in the literary canon, on the critical agenda, in the university curriculum'. As a result of Eliot's intervention, Taylor argues that modern English play-writing, from Harold Pinter to Edward Bond and Joe Orton, displays a renewed Early Modern harshness, through shared indebtedness to Middleton.[13] In terms of Eliot's theological interests, Sophie Read has recently noted that the work of Lancelot Andrewes had languished, 'unread and unthought-about', until Eliot's attempted 'rehabilitation' of him—a rehabilitation which, as we shall see later in this book, had important consequences for the sound-world and punning paradox of Eliot's mature work.[14]

These, and similar instances, are all attributions to Eliot of founding cultural significance in his concentration upon Early Modern works; a founding significance with which he was uncomfortable. In nearly his last critical pronouncement, the reflective lecture 'To Criticize the Critic' (1961), Eliot points out that no single critic can create a taste in literary appreciation for any specific generation of readers. The taste for Donne, and for the minor Elizabethan and Jacobean dramatists to which he had recourse, was an established one to which his own critical writing and poetry merely added. The taste itself had been created, Eliot points out, by critics in the nineteenth century.[15] It had begun with the rediscovery of the significance of Early Modern writing by Coleridge and Lamb, and thence continued into the criticism by critics closer to Eliot's generation, such as Edmund Gosse on Donne, and George Saintsbury on the poetry more broadly, and on the drama (*TCC*, 21). By recovering that critical context contemporary to Eliot, as he started out as a writer—and by tracing the ways in which, through his reviewing,

---

[11] Richard Halpern, 'Shakespeare in the Tropics: From High Modernism to New Historicism' *Representations* 45 (Winter, 1994), 1.

[12] John Stubbs, *Donne* (London: Viking, 2006), 473.

[13] Gary Taylor, 'Lives and Afterlives', in Thomas Middleton, *The Collected Works* (Oxford: Clarendon Press, 2007), 55.

[14] Sophie Read, 'Puns', in *Renaissance Figures of Speech*, ed. Sylvia Adamson, Gavin Alexander, and Katrin Ettenhuber (Cambridge: Cambridge University Press, 2007), 85.

[15] J.B. Bullen has pointed out that the term 'Renaissance' to describe such 16th–17th century work, itself was only introduced in the 1840s, probably by Pugin. Key figures of the Victorian period were not immediately able to adjust to the new 'historical perspective which its use demanded'. It was only with Browning, Swinburne, Ruskin, and, later, with Pater, that some larger understanding of the earlier period developed (*The Myth of the Renaissance in Nineteenth-Century Writing*, Oxford: Clarendon Press, 1994, 10, 151, 155).

article-writing, and broadcasts, he became an interlocutor within such debates—it will be possible to give a grounded account of Eliot's engagement with the Early Modern era, and to understand better the distinctiveness of his responses to that period. For the first time at any length, this study will account for Eliot's various resistances to certain aspects of that contemporary presentation, but will also consider his intrigued, and sometimes deliberately contentious, interventions into, and furtherings of, established understanding.

ELIOT'S EDUCATION IN THE EARLY MODERN

As the anecdote about Henry King recounted by Eliot in his 1957 BBC broadcast intimates, there is a good deal of the enthusiasm of the autodidact about Eliot's imbruement in Early Modern drama and poetry. Documentary sources relating to his early education suggest the degree of his determination to explore on his own initiative the work from the earlier period that, even then, most engaged him. In a handwritten note by him, about his record at Smith Academy, Eliot mentions studying *Othello*—a play which, as we shall see, consistently underwrote his mature literary interests—, *Macbeth*, Palgrave's *Golden Treasury*, and Milton's Minor Poems (*LI*, 5). Yet, in her letter recommending the young Eliot (aged sixteen) to the headmaster of his next school, Milton Academy, his mother felt confident in reporting that her son had read most of Shakespeare by that point, and that he had also 'memorized' it (*LI*, 4). At Milton Academy for a year, it would seem that Eliot did not formally study for those courses in which he had already passed the examinations for university entry, including Latin, Greek, and English (*LI*, 8). Thereafter, similar private enthusiasm for the plays of Shakespeare and those of the early seventeenth-century dramatists who wrote in his wake, as well as for the poetry of the same period, would seem to have to have sustained Eliot when he studied at Harvard University from 1906.

However, Eliot did not enrol for many English courses at the university, although in his third year he did take Comparative Literature 6b, 'The Literary History of England and its Relation to that of the Continent from Chaucer to Elizabeth'. But, as Dayton Haskin's researches have revealed, that course, although it included Spenser (later source for *The Waste Land*), established a firm barrier between the values of the Elizabethan period and those of the succeeding one, which predominantly engaged Eliot at this time and subsequently. Another course he took, on 'Tendencies of European Literature in the Renaissance', ended its focus late in the sixteenth century. Only English 28, 'History and Development of English Literature'—the course on which Haskins speculates that Eliot first encountered the work of John Donne—offered lectures in the relevant area. Six lectures covered Donne, Jonson, minor poets of the time, some prose, then Milton, and Dryden, with an emphasis on Donne as the precursor of a new momentum.[16]

---

[16] Dayton Haskin, *John Donne in the Nineteenth Century* (Oxford: Oxford University Press, 2007), 224–5.

The consequences of Eliot's early encounter with Donne's work will be considered fully in the opening section of Chapter Two below; those of his private enthusiasm as a young man for Early Modern drama upon the first of his poems to be collected in a book, *Prufrock and other Observations* (1917), in the opening sections of Chapter Three. The poems written up in the Notebook *Inventions of the March Hare*, and not subsequently published in book form, however, seem to confirm the point made in the discussion below. Although, in his first poems, in his Harvard writings, and in those of his early years in London, Eliot's work shows his familiarity with (often quite obscure) Early Modern poetry but drama especially, the predominantly Laforguian poetics he adopted until later in the 1910s largely restricted the impact of his other guiding literary interest to glinting and ironic allusion. The Hamlet of 'The Love Song of J. Alfred Prufrock' itself seems indebted to the dandyish figure included in Laforgue's obsessive late collection, *Des Fleurs de Bonne Volonté*, rather than to the tragic metaphysician of Shakespeare. The appropriation of Romeo's paean to Juliet's eyes (II.ii.15–17) in 'Second Caprice in North Cambridge' (1909), as a way of 'entreating' a reader's engagement with the fact of the tawdry waste lands of the modern city, might stand as example, here, of the savagely ironic purpose perpetuated by Eliot's allusion to the richness of Early Modern dramatic discourse at this early stage of his career (*IMH*, 15).

Only the paired poems, the 'First Debate between the Body and Soul' (1910) and 'Bacchus and Ariadne: 2nd Debate between the Body and Soul' (1911), come close to Eliot's later concern with metaphysics. 'Bacchus and Ariadne' takes up from one of the obvious sources for this style of 'encounter', Andrew Marvell's 'Dialogue between the Soul and Body', the notion that the physical world is 'drumming' on, and dinning out, the potentiality for a higher purpose amongst humanity (a notion later taken up by Eliot again in 'Whispers of Immortality'). Eliot's reduction of Marvell's original 'dialogue' to the terms of a 'debate', and his wry inversion of the earlier poet's 'Soul and Body' to 'Body and Soul', suggest, however, the persistence of Laforgue's 'débats' behind the unresolved (and in the 'First Debate' scurrilous) 'terms' of engagement in Eliot's exercises. Once again, in form and in matter, these early works advertise with some humour their diminished and enervated situation, when measured against the potential of Early Modern writing. Amongst the poems included by Eliot in *Inventions of the March Hare*, it is only perhaps 'The Love Song of St. Sebastian' (1914) that has the ability to disturb through its references to the Early Modern, in ways which will become a feature of the integrative, structuring role that those early texts acquired in the later 1910s, and from 'Gerontion' onwards, as we shall see later in the book (*IMH*, 78). The ghosting of the Saint's 'Love Song' by the obsessive and jealous desire of Othello for Desdemona, in a poem that seems otherwise engaged with Victorian tropes of harm and suffering in love from such as Swinburne and Browning, proffers an example of that originating recourse which, across this book, will be seen to mark such returns by Eliot. As Chapter One will argue, it was not until opportunity afforded in 1919 that Eliot's private self-education took on a renewed, and concerted, purpose as determining his mature poetics, in the years across which *The Waste Land* was being developed, and beyond.

THE 'RENAISSANCE' IN CRITICISM,
PATER, AND THE 'HISTORICAL SENSE'

Dialogue with Early Modern writing, but also, as we shall see, with contemporary criticism upon it, in its turn, had a definitive impact upon Eliot's own poetry and drama in a more concentrated way from the end of the 1910s onwards—but that concentration also reflected back upon Eliot's early encounters with late Victorian formulations about the earlier period. For instance, in the collection of draft manuscripts relating to *The Waste Land*, we can see that 'The Fire Sermon' originally opened with a dismissive, misogynist, satiric passage, recounting the morning levee of a decadent society woman, Fresca. The pastiche eighteenth-century couplets of the rejected passage take a surprising turn, however, as Fresca's literary pretensions come to the fore. Then, she is envisaged, spiritually, as drowning in the opaque waters of the work of Walter Pater, John Addington Symonds, and Vernon Lee (*WLFT*, 27). Fresca's decadent sensibility, in other words, is posited in these drafts as deriving from the aestheticism of a range of late nineteenth-century criticism about Renaissance Italy. This is a telling association in Eliot's mind.[17] The sarcastic and aggressive tone of this pastiche poetry, the modernity of the conception of the literary artist that is implied by it, operates in nominal contrast to Fresca's languidness. But that modernity is declared through writing off recent critical consensus around approaches to the Early Modern period.[18] There was a consensus of approach, in other words, one typical of literary salon culture, which was emblematic of all that a declaratively modern poet like Eliot was anxious to escape.

Yet such breathlessly witty dismissal of a salon consensus in the drafts of 'The Fire Sermon', and the profession of a new countering clarity, which might replace the cloudy incoherence of these late nineteenth-century precursors, of course itself obscures complexities within Eliot's engagement with them. It is a complexity of engagement with the earlier period, as it was initially figured for him in Italian, and then later, in English critical contexts. Although Eliot seems never to have engaged with Vernon Lee's work, beyond this glancing dismissal, John Addington Symonds retained a more substantial presence in Eliot's thinking, as will be discussed in Chapter One. Symonds figures, not least, as critic and editor of some of the Early Modern dramatists Eliot consistently referred to in his own mature essays.[19]

[17] Pater's *Studies in the History of the Renaissance* had appeared in 1873, and gone through several new editions before the century's end. John Addington Symonds's seven-volume *Renaissance in Italy* had appeared between 1875 and 1886. Vernon Lee was the pen name for Violet Paget, whose essay collections on English and European Renaissance art and literature appeared as *Euphorion: studies of the antique and the medieval in the Renaissance* in 1884, and *Renaissance Fancies and Studies: a sequel to Euphorion* in 1895. Eliot's dandified speaker in his early 'Suite Clownesque' III is mocked through his own identification of himself, as he strolls Broadway, as a modern Euphorion (*IMH*, 35).

[18] Languor is one of the qualities for which Eliot criticized Pater, in his 1930 essay 'Arnold and Pater'. Here, Eliot indicts Pater for following Arnold in seeing Culture as a modern replacement for Religion (*SE*, 443).

[19] Symonds's *Shakespere's Predecessors in the English Drama* (London: Smith Elder, 1884, reprinted 1920), for instance, appeared on Eliot's course outline for his Elizabethan Literature Extension Lectures, 1918-9. The prospectus for the lectures is given in Ronald Schuchard, *Eliot's Dark Angel: Intersections of Life and Art* (New York: Oxford University Press, 1999), 45-9.

Of these three decadent critics, Walter Pater's writing, in particular, seems to have had a marked and continuing bearing upon Eliot's need for saturation in the Early Modern. It thence affects his poetic character, however much Eliot later resisted the implications of Pater's aesthetic or ethical position.

Eliot's mother had bought him the first, 1873, edition of Pater's *Studies in the History of the Renaissance*, when he was a teenager, at a sale of surplus books in St Louis.[20] His marked-up copy, now held in the Hayward Bequest at King's College, Cambridge, reveals that Eliot probably paid considerable attention to Pater's book. The notorious 'Conclusion' to this 1873 version, for instance, has the variant readings from later editions pencilled over the printed text.[21] But Eliot's textual interest hints that Pater's *Studies* had a major impact upon him. As a marker of Eliot's abiding equivocation about the significance of Pater's ideas behind his own, the iconic phrase about the ideal life of experience from Pater's 'Conclusion' ('to burn ever with a hard gem-like flame') appears repeatedly in his work. It features not only uncertainly in the brief prose of 1917, *Eeldrop and Appleplex*, but as a vision of creative possibility asserted both by Agatha, in Eliot's 1939 play, *The Family Reunion*, and by Celia, about to set upon her path of religious duty, in the subsequent play *The Cocktail Party* of 1949.[22] Antithetically, Eliot was also fascinated, as Frank Kermode perceptively noted, by 'the simultaneous enchantment and loss' in lines from what he and others at the time thought to be Cyril Tourneur's *The Revenger's Tragedy* (the work is now commonly ascribed to Middleton). Eliot was fascinated by the phrase in the play, 'bewildering minute'.[23] But, more broadly, if we take Pater's book as Eliot's early means of engaging with that period of artistic history which was to preoccupy him over much of his writing life, certain elements of Pater's approach speak emblematically within what we now conceive as Eliot's modern poetics.[24]

---

[20] See John J. Soldo, *The Tempering of T.S. Eliot* (Epping: Bowker, 1983), 32. A footnote in 'Arnold and Pater' tells us that Eliot was using the first edition of Pater's *Studies* in his quotations for the essay, suggesting that he was aware of the complex textual history of Pater's book, but also that he continued to work with this edition, the present from his mother (*SE*, 436).

[21] Hayward Bequest, King's College Library, Cambridge, HB/B/21.

[22] *Eeldrop and Appleplex* stages a knockabout discussion about the modern artist around the reminiscence of a former love object, Edith. She is recalled memorably and absurdly by Eeldrop through the fact that she gave her view of life which ran together two key Pater phrases—one from Chapter IX of his 1885 novel *Marius the Epicurean*, the other from the 'Conclusion' to *Studies in the History of the Renaissance*: 'Edith . . . I wonder what has become of her. "Not pleasure, but fullness of life . . . to burn ever with a hard gem-like flame," those were her words.' *The Little Review*, IV.5 (September 1917), 16. Agatha speaks about the 'present moment of pointed light/When you want to burn' in *The Family Reunion* (London: Faber, 1939), 96; Celia speaks of 'moments' when 'the ecstasy is real' in *The Cocktail Party* (London: Faber, 1950), 123.

[23] *The Selected Prose of T.S. Eliot*, ed. Frank Kermode (London: Faber, 1975), 13. In 'Cyril Tourneur' (1930), Eliot noted his long-term preference for 'bewildering' over the 'bewitching' that several editors held to be the text's original word (*SE*, 192). 'Bewildering' appeared in the Mermaid text of *Webster and Tourneur*, ed. John Addington Symonds (London: Vizetelly, 1888). The phrase appears on p. 392 of that edition.

[24] Denis Donoghue has argued that it is Pater, rather than his contemporaries Arnold, Tennyson, or Ruskin, who was responsible for setting modern literature upon an 'antinomian', 'antithetical', course—which, with tonal differences, manifests, for instance, in Eliot's 'The Love Song of J. Alfred Prufrock' (*Walter Pater*, New York: Alfred. A. Knopf, 1995, 7).

Pater's book was one important influence, and one operative in relation to the era most important to him, for Eliot in establishing that historical understanding was, in itself, a principle of value.[25] When considering the difficulty he feels with earlier critics' work on the fifteenth century, Pater introduces a concept that later underwrites also Eliot's sense of his relation to the past, as evidenced, for instance, in key essays such as 'Tradition and the Individual Talent' (1919):

> They lacked the very rudiments of the historical sense, which by an imaginative act throws itself back into a world unlike one's own, and judges each intellectual product in connection with the age which produced it; they had no idea of development, of the differences of ages, of the gradual education of the human race.[26]

Pater's essays on the Italian Renaissance, therefore, cast themselves as acts of trans-historical dialogue and recovery. They bring to the fore, as Eliot's essays and reviews would later do, the necessity of situating the work under consideration within the context of those works that have led up to it, as well as in its relation to works from the period in which it was produced. This is a dual insistence that Eliot sustained, after Pater. As late as 1926, for instance, Eliot noted in a review of a book on Early Modern thinkers, that the Tudor churchman and theologian, Richard Hooker, had displayed a quality of historical thinking that had been matched by his modern critic. However, Eliot contends that, elsewhere in the book under review, such historical thought was lacking:

> Perhaps the final problem for historical students is a problem of imagination—that is, to reconstruct for ourselves so fully the mind of the Renaissance and the mind of the pre-Renaissance, that neither of them shall be dead for us—that is to say, unconscious parts of our own mind—but shall be conscious and therefore utilizable for our further development.[27]

The similarities between the vocabulary of this passage, and that of the passage in Pater's work with which Eliot had become familiar as a teenager, is striking. Imagination is seen by both writers as the necessary quality for determining and defining the historical understanding. It is crucial to the 'reconstruction' of a past. The model for both is, perhaps surprisingly, Darwinian. Eliot's further assertion, that the dead form the unconscious minds of the living, then establishes the ways in which his poetry's historical understanding is at least partly derived from the neces-sity, for him, to bring the past into defined perspective, as an organizing principle for the new text. This quality of historical thought, consistently attributed to Early

---

[25] See James Longenbach, *Modernist Poetics of History: Pound, Eliot and the Sense of the Past* (Princeton: Princeton University Press, 1987), for a full exploration of the philosophical origins of Eliot's perspective.

[26] Walter Pater, *Studies in the History of the Renaissance* (London: Macmillan, 1873), 22. Subsequent references to this edition given in the text.

[27] 'Hooker, Hobbes and Others', unsigned review of *The Social and Political Ideas of Some Great Thinkers of the Sixteenth and Seventeenth Centuries*, ed. F.J.C. Hearnshaw, *TLS*, 11 November 1926, no. 1, 293, 789. Similarly, in a review of an edition of the poems of Henry Vaughan by Edmund Blunden, Eliot chided the editor for failing to 'project himself into the seventeenth century'. Blunden had, rather, erred by 'tearing a figure' out of the earlier time, in order to 'assimilate' 'to himself' in the present. 'Henry Vaughan: The Silurist', *The Dial*, September 1927, 262.

Modern writing by Eliot, was, in its turn, to become the mythic method of Eliot's sense of modernity, as discovered, for instance, by him in James Joyce's *Ulysses*.[28]

It is the purpose of Pater's 'historical sense', therefore, that his essays seek to render moments from history into the present. From the outset, Pater had emphasized the 'relative' over the 'absolute', within paradigms of knowledge; his 1865 essay 'Coleridge' maintained that:

> The philosophical conception of the relative has been developed in modern times through the influence of the sciences of observation. Those sciences reveal types of life evanescing into each other by inexpressible refinements of change.[29]

The historical sensibility is one, therefore, which discovers 'truth' about the past for its own time, whilst relinquishing claims to a universality within that discovery.[30]

This version of reading in history is familiar across the Victorian understanding of the Italian Renaissance, both as Eliot understood that perspective and as he took his core adherences from it. George Eliot's novel *Romola* is aptly cited by T.S. Eliot, in his Introduction to the published version of his mother Charlotte Eliot's *Savonarola: A Dramatic Poem* (1926). T.S. Eliot presents *Romola* as exemplary of the fact that works of historical fiction are unique. *Romola* allows twentieth-century readers a rare 'third' level of critical understanding. They can witness an earlier period, which the Victorian had already become, as it—the Victorian period—encounters a still earlier time, in this case the Italian Renaissance, in which George Eliot's fascination with the rebel monk Savonarola is encapsulated. That fascination gains a new moment in Charlotte Eliot's re-rendition. Yet George Eliot's 'Proem' to her novel, in its turn, famously plays upon the complex association of present to past. The 'Proem' invokes a timeless 'Shade' or 'Spirit', a typical Renaissance citizen who might 'revisit', having been reborn in the present, the Florentine scenes amongst which Savonarola's rebellion was played out. George Eliot's inception to her novel thereby initiates a sense of continuation between present and past in a single place, 'fellowship and understanding for him among the inheritors of his birthplace'.

---

[28] '"Ulysses", Order, and Myth', *Selected Prose of T.S. Eliot*, ed. Frank Kermode, 177. F.O. Matthiessen early highlighted that Eliot's deployment of 'so many reminiscences of other poets' in his work was towards accomplishing 'interpretation' of the modern experience. Eliot can 'increase the implications of his lines by his tacit revelation of the sameness (as well as the contrasts) between the life of the present and that of other ages'. *The Achievement of T.S. Eliot: An Essay on the Nature of Poetry* (New York: Oxford University Press, Third Edition, 1959), 35.

[29] Jeffrey M. Perl has described Eliot's 'philosophical perspective' as one of 'radical skepticism', in *Skepticism and Modern Enmity: Before and After Eliot* (Baltimore: Johns Hopkins University Press, 1989), 63. As this book argues, especially in the work from the mid-1920s onwards, Eliot's reference to Early Modern writings enjoins such scepticism as the critical potential within his poetry. This is the philosophical version of the self, which Eliot was familiar with. F.H. Bradley, in *Appearance and Reality: A Metaphysical Essay*, claimed that the self was 'appearance', 'too full of contradictions to be the genuine fact' (London: George Unwin, 1916 edition), 75.

[30] Walter Pater, *Appreciations: With an Essay on Style* (London: Macmillan, 1910 edition), 66. F.C. McGrath has pointed out that although, in *Plato and Platonism*, Pater had proclaimed an Hegelian 'historical method', which would place figures of intellectual culture 'in the group of conditions, intellectual, social, material', his writing practice focused more upon 'individual genius' above that emphasis. McGrath links this to the emphasis of 'Tradition and the Individual Talent'—but it also describes Eliot's 'method' which, like Pater's, tends towards essays entitled with individuals' names (*The Sensible Spirit: Walter Pater and the Modernist Paradigm*, Tampa: University of Southern Florida Press, 1986, 124, 131ff.).

However, as George Eliot's 'Proem' continues, questions about the innovations wrought by change in the intervening centuries also become increasingly frequent and loud. Differences between the Victorian and the Renaissance worlds become more evident, until, finally, the timeless 'Shade' is told that Florence is too alien now for his attendance: 'Go not down, good Spirit! for the changes are great and the speech of Florentines will sound as a riddle in your ears.' Yet such rebuttal underscores only one perspective within George Eliot's historical perception. The continuities between past and present, which George Eliot contrarily ends by invoking, are those to be found in 'the sunlight and shadows', amongst children, or in the perpetuation of worship in the city's churches; all other 'change' seems resistant to the present, and potentially, too, to the approach of the historical novelist.[31]

Such complexities of acceptance and resistance in the historical imagination carry forward in those works involving historical reconstruction of the sixteenth and seventeenth centuries with which Eliot was familiar from his own time. *Elizabeth and Essex: A Tragic History*, by Eliot's friend Lytton Strachey, contains in its early pages several meditations on this issue. Claiming that 'everybody knows' the superficial qualities of the Elizabethan age, Strachey immediately seeks to strike deeper:

> More valuable than descriptions, but what perhaps is unattainable, would be some means by which the modern mind might reach to an imaginative comprehension of those beings of three centuries ago—might move with ease among their familiar essential feelings—might touch, or dream that it touches (for such dreams are the stuff of history) the very 'pulse of the machine'. But the path seems closed to us.

Having made the general case for the irredeemable difficulty confronted by the historical imagination, Strachey rapidly moves, however, to identify the specific barriers faced in the Elizabethan case, 'the contradictions of the age that baffle our imagination and perplex our intelligence.... The inconsistency of the Elizabethans exceeds the limit permitted to man.'[32] Eliot's warm review of Strachey's book for the *TLS* picks up on that word 'inconsistency', to describe the difference between the Elizabethan and modern ages, but also, paradoxically, to turn the 'inconsistency' towards descriptive relevance. The modern age, with its strong narratives from moral philosophy and from psychology, is, Eliot wrote, unable to grapple fully with the earlier period. But 'inconsistency' in the Elizabethan age characterizes, Eliot also claimed in this review, the dramatists of that period, including Shakespeare, as well as the poets, including John Donne: and 'we', the

---

[31] George Eliot, *Romola* (Harmondsworth: Penguin, 1996), 2, 7. See T.S. Eliot's Introduction to Charlotte Eliot, *Savonarola: A Dramatic Poem* (London: R. Cobden-Sanderson, 1926), vii. According to the inventory of Eliot's library prepared by Vivien Eliot, *c*.1933, a copy of *Romola* stood on Eliot's shelves (Bodleian Library, Oxford, MS Eng. Lett B 20).

[32] Lytton Strachey, *Elizabeth and Essex: A Tragic History* (Harmondsworth: Penguin, 1971), 11–12. George Eliot has a long meditative passage, in which contradiction is seen to characterize Savonarola, whose 'nature was one of those in which opposing tendencies coexist in almost equal strength: the passionate sensibility which, impatient of definite thought, floods every idea with emotion...alternated in him with a keen perception of outward facts' (*Romola*, 521).

moderns, would not find the Elizabethan age appealing were it not that it remained 'latent' in ourselves.[33]

From George Eliot, Pater, and, latterly, from such as his mother's work and Strachey's, T.S. Eliot understood that the historical reimagining of the Early Modern period confirmed the ontological perplexities involved in the necessity of reading in and through history. These are perplexities necessarily shared by inconsistent ideas amongst all modern citizens, but, most particularly, exercise the modern writer. The sense that the unresolvedness and contradiction of the Early Modern remain buried in 'us', beneath the modern consciousness, seemingly attuned to our dreams and nightmares, but also to 'our' creative modalities, therefore forms the figural attention of much of this book, in its reflection on the Early Modern traces in Eliot's thought and poetry. Such perplexities, as we shall see, are implicated, further, in the various distance and proximity that the Early Modern period was felt to sustain for Eliot, writing at the turn of the twentieth century. Versions of the earlier period might help 'us', the moderns, to attain a critical distance upon the similar transitions and cultural changes occurring in the shocked, contemporary world just after the end of World War I. But, contrarily, the modern age might seem a simple repetition of the dissociations and malaise of the Early Modern times, and of its writers. Eliot's understanding of the Early Modern writing shifted between these antithetical possibilities, and created, through allusion and the compulsive summoning of previous literary contexts, consciously 'modern' and metaphysical poetics from them. In this, again, his ambition seems partly consonant with the thought of the generation previous to his own, thought with which he became familiar at an early stage of his development, through the assiduity of his mother, and his determined following through of his own literary interests.

The scope of Eliot's interests in the Early Modern as mediated by Victorian writers was notably broad, and spoke to his own particular Christian values as they emerged in the mid-1920s. Eliot had been fascinated by the Early Modern as a high point of religious writing from at least the late 1910s, and in this again he was following an established tradition of understanding carried over from Victorian times. His own choice of basic history book through which to comprehend the earlier age makes this clear. J.A. Froude's history of Tudor England and its monarchs, in the recent Everyman edition, was recommended as the text to provide historical background, when Eliot mounted his own course of lectures and classes on 'Elizabethan Literature' in 1918–9. Froude's account of Elizabeth and Leicester on the Thames is thence quoted as a gloss for line 279 of *The Waste Land* (1922). Froude's history casts the period, from 'The Accession of Elizabeth', as one definitively marked by 'differences of religion' between Catholicism and Protestantism in England, differences that mirrored the 'sharp antitheses which were dividing Christian Europe'. For Froude, this division accounted for the extreme flexibility of the English language at that time, since 'words could be used which admitted of uncertain interpretation, so long as there was no authority to invest them

---

[33] 'Elizabeth and Essex', unsigned review of *Elizabeth and Essex: A Tragic History* by Lytton Strachey, *TLS*, 6 December 1928, no. 1, 401, 959.

with a definite meaning'. Elizabeth's own struggle across her life was to re-establish the 'spiritual jurisdiction of the crown'.[34] For Eliot, uncertain from the outset as to how to determine 'meaning' in his own times (as key essays like 'The Metaphysical Poets' make clear), the religious reach, and the intonations of Early Modern religious writing, always informed his poetry from the youthful poems of martyrdom ('The Death of Saint Narcissus', 'The Love Song of St. Sebastian'), with broadening urgency from 'Gerontion' onwards. Those Early Modern religious works to which he had frequent recourse, and to which he made allusion, will, therefore, inform this study of his sources, and also its consideration of the original contexts out of which his work is created.

ELIOT STUDIES, ALLUSIVENESS, AND A DIFFERENT METHODOLOGY

My approach in this book, which is derived from Eliot's attunement to a particular historical understanding of Early Modern writing, to an extent runs counter to the context of established criticism on this poet. There has been a tendency in Eliot Studies to assume that the nature and context of the originating source for many of his allusions has no relevance, within the new location that he provides for them. Helen Gardner, in 1949, for instance, argued that we should show 'some regard' for the sources of *The Waste Land*, since Eliot indicated them in his 'Notes'. However, when reading the later work, including *Four Quartets*, she felt that the allusive quality of the poetry was overridden by its 'musical' ambition: 'The sources are completely unimportant. No knowledge of the original context is required.'[35] But this fails to explain why Eliot's later work continued in its allusive, palimpsestic, patterning, or why those allusions (including those to Early Modern texts) are less important in the later, than they were in the earlier, poetry. It also fails to explain how *The Waste Land*, although more obviously to be regarded, according to Gardner, on account of its shrewd deployment of its sources, is not itself 'musical'.

Most notorious in this dismissive vein regarding Eliot's allusion is, perhaps, F.W. Bateson's attack upon the 'pseudo-learning' which he felt that it displayed. The fragmentary nature of Eliot's work, Bateson contended, was a result of his (and Pound's) determination to display, within the poetry itself, a form of scholarly approach to past texts, in order to 'eke out' 'material that is subjectively and emotionally "thin"'. Yet this scholarship (Bateson notes that both poets are American) is, if 'wide-ranging', also 'often superficial and inaccurate': Eliot's literary essays contain many 'factual' and textual mistakes, and this tendency is repeated in his poetry.[36] The admitted 'verbal brilliance' of some of Eliot's passages is, therefore,

---

[34] James Anthony Froude, *The Reign of Elizabeth* (1858) (London: J.M. Dent, Everyman Edition, 1912), vol. I, 6, 17.

[35] Helen Gardner, *The Art of T.S. Eliot* (London: Faber, 1968 edition), 54.

[36] Christopher Ricks has brilliant pages on Eliot's creative tendency to 'mistakes' in relation to his quotation from earlier texts in 'Walter Pater, Matthew Arnold, and Misquotation', *The Force of Poetry* (Oxford: Oxford University Press, 1984), 414–6.

somehow dishonest, founded upon a form of 'plagiarism'. This is a 'plagiarism' which, Bateson acknowledges, itself comes with a history that dates back to the Early Modern period, where others' best writings were frequently appropriated by authors and integrated into new work. But it is a 'plagiarism' that, for Bateson, is nonetheless a 'defect' in any poetry, and a kind of 'bluff' which does not deceive the 'critical reader'.[37] The possibility that poetry might find its subjectivity and emotional locus *through* past texts, and that this is an inevitable consequence of its conscious engagement, as a piece of new writing, with tradition, is not one which engages Bateson's interest. It is, however, a possibility that forms a driving consideration in the present study, which takes Early Modern creative practices as pertinently descriptive of modern poetic characteristics.

The view that Eliot's poetry needs to be dealt with solely on its immediate terms has, however, persisted to some degree across subsequent Eliot Studies, and in many of its sympathetic, rather than its prejudicial, accounts. Ronald Bush, for example, describing the image of the 'Shadow' that appears in the final section of 'The Hollow Men', warns against thinking of it in relation to its potential sources in St. Luke's Gospel or Shakespeare's *Julius Caesar*:

> Once more Eliot's allusion merely juxtaposes a tangential and suggestive analogue to the experience presented in the action of the words on the page.[38]

The disdainful 'merely' is troubling here. The suggestion is that Eliot, if conscious of his sources for the image of the 'Shadow', would not have been concerned to engage, as part of the imaginative process through which he synthesized his 'words on the page', with the context, and thence the resonances, of his primary material. And yet, as in the discussion of the passage from Chapman's *Bussy d'Ambois* mentioned above, and elsewhere in this book, it is evident that Eliot was assiduous, from early on in his career, at tracing the sources of those passages that spoke most directly to him: significantly, he often redeployed those sources in the context of his own poetry. In this allusive instance from Chapman, for example, the *Hercules* plays of Seneca are the focus of two major essays of 1927, 'Seneca in Elizabethan Translation' and 'Shakespeare and the Stoicism of Seneca'. *Hercules Furens* then provides Eliot's poem 'Marina' (1930) with its epigraph, and with its opening line, which translates the Latin.

My contention, here, as across the book, is that, rather than being 'tangential' or analogical to 'the action' of Eliot's words, as Bush contends, the poet's Early Modern sources particularly—in and of their nature as he came to understand it—form a conscious and informing part of, a context for, that 'action' (leaving aside, for one moment, the question of what such an 'action' in a poetic text might be).[39]

---

[37] F.W. Bateson, 'The Poetry of Learning', *Eliot in Perspective: A Symposium*, ed. Graham Martin (London: Macmillan, 1970), 31, 39, 42, 43.

[38] Ronald Bush, *T.S. Eliot: A Study in Character and Style* (New York: Oxford University Press, 1983), 101.

[39] Ezra Pound felt that it was Eliot's concern to 'go back' to 'the original' sources when considering any later text which gave his criticism a rare and outstandingly 'vivid power'—especially so in the case of Eliot's hunting out of the Senecan sources of Elizabethan literature, which gave his writing in that area its special insight ('Prefatio Aut Cimicium Tumulus', *Selected Prose 1909–1965*, ed. William Cookson (London: Faber, 1973), 369.

We might cite here also Eliot's own concern to encourage and assist those critics who sought to consider the sources of some of his lines, as an important factor in understanding the purpose and meaning of his poetry. From George Williamson in 1930, through F.O. Matthiessen, Herbert Howarth, Grover Smith, and B.C. Southam, Eliot's keenness to provide information about references, and his concern to ensure that the sources are correctly identified, is amply evident.

Perhaps the most subtle interpreter of Eliot's intention regarding his allusions to earlier texts is Louis Menand. Menand has acknowledged the 'ingenious' nature of Eliot's allusiveness, seeing it as an 'answer' to a key issue with which he, like other early twentieth-century poets, was confronted. This was the 'question of sincerity', or of how to translate a poet's personal experience and sense of the world, into an environment that did not recognize the legitimacy of either:

> What is most typical of Eliot's poetic practice is the way...allusion...answers the question of sincerity by referring it back to an anterior authority. This tactic has the curious effect of establishing Eliot's own sincerity, since we cannot accuse him of manufacturing a literary emotion when he has declared his poem's literariness in advance.

Menand's more theoretically sophisticated understanding of the origins of Eliot's creativity provides convincing answers to objections such as Bateson's. The *literariness* of the poems is advertised by the poems themselves—hence their sincerity. This insight will form a crucial part of the discussion of Eliot's derivation of literariness, from his engagement with Early Modern writing, in this book. Menand's model of reading is, however, ultimately and unacknowledgedly, related to the studies of influence by Harold Bloom. For Menand feels that Eliot always needs to 'revise' an 'older poem' referred to by his own poetry, 'by filling the familiar form with slightly ill-fitting content'.[40] Eliot's relation towards his source texts, is, therefore, for Menand, one of 'ambivalence'; he fears their becoming an 'obsession' within his own work.

Without wishing to engage the undeveloped psychology of these issues, as presented by Menand, if not by Bloom, it is questionable whether the model of influence that Menand expands upon here in connection with Eliot's early poetry holds across all of his writing. Firstly, whilst it would be unwise to venture the word 'obsessive' in relation to it, Eliot's career shows him repeatedly returning to the same earlier sources, but then placing them in *different contexts and perspectives*, rather than 'revising' them in order to overcome them. The word 'axletree', from the final speech of George Chapman's *Bussy*, for instance, recurs in earlier and later Eliot: in 'Burbank with a Baedeker: Bleistein with a Cigar' (1919) and in *Burnt Norton* II (1935). Different implications may be drawn from each appearance of

---

[40] Louis Menand, *Discovering Modernism: T.S. Eliot and His Context* (New York: Oxford University Press, Second Edition, 1987), 16. Menand's related assertion (p. 18) that allusion only works because it is recognized as such by an audience, and, therefore, that the source text must already enjoy a cultural status, seems only partially valid for Eliot's encounters with Early Modern texts, however. As has been noted above, Eliot is credited by many subsequent critics with having *established* the cultural status of those earlier texts to which he alludes. The sources of the allusions are sometimes, therefore, not so immediately evident to readers, and are more implicated in the author's processes of creating poetry, rather than in readers' understanding of it. Ultimately, however, the two are never estranged the one from the other.

this odd word in Eliot's poems, implications drawn from the new context within which the allusion is made to appear. Further, those implications relate, not just to the specific use of the word 'axletree' in each new context created by Eliot, but also to the context in which the word originally occurred in Chapman. And, further, Eliot's understanding of the implications of the word is, at least partly, informed by the ways in which Chapman's play had been mediated to him. This mediation occurred via the editions of it with which we can establish that he was familiar, and by the critical studies of *Bussy d'Ambois* that he read for his own interest, or as an occasional lecturer, and frequent reviewer of work from the Early Modern period. It is this multiple perspective that the present book will engage, keeping Eliot's own poetry and poetic drama, as it is vividly informed by these multiple, but subtly connected, contexts, as its central focus.

This is not to say that Eliot would necessarily himself have seen the worth of such a study as this one. In his 1956 lecture on 'The Frontiers of Criticism', Eliot discussed J. Livingston Lowes' book on Coleridge, *The Road to Xanadu*. Lowes, Eliot acknowledged, had performed a valuable piece of detection in 'ferreting out' the books that Coleridge had read, and from which he derived images or phrases for his own work. Coleridge emerged from Eliot's reading of Lowes' book as a proto-modernist poet. Eliot claimed that Lowes had proved that poetic originality in Coleridge was paradoxically about 'assembling the most disparate and unlikely material to make a new whole'. But, Eliot contended, Lowes' book aids no one in reading *The Ancient Mariner* 'better'. Lowes' book is an 'investigation of process', the process through which Coleridge, consciously or unconsciously, derived his poetry. For Eliot, this placed Lowes' work beyond the 'frontiers of criticism', which protect an activity engaged with responding to the poem as it eventually stood on the page, rather than one engaged in exploring how it came to be what it was (*OPP*, 108–9). In this delimitation of the critical field of possibility, as we have seen, Eliot was followed by the New Critics, by Gardner and by Bush, as well as, to an extent, by theoretically inclined writers like Menand. However, this current book is offered in the belief that, through exploring further the different critical and creative contexts outlined above, and through focusing upon readings in that period fundamental for Eliot's development of his own poetic, the Early Modern, it is possible to say something *more* about the recurrent grounds for his poetry and drama. By considering empirical examples of his recurrence to the Early Modern in obvious, but also in occluded, ways, it is possible to bring to light those facets of the earlier writing with which Eliot continued to be engaged.

That this involves the 'process' through which literature is originated becomes inevitable in Eliot's case. For, intriguingly, the Early Modern influence is most evident in those formative aspects of Eliot's writing that were often excised by him once he had settled upon final versions of his writing for publication. The suppressed epigraphs, the allusions to the works of the earlier period in drafts and typescripts, often display, more overtly than the published texts, the shaping role that Early Modern poetry or drama has played in his initial thoughts, from his first poetic sequences through to the mature dramas of the 1950s. Those initial thoughts and inflections then retain a vestigial afterlife in the final published versions. It is one major purpose of this book to delve back to those original impulses behind the Eliot canon, and to set them in the full context provided by early twentieth-century criticism, and Eliot's own ephemeral writing, the reviews and Prefaces that will not finally be gathered until completion of the Faber *Collected Prose* project. For Eliot's engagement with the Early Modern period continued, even as the 'public' nature of his poetry (to adopt Menand's term for the allusive bases of Eliot's work) shifted from its origins in *Inventions of the March Hare* through to the late dramas, and from his early critical essays on Marlowe and Jonson through to the last book, on George Herbert.

Of course, as is proven in the opening example given here—the example of reference in Poe's Tale to Early Modern works, works that then acquire renewed potential in Eliot's poetry—influence is never a simple or single thing. Eliot's work creates a space in which several distinct backgrounds of influence come together. These include notoriously, work from the post-Baudelairean poetic tradition in France, work that Eliot, and critics he was familiar with, often perceived within the same paradigm as English writing of the sixteenth and seventeenth centuries. Dante's is the most obvious influence, from the early work onwards. Eliot's work on philosophy, and particularly that towards his doctoral thesis on F.H. Bradley, offered further conceptual impetus. It would take a study several times the length of this one to interweave the likely resonances from even these sources into my discussion of each instance of the Early Modern presence in Eliot's thought and writing. Others, better qualified to do so than I am, have traced those influences previously.[41] This book is designed to present, through a chronological survey of Eliot's career as a poet, the narrative of the inflections from a range of sixteenth- and early seventeenth-century poems and plays that entered Eliot's writing, and which were continually being newly heard, or put into new contexts, as his work developed. His engagement with the Early Modern altered as his own thoughts developed, but also as the inevitable comparison between the Early Modern, and his contemporary age, evolved in Eliot's own work, and in that of critics and poets whose writing he was attentive to. The Early Modern was Eliot's declared 'favourite literary period'; this study continually reflects, however, the ways in which that period was further nuanced, for him, by the understanding of the Early Modern in recent criticism (*LI*, 263).

THE STRUCTURE OF THIS BOOK

The two opening chapters of the book consider the origins and intersections of the two generic strands of Early Modern writing that most influenced Eliot's poetry: the drama and the metaphysical lyric. Chapter One establishes one important

---

[41] Dominic Manganiello, *T.S. Eliot and Dante* (Basingstoke: Houndmills, 1989), remains a definitive study. Edward J.H. Green, *T.S. Eliot et la France* (Paris: Editions Contemporains, 1951), remains valid for drawing attention to many sources; more recently, Piers Gray has some percipient remarks on Eliot and Jules Laforgue in *T.S. Eliot's Intellectual and Poetic Development 1909–1922* (Brighton: Harvester, 1982), 1–22. Jewel Spears Brooker has traced the legacy of F.H. Bradley in Eliot's thought, most specifically in *Mastery and Escape: T.S. Eliot and the Dialectic of Modernism* (Amherst: University of Massachusetts Press, 1994).

ground for this study, since it reviews Eliot's early understanding of the Early Modern period by outlining the books upon it that he owned, and which he constantly referred to. Further, it outlines the contemporary publishing situation around Early Modern literature. It then goes on to consider the critical context for the determining genre for him, even at this stage, namely drama, a genre that was itself considered central to contemporary reconsiderations of the earlier period. Issues of national unity, relations between author and audience, but more particularly those relating to formal coherence are implicated, and considered here through their impact on Eliot's ideas and generic choices.

Chapter Two then opens up the notion, through issues of poetic technique but also its ethos, of an intersection between the lyric and the dramatic in the Early Modern period. This is an intersection that is, in its turn, translated directly into Eliot's poetry. The chapter opens with a consideration of the contemporary critical context around Donne, the key non-dramatic writer for Eliot to about 1930. It considers the impact of contemporary editions of the poet, before homing in upon contemporary critical preoccupation with Donne's metrics. This proves the point of intersection, the entry of the lyric into the dramatic. Comparison is made between Donne and Christopher Marlowe, the accepted innovator in the drama around experimental technique, and this comparison raises the issue of Eliot's own understanding of *vers libre* towards the end of the 1910s. Marlowe was also central to contemporary debates about allusion and literariness, and the chapter considers Eliot's promotion of a contemporary practitioner of a criticism that placed the interlayered textuality of Early Modern drama at the heart of its creation, J.M. Robertson.

Chapter Three looks at Eliot's use of quotations from Early Modern drama as the source of epigraphs in his early poetry to *Poems, 1920*. It also explores the original contexts for those citations, and discovers the beginnings of a practice that will continue across Eliot's career, through which related quotations from single sources provide undercurrents of connection between various of his poems. The chapter includes extensive consideration of 'Gerontion', particularly in its deployment of an epigraph from Shakespeare's *Measure for Measure*, and allusion to two sermons by Lancelot Andrewes. 'Gerontion' represents a very significant moment in the development of Eliot's writing. It is a development derived from the means provided him by his Early Modern sources to engage with, and also to reflect upon, the pressures of modern history and untimeliness—a development that lays the ground for the procedures of *The Waste Land*.

Chapter Four continues the momentum from the discussion of 'Gerontion', to consider Eliot's development of a method to structure a long sequence confronting contemporary history, a method founded on the principles of metaphysical poetry, 1920–2. *The Waste Land* deploys those Early Modern facets of 'wit' and 'conceit' that were receiving particular definition from Eliot's concurrent critical attention, across the time he was working on the new poem. This period also saw Eliot achieving greater concision in his understanding of the role of allusion in relation to these other technical facets, and his development of the notion of the 'cryptogram' to explore how allusions might be re-made and interconnected in the structure of modern work. Subsequently, Chapter Five discusses these methods in relation to *The Waste Land* itself, and the interlinked aftermaths, *Sweeney Agonistes* and 'The Hollow Men'. Eliot's move towards a more overtly dramatic interest, from 1923 onwards, is shown to operate alongside a purgatorial siting of the poetry. The chapter involves a full review of *The Waste Land* manuscript, in order to discover the thread of interconnection around Eliot's Early Modern sources that resonates behind the 'final' version of the poem.

Chapter Six demonstrates the considerable redirection that Eliot's engagement with the Early Modern took, in the time immediately before and after his acceptance into the Church of England, and assumption of British citizenship. He now saw the formerly integrative qualities of wit and the conceit, which he had derived from his considerations of the metaphysical poetry of Donne and Marvell, as, rather, unable to sustain work that displayed, when compared to Dante's, 'disintegration of the intellect'. The chapter reviews the alternative models of poetic relationship evolved by Eliot at this time, the 'doubleness' or 'planes of relation' derived, again, from Early Modern sources, and from critical commentary upon them. Such 'doubleness' is discussed particularly with regard to Eliot's ambition to unite a stoical with a Christian world view, in the poems written immediately after his confirmation: *Ash-Wednesday*, the Ariel poems, and 'Coriolan', all of which find particular Early Modern precursor texts for their new adaptation, towards the creation of religious pattern.

Chapter Seven carries forward the metaphors of 'doubleness' and 'planes in relation', as the poetic and integrative strategies underlying Eliot's later work, to consider their literal and practical application within his poetic dramas. Both strategies take on an ontological aspect through their utilization, in *The Rock* and *Murder in the Cathedral*, to figure spiritual possibility historically, and in the interruptive contexts of the modern world. The final chapter discusses several of the practical aspects of Eliot's saturation in the imagery and stagecraft of Early Modern drama, in connection with his last four plays, and in the theatrical conceits of *Four Quartets*. Again, themes of untimeliness, and its antithesis, 'measure', come to the fore, in these extensive late meditations on identity, and its relation to the multivocal past to be figured, for Eliot, from his engagement with the era of English literature with which he was most fascinated.

The Early Modern period presented a perspective upon the increasingly disordered world that the early to mid twentieth century found spoke to its situation. Eliot's method of integrating that perspective into his poetry, most emblematically in *The Waste Land*, was, this book suggests, largely derived from particular Early Modern sources, and from the inflections which those sources had received in the intervening periods, most particularly in the thirty years before he wrote his first poetry. The approach attends to those receding frames of perception, seeing back through Eliot's work, then that of recent critics, to the Early Modern plays and poems which most fascinated him, and which underwrote his poetry. The modern writer is, throughout this study, a highly informed and consciously prepared reader. Eliot's poetry thus becomes a way of reading the Early Modern, a response which, as a result of the involved sophistication of its understanding, and Eliot's brilliant ability to remake his sources into something new, proved compelling for subsequent poets, novelists, and playwrights.

Through its discovery of the particularity of Eliot's inter-layered reading in the Early Modern period, the book further presents a radical new approach to the consideration of influence in modern poetry. It focuses the material force of the translation of Early Modern form and content together, into the new context of Eliot's work. Media that to date have not been investigated in studies of literary influence—in this case, the editions of poems, plays, and novels with which Eliot was familiar, and the criticism of Early Modern work to which he attended in his essays and reviews—are cited to establish the approach. Eliot referred to particular passages in Early Modern texts repeatedly across his writing life. He saw interconnections between them, which then become threads of connection between various of his own poems.

When thinking about Shakespeare, or George Herbert, Eliot felt that it was necessary to see, primarily, the integrations achieved through their careers as a whole, rather than creating a response founded upon taking their plays or poems one by one. The material, and text-based, focus of the current study therefore uniquely reveals those Early Modern undercurrents, frequently reviewed or reconsidered from a different angle, which provided the integration between thought and technique of Eliot's innovative poetry across his writing life. Eliot could of course be inconsistent and contradictory in his views of Early Modern writers and writing, but always in a manner to move his own creativity forward into different territory. The strikingly modern voice of Eliot's poetry listens to those voices that are making themselves heard through it, Early Modern voices which remain distinct, but which are set in dialogue with, and generate, the constantly new voice of later poetry, as it develops and responds to the pressures of the modern age.

1

'Without a Harmonising Medium'
Eliot in 1919, and Contemporary Criticism of Early Modern Drama

1919: THE EXTENSION LECTURES ON 'ELIZABETHAN LITERATURE'

The year 1919 was a crucial one for T.S. Eliot's engagement with English Early Modern literature. A year after the end of World War I, Eliot's literary interests were refocused in ways that took his poetry into a new mode. His reversion to his favourite literary period at this moment enabled him, as an American writer seeking to integrate himself into English literary culture, to establish a grounded sense of a former national literary tradition. This was a tradition in which aesthetic merit was taken to presume other types of historical and political coherence.

As this chapter will show, in this reversion at this moment, Eliot drew upon a settled vein of criticism regarding the Early Modern, which had come down from late Victorian and Edwardian sources. These sources now enabled Eliot to remake his sense of modern poetry's form and possibilities. Paradoxically, recent criticism about the development of Early Modern work, and particularly about the genre that most interested Eliot, drama, found crucially that the coherent national context out of which the earlier plays had appeared was not reflected in the formal nature of the works themselves. This chapter will delineate the immediate critical background out of which Eliot's mature criticism, and his determinedly modern poetry, appeared. It will do so partly by considering the Early Modern texts, and criticism on them, which we can establish that Eliot owned. This material context provides a means to root that definitive set of textual inter-layerings, from which his poetry is derived, and which this study therefore adopts as its own basis for discussion.

In May of 1919 the University of London Extension Lecture course that Eliot had been tutoring in 'Elizabethan Literature', a course which had begun the previous autumn, came to its end.[1] Over the summer and autumn after his teaching had finished, Eliot used his close association with the *Nation and Athenaeum*, and his contributions to other cultural journals, to write up his reflections on some of the

---

[1] Ronald Schuchard pioneered study of Eliot's Extension Lectures, and of the syllabi and Reading Lists that Eliot provided for them, in an article reprinted as 'In the Lecture Halls' in *Eliot's Dark Angel: Intersections of Life and Art* (New York: Oxford University Press, 1999), 25–51.

topics and texts discussed during the Extension Lectures.[2] Slightly altered versions of several of these journal pieces then went on to form the core essays of Eliot's first critical book, *The Sacred Wood* (1920). Essays on Marlowe, Hamlet, and Jonson are amongst these, as are the opening part of 'Imperfect Critics' (which had first appeared as 'Swinburne and the Elizabethans'), and ' "Rhetoric" and Poetic Drama' (originally 'Whether Rostand Had Something About Him').[3] This last contribution is indicative of the way in which, at this time as later, Eliot could deploy his reflections upon Early Modern literature even when his ostensible subject was removed from it, or rather *because* his subject was removed from it. The Early Modern period served, both now and later, as the major reference point for his thinking about literary style and history. This is a tendency exemplified, in 1919, by Eliot's review of a collection of work by soldiers fighting in World War I, 'The New Elizabethans and the Old', and in his piece 'Reflections on Contemporary Poetry'.[4] A significant culmination of Eliot's already long-term engagement with John Donne also appeared in this year, in a review-article on Donne's sermons, 'Preacher as Artist'. Finally, 'Tradition and the Individual Talent' appeared in two parts in *The Egoist* during September and December.[5] That essay reserves its only passages of close reading for lines from *The Revenger's Tragedy*, now assumed to be by Thomas Middleton, but during Eliot's time commonly attributed (as it was by Eliot himself) to Cyril Tourneur.

It is not only Eliot's criticism in this year that is informed by his reading, at this time and earlier, in the literature of the Early Modern period. 'Burbank with a Baedeker: Bleistein with a Cigar', the last written of the group of quatrain poems begun in 1917, includes reference (amongst others) to the playwrights John Marston and George Chapman, to Shakespeare's *Othello* and to *Antony and Cleopatra*. 'Gerontion', with its epigraph from *Measure for Measure*, was completed in the summer of 1919. 'Gerontion' was the first poem by Eliot exclusively to adopt a variation on the blank verse of Early Modern drama as its metre, and the first poem to move decisively beyond the Laforguian ironies of Eliot's earlier long poems.[6] Valerie Eliot has dated the first mention by Eliot of what would become *The Waste Land* to 5 November 1919; to a short time, in other words, after the

---

[2] Eliot reports having been offered the assistant editorship of the *Nation and Athenaeum* by its editor, John Middleton Murry, in a letter to his mother of 12 March 1919 (*LI*, 327). The two-year contract, offered at £500 per annum, was not secure or well-paid enough to lure him from Lloyd's Bank, however. Instead of taking up the offer, Eliot agreed to contribute frequently to the journal (*LI*, 330).

[3] 'Whether Rostand Had Something About Him' appeared in the *Nation and Athenaeum* no. 4656 on 25 July 1919; 'Swinburne and the Elizabethans' in no. 4663 on 19 September; 'Hamlet and His Problems' in no. 4665, 26 September; 'The Comedy of Humours' on Jonson in no. 4672, 14 November. 'Some Notes on the Blank Verse of Christopher Marlowe' appeared in *Arts and Letters*, vol. II, no. 4, Autumn 1919.

[4] 'The New Elizabethans and the Old' appeared in the *Nation and Athenaeum* no. 4640, 4 April 1919; 'Reflections on Contemporary Poetry' in *The Egoist*, vol. VI, no. 3, July 1919.

[5] 'Preacher as Artist' appeared in the *Nation and Athenaeum* no. 4674, 28 November 1919; 'Tradition and the Individual Talent' in *The Egoist*, vol. VI, nos. 4 and 5.

[6] The dating of these poems is as given by Christopher Ricks (*IMH*, xlii), and agreed by Laurence Rainey, *Revisiting The Waste Land* (New Haven and London: Yale University Press, 2005), 198.

publication of the Hamlet essay, and around the period at which Eliot must have submitted his copy for the Jonson and (perhaps) the Marlowe pieces. *The Waste Land*, as it was first developing, contained extended passages in the verse form already evolved for the recently completed 'Gerontion' (*WLFT*, xvii).[7]

Eliot's reading and thinking about the Early Modern period, at the time of the Extension Lectures and beyond, clearly, therefore, had a decisive impact at this moment. This impact is evident upon both the nature of his identity, as a critic seeking to emerge in the (to him alien) English milieu at the time, and upon his ambition as a poet. It is an impact that would extend across the term of his writing career. Eliot's letters at this point provide a sporadic record of his critical engagement with the period, as he considered how best to shape the essays that might be derived from his teaching involvements, and (presumably) out of his preparatory materials for the Lectures. He began preparing for the course in the summer of 1918, re-reading Jonson; by 3 January 1919 he aspired to produce a book on Elizabethan blank verse (this evolved into a projected book on *Studies in Elizabethan Literature* by 14 September). After the course of lectures had finished, he recorded, in July, reading little 'at present' beyond Tudor drama and prose and Gibbon— presumably he remains keen, after preparing the lectures, to write some kind of book on the period discussed in them (*LI*, 314, 374, 396).[8]

The Reading List that Eliot prepared for his Extension students gives some indication about his initial understanding of the earlier period's range. Eliot followed contemporary critical practice in adopting a synoptic approach towards his subject, tracing literary development from medieval drama through to Jonson and Jacobean tragedy.[9] Even by these models, however, Eliot's course seems particularly ambitious. He sought to cram into its eighteen weeks some reading of the period's prose (Bacon, Hooker, Sidney, Raleigh, Florio's Montaigne), and poetry (Marlowe's *Hero and Leander*, Shakespeare's *Venus and Adonis*, Spenser's the *Fairie Queene*, alongside selected lyric poets), as well as providing detailed discussion of the course's predominant generic focus, which was the drama.

---

[7] Eliot obviously dallied with the notion of printing 'Gerontion' as a 'prelude' or 'preface' to *The Waste Land* at one stage, but was dissuaded from doing so by Pound (*WLFT*, 127). Ricks dates 'The Death of the Duchess' and 'Dirge', parts of *The Waste Land* manuscripts which were later rejected, to 'Summer 1919' (*IMH*, xlii). Rainey, however, dates the former to 1916 and the latter to 1921 (200–1). The issue of the dating of *The Waste Land* drafts, and their relation to Eliot's thinking on the Early Modern period, will form part of the discussion of Chapter Four.

[8] Other letters written during the time of the lectures show Eliot re-familiarizing himself with works not included on the course, presumably for contextual purposes, such as *The Yorkshire Tragedy* (*LI*, 328), attributed to Thomas Middleton.

[9] A synoptic approach was recommended by several of the critics mentioned on Eliot's Reading List for the course, notably Felix E. Schelling, *Elizabethan Drama 1558–1642*, vol. I (Boston: Houghton, Mifflin, and Co., 1908), 1. Such an approach was inevitable for those critics, like John Addington Symonds, also on the Reading List, who adopted an organic model of the development of literary history. Symonds sees drama as progressing according to 'laws of artistic evolution' and a 'law of growth', in *Shakspere's Predecessors in the English Drama* (London: Smith Elder, 1884), 7. Such organic models prevailed in the literary histories of this time. Writing of another critic, J.M. Robertson, who was also much favoured by Eliot (as the next chapter will show), Odin Dekkers provides a useful overview of the quasi-scientific claims being made for literary criticism at this time (*J.M. Robertson: Rationalist and Literary Critic*, Aldershot: Ashgate, 1998, *passim*).

As his Reading List for the course also demonstrates, Eliot thoroughly re-familiarized himself with recent literary criticism on his chosen period when preparing for lectures. Yet his respect for this criticism seems, from the guiding comments entered on the Reading List, to be at best equivocal. His unguarded view of these recommended critics' attempts to describe the literature of the earlier period is given, though, in a piece he wrote on 'Studies in Contemporary Criticism II' from November–December 1918. Of the critical books mentioned also on the Reading List, he wrote that Swinburne's *Age of Shakespeare* was 'neither scholarship nor criticism'; J.A. Symonds's *Predecessors of Shakespere* (sic) was 'absurdly long'; in F.S. Boas's *Shakespeare's Predecessors* 'the literary criticism is negligible'; and that Felix Schelling's *Elizabethan Drama* is 'the most painful of all'.

For Eliot, then, the critical 'field' of his topic remained in his view outmoded at best, and void of critical understanding. It was a field, in other words, that could rapidly be occupied by a new writer who was fascinated by the Early Modern period, and by an American citizen anxious to assimilate himself to Old World 'tradition'. Eliot was not entirely innocent of the potential for opportunism provided by this situation. For him, the common vice shared by these current, and by similar, studies was that they conformed to 'some official ideal of "criticism"', rather than their authors' writing simply and conversationally 'what they think'. Eliot's evident impatience with the nature of recent criticism of the Early Modern period, as well as his sense that it also provided a definitive exemplar of all recent critical activity, is reflected in his summary dismissal of it, in 'Studies in Contemporary Criticism II', as either 'superfluous or grossly inflated'.[10] This is the tone he adopted, also, in the comments he entered on the Extension Lectures Reading List, where his students are told, for instance, that 'there is very little good criticism of Elizabethan and Jacobean drama'.[11]

Eliot's evident impatience, in its turn, underlies his advocacy of an Aristotelian method of criticism in 'Imperfect Critics' in *The Sacred Wood* (1920)—the essay which reprints, as its first part, Eliot's attack on Swinburne's *Age of Shakespeare* published in 1919. At this key moment in Eliot's own thinking, therefore, it is clear that part of his drive more fully to write up material deployed in his Extension Lectures is to put forward a new standard of criticism both for the Early Modern Period and, therefore, more generally in the English context. He wished to avoid the afflatus, tedious length, and plot-summary-led characteristics of the available writing on the earlier period. His equivocation about producing a book-length study, which continued at least down to 1926, must in part derive from his unease at the laborious and lengthy contemporary approach that seemed inevitable in order to complete this task.[12]

---

[10] Eliot, 'Studies in Contemporary Criticism II', *The Egoist*, vol. V, no. 10, November–December 1918, 132.

[11] Schuchard, *Eliot's Dark Angel*, 49.

[12] The idea that he might write longer studies about the period covered in his lectures persists in Eliot's letters across consequent years. In 1921 he wrote to John Middleton Murry proposing *two* volumes, one on 'Elizabethan' and another on 'Seventeenth Century' literature (*LI*, 553). Similar plans are presented in other letters (see *LI*, 263, 320, 374, 396, 475; *LII*, 222–3, 254, and the Prefaces

SOURCE MATERIALS

It is vital to realize that, whatever the definitive nature of the impact of Eliot's engagement with Early Modern literature, especially in 1919, upon his critical writings, and upon his poetry, his designation of this as his 'favourite literary period' reflects his already-established knowledge of the subject of his 1918–9 lectures. This was an understanding and knowledge that involved thorough familiarity with primary texts. But it *also* involved a deep awareness of the relevant contemporary critical debate on the subject, debate that had appeared across the previous thirty years, initially from amateur, and then from increasingly professional (and university-based) critics.[13] This understanding and awareness is clearly derived from, and partly reflected by, the comparatively high number of Early Modern texts and criticism that Eliot actually owned, even as a young poet-critic. During the preparations of Eliot's mother for a house-move around August 1920, she sent Eliot a list of those books of his that remained at the family home in St Louis. This list includes works by Marlowe, Jonson (3 volumes), Shakespeare (38 volumes), Hooker's *Ecclesiastical Polity*, *England's Helicon* (an anthology of Early Modern lyrics), collections of Wither, Carew, Marvell, Campion; J.M. Manley's *Specimens of Pre-Shakespearean Drama* (a named source of texts for the Extension Lectures); Browne's *Religio Medici*; three volumes of Walter Pater, and 'Spingarn's Renaissance', the American critic's *A History of Literary Criticism in the Renaissance* (*LI*, 486–7).

To an extent, Eliot's absorption in the Early Modern period reflected, but also resisted, an upsurge of interest that had been developing for some time. The last decades of the nineteenth century, and the first decades of the twentieth, saw a reappearance of editions of Early Modern drama and poetry, as well as an increasing quantity of secondary criticism on it. Earlier editions of the dramatists, like those of A.H. Bullen and Alexander Dyce, were now replaced by popular editions such as the Mermaid Best Plays Series, under the General Editorship of Havelock Ellis, and later by Ernest Rhys's Everyman Library editions, which also included a full coverage of Early Modern poetry and prose. These more popular editions gathered around them, as editors and writers of introductions, a considerable, if eclectic, group of scholars (some of whom would later produce definitive editions of Early Modern authors who were reviewed by Eliot in the 1920s). Aside from the Mermaid volumes that Havelock Ellis chose to edit himself (Ford, Middleton II), for instance, he recruited a team of critics that included Brinsley Nicholson and C.H. Herford (Jonson), Rhys himself (Dekker), A. Wilson Verity (Heywood), and John Addington Symonds (Webster and Tourneur). He also recruited the poet-critics Algernon Swinburne

---

to *Homage to John Dryden* and *The Varieties of Metaphysical Poetry*). But Eliot also seems to have been contemplating writing an extended study of this period *before* the opportunity arose to discuss it in the Extension Lecture course. A Notice was printed in *The Egoist*, August 1917, heralding a series of six articles by Ezra Pound on the 'Elizabethan Classicists' (which did appear), to be followed by 'a series of articles on Elizabethan drama' by Eliot (which did not) (*The Egoist*, vol. IV, no. 7, 101).

[13] Hugh Grady has written interestingly in this light about the relation between Shakespeare criticism, the institution of English as a subject within the academy, and modernism (*The Modernist Shakespeare*, Oxford: Clarendon Press, 1991, ch. 1).

(Middleton I) and Arthur Symons (Massinger, *Nero and Other Plays*). Swinburne and Symonds's book-length studies of this period's drama were then reprinted in the late 1910s. As later in his criticism, his review-articles on these books formed Eliot's reflections on critical and poetic methods in *The Sacred Wood*.[14]

These popular editions of the dramatists were recommended by Eliot for the Extension Lectures Reading List, as were more expensive recent editions, such as J.M. Manley's *Specimens of the Pre-Shakespearean Drama*, and C.F. Tucker Brooke's *The Shakespeare Apocrypha*. The editorial and critical interest that late Victorian and Edwardian *poets* had in the Elizabethan and Jacobean periods is again advertised in Eliot's recommendations for his Extension Lectures course, which feature Rupert Brooke's posthumous *John Webster and the Elizabethan Drama* (1916) and the 1909 Everyman *The Plays of Christopher Marlowe*, introduced by Edward Thomas. The views expressed in these editions by these slightly older poets do not simply provide points of debate for Eliot's subsequent critical essays, however. Their interpretations figure consistently behind that evolving understanding of the Early Modern period which, in 1919, reshaped Eliot's thinking about the poetry he might write. This upsurge of cultural interest in Early Modern at the time, and particularly in non-Shakespearean drama, exemplified in these new editions and critical works, was generally credited, and repeatedly credited by Eliot, as deriving from a sole source. Charles Lamb's *Specimens of English Dramatic Poets* went through several reprints at this time, most notably perhaps in the edition by Israel Gollancz in 1893, and Lamb's example in treating of his 'specimens' will be discussed below.[15]

That other key genre for Eliot, lyric poetry from the Early Modern period, was now also available in cheaper editions, with the established Muses Library collections vying with the newer Everyman and Oxford texts. Spanning the century's turn, Edward Arber presented ten volumes of *British Anthologies* of lyric verse, including several from the Early Modern period. He also reprinted original anthologies from the period, such as *Songs and Sonnettes*, which he produced as *Tottell's Miscellany* and *England's Helicon*, both in their original form.[16]

---

[14] The Mermaid series' original publishers, Vizetelly and Co., were renowned as important avant-garde publishers at the time of Ellis's editorship. They were especially important for publishing early translations of Zola and of *Madame Bovary*. The Mermaid Series as originally planned, and Ellis's editorship, actually ended when Vizetelly was jailed and fined for obscenity for publishing a translation of Zola's *La Terre*: he was only freed after petitioning from Leslie Stephen, Thomas Hardy, Olive Schreiner, and others. Ellis's editorship of the Mermaid drama series obviously attuned itself to this atmosphere. The title pages of the individual volumes each bear the proclamation 'Unexpurgated Edition'. This prurient claim is dubious; as Ellis's biographer Phyllis Grosskurth acknowledges, Ellis's own grasp of some of the editorial issues raised by the plays was unsteady, and the editions were largely dependent on, if not actually pirated from, earlier series such as those by Bullen and Dyce (*Havelock Ellis: A Biography*, London: Quartet Books, 1980, 112–3).

[15] Lamb is repeatedly acknowledged by Eliot for this instigation, through to as late as 'To Criticize the Critic' (1961). He alone, Eliot had maintained in 1924, was responsible for the continuing 'enthusiasm' for this drama (*SE*, 109–10).

[16] Such editions had considerable popularity amongst modernist writers. Virginia Woolf's copy of Arber's multi-volume *English Garner* (which again gathers much Early Modern work) was a favourite source for quotation in her novels. She had to have her set repaired and rebound, so frequently did she refer to it (Alice Fox, *Virginia Woolf and the Literature of the English Renaissance*, Oxford: Clarendon Press, 1990, 159).

Arber's 'Surrey and Wyatt', 'Shakespeare', and 'Jonson' selections all appear on the Extension Lectures Reading List.

The other document that aids our knowledge of the Early Modern materials Eliot owned in the first part of his career, is an inventory of Eliot's library, prepared *c*.1933 by Vivien Eliot. As the inventory shows, Eliot owned many of these popular editions of plays and poems, as well as some of the more expensive and scholarly anthologies. By that point, he owned 'ten volumes of the thin paper edition of the "Mermaid dramatists"'; the Muses Library volumes of Vaughan, Campion, Drummond, Crashaw, Donne, Marvell; twenty-two volumes of the Temple Edition of Shakespeare; all three volumes of *The Minor Caroline Poets* edited by George Saintsbury; *Some Longer Elizabethan Poems* edited by Bullen; and reprints of lyric anthologies, including *Parnassus Biceps* and *The Phoenix Nest*.[17] These were the editions (later supplemented by some borrowed from the London Library) to which Eliot referred, when writing his essays on the Early Modern period; or when checking a quotation from its writings that might then be stolen for his own poetry. Obviously, Vivien Eliot's inventory is incomplete: absent from it are Early Modern theological and educational works by such as John Bramhall, Lancelot Andrewes, Thomas Browne, or Donne's sermons and Sir Thomas Elyot's *The Book Named the Gouvernour*, which are all referred to in the Extension Lectures Reading List, and then that relating to Eliot's Clark Lectures (1926). These works all feature, as we shall see, in Eliot's poetry as well.[18]

We can gather a reasonable understanding of the breadth of Eliot's knowledge of Early Modern literature from this inventory, whilst noting also that he retained many of the copies of the critical books on the period which he chose to review from at least 1919. The popular editions of the drama, poetry, and prose of the earlier period which Eliot owned rarely included full textual apparatus. They did, however, contain substantial critical introductions, to which Eliot responded in his mature essays, right into the 1940s.[19] These, and other critical materials available to him on the Early Modern period, provided, therefore, a point of reference, and a formative presence, in his own critical thinking and in his relatively changing poetic, across his active writing career.

---

[17] Bodleian Library MS Eng. Lett B 20. The inventory also includes unidentified editions of Hooker, Bacon, Marvell, Crashaw, Charles Cotton, Beaumont and Fletcher (the Extension Lectures recommend the Everyman), Massinger and Ford, Sidney, Puttenham and Webbe, Spenser (the Extension Lectures recommend the Oxford edition), Wither, Carew, Dryden—as well as major multi-volume editions more recently produced at the time the inventory was made. These included Herford and Simpson's Jonson and F.S. Lucas's Webster, presumably the review copies he had received at the time of their publication. The impact of these later editions upon Eliot's mature thinking about the Early Modern period will be discussed in Chapter Six.

[18] The Clark Reading List appears in *VMP*, 64–5, including Ron Schuchard's notes.

[19] For example, Eliot praises but disagrees with Havelock Ellis's 'excellent introduction' to the pertinent Mermaid volume in 'John Ford', 1932 (*SE*, 202); he mentions Symonds's introduction to the Mermaid *Webster and Tourneur* in a 1941 radio talk on 'The Duchess of Malfy' [sic] (*The Listener*, vol. XXVI, no. 675, 18 December 1941, 826).

EARLY MODERN LITERATURE AND THE NATION

What emerges from the material constituting Eliot's library, and from his Reading List of secondary criticism for the Extension Lectures, is a canon-forming view of the earlier period, which often feels now familiar to us, largely because of Eliot's particular formulations and critical positions. When, aged thirty, Eliot reread books for, and prepared, his Lectures on 'Elizabethan Literature', and for the spate of critical prose of 1919, which would also result in significant rethinking of his poetic method, he was drawing upon a considerable amount of informed, private, absorption in the earlier period. This was an absorption already reflected, as Chapter Three demonstrates, in the allusions and epigraphs given to his early poetry. That absorption was, inevitably, mediated through the critical apparatus of the editions of Early Modern texts which Eliot owned and from which he quoted in his essays. It was also mediated by the scholarly and critical work on the earlier period reflected in his Reading List for the Extension Lectures. For, his reading in this scholarship, however resistant he was to its extent and critical approach, was something which he had also absorbed. This chapter will therefore review Eliot's understanding of the Early Modern period by 1919, not just through the lens of the literary texts that he set for his Extension Lectures, but also through some of the critical reading he had absorbed up to that point. It will pursue, specifically, ideas about the drama, the genre that predominated in Eliot's critical thinking now as later. These are ideas that are often encapsulated by him in terms that then resonate across Eliot's ideas about *all* genres.

Alongside its adoption of an organicist model of literary-historical development, John Addington Symonds's *Shakespere's Predecessors in the English Drama* (first published in 1884 but reprinted four times down to 1920) presents, despite Eliot's quibbles over its length, a view of the Early Modern period that is representative, in the context of the later studies published into the first decades of the twentieth century. In many ways, Symonds's perspective resonates with Eliot's understanding of this literature, and of relevant cultural history, as given in his most famous essays. For Symonds, the unique achievement of what he called Elizabethan literature was that it arose from a 'spirit of nationality mature and conscious'. It derived from a unified England that was shortly to pass away, an England:

> perplexed as yet by no deeply reaching political discords such as those which later on confused the hierarchy of classes and imperilled the monarchical principle. It was a spirit in which the loyalty to the person of the sovereign was at one with the sense of national independence. A powerful grasp on the realities of life was then compatible with romantic fancy and imaginative fervour. The solid ground supported the poet.

In ways that speak typically, and perhaps surprisingly, to Eliot's historical understanding, Symonds sees being raised from this sturdy national foundation the robust and exciting style of Elizabethan and Jacobean literature, its 'extraordinary vigour and vividness in the use of language, running riot often in extravagance and verbose eccentricity'. Yet such uncontainable exuberance, for Symonds, further heightened the role of the drama in drawing the country together:

it grew up beneath the patronage of the whole nation; the public to which these playwrights appealed was the English people, from Elizabeth upon the throne down to the lowest ragamuffin in the streets.[20]

Symonds's view of these matters was commonly shared at around this time. For the American critic Felix Schelling, this perceived unified appeal in the Elizabethan drama allowed for a negative commentary, in a style close to Eliot's later comparisons, on recent work. For Schelling, the Elizabethan material marked a forcible contrast to literature from the late nineteenth century. Elizabethan writing was 'focused in the activities of the age itself and was literally a great national utterance'. 'Modern drama,' however, is 'less interesting' and contains 'more of the individual less of the time'. It 'intellectualizes emotion... in the curious minutiae of the psychologist'.[21] In Thomas Seccombe and J.W. Allen's two-volume survey, *The Age of Shakespeare (1579–1631)* (recommended by Eliot, along with the Symonds and the Schelling, for the Extension Lectures), the sudden flourishing of drama, particularly in the late sixteenth century, is predicated upon England's new national status:

> England had successfully asserted its independence of any foreign power or prelates. It had become self-conscious as never before, and proud of its past and its present. Its developing sea power gave it an increasing sense of security. Its freedom from internal strife enabled it to concentrate its energies upon expansion in all directions. In the monarchy the new-born self-conscious unity, the self-sufficing isolation of the people, was symbolized and all but worshipped.[22]

Seccombe and Allen's survey, like the Symonds, was a popular one—it went through six editions in its first eleven years. Its implication is clear: a unified, stable national structure, under a stable monarchy, provides the basis for literary excellence. 'Internal strife' destroys self-sufficiency. Such imperialist statements recur across criticism of the Early Modern period at this time. Symonds's General Introduction to the Mermaid Series, for instance, reinforces its justification for reprinting the earlier drama straightforwardly:

> The spontaneity and freedom... of which I have been speaking, form so conspicuous a note of Elizabethan literature that when the genius of our race and language takes a new direction under conditions favourable to liberty, as may be seen at large in the

---

[20] John Addington Symonds, *Shakespere's Predecessors in the English Drama* (London: Smith Elder, 1884; 1908 edition), 16, 54. Subsequent references to this edition appear in the text. Symonds made a similar point about the drama's centrality to, and availability for, the nation, in the General Introduction he wrote at Havelock Ellis's request to the Mermaid Series, as published in the initial volume, *Christopher Marlowe* (London: Vizetelly, 1887, xi–xii).

[21] Schelling, *Elizabethan Drama 1558–1642*, vol. I, lxii. Subsequent references to this edition appear in the text. A. David Moody has suggested that Ezra Pound, Eliot's interlocutor from the mid 1910s about poetry, conceived an immense personal dislike for Schelling, when he encountered him as a tutor for Renaissance Literature at the University of Pennsylvania. This deterred Pound from taking any interest in Schelling's main subject, Elizabethan drama. See *Ezra Pound: Poet. A Portrait of the Man and his Work. The Young Genius 1885–1920* (Oxford: Oxford University Press, 2007), 29.

[22] Thomas Seccombe and J.W. Allen, *The Age of Shakespeare (1579–1631)*, vol. II (London: G. Bell & Sons 1903; 1914 edition), 3.

history of the present century, poets turn their eyes instinctively to the old dramatists, assimilate their audacities, and do not show their imperfections.[23]

Symonds's approach, which derives the pertinence of the Early Modern drama through its influence upon key contemporaries such as Browning, Dowson, and Swinburne, initially seems remote from the determinedly modern note of Eliot's 1919 essays, with their scientific analogies for creativity, and their calls for Aristotelian 'intelligence' to set against the sensationalism of contemporary criticism.[24] And yet the polemical implications of such readings as Seccombe and Allen's, or Symonds's, are not remote from Eliot's own key historical theories about the earlier period, as formulated in 'The Metaphysical Poets' (1921). There, Eliot notoriously asserted that a 'dissociation of sensibility', a split between the emotions and the intelligence, entered English culture at the time of the English Civil War, and could be perceived subsequently in Milton and Dryden (*SE*, 288).[25] Metaphysical poetry, though it bore intimations of just such a dissociation (and Eliot was increasingly from 1926 to highlight that fact), nonetheless was free of it.

But Eliot's theory about a 'dissociation of sensibility' also seems to have been, at least partially, inflected by the contemporary revivification of such critical readings of earlier literary history, in 1919, at the time of his first essays on its literature. For notions of the exemplary, inspirational, and recuperative potential of Early Modern literature had reappeared in debates of which Eliot was crucially aware, in the immediate aftermath of the catastrophic cultural breakdown that occurred with World War I. A series of articles ran from July through October 1919 in *The Nation and Athenaeum*, called 'Our Inaccessible Heritage'. The series formed a debate, conducted between publishers and readers, largely through the 'Letters' column. This was a debate about the fact that, in the aftermath of the Great War, there were now again few cheap editions of the classics, and more specifically editions of the English literary classics, currently available.

Eliot contributed a wry letter to this debate on 24 October 1919. He noted that, given the paucity of available texts, it would be helpful were the lending libraries to extend their opening hours, so that businessmen like himself might borrow books in the evening. And yet the terms of this debate about literary heritage, as signalled in a leading article by John Middleton Murry of 11 July, were provocative for other reasons. Eight months from the end of the war Murry claimed, whilst acknowledging the platitudinous nature of what he was saying, that 'the Englishman's most magnificent heritage is English literature'. Murry's elision of national history into literary history then further focused itself, as he made it evident that he had in mind only one phase of English literature:

---

[23] Symonds, General Introduction, *Christopher Marlowe*, xii.

[24] Eliot, 'The Perfect Critic' (*SW*, 9, 18).

[25] Swinburne identifies a similar phenomenon of dissociation emerging in the work of Webster, in *The Age of Shakespeare* (London: Chatto & Windus, 1908, 46); Symonds, in *Shakespere's Predecessors*, attributes literary decline to 'the civil wars': 'Political and religious interests, more grave than those of art, consigned the dramatists and poets of the sixteenth century to oblivion for a time.... But the spirit of England has revived in this age of Victoria.' (58–9).

> With all their faults the Elizabethans are the fountain-head of English literature, a perennial source of reinvigoration to the English language. If they are made inaccessible, contemporary literature is to some extent inevitably starved.[26]

Eliot's continued espousal of the Early Modern period, in his poetry and in his critical essays, was, therefore, largely in agreement with the political and nationalist resonances of these debates, from the late nineteenth century into his own day. This was a view he was consciously signed up to, at least until 1921, when *The Waste Land* was largely complete (and echoes continue down to the last of the *Four Quartets*, written during the early years of World War II).[27] At this time, in other words, Eliot's Early Modern interests were complicit with national questions, and he was following a contemporary strain of critical thought in conceiving this to be so. However, despite the inclusive drive of this shared ambition around the renewal of Early Modern writing in contemporary work, it is noticeable that neither the turn-of-the-century critics, nor Eliot himself, see that writing as offering viable models of unity, formal coherence, or wholeness per se (vide Murry's 'faults').

THE NATURE OF EARLY MODERN DRAMA

For the late nineteenth-century critics, it is the *mass* of Elizabethan drama that warrants its unrepeatable phenomenon as 'national utterance,' not (outside perhaps examples from Shakespeare and Jonson) the individual play. The texts of Early Modern drama, in fact, are often seen as fragmentary, inconclusive, or only momentarily brilliant. Again, Symonds's *Shakespere's Predecessors in English Drama* determines the ground for the critical texts with which we know Eliot to have been familiar:

> Reviewing this unique achievement of our literary genius [the Early Modern drama], the critic is puzzled not only by its complexity, but also by its incompleteness as a work of art. The Drama in England has no Attic purity of outline, no statuesque definition of form, no unimpeachable perfection of detail. The total effect of those accumulated plays might be compared to that of a painted window or a piece of tapestry, where the colour and assembled forms convey an ineffaceable impression, but which, when we examine the whole work more closely, seems to consist of hues laid side by side without a harmonising medium. The greatness of the material presented to our study lies less

---

[26] John Middleton Murry, 'Our Inaccessible Heritage', *The Nation and Athenaeum*, no. 4654, 11 July 1919, 581. Eliot's contribution to the debate appeared in no. 4669 (1076). In his 'Reflections on Contemporary Poetry', which appeared in this July issue, Eliot rehearsed some of the arguments given classic statement in 'Tradition and the Individual Talent' which was to be published later in 1919. Eliot does so in terms not remote from Murry's argument here, as he deplores the lack of a visible sense of tradition in contemporary poetry ('No dead voices speak through the living voice, no reincarnation, no recreation'), and then gives a countering example of the 'saturation' in Seneca to be found in Chapman (39). David Goldie has some insightful pages on Murry's steady stewardship of the journal amidst the 'radical uncertainty of the post-war world', in *A Critical Difference: T.S. Eliot and John Middleton Murry in English Literary Criticism 1919–1928* (Oxford: Clarendon Press, 1998), 37ff.

[27] Carly di Pietro has drawn scholars' attention to another debate in 1919, which prioritized the significance of the earlier period (although di Pietro does not mention the *Nation and Athenaeum* exchanges). The *TLS* ran a series of exchanges about the authority of Shakespeare's Folio; di Pietro, *Shakespeare and Modernism* (Cambridge: Cambridge University Press, 2006), 148).

in the parts than in the mass, less in particular achievements than in the spirit which sustains and animates the whole... it is the multitude of fellow-workers, and the bulk of work produced in concert, that impress the mind; the unity not of a simple and coherent thing of beauty, but of an intricate and many-membered organism, striving after self-accomplishment, and reaching that accomplishment in Shakespere's art, which enthrals attention. (11)

Later in his study, Symonds attributes this lack of classical formal unity in his period of study to the loss of a religious or ritual fascination to the drama, as it developed away from one of its origins, identifiable in the medieval mystery plays.[28] Forgivingly, he concludes that, given their comparatively early place in literary development, 'It is not to be wondered that the works of our Elizabethan playwrights should be incomplete and fragmentary, grandiose by accident, perfect only in portions.' (252)[29] In his comparable survey, Felix Schelling bemoaned the 'lack of finish' of nearly every Early Modern play (xli). Seccombe and Allen, too, lament the fact that non-Shakespearean drama 'is a drama of passages, of passionate or joyous moments, of inspirational flashes. It is amazingly unequal, crude'. (146) In similar vein, when introducing the first volume of the Mermaid *Thomas Middleton*, Swinburne admitted the 'extreme inequality and roughness' of his subject's output.[30]

This overriding and established approach to criticism of Early Modern drama sets itself, therefore, to distinguish the location, and the specific quality, of its 'inspirational' scenes or passages, as opposed to discovering formal coherence amidst what is perceived as wayward and often chaotic writing. Perhaps surprisingly, this approach is an exercise in taste not alien to Eliot's own method, from the outset of his professional critical writing. 'Reflections on *Vers Libre*' (1917) finds Eliot celebrating passages in Webster and Middleton where the irregularity of metre and shortening of lines work, he claims, to produce the 'highest intensity' of dramatic effect. Alternately, he berates the same playwrights in the same plays for producing passages where the drama is 'spoilt by regular accentuation' (*TCC*, 187). Exactly a decade later, we find Eliot deploying the same critical methodology, in his essay on 'Thomas Middleton', praising certain moments in the plays, whilst complaining about the 'mixture of tedious discourse and sudden reality', the lack of sustained rhythm and tone, even in the work of this, amongst his favourite of playwrights (*SE*, 162).[31]

---

[28] Speaker 'E', in Eliot's 'Dialogue on Poetic Drama' (1928), claims that perfect 'drama springs from religious liturgy'. Speaker 'B', however, condemns this confusion of literature with religion (*Of Dramatick Poesie: An Essay 1668* by John Dryden. Preceded by a Dialogue on Poetic Drama by T.S. Eliot (London: Frederick Etchells and Hugh MacDonald, 1928), xv–vi.

[29] Symonds makes a similar point with reference to his playwrights in his Introduction to the Mermaid *Webster and Tourneur*: 'Both playwrights have this point in common, that their forte lies not in the construction of plots, or in the creation of characters, so much as in an acute sense for dramatic situations. Their plots are involved and stippled... and do not rightly hang together.' (London: Vizetelly, 1888, xii. See also xix).

[30] Algernon Charles Swinburne, Introduction to *Thomas Middleton*, vol. I, ed. Havelock Ellis (London: Vizetelly, 1887), viii.

[31] As late as 1953, Eliot provided a laudatory Foreword to the English translation of Henri Fluchère's *Shakespeare*, in which the French critic consistently measures the 'illogical' plots of Elizabethan drama, and of Shakespeare himself, against classical (Attic and French) models (London: Longman, 60, 114). Such views had already become commonplace a decade into Eliot's critical

Eliot's critical method, when treating Early Modern drama, would seem to be very responsive, therefore, to the real issue about it as identified by the preceding genera-tion of critics. Yet he could also be more equivocal and sceptical, particularly when considering the example set by Lamb, the credited renewer of interest in these works. Eliot criticized the vogue of criticism established in *Specimens of English Dramatic Poets*, at the same time as he acknowledged its historical and recuperative signifi-cance. Lamb's method did precisely what the late nineteenth-century critics sought, by presenting for examination key scenes or passages from the drama, and so reduc-ing the source plays to intense and illuminating moments of poetry. Eliot complains in 'Four Elizabethan Dramatists' (1924) that this method suggests that the plays are best enjoyed as private celebrations of poetic worth, rather than as works to be per-formed on the public stage. For him, Lamb resurrected those plays for modern read-ers, but single-handedly 'ruined' the prospects for modern poetic drama in production. This blurring of intention is something that his own dramatic writing, inaugurated with *Sweeney Agonistes*, upon which he was working in 1924, strove to counter (*SE*, 110). And yet, Eliot's identification of unevenness of tone and quality, his singling-out of representative passages of poetic excellence, and his often-repeated reversion to the same scenes and even speeches from his favoured Early Modern works (a rever-sion that this current study will identify and consider later), show an essential ambi-guity in his critical method, when approaching the drama. As we shall see, this uncertainty of approach critically then feeds into tension around the structuring of Eliot's longer poetic sequences, from 1919 onwards.[32]

Such tension, in its turn, also fed into the initial reception of Eliot's writing within academic circles. His poetry was immediately seized upon by the emerging school of American New Criticism, as offering contemporary examples of the much-valued principles of achievement and resolution in poetic form. Eliot's criti-cal writing seemed to warrant the New Critics' discovery of such unities in Early Modern writing.[33] Yet, the critical texts on the Early Modern period with which Eliot was familiar rooted the achievement of that period in opposite qualities. The terms and phrases adopted by such as Symonds, when considering the earlier drama ('complex', 'incomplete', 'fragmentary', 'mosaic', 'without a harmonizing medium'), look forward to Eliot's terminology about the necessary nature of mod-ern poetry in 'The Metaphysical Poets' and elsewhere, and also prefigure debates that have surrounded his poetic practice.[34] Eliot's poetic sequences, from 'Gerontion'

---

engagement with the Early Modern period, however. For example, F.L. Lucas's General Introduction to his multi-volume *The Complete Works of John Webster* insists that the popular audience for the origi-nal performances wanted 'a succession of great moments... on the stage, not a well-made play'. This is a desire Lucas sees shared by contemporary cinema audiences (London: Chatto and Windus, 1928, 17). Eliot reviewed this edition twice.

[32] Bernard Bergonzi has noted what he calls the 'paradox' in Eliot's position on Lamb, in *T.S. Eliot* (New York: Macmillan, 1972), 60.

[33] See, for example, Cleanth Brooks, *Modern Poetry and the Tradition* (Chapel Hill: University of North Carolina Press, 1939), 173–6.

[34] That such qualities were also being highlighted with regard to some *lyric* writing in the earlier period is exemplified, for example, in Canon Beeching's Introduction to the *Poems of Henry Vaughan, Silurist*, in the Muses Library edition which Eliot owned: 'Indeed, if truth must be told, Vaughan is

through to *Little Gidding*, operate, of course, through verse paragraphs containing varied tones and materials, whose integration or otherwise it remains the task of his readers to determine.[35] The episodic nature of Eliot's sequences, moving freshly but unpredictably, as they do, between materials whose relation is often obscure or cryptic, and often threaded upon a constellation of references or allusions around similar themes, seems closer to the received notion of Early Modern heterogeneity than it does to the notion of New Critical completion.

RHETORIC AND REALISM IN DRAMA

Criticism of the Early Modern drama contemporary to Eliot defined, then, for him, a broader and linked set of complexities about poetic coherence and, alternatively, the impressionistic enjoyment of the moments of poetry as they pass. At the core of these debates lies the balance (or lack of balance) identified as crucial by Eliot in 'Thomas Middleton': the relation in the Early Modern period between literary discourse, or rhetoric, and reality. It is a balance that Ronald Bush has seen as crucial to Eliot's early critical arguments, and so to his developing poetic method, across the later 1910s.[36] It is also a balance that much exercised the previous generation of critics to Eliot when considering the Early Modern period. These were critics to whom Eliot's personal library, Reading Lists for lectures, and essays draw attention. Rupert Brooke, for instance, when writing on John Webster, in the book recommended by Eliot for the Extension Lectures, picked up a familiar point about incoherence in Webster's plotting, with characters' speeches in *The White Devil* seen to be particularly unrevealing of their motives. But Brooke saw this, surprisingly, as an *advantage*:

> On the whole this is a virtue; or seems to be in the modern mind. Characters in a play gain in realism and a mysterious solemnity, if they act unexplainedly on instinct, like people in real life, and not on rational and publicly-stated grounds, like men in some modern plays.[37]

very much the poet of fine lines and stanzas, of imaginative intervals.' That last phrase might apply to the episodic nature of some of Eliot's passages (London: George Routledge, 1905, vol. I, xlviii).

[35] Jewel Spears Brooker's chapter on 'The Structure of Eliot's "Gerontion": An Interpretation Based on Bradley's Doctrine of the Systematic Nature of Truth', in *Mastery and Escape: T.S. Eliot and the Dialectic of Modernism* (Amherst: University of Massachusetts Press, 1994), 81ff, for example, offers a fine reading of Eliot's poem, whilst also exemplifying the issue I am referring to here.

[36] Ronald Bush, *T.S. Eliot: A Study in Character and Style* (New York: Oxford University Press, 1983), Chapter Two, 'The Pathology of Rhetoric', 17–31.

[37] Rupert Brooke, *John Webster and the Elizabethan Drama* (London: Sidgwick and Jackson, 1916), 92. Eliot's recommendation of this book on his Extension Lectures Reading List is equivocal. He brackets it with Swinburne's *Age of Shakespeare* and *Ben Jonson* as 'interesting though misleading' (Schuchard, *Eliot's Dark Angel*, 49). He would presumably have been uneasy about Brooke's repeated and unqualified reversion to 'instinct' when seeking to explain characters' motivation. As a former member of Cambridge's Marlowe Society, Brooke defended Webster's texts as works for performance (23). But, perhaps paradoxically, he neglected the poetry in Webster, seeing him instead as a proto-novelist. Eliot would presumably have found such a remark as this both interesting *and* misleading: 'Webster's literary skill, his managing genius for incorporating fragments of his experience, his "bitter flashes" and slow brooding atmosphere of gloom, would have been more tremendous untrammelled by dramatic needs.' (80).

Brooke's contention that it is the mimetic realism of Elizabethan drama that makes it exceptional, but that this has considerable formal consequence, looks back at least as far as the Romantics. Coleridge (who, according to Eliot's 1918 Reading List, wrote 'the best criticism' available of Early Modern drama) found these qualities most strongly in Shakespeare, where:

> the heterogeneous is limited, as it is in nature.... He entered into no analysis of the passions or faiths of men, but assured himself that such and such passions and faiths were grounded in our common nature, and not in the mere accidents of ignorance or disease.[38]

Lamb, when justifying his choice of these particular *Specimens* over potentially thousands of others, wrote of his preference for those moments in the dramas that 'treat of human life and manners, rather than masques, and Arcadian pastorals'. As a result, his selections derive from 'tragic rather than comic poetry'. This tendency towards the tragedies left its mark on the predilection of later nineteenth-century writers, and, thence, upon the critical emphasis of Eliot himself.[39] The comparative realism of Early Modern dramatic writing had become a measure of its value, within much criticism, by the end of the nineteenth century; one version of it clearly formed part of the appeal of that writing for Eliot, who immediately translated an instance of this realism into his poetry in 1919.[40] Yet, beyond implying that Elizabethan writing had modern pertinence through its 'realism' alone, the preceding generation of critics to Eliot took debates about 'realism' into specific consideration of Jonson and Donne, two writers particularly at the forefront of Eliot's critical thinking at the time of the Extension Lectures. (Donne's complicated importance in this regard will be discussed more fully in the next chapter.)

For these critics the high status that Jonson had been accorded in the Early Modern period remained unchallenged.[41] But the *nature* of his achievement, particularly when deploying his characteristic comedic Humours, seems more difficult to quantify, given the value placed at this time upon 'realism' above all other qualities. Seccombe and Allen, who ranked Jonson's perfection next to Shakespeare's, seek to draw a fine distinction between the two:

[38] Samuel Taylor Coleridge, *Essays and Lectures on Shakespeare and Some other Old Dramatists* (London: Dent, 1907), 56.

[39] Charles Lamb, *Specimens of English Dramatic Poets* (London: Routledge, 1927 edition), xix.

[40] Schelling notes the dramatists' 'uncompromising realism' (xix); Havelock Ellis found John Ford 'a sensitive observer who had meditated deeply on the springs of human nature, especially in women', in his Introduction to the Mermaid *John Ford* (London: Vizetelly, 1888, xvi). The edition of the medieval plays, *Everyman and Other Interludes*, which Eliot set on the Extension Lectures list, finds Ernest Rhys promoting the continuing relevance of the plays since they 'hide under their archaic dress the human interest that all dramatic art... can claim when it is touched with our real emotions and sensations' (London: Dent, 1909, vii).

[41] Eliot's first poem, 'A Lyric', written at school, was an imitation of Jonson's poetry (*LI*, 3; *CPP*, 590). James E. Miller Jr thinks that the model is the alternating four- and three-stress iambic of 'Drink to me only', in *T.S. Eliot: The Making of an American Poet 1888–1922* (Pennsylvania: University of Pennsylvania Press, 2005), 39. Eliot's first attempt at verse therefore bears striking resemblance to his practice of rewriting Early Modern sources, through to the lyric Part IV of *Four Quartets* (see Chapter Eight).

it would hardly be exaggeration to say that Jonson takes a master-passion, a 'humour', and constructs a man by tricking it out with an elaborate and complex outfit of realistic detail, phrase, manner, habit and surroundings. The result is something that will pass very well if not looked at too closely.[42]

When compared by these critics to Shakespeare, Jonson does not offer us living characters, 'familiar acquaintance'. But nor does he present something unrecognizable. C.H. Herford, in the introduction to the three-volume Mermaid edition of Jonson's plays, acknowledged Jonson's feat in depicting the nature of contemporary life in works such as *Every Man in his Humour*, which employs, as Jonson hoped it would, 'deeds and language such as men do use'. But Jonson is also remote, for Herford, from creating the 'full-bloodedness' of a Falstaff:

> Jonson's conception of character ended... where it began, at the 'Humour' stage.... Of the more complex forms of character, and of the subtler development which is only a continuous effort to reconcile the inconsistencies, he had no conception.[43]

For Herford (later a major editor of this playwright), Jonson, with his 'satiric habit' of mind, displayed 'criticism', rather than 'sympathy', as his chief characteristic. Yet Herford also sees Jonson's 'critical' approach, his ambition to 'define' qualities of life rather than to display them through his dramatic personae, as being related to his exceptional appeal and relevance, then as now.[44]

The distinctions this line of criticism draws between Jonson and Shakespeare are perhaps only interesting here in that they receive renewed currency in Eliot's review article, 'Ben Jonson', originally published in 1919. Eliot makes the same distinctions: in the works of Shakespeare, the characters '*act upon*' each other; in Jonson, the drama is contained in the way in which the characters '*fit in*' with each other (Eliot's italics). This leads Eliot into a startling claim of advocacy, partially driven perhaps by his feeling that the book under review, G. Gregory Smith's *Ben Jonson*, in the popular 'Men of Letters' series, had done little to increase the relevance of its subject. Jonson, for Eliot, was the Early Modern playwright who is likely, despite expectations, to prove most sympathetic to the early twentieth century, for his 'brutality' (*SW*, 95, 102).[45] After finishing his run of quatrain poems in the summer of 1919, therefore, and as he completed 'Gerontion', Eliot continued in a mood into that autumn which viewed Jonson's contemporaneity as continuous

---

[42] Seccombe and Allen, vol. II, 46.

[43] *Ben Jonson*, ed. Brinsley Nicholson with an introduction by C.H. Herford (London: T. Fisher Unwin, 1893), xliii, lx. A related approach to character is identified by Symonds in his introduction to the Mermaid *Webster and Tourneur*: 'their characters, though forcibly conceived, tend to monotony, and move mechanically' (xii).

[44] Swinburne makes this same link in *A Study of Ben Jonson*, recommended for the Extension Lectures, but views it negatively. Swinburne sees Jonson's lack of 'casual inspiration' as leading to a 'tedious and intolerable realism', and to too close an involvement with the issues of his day: *Prose Works*, vol. II, ed. Edmund Gosse and Thomas James Wise (London: Heinemann, 1926), 7.

[45] Whatever Eliot's feeling about the insipidity of Smith's book on Jonson, Smith does make a similar point about Shakespeare and Jonson to his own: 'In Shakespeare a character does not end where it begins. In Jonson the single whim or temper persists, and when the scheme is to be enlarged, fresh characters are added, it may be partly like the others, but plainly preserving their individuality. In this synthesis of many elements he is driven by an imperturbable logic.' (London: Macmillan, 1919, 61).

with his satirical, 'brutal', version of character.[46] From this perspective, Eliot's own Sweeney (and Gerontion to a lesser extent), like Jonson's Bobadil, are Humour characters, as they had been understood by the previous generation of critics, and recently valorized by Eliot himself.

The main persona in 'Sweeney Erect' is determined by the world around him, and unable to affect it. For this Sweeney, also for Jonson as Eliot chose to defend him, what appears on the surface, the Emersonian 'shadow of a man', is all we have to countenance. The language of Eliot's poem is both polished, and deliberately rhetorical, in its strained or exotically inappropriate use of language (Sweeney is 'straddled' to produce his shadow) (*CPP*, 43).[47] This particular Jonsonian inflection is more specifically evident in 'Gerontion'. Gerontion's use of the word 'merds', when contemplating the field above his house, recalls the listing of 'Hair o' the head, burnt clouts. Chalk, merds and clay' amongst the 'strange ingredients' available to Jonson's *The Alchemist*. Gerontion's aged senses, having cooled, lead him to contemplate that he might 'multiply' an alternative sensual 'variety/In a wilderness of mirrors' (*CPP*, 38). Gerontion's afflatus recalls Sir Epicure Mammon's effusively lascivious contemplation, in Jonson's play, of 'my glasses/Cut in more subtle angles, to disperse/And multiply the figures as I walk/Naked between my *succubae*.' Mammon fantasizes deludedly about his life once he has received what he believed to be the philosopher's stone, for which he has paid copious money to the alchemist.[48] Jonson's original, in other words, both expands and ironizes the grounds out of which Eliot's character speaks his understanding of *his* occasion and circumstance.

Eliot's defence of Jonson, which was typically a defence by Eliot of himself at this moment of his poetic career, was fraught with unease. He feared that Jonson's learned and critical manner, taken to be 'modern' and immediately pertinent, was in fact awkwardly unfamiliar and inappropriate to his age's demands—which is, of course, also part of its interest and potential significance. Like the Noh drama translated and introduced into wartime London by Pound and Yeats, and celebrated by Eliot in *The Egoist*,[49] Eliot acknowledged that a revival of Jonson would have limited impact, appealing only to relatively few people. But 'learning' and

---

[46] James Longenbach provides a timely caveat that such tonal and generic decisions and developments are never simply identifiable through one strand of influence. He reminds us that Edith Wharton's satire in her novel *Summer*, upon which Eliot wrote a brief notice in January 1918, might also be the source for the manner of the later quatrain poems. See '*Ara Vos Prec*: Satire and Suffering', in Ronald Bush, ed., *T.S. Eliot: The Modernist in History* (Cambridge: Cambridge University Press, 1991), 49–52.

[47] Eliot offers in 'Ben Jonson' a directly aimed dialectical variant of Herford's case about Jonson's language. He says that the first five hundred lines of *Volpone* are *not* 'language such as men do use', but neither are they mere rhetoric. When seen as a part of the play they manifest 'shocking and terrifying directness' (*SW*, 97).

[48] In both instances, the references (taken from Act II of Jonson's play) ironize the seeming assurance of Gerontion's rhetoric. References here to *The Alchemist* are taken from Eliot's recommended edition, the Everyman *Complete Plays*, ed. Felix Schelling (London: Dent, 1910), vol. II, 28, 21.

[49] Noh plays, according to Eliot, display 'real personalities'; their ghostly lovers have 'as fine a strangeness...as any lovers of Webster or Ford' ('The Noh and the Image', *The Egoist*, vol. IV, no. 7, August 1917, 10).

'rhetoric', through their limitation, have critical, if not emotional impact, under this aegis. 'Rhetoric' does not, importantly for Eliot's own development, detract from 'reality' or contemporaneity; Jonson's importance for his work, and for his consideration of dramatic character, did not recede, and shaped to an extent his own drama, as the discussion of his play *The Cocktail Party* in Chapter Eight reveals.

For turn-of-the-century critics, as for Eliot himself, these qualities of learning and rhetoric link Jonson's writing to that of two other of his contemporaries particularly: George Chapman and John Donne. Although Chapman's writing is gestured towards in Eliot's work to the end of 1919—like Donne's, his work has a quality of 'thinking through the senses', we are told in 'Imperfect Critics' (*SW*, 19)—his role in helping evolve a new poetic after *The Waste Land* is more crucial. The next chapter will, therefore, initially pursue the early importance of Donne in Eliot's reading and thinking, especially as it impacts upon the discovery of a metre, and a drama in the lyric, which enables him to move beyond the Laforgue-influenced range of his work across the 1910s.[50]

---

[50] That early influence from Laforgue and the Symbolist Movement in French literature never, of course, entirely recedes. G.K. Hunter has pointed out that Eliot's engagement with critical writing by such as G. Wilson Knight from the early 1930s shows him developing an aesthetic which reflects back positively to these early interests. See 'T.S. Eliot and the Creation of a Symbolist Shakespeare', *Dramatic Identities and Cultural Tradition: Studies in Shakespeare and his Contemporaries* (Liverpool: Liverpool University Press, 1978), 289, 294.

2

'I Am Not All Heere'

Donne, Marlowe, 'Disintegration', and the Development of Dramatic Lyricism by Eliot

DONNE, PERSONALITY, AND IMPERSONALITY

T.S. Eliot's long dialogue with the work of John Donne took the 'realism', which he relished in the late 1910s in the work of Ben Jonson, George Chapman, and others, into new territories. Recent criticism of Donne's work, at this point, projected the emotional and sexual sincerity of the songs and sonnets as evidence of the poet's modernity, and relevance for twentieth-century readers. That modernity, in its turn, was perceived to have a specific outcome, one that enabled Donne to break from the artifice and convention of his immediate predecessors. Eliot's readings of Donne reflect this perception. As a determinedly modern poet (and an American one seeking assimilation into a new culture), Eliot gained much from Donne's example, which was instrumental, in that it allowed him to overcome impatience with late nineteenth-century preciousness (as exemplified in the deleted Fresca section of *The Waste Land*, discussed in the Introduction). For Eliot's contemporaries Donne's innovations carried precise technical implication, in terms of the exploitation of new rhythmic possibilities, ones that linked the lyric to a more dramatic voice. In this, again, Eliot was licensed in his quest to present a resolutely modern voice, but one aware of its revolutionary precursors, in his poetry. This chapter, then, discovers the Early Modern origins of Eliot's enduring technical preoccupations, by considering early twentieth-century critical discussion of first Donne, and then of the dramatists most engaged in these debates. Specifically, it explores the relation between the scoring of a dramatic lyricism, and contemporary presumptions about the paradoxically allusive nature of a poetry of sincerity, as they were to be understood through critical discussion about Early Modern works.

Several of the contemporary critical books discussed in the previous chapter were clearly acquired by Eliot during his undergraduate years at Harvard. Many would have been needed during 1908–9, when he attended Comparative Literature 66, 'The Literary History of England and its Relations to that of the Continent from Chaucer to Elizabeth', and the course on 'Tendencies of European Literature of the Renaissance'.[1] Eliot's undergraduate years also supplied him with a particular interest, as he himself recalled in 'Donne in our Time' (1931):

---

[1] Herbert Howarth, *Notes on Some Figures Behind T.S. Eliot* (London: Chatto and Windus, 1965), 81.

Professor Briggs used to read, with great persuasiveness and charm, verses of Donne to the Freshmen at Harvard.... his own words and his quotations were enough to attract to private reading at least one Freshman who had already absorbed some of the Elizabethan dramatists, but who had not yet approached the metaphysicals.[2]

Dayton Haskin's invaluable research into Briggs's Harvard lecture on Donne obliquely suggests several possible motivations behind the young Eliot's interest. According to Haskins, Briggs spent much time at the podium in consideration of Donne's 'decadent' style, his lewdness and lustfulness. Beyond the immediate appeal of such a sensationalist approach, however, Briggs addressed the metrical uniqueness of Donne's satires and lyrics, and the relation of their metrics to the complexity of thought that Donne's poetry mediates. Primarily, Briggs's approach to Donne was not proscriptive: as Haskin has it, 'to Briggs's mind Donne was important for what he could provoke readers to imagine'.[3] Briggs pointed his audience particularly in this regard towards the first and second 'Anniversaries', 'The Dream', and 'The Relique'. These poems all played an important part in Eliot's development as a writer. The 'Anniversaries' were picked out several times, as this book will show, in Eliot's criticism on Donne; 'The Relique' was soon to be echoed in 'The Love Song of J. Alfred Prufrock' and at later key junctures, including the essay where it is used as a primary example, 'The Metaphysical Poets' (1921).

Eliot's account, from 1930, of his early encounter with Donne's poetry in Briggs's lecture, is suggestive in other ways. His recollection that the professor's quotations 'attracted' him 'to private reading' demonstrated that much of Eliot's interest in the Early Modern period was determined by his pursuing personal fascinations, outside of the curriculum. His being made aware of Donne's work led to wider reading of metaphysical lyrics from that period. Then, his sense of having, as a Freshman, already 'absorbed' some of the Elizabethan dramatists, looked forward to his use of that related noun, which the mature Eliot would repeatedly call upon when describing the overwhelming nature of his encounters with Early Modern writing: 'saturation'.[4] Even as a student at Harvard, Eliot recalled having become imbued with, and steeped in, the rhythms and content of the earlier period—become imbued with while also making that poetry a part of himself.

---

[2] Eliot, 'Donne in our Time', *A Garland for John Donne 1631–1931*, ed. Theodore Spencer (Cambridge: Harvard University Press, 1931), 5.

[3] Dayton Haskin, *John Donne in the Nineteenth Century* (Oxford: Oxford University Press, 2007), 224, 230.

[4] Eliot used the term in several ways, both when describing how Early Modern texts related to their precursor sources, and when promoting the approach towards understanding Early Modern texts he felt to be necessary for the modern reader. An example of the former is his 1919 article 'Reflections on Contemporary Poetry' where, addressing George Chapman's use of Seneca, Eliot laments that modern poets lack 'even the *saturation* which sometimes combusts spontaneously into originality' (his italics, *The Egoist*, vol. VI, no. 3, July 1919, 39). An example of the latter is Eliot's advocacy of Ben Jonson, where he suggests that, instead of making dry reflections about Jonson's classicism, critics need 'intelligent saturation' in the complete Jonson oeuvre (*SW*, 89–90).

As noted in the Introduction, Eliot's late reflection back on his own career as an essayist, 'To Criticize the Critic' (1961), elegantly demurred on the point that he alone invented the vogue for John Donne that had continued across his career. Instead, he pointed his audience to two sources from the turn of the twentieth century for that renewed popularity, as well as again mentioning the personal importance for him of the advocacy of Dean Briggs at Harvard. Those sources are Gosse's *The Life and Letters of John Donne* (1899) and Herbert Grierson's two-volume edition of Donne's *Poems* (1912) (*TCC*, 21). Both of these sources would have raised for Eliot, when he first encountered them, issues with which he battled throughout his life. Both sources would have alerted him to the difficulties and tensions inherent in writing a poetry of metaphysical ambition—tensions that are manifest in Eliot's own criticism of the Early Modern period, and are, from the outset, to be found in his poetry.

For Gosse (Eliot's 'Perfect Critic' in his ironically titled 1919 essay), there was no poem by Donne, 'however cryptic it may seem,' which 'cannot be prevailed upon to deliver up some secret of his life and character'.[5] Hence Gosse's ratification of the approach taken in the *Life and Letters*, which justified reading Donne's biography *out* of the poems, and, via the letters, also *back into* the poems. Gosse's whole quest was to elucidate the poems' personal 'secrets' and instigations. To this end, he consistently singled out the 'aggressive realism' that distinguished Donne's poetry from the beginning, 'his determination to substitute for classical and romantic metaphors images drawn from the life'. Donne's modernity, for Gosse, lies in his ability to escape the artifice of the poetry he inherited, and to substitute directness and honesty for its stale convention:

> he was, above all things, sincere. His writings, like his actions, were faulty, violent, a little morbid even and abnormal. He was not, and did not attempt to be, an average man. But actions and writings alike, in their strangeness, their aloofness, were unadulterated by a tinge of affection.[6]

Such morbidity, however satirically figured or otherwise, underscores Eliot's tensely apocalyptic depiction of the modern city via 'bones cast in a little low dry garret'. The fact that Donne, as Gosse presumed, 'knew the anguish of the marrow' obviously appealed immediately to the sensibility of Eliot, as did the 'strangeness' and 'aloofness' of Donne.[7] Strangeness and aloofness were also identified as distinctive Donne qualities by Herbert J.C. Grierson in 'The Poetry of Donne', the extended defence he mounted as the 'Introduction and Commentary' to his hugely influential 1912 edition of Donne's *Poems*. 'It is not true,' Grierson averred, 'that the

---

[5] Edmund Gosse, *The Life and Letters of John Donne* (London: William Heinemann, 1899), vol. I, 62.

[6] Ibid., 41, 57. Dayton Haskin has an illuminating section on Gosse's *Life and Letters*, including commentary on its contemporary reception, and discussion of its reading of Donne's conversion, 165–83.

[7] Eliot, 'Whispers of Immortality' and *The Waste Land* (*CPP*, 52, 67). A similar appeal is made, as we shall see, in Eliot's responses, as when, for instance, in a review of *The Plague Pamphlets of Thomas Dekker*, he copies out a long quotation beginning 'What an unmatchable torment were it for a man to be bard up every night in a vast Charnell-house?' (*TLS*, 5 August 1926, no. 1279, 522).

thought and imagery of love-poetry must be of the simple, obvious kind', or 'that any display of dialectical subtlety, any scintillation of wit, must be fatal to the impression of sincerity and feeling'.[8] According to Grierson, Donne's difficulty with, and 'abnormality' around, the treatment of emotion, which paradoxically also ratify his directness and honesty, are what underscored the immediacy of the poet's writing. Indeed, for Grierson, it is these qualities that reinforce the 'winning' and unique version of individuality Donne presents for early twentieth-century readers:

> It is only the force of Donne's personality that could achieve even an approximate harmony of elements so divergent as are united in his love-verses. (xlvii)

Such terms as 'sincerity' and 'personality' seem remote from the classical emphasis that Eliot, in the late 1910s and early 1920s, gave to subjects such as tradition, the modern artist's nature, and Donne himself—at least in the version of that younger self which Eliot sought to preserve through the reprinted editions of *The Sacred Wood* and of *Selected Essays*. Donne has a 'quality of sensuous thought, or of thinking through the senses, or of the senses thinking', we are told, in a sequence that removes the process of 'thought' from any 'personal' origin or implication ('the...the') (*SW*, 19).[9] The most familiar comments about the necessary impersonality of the artist appear in 'Tradition and the Individual Talent' (1919), and in related essays of that year: 'The existing order is complete before the new work arrives'; poetry 'is not the expression of personality, but an escape from personality' (*SE*, 15, 21). But Eliot's immediate return upon himself after the latter of these comments, which comes in the *second* part of 'Tradition and the Individual Talent' ('only those who have personality and emotions know what it means to want to escape from these things'), establishes a crucial complication within, and against, the *im*personal drive towards critical modernity in these classic essays. There is a divide, in other words, between the treatment of 'personality' in 'Tradition and the Individual Talent' I and that in 'Tradition and the Individual Talent' II, which is more qualified about these matters. Yet this is a return upon himself by Eliot, between parts I and II, behind which the reading of Donne by early twentieth-century critics loomed strongly.

---

[8] Herbert J.C. Grierson, 'The Poetry of Donne', *The Poems of John Donne*, vol. II: Introduction and Commentary (Oxford: Clarendon Press, 1912), xxxii. Subsequent references to Grierson's essay are given in the text. See the current author's '"Passionate Improvisations": Grierson, Eliot, and the Byronic Integrations of Yeats's Later Poetry', *English* (vol. 49, no. 194, Summer 2000), for further discussion of Grierson's importance for the development of modernist poetry.

[9] This view of Donne, more simply conveyed by Eliot in 'The Metaphysical Poets' (1921) (*SE*, 287), is one that he had been developing from at least September 1917, in 'Reflections on Contemporary Poetry I'. Quoting his perennially favourite line from Donne's 'A Relique', 'A bracelet of bright hair about the bone' (also to appear in 'The Metaphysical Poets' and many other places in his criticism), Eliot pronounced that in this phrase 'the feeling and the material symbol preserve exactly their proper proportions' (*The Egoist*, vol. IV, no. 8, 118). Eliot's praise of Donne here looks forward to his notion of the 'objective correlative' delineated in the essay on 'Hamlet and his Problems' (1919) (*SW*, 86–7).

DONNE AND THE EMERGENT
POETRY OF MODERNITY

The crucial complication in this area is reflected by Eliot in the review of a volume of selections from Donne's Sermons, 'The Preacher as Artist', which appeared on 28 November 1919—that is, between the two parts of the original publication of 'Tradition and the Individual Talent' in the September and December issues of *The Egoist*.[10] Eliot's signal return upon himself about the role of personality within the artist's work appeared, then, *after* his review of passages from Donne's Sermons. He had been mulling over the September, Part I, of 'Tradition and the Individual Talent' since at least early July of that year (*LI*, 378). This opening part had been much more adamant about the necessary 'self-sacrifice', and the continual 'extinction' achieved in the finished work in a complete and ordered tradition (*SE*, 17). It might be impossible to tell the process of Eliot's drafting of the full essay on Tradition, in relation to his work towards the Donne review. However, it seems that Eliot's discussion and terminology in the latter are interrelated with the complication and contradictory returns upon the self between the two parts of the former, the revisiting and emendation of the relation of the later poet to the 'existing' order.

'The Preacher as Artist' opens by declaring that Eliot has 'no objections' to the portrait of Donne that Logan Pearsall Smith offered in his Introduction to *Donne's Sermons: Selected Passages*.[11] In that Introduction, Smith recognized the critical divisions of opinion which exist about Donne's writing. To some, Donne's poems, he said, can seem 'harsh', 'crabbed', 'frigid', 'cynical', and to operate through 'forced conceits'. Others, so Smith challenged, see these seemingly negative qualities as virtues, conveying 'realism', 'subtlety', and the 'modern and intimate'. Smith isolated 'Sin and Death' as the special themes of Donne's Sermons. The former he found conveyed with 'a modern subtlety of analysis'; the latter he took to allow Donne freely to 'indulge his taste for the grotesque and disgusting' in a wholly fascinating way.[12]

What Smith particularly emphasized as Donne's achievement in the Sermons is the deployment of a public form—sermons were often preached in the open air to large crowds—to achieve a *staging* of versions of selfhood. He described Donne's Sermons as strategic performances of a dramatized self, one that mediates scriptural

---

[10] The review-article on 'Ben Jonson,' which treats of similar issues, also dates to this November. Eliot's letters suggest that 'The Preacher as Artist' was completed around 18 November 1919, and the second part of 'Tradition and the Individual Talent' on 18 December (*LI*, 417, 424).

[11] As he revised his view of Donne in the 1926 Clark Lectures, however, Eliot's attitude changed in this instance. The Pearsall Smith selection is included on the Lectures' Reading List as supplied by Eliot, but we are told that he does 'not recommend' the 'L.P.S. preface' (*VMP*, 64).

[12] *Donne's Sermons, Selected Passages*, with an essay by Logan Pearsall Smith (Oxford: Oxford University Press, 1919), xiii, xxvi. Smith's portrait of Donne carries something of the resonance of Eliot's definitive later version of 'Baudelaire' (1930): 'Baudelaire perceived that what really matters is Sin and Redemption.' (*SE*, 427) Versions of Donne's 'special themes' of 'Sin and Death' then appear as keynotes in Eliot's mature dramas, beginning with *Murder in the Cathedral* (1935).

lore at a particular moment in time.[13] The nature and occasion of the sermon form, in other words, enabled in Donne dramatic intensity to what is being said. But what, for Smith, was compelling, is Donne's harnessing of such intensity 'to preach himself' with 'a curious modern note or quality', which displays:

> a subtlety of self-analysis, an awareness of the workings of his own mind.... We hear him confessing, for instance... how, while he is preaching, he is partly in the pulpit, partly in his library at home.[14]

Smith's reference here is to the selection he gives as no. 3 in his anthology of selected passages, for which he provided the title 'I am not all Heere', from a passage in a sermon preached by Donne at Lincoln's Inn 1620:

> I am not all here, I am here now preaching upon this text, and I am at home in my library considering whether *S. Gregory*, or *S. Hierome*, have said best of this text, before.

For Smith (and consequently for Eliot), this passage, encompassing the self simultaneously as scholar and performer, provided evidence of Donne's multiplicity of personality.[15] This is multiplicity evident, most famously, in the switch Donne made from his earlier self, the lover and sensualist Jack Donne, to his later self, the preacher.[16] Smith saw the Sermons containing, not excluding, all of Donne's earlier experience, which then contentiously becomes central to Donne's staged profession of religious faith, and central to the Sermons' distinctive rhetoric.

Eliot's review-article on the selection covered much of the territory of Smith's Introduction. He recognized Donne's Sermons as forming an important departure in the history of English prose.[17] He pointed out Donne's 'uncommonness' and 'direct personal communication'. But he bemoaned the fact that Smith does not allow us fully to see the uniqueness and significance of Donne's style, because the Introduction to *Selected Passages* does not compare the Sermons with examples by contemporaries, such as Hugh Latimer and Lancelot Andrewes. 'The comparative study would educe... that a great deal in Donne's predicatory style is traditional':

---

[13] Donne's near contemporary, the theologian Richard Hooker, confirms this in a passage which demonstrates his uneasiness with the dependence of the relaying of the Word of God to the people through sermons: 'the vigour and vital efficacy of sermons doth grow from certain accidents which are not in them but in their maker: his virtue, his gesture, his countenance, his zeal, the motion of his body, and the inflection of his voice who first uttereth them as his own, is that which giveth them the form, the nature, the very essence of instruments available to eternal life.' *Of the Laws of Ecclesiastical Polity*, Book V, ed. Ronald Boyce (London: J.M. Dent, 1907), 104. This is an edition which, Ronald Schuchard has noted, Eliot owned (*VMP*, 65). Eliot discussed the founding importance of Hooker's writing in 'The Genesis of Philosophic Prose: Bacon and Hooker' (*The Listener*, 26 June 1929).

[14] *Donne's Sermons, Selected Passages*, xxxi.

[15] In its original context, however, the passage from Donne is drawing a contrast between the earthly situation of distraction and the heavenly. After the Resurrection, all aspects of the self will be reunited: 'I cannot say, you cannot say so perfectly, so entirely now, as at the Resurrection, *Ego*, I am here; I, body and soul; I, soul and faculties.' *The Sermons of John Donne*, edited by George R. Potter and Evelyn M. Simpson (Berkeley: University of California Press, 1957), vol. III, 110. Pearsall Smith cuts off his selection before this heavenly aspect is given.

[16] Eliot repeats something of Donne's pattern of movement from worldly youth to spiritual maturity within his portrayal of Becket in *Murder in the Cathedral*, as Chapter Seven will show.

[17] This is a theme which Eliot would return to a decade later, in his radio talk 'The Prose of the Preacher: The Sermons of Donne' (*The Listener*, vol. II, no. 25, 3 July 1929).

Not until we see this can we understand the difference between certain passages: the difference between Donne as an artist doing the traditional better than anyone else had ever done it, and Donne putting into the sermon here and there what no one else had put into it.[18]

Comparison, in other words, draws the true relationship between tradition on the one side and Donne as an (or *the*) individual talent on the other. Eliot showed that the Sermons' characteristic practice of using repetition and analogy is 'traditional', because it is a practice shared at the same time by Latimer and Andrewes.[19] But comparison also shows, in Eliot's opinion, the uniqueness of other passages from Donne in the selection under review, 'such as Mr Pearsall Smith has done well to put first, which carry him out of [such analogy]: I am not all here'. Repetition and analogy in other words, those central features in the performance of Eliot's own poetry, do not debar, but rather license, the staging of a complex selfhood through writing, at particular moments of insight or intensity.

Eliot's gloss on this passage in Donne is revealing for the way it negotiated formulations about tradition, and escapes from it into 'talent'. It also revealed the staged and multiple version of personality that he felt was conveyed in and through metaphysical writing, which would soon include his own. This Donne passage is rare, Eliot argued, because it encapsulates 'the sense of the artist as an Eye curiously, patiently watching himself as a man. "There is the Ego, the particular, the individuall, I"', as the first of Pearsall Smith's selections, 'The Preacher', concludes. The 'I' emerges through a process of vigilance, a play of presence and absence, and division. This is the vigilance which is concurrently underpinning Eliot's discussion of tradition, prefiguring both the presence or otherwise of Eliot himself in his declaratively modern poetry, and also the ghostly appearance of earlier texts within it. The 'particular, the individuall, I' is incomplete, the work of art unfinished, without this 'patient watching' of self by self (or by God, in Donne's original conception), a form of distraction described as 'curiously modern' when it is advocated by Pearsall Smith.[20] In a later comment on Donne, Eliot found an interesting further analogy for this interchange. Seeking to resist the mistaken notion that Donne's poetic subject matter means that readers might get closer to his personality than they do in others' work, Eliot countered with the example of Browning's dramatic monologues (of which 'My Last Duchess' is

---

[18] Eliot, 'The Preacher as Artist', *The Athenaeum*, no. 4674, 28 November 1919, 1252.

[19] This is a method which Eliot sees in all three preachers, and for which he finds analogy (significantly for *The Waste Land*, which he begins to draft at exactly this moment) in the Fire Sermon preached by the Buddha.

[20] Eliot recalls the passage 'I am Not all Heere' in Pearsall Smith's selection, and its relation to Andrewes, seven years later in 'Lancelot Andrewes' (1926). He says the passage expresses a thought of which Andrewes was incapable, since he lacked Donne's 'personality' and therefore was less 'modern'. However, within the context of his own conversion, perhaps, Eliot now doubted whether Donne was not more 'dangerous' than Andrewes, since he sought 'refuge in religion from the tumults of a strong emotional temperament', whereas Andrewes remained 'contemplative' and subsumed himself in his text (*FLA*, 23–5). In the radio talk of 1929, Eliot quoted that passage again, this time as evidence of Donne's 'curious knowledge of the human heart', comparable only to Shakespeare's ('The Prose of the Preacher: The Sermons of Donne', 22).

perhaps the most well-known example), in which readers imagine a scene while the poems' speaker addresses 'someone else'.[21]

In a recurrence of his argument that the literary medium could be inadequate to express the pressure of intense (and probably personal) content, the argument which had underwritten 'Hamlet and his Problems' in September 1919 (two months before this piece appeared), Eliot maintained that Donne was unable to give this insight 'complete expression', since 'English prose was not sufficiently developed…for this introspective faculty of Donne to tell its tale' (note the last verb, seemingly operating independently of Donne himself). Whilst 'Tradition and the Individual Talent' measures an artist's perfection by the absolute separation between 'the man who suffers and the mind which creates', the essay does not exclude or preclude a Donne-like vigilance ('only those who have personality and emotions know what it means to escape those things'). What Pearsall Smith called modern 'self-analysis' was taken by him, *and* by Eliot, as integral to the process of artistic creation, separating selfhoods, transmuting or staging them. The self writing or speaking at any one moment is also the self enquiring elsewhere about others' responses to similar ideas or emotional insights, be they responses captured in texts or in intense personal 'experience'. As this study shows, Eliot was drawn back repeatedly to particular moments in Early Modern plays, often those moments involving various kinds of reflection, or of self-vigilance just before death. These are moments that obviously contain a latent content and appeal, both *as* poetry and *as* they convey distinctive and complex 'experiences'. The self's authority in the text is not so much displaced or dissociated, as spread between multiple perspectives, voices, or rhetorics.[22] This is the essence of Eliot's modern poetic, now as later.[23]

The identification of such qualities in Donne, partly via Pearsall Smith's selection and Introduction, endure in Eliot's admiration for Donne across the time of his writing *The Waste Land*, and also in the poems leading up to 'The Hollow Men', as well as in his prolonged wrestling with the incomplete drama, *Sweeney Agonistes*. In the next major review of 'John Donne' in 1923, Eliot enquired into the reasons for Donne's popularity at the time. Donne displays, Eliot said, 'fidelity to emotion as he finds it', and 'recognition of the complexity of feeling and its rapid alternations and antitheses'. It is impossible, furthermore, to isolate what is 'conventional' in Donne from what is 'individual' (the 'individuall, I', again). Donne was 'responsible' in his deployment of 'difficult consciousness and honesty'. To this extent, he and his contemporaries offer 'us' 'instruction and encouragement'.[24]

---

[21] 'The Devotional Poets of the Seventeenth Century: Donne, Herbert, Crashaw', *The Listener*, vol. III, no. 63, March 1930, 552. The article, a version of a recent radio talk by Eliot, is accompanied by a picture of the Anglican nunnery at Little Gidding.

[22] In his radio talk, 'The Prose of the Preacher', Eliot continued to see the 'mixture' of various professional selves evident in Donne as 'crucial' to the 'fascination' of his work.

[23] Eric Sigg has noted the similarity between some of Eliot's statements about the self and the chapter in William James's *The Varieties of Religious Experience* called 'The Divided Self': 'a stable, serious, spiritually ambitious self competes with one immersed in dramatic, role-playing, social enterprise'. See *The American T.S. Eliot* (Cambridge: Cambridge University Press, 1989), 71.

[24] Eliot, 'John Donne', *The Nation and Athenaeum*, vol. XXXIII, no. 10, 9 June 1923, 331–2.

In a contradictory fashion that this book shows to be particularly his, when Eliot is moving his own poetry into new possibilities, at the same phase in his own career as 'The Metaphysical Poets' (where he described Donne as a classic exemplar of the unity of thought and feeling in poetry), he was *also* working from a different model of the earlier poet, one closer to his own understanding of the nature of poetic creativity. This is a creativity in which 'difficult consciousness', and 'patiently watching', are the predominant and defining qualities. This 1923 review presented a Donne closer to the versions of him promulgated by Gosse and Grierson than to the purely 'traditional' version given by Eliot at other moments in his career, and in his formation of a declaredly modern canon of his own selected prose work. From the criticism of the time, then, and from Eliot's response to it, Donne emerged as an exemplar who offered Eliot a more complex way of understanding the relationship between writing and experience, self and artistic creation, literary presents and pasts, than had been available in the skittish, self-ironizing method of his earlier Laforguian mode. What Donne offered also within the conception of lyric poetry, crucially for Eliot, from the outset, was a different way of staging the speaking voice, within and against formal constraints, from that available in late Victorian and Edwardian poetry. Donne's handling of poetic form was commonly perceived by critics at this time as what guaranteed the immediacy, the 'honesty', but also the relevance and the *modernity*, of his writing for the early twentieth century. Grierson's 'The Poetry of Donne' strings all of these possibilities together, when pointing to the fact that 'the natural accent' of Elizabethan lyric was 'song'. Yet Donne excelled:

> in the clear and pointed yet easy and conversational development of his thought, in the play of wit and wisdom [and] in the power to leave on the reader the impression of a potent yet winning personality. (xiv)

Gosse saw Donne's revolutionary metrics as being of a piece with his dissatisfaction with 'mellifluous, sensuous, and soft' poetry, its unerringly predictable rhythm: the poetry, in other words, which Donne inherited from Sidney and Spenser. Instead, 'Donne thought that the line should be broken up into successive quick and slow beats.' The opening line of Donne's 'Twickenham Garden' ('Blasted with sighs and surrounded with tears') seems, to the 'ordinary reader', not to be 'iambic verse' at all, but 'we have to recognise in it the poet's attempt to identify the beat of his verse with his bewildered and dejected state'.[25] What we find in Donne, then, according to these important critics, is a determination to deploy a mimetic metre, close to a performative or dramatic expressiveness, in which rhythmic expectations are constantly being strained and altered by the staged presence of a responsive speaking, conversational, voice.

DRAMA AND THE LYRIC

Eliot, who had discovered similar rhythmic qualities to those in Donne promoted by Gosse and Grierson, from Early Modern drama in 'Reflections on *Vers Libre*' (1917) on, remained attuned to this potential in Donne's verse, over the next decade

---

[25] Gosse, *The Life and Letters of John Donne*, vol. II, 334.

and more. That is to say, he remained attuned to it through and beyond his increased scepticism from the mid-1920s about the philosophical or emotional worth of Donne's writing (to be discussed in Chapter Six), or that of the Early Modern period more generally, in comparison to the ordered religious world view of medieval culture, and of Dante in particular. In 1923, Donne's vocal potential was taken as admonitory, seen as something that the modern age 'lacks', however much elsewhere 'we' might feel 'we' recognize something significant in Donne's poetic content: 'A style, a rhythm, to be significant, must embody a significant mind, must be produced by the necessity of a new form for a new content.'[26] Yet, as late as 1931, Eliot perceived Donne's versification as laying the grounds for a revised scoring of poetry in relation to *'normal* English speech', grounds upon which the perhaps unlikely figure of John Dryden is claimed to have conceived his own poetic. Donne, Eliot wrote, 'introduced into lyric verse a style of conversation, of direct, natural speech', and, for these reasons, attracted Dryden's attention and admiration.[27] By this process, here, as crucially in the early 1920s, which Chapter Four will show, Dryden was co-opted by Eliot, as a kind of belated Early Modern writer. But, to Eliot's ear, Donne's style was never remote from the revolution in versification that appeared at roughly the same moment in literary history: in the next clause to that lauding Donne's introduction of 'direct, natural speech', Eliot made the connection himself. Donne was effecting a revolution 'comparable to the development of blank verse into a conversational medium, from Kyd to the mature Shakespeare'.

In the immediate context of the later 1910s, it is this 'revolution'—which Eliot at that time perceived more in pre- and non-Shakespearean drama than in Shakespeare himself—that particularly exercised his attention. It is a 'revolution' that brought Eliot's conception, via Donne, of the multiple self in *lyric* sequences, into the realm of his other major generic interest across his life, the vocalization of the self in poetic drama. The near-contemporary criticism, with which he was often in dialogue, time and again rooted the excitement of Elizabethan and Jacobean drama in its vocal flexibility with regard to staging character. For these critics, Christopher Marlowe, whose blank verse formed the subject of Eliot's essay in 1919, was the key innovator. Edward Thomas made this point in his Introduction to Marlowe's *Plays* for Everyman (the set text for Eliot's Extension Lectures), saying that Marlowe's versification proves 'for the first time' that poetic style can be made 'well suited to natural dialogue'; it is at once 'of great beauty' and 'direct'.[28] Swinburne, in *Contemporaries of Shakespeare*, praised Marlowe as 'the absolute and divine Creator of English blank verse, one of the highest forms of verbal harmony or expression'.[29] Thomas Seccombe and J.W. Allen saw the two parts of *Tamburlaine* as

---

[26] Eliot, 'John Donne,' 332.

[27] Eliot, 'John Dryden I—The Poet Who Gave the English Speech', *The Listener* (vol. V, no. 118, 15 April 1931), 622. Eliot's interest in this aspect of Dryden is a more expansive version of his view in 'John Dryden' of a decade earlier, where Dryden's poetry is simply held up, in contrast to the 'artificiality' of Milton's and Pope's, as 'natural' (*SE*, 310).

[28] Edward Thomas, Introduction to *Christopher Marlowe, Plays* (London: Dent, 1909), viii.

[29] Algernon Charles Swinburne, *Prose Works*, vol. II, ed. Edmund Gosse and Thomas James Wise (London: Heinemann, 1926), 239.

having freed metre 'at one stroke from useless mechanical trammels and conventional restraints'. As a result of this breakthrough, they claimed that the evolution of Shakespeare's prosody was to create a verse 'continually more flexible and free, more various in cadence.... The verse pauses everywhere, at irregular intervals.'[30]

John Addington Symonds also acknowledged Marlowe's revolutionary place in the growth of English drama, in general reflections that are pertinent to Eliot's own poetic development, across the later 1910s and towards *The Waste Land*. Writing of Marlowe's metrics, Symonds notes that:

> It is clear that the line which forms the unit of the measure is, to say the very least, an exceedingly licentiate iambic. So long as our nomenclature of prosody remains what it is, we may feel obliged, when thinking of the normal blank verse line, to describe it as an iambic, with laws and licences different from those of the Greek tragic metre. But this necessity should not make us forget that those laws and licences, on which its special quality depends, are determined by the fact that it is accentual and not quantitative; and that, though accent may be made to do the work of quantity, it imposes different conditions on the prosody of which it forms the natural basis.[31]

Eliot thought similarly about both Marlowe and the general metrical implications of this innovation. In his 1919 essay, originally called 'The Blank Verse of Christopher Marlowe', Eliot's discussion of Marlowe's allusiveness defined the effects of the playwright's prosody, and explored its development across Marlowe's brief writing career: 'he gets a new driving power' in *Tamburlaine* 'by reinforcing the sentence period against the line period'. *Dr Faustus* is even more innovative, however, since 'he broke up the line' in order, for the first time, to achieve a 'conversational tone' in the drama (*SW*, 76–7).

But a general explanation, like that succinctly expressed by Symonds, of the relationship between metrical expectation and flexibility, between accent and quantity, in dramatic verse after Marlowe, brings us more absolutely to the foundation of Eliot's mature poetics, and their relation also to Donne. As 'Reflections on *Vers Libre*' has it, 'freedom', in metrical as in other matters—physical, political, and metaphysical—'is only truly freedom when it appears against the background of an artificial limitation' (*TCC*, 187). It is this variety within constraint that Eliot was attempting in the introduction of modern materials into his quatrains in *Poems, 1920*. It is, though, more evident in the concerted echoes of Early Modern blank verse that emerged in 'Gerontion', itself begun in 1917:[32]

---

[30] Thomas Seccombe and J.W. Allen, *The Age of Shakespeare (1579–1631)*, vol. II (London: G. Bell & Sons 1903; 1914 edition), 38, 114. This argument about the teleology of Shakespeare's evolutionary metrics has a distinguished nineteenth-century heritage. Coleridge, in his 'An Outline of An Introductory Lecture Upon Shakespeare', noted the 'impetuosity of thought, producing a flowing metre and seldom closing with the line', which inhered particularly in Shakespeare's mature plays; Samuel Taylor Coleridge, *Essays and Lectures on Shakespeare and Some other Old Dramatists* (London: Dent, 1907), 57.

[31] John Addington Symonds, *Shakespere's Predecessors in the English Drama* (London: Smith Elder, 1884), 478–9.

[32] A. David Moody has noted that the opening lines of the poem are 'close to the norms of Jacobean drama', in *Thomas Stearns Eliot: Poet* (Cambridge: Cambridge University Press, 1994, 2nd edn), 66. Eliot's early poetry is partly striking for its spontaneous variety of rhythm and line length. 'The Love

Here I am, an old man in a dry month,
Being read to by a boy, waiting for rain. (*CPP*, 37)

Eliot's re-scoring of his prose source, A.C. Benson's *Edward Fitzgerald* ('Here he sits, in a dry month, old and blind, being read to by a country boy, longing for rain'), makes the original's rhythm more various. The pauses are unpredictable, the commas, acting as unequally placed caesuras to break up the lines, also sustain the sentence flow between the lines. Part of the development of Eliot's metrics in the early 1920s is towards further experimentation with such variation and movement between lines; not least once he makes the lines themselves the units of pace and pause in the sparsely punctuated verse from 'The Hollow Men' onwards. Variation, and vowel music, aided by repetition (that rhetorical feature noted in the Sermons of Donne and Andrewes), and parallelism of sound pattern and rhythm between lines—this is the vocal drama of Eliot's mid-career work, and a major part of his exploration of ritualistic rhythm and vocalization in the verse dramas of the 1930s.

As Eliot's indication of Marlowe's poetic debts to Spenser in 'The Blank Verse of Christopher Marlowe' makes evident, however, the purported immediacy and presence implied by the conversational qualities of such metrics are *always* also otherwise-inflected, over-written, and pre-scripted. Critical work such as Schelling's or Symonds's overviews of the evolution of English drama would have alerted Eliot to the fact that the pragmatics of hasty theatrical production in the Early Modern period required, as Schelling put it, that 'a single play was let to two or three authors to be cobbled up', and that 'incessant revision, excision, and recasting followed'. Theatrical companies were the real owners and developers of plays, not single authors. Symonds finds 'genuine collaboration' to be the essence of this moment in literature, and of this moment alone. Collaboration was, of course, also the essence of Eliot's literary friendship with Pound, at least from the time of 'Gerontion' through to *The Waste Land*.[33] But, for Eliot, from the start of his thinking about Early Modern literature, such issues also took on further, directly *textual* and technical implications.

ALLUSION AND 'DISINTEGRATION'

When, in 'The Blank Verse of Christopher Marlowe', Eliot sought to explain the variable quality of the output from 'this bard of torrential imagination', he oddly turned to thoughts about how it was that Marlowe not only 'recognized', but 'reproduced', 'best bits' of verse by himself and by others, and how he sought to

Song of J. Alfred Prufrock', for example, contains lines ranging from three syllables to the loose versions of fourteeners, the standard metric which preceded Marlowe's innovation, the metric for early tragedies in English and for Chapman's Homer: 'I shall wear white flannel trousers, and walk upon the beach'. (*CPP*, 16)

[33] Felix Schelling, *Elizabethan Drama 1558–1642*, vol. I (Boston: Houghton, Mifflin and Co., 1908), xli; Symonds, 236. Richard Badenhausen has noted, in passing, Eliot's interest in the collaborative nature of Early Modern drama, but does not develop the point or seek the origins of this interest in Eliot's thought and reading; *T.S. Eliot and the Art of Collaboration* (Cambridge: Cambridge University Press, 2004), 122, 206.

improve his source materials in the process. Marlowe's achievement, in other words, was at least partly 'synthetic'—and in this he was typical, in Eliot's view (*SW*, 73–5). As we saw in Chapter One, such ideas about Early Modern writing, its reproduction of others' 'best bits' within its own materials, were a critical commonplace at this time. As Eliot would also have been aware, from the editions of Early Modern playwrights on his bookshelves, such 'enrichment' was a common quality of, for example, those Shakespeare plays he most favoured. In the Temple Classics edition of *Coriolanus*, from the series Eliot began to collect (somewhat reluctantly) as a boy, the Preface by Israel Gollancz pointed out that Shakespeare's plot 'was directly derived from Sir Thomas North's famous version of Plutarch's "Lives"'. More pertinently here, Gollancz reminded his readers that Shakespeare frequently took into his own characters' speeches 'many of North's words in their [original] order'.[34] What is particularly startling in Eliot's first ten years or so as a critic of Early Modern literature, is the advocacy for the work of other critics to which this interest in the allusive nature of Early Modern texts led. This was an advocacy that had a direct and obvious impact upon his developing self-awareness about the dramatic use of allusions in his poetry.

When discussing Marlowe's indebtedness to the 'best bits' of Spenser, Eliot half-acknowledged his own debt to the Scots critic J.M. Robertson for this insight. Robertson's populist study *Elizabethan Literature* (1914), in the Home Library of Modern Knowledge, had a chapter on Spenser that considered the 'varying quality' of that poet's output (such unpredictable 'quality' was also the focus of Eliot's later essay on Marlowe). This is the part of Robertson's chapter from which Eliot directly borrowed, when citing examples of Marlowe's indebtedness to Spenser.[35] More immediately, Robertson pointed out that poets like Spenser frequently borrowed lines from themselves, nearly as much as they did from others. This was a point noted by Eliot about Marlowe, again, a note which—as this book will later argue—came into play in Eliot's own work, as a structuring principle of the poetry, from the late 1920s through to *Four Quartets*.[36]

But the impetus generally towards evaluation of poets' work through indebtedness and allusion underlay Robertson's critical approach across his career, which

---

[34] The Temple Shakespeare, *Shakespeare's Tragedy of Coriolanus*, with a Preface and Glossary by Israel Gollancz (London, 1896), vi. In a letter of 1919 to Mary Hutchinson in which he enclosed 'Burbank with a Baedeker: Bleistein with a Cigar', Eliot pointed out that 'I can show you in the thing I enclose how I have borrowed from half a dozen sources just as boldly as Shakespeare borrowed from North.' (*LI*, 372).

[35] J.M. Robertson, *Elizabethan Literature* (London: Williams and Norgate, 1914) 72. Elsewhere, Robertson's chapter reveals opinions similarly congenial to Eliot's poetic sensibility—he notes the 'fluid and limpid blank verse', and the 'irregular lines' of Spenser's du Bellay translations, for instance. He praises the Prothalamion and Epithalamion, for their 'variety of melody', above all other work by Spenser, but notes the sad, 'elegiac', 'prevailing bias' of Spenser's imagination (68, 72, 80). These judgements play, in their turn, into Eliot's quotation from the Prothalamion at the opening of Section III of *The Waste Land*, 'The Fire Sermon'.

[36] Eliot's attention was redrawn to this from the evidence of a review: 'Poets frequently, if not always, borrow from other poets; we need to be reminded to what extent they do, and must, borrow from themselves', 'Poet's Borrowings', *TLS*, 5 April 1928, no. 1366, 255. These issues will be developed in Chapter Seven.

was one that Eliot followed closely, praised, then promoted practically, from 1919 for nearly the next decade. For Robertson was a late exponent of what became known as the 'disintegrationist' trend in Early Modern studies. 'Disintegration', as a practice, had grown up around the New Shakespere [sic] Society, founded by F.J. Furnivall in 1874.[37] It deployed a range of metrical analysis, examination of line-endings, and a study of playwrights' vocabulary, in order to achieve 'scientific' proof of the authorship (or of the multiple authorship) behind any one passage in an Early Modern play. The practice was aimed primarily at seeking to establish which are the 'authentic' plays in the Shakespeare canon, or which parts of multiple-authored plays were scripted by him. Disintegration was prevalent in the last decade of the nineteenth century, and the first of the twentieth, although it attracted both positive support and negative comment throughout this period.[38] 'Disintegration', and particularly Robertson's promulgation of it, finally received its most devastating critique in E.K. Chambers' British Academy Shakespeare Lecture of 1924, on 'The Disintegration of Shakespeare'. Yet Eliot's support for Robertson's views continued even after Chambers' attack, and through to 1927 at least.[39]

When reviewing Robertson's *The Problems of the Shakespeare Sonnets* in 1927, Eliot felt pressed to indicate his continuing (if now somewhat wary) support:

> I admit that I have always agreed (in the rough) to Mr Robertson's 'disintegration' of the Shakespeare canon, though I may question, or at least marvel at, the precision with which he and other specialists in Elizabethan textual criticism identify line by line...[40]

Such wariness was, however, absent from Eliot's enthusiastic first public advocacy of Robertson, whose work on another 'problem', that of Hamlet, formed the basis (along with a briefly mentioned book by E.W. Stoll) of Eliot's essay originally called 'Hamlet and his Problems' (1919). In its first publication, in *The Nation and Athenaeum*, Eliot's review article on Robertson opened with a sly sentence that was omitted when the piece appeared in *The Sacred Wood*. 'We are very glad to find Hamlet in

[37] See Carly di Pietro, *Shakespeare and Modernism* (Cambridge: Cambridge University Press, 2006), 36, for further discussion of the origins of 'disintegration'.

[38] C.F. Tucker Brooke, for example, in his introduction to *The Shakespeare Apocrypha*, deploys what he acknowledges are 'disintegrationist' techniques to identify the authorship of *Edward III* (Oxford: Clarendon Press, 1908, xxiii); Swinburne, however, scorns the practice as 'silly', 'shallow', 'pedantic', and 'mechanical' (*Prose Works*, vol. II, 213).

[39] Gary Taylor has, however, taken such doubts further, and argued that 'disintegration' was out-moded even before Eliot's interest was aroused; *Reinventing Shakespeare: A Cultural History from the Restoration to the Present* (London: Vintage, 1988), 282.

[40] Eliot, 'The Problems of the Shakespeare Sonnets', *The Nation and Athenaeum*, vol. XI, no. 19 (12 February 1927), 664. A further promoter of 'disintegrationist', 'scientific', critical techniques who received (brief) interest from Eliot was A.C. Bradley. Bradley's *Shakespearean Tragedy* (1904), with its exhaustive character analysis and extensive notes on textual matters, was described as an 'excellent study' on Eliot's Extension Lectures Reading List. See Ronald Schuchard, 'In the Lecture Halls', in *Eliot's Dark Angel: Intersections of Life and Art* (New York: Oxford University Press, 1999), 49. Eliot seems finally to have renounced Robertson's approach only in 1930, as he became persuaded by new thinking about Shakespeare's symbolism, and different forms of textual criticism, in the work of younger critics including G. Wilson Knight and John Dover Wilson. *The Criterion* carried an attack on Robertson in July 1930 (vol. IX, no. 37), although Eliot allowed Robertson to reply in April 1931 (vol. X, no. 40).

the hands of so learned and scrupulous a critic as Mr Robertson.'[41] 'Sly', because, of course, the 'disintegration' that Robertson's book *The Problem of 'Hamlet'* practised on Shakespeare's most famous play (as he had earlier on *Titus Andronicus*, *Timon*, and 'A Lover's Complaint'),[42] aimed to prove at the least that *Hamlet* is a very uneven and composite work of art. Robertson traced the lack of 'aesthetic consistency' in the play, the unbalancing of its form through concentration upon Hamlet's conscience and psyche over the revenge action, to Shakespeare's having adapted a previous play, based upon yet further earlier stories, in order to construct his own. This ur-*Hamlet* Robertson saw as possibly by Thomas Kyd, a 'fact' evidenced from the use of similar material in Kyd's surviving play, *The Spanish Tragedy*.[43] Robertson reflected:

> The history of the play is thus vital to comprehension of it. A real life is the life of an organism; and a biography, whether general or episodic, is a necessarily imperfect and selective presentment of a life by way of narrative, document, and explanation. . . . In a word the dramatist is conditioned on the one hand by his qualities, congenital and acquired, and on the other hand, by his matter; and when the matter emerges as a prior play, with striking situations which constitute its 'drawing' power, the conditioning on that side is apt to be constringent.

This concatenation soon finds direct dramatic example in Eliot's own poetry, as a similar correlation as that made here by Robertson between *Hamlet* and Kyd's play hovers behind the 'madness' theme of *The Waste Land*. References to Ophelia, and to Hieronymo's Hamlet-like playwriting, provide undercurrents that link various parts of Eliot's poem, as Chapter Five will demonstrate.[44]

But, having opened up the 'history' of *Hamlet* for scrutiny, Robertson soon 'disintegrated' the supposed 'prior play' (a lost *Hamlet* of 1598, we learn), which had left its mark upon the 'Shakespeare' play as we have it. Writing of the performance of the players before Claudius the king, for instance, Robertson averred:

> the existing play-scene I take to be Chapman's work. The absolute echo of Greene in the opening lines raises the question whether that poet may here have collaborated

---

[41] T.S. Eliot, 'Hamlet and his Problems', *The Nation and Athenaeum*, no. 4665, 26 September 1919, 940.

[42] See J.M. Robertson, *Shakespeare and Chapman: A Thesis of Chapman's Authorship of 'A Lover's Complaint' and his Origination of 'Timon of Athens' with indications of further problems* (London: T. Fisher Unwin, 1917). Intriguingly, when discussing Chapman's supposed input to Shakespeare's 'oeuvre', Robertson focuses at one point in this book on the sole use of the word 'axletree' in *Troilus and Cressida* (I.iii, 66–7), and notes it to be 'one of Chapman's tags' as well as being 'often used' by Marlowe (206). See the Introduction for further discussion of Eliot's use of this rare term. 'Axletree' also appears in Marlowe's *Tamburlaine Part I* (IV.ii.49).

[43] This view seems to have been widely held in the literature about *Hamlet* with which Eliot was familiar: the Preface by Israel Gollancz in the Temple Shakespeare repeats the claim, and suggests that 'the lost *Hamlet*' was written by Thomas Kyd, since *Hamlet* and *The Spanish Tragedy* are 'twin-dramas' (*The Larger Temple Shakespeare*, vol. 10, London: J.M. Dent, 1900, unnumbered pages). It is a view which continues today; see Harold Jenkins' remarks in his Introduction to the Arden edition of *Hamlet* (London: Methuen, 1982), 82–4.

[44] J. M. Robertson, *The Problem of 'Hamlet'* (London: George Allen & Unwin, 1919), 11, 30, 33. More broadly, we might note in passing that it is this kind of (albeit historically more remote) 'constringent' condition, envisaged in the process of adaptation by Robertson, which Eliot entered upon with his own dramas from *The Family Reunion* onwards, all of which are founded upon ancient Greek originals.

with Kyd in the original play, or added something as he seems to have done to some extent in ARDEN. But if so Shakespeare or another had rejected Greene's work to begin with, for the version in the First Quarto differs entirely at the outset from that in the Second, the Greene lines being absent.[45]

It is important to remember, amid this dizzying play of authorial absences and presences—an Eliot-like shadow-life of prior lines and ideas within the 'finished' text—that Robertson's belief in his 'scientific method' never waned. Despite his revealing vagueness sometimes ('he seems to have done to some extent'), Robertson expected that the source of any line might be revealed, and that that revelation would inform readers about the 'history' of any text. Presumably, the more aesthetically 'complete' a text, the less easy it would be to 'disintegrate': Robertson notably honed his critical technique on Shakespeare's 'uneven' early plays, and upon the notoriously problematic mid-late work like *Hamlet* or *Timon of Athens*.

It is hard to see Eliot's criticism in this light as actively 'disintegrationist', although it is true that he was knowledgeable about the contemporary critical desire to ascribe authorship in the Early Modern period. His own essays on 'Thomas Middleton' (1927) and 'Thomas Heywood' (1931) both open with pages pondering the latest scholarship on this matter. But it is also true that his 'scientific' critical (and poetic) thinking in the later 1910s and early 1920s envisaged 'heritage' or 'tradition', and the establishment of the 'newness' of the 'modern' text, as founded upon similar issues and enquiries. Such a notion of course lies beneath the surface of the classic statements in 'Tradition and the Individual Talent' (1919), and the call for allusiveness in 'The Metaphysical Poets' (1921). But it is stated as Eliot's credo at the opening of the 1923 review, 'The Beating of a Drum':

> If literary critics, instead of perpetually perusing the writings of other critics, would study the content and criticize the methods of such books as 'The Origin of Species' itself, and 'Ancient Law', and 'Primitive Culture', they might learn the difference between an interpretation and a fact. They might learn also that literature cannot be understood without going to the sources: sources which are often remote, difficult, and unintelligible unless one transcends the prejudices of ordinary literary taste.... That the *nature* of the finished product ('finished', of course, is relative) is essentially present in the crude forerunner, is an assertion which the prompt disposers of values do not make.[46]

The dead voices speak through the living voice, in Eliot's prescription, and in the method of this book, which reviews how those dead voices are mediated to the new, modern, poet. For both Robertson and Eliot, the 'problem' of *Hamlet* was that it is an imperfect adaptation of its source(s), and so is uncontrolledly over-written by the multiple voices of earlier adapters of its narrative material.[47]

---

[45] Robertson, *The Problem of 'Hamlet'*, 60.

[46] T.S. Eliot, 'The Beating of a Drum', *The Nation and the Athenaeum*, vol. XXXIV, no. 1, 6 October 1923, 11.

[47] This is the conclusion also of E.E. Stoll, in the other book Eliot had under review in 'Hamlet and his Problems'. Stoll sees *Hamlet* as indeed based upon a lost Kyd play, but emphasizes the 'obscurity and contradiction' involved in Shakespeare's adaptation and in Hamlet's resultant character. Stoll, further, examines the alterations of Shakespeare's play between the Quartos and the Folio—an examination which proves for him that, in all of these processes, Shakespeare 'has not made it a more

For Robertson, as for Eliot, the focus upon the traumatic interaction between Hamlet and his mother Gertrude, which formed Shakespeare's innovative addition to his known source material, along with the psychologically charged soliloquies, distorted the 'primitive' 'revenge' *'nature'* of the play unbearably. As Robertson concluded, in words which presumably resonated strongly with the creator of that later highly-strung character, 'J. Alfred Prufrock':

> Shakespeare *could not* make a psychologically or otherwise consistent play out of a plot which retained a strictly barbaric action while the hero was transformed into a super-subtle Elizabethan.[48]

For Robertson, it was the very *modernity* of Shakespeare's version that undermined the play's coherence: for Eliot, notoriously, there is a hint of hidden 'compulsion' in Shakespeare's (necessarily failed) attempt to 'express the inexpressibly horrible'.[49] Whatever the unrevealed psychological or biographical drive which Eliot hints lay behind *Hamlet*, however, it is clear that his complex engagement with Robertson's critical method in *The Problem of 'Hamlet'* involved him in a detailed experience of 'authorship' as adaptation, and of seeing a key text in the 'tradition', *Hamlet*, as shadowed by earlier versions of the iconic story, and by individual lines and passages lifted entirely from several other writers. Robertson's method cast the Early Modern dramatic text as, in other words, a composite of fragments that did not ultimately or necessarily cohere into a consistently vocalized whole.

Robertson's Hamlet, and Eliot's response to him, do not, then, necessarily contradict the dandyish ironist of Laforgue's version of the same character, the version so present in Eliot's early poetry.[50] But they added the significant contention that

---

coherent and consistent play'; *Hamlet: An Historical and Comparative Study* (Minneapolis: University of Minneapolis Press, 1919), 3, 30, 71ff.

[48] Robertson, *The Problem of 'Hamlet'*, 73. This is exactly the way of putting the 'problem' of the play which Eliot as editor allowed Robertson to repeat later in 'The Naturalistic Theory of Hamlet': 'to rewrite a tragedy of barbaric revenge is to make it the tragedy of a soul...was to undertake what could not be brought into all-round consistency' (*The Criterion*, vol. III, no. 10, January 1925, 189). This number also included 'Three Poems' by Eliot, the first publication of what was to become part of 'The Hollow Men'.

[49] T.S. Eliot, 'Hamlet and his Problems' (*SW*, 87). Robertson was notably more indifferent towards the 'failure' of the play than Eliot—to pick up the description the-poet-as-coat-trailer used several times in his essay. Robertson concluded that, as a dramatist, adapter, and workman-like presenter of plays for the Elizabethan stage, 'it would be idle to pretend that Shakespeare was concerned to secure perfect artistic consistency' (*The Problem of 'Hamlet'*, 84). Notably, however, in his follow-up book, *'Hamlet' Once More*, Robertson was moved to defend both Eliot and himself on this aspect of their reading of the play in the face of an onslaught by Arthur Clutton-Brock against their position's seeming absurdity: '"Failure", like so many other words, carries different meanings in respect of *relative* forces....But whereas "a failure" frequently suggests mere disaster, I imagine that Mr Eliot meant no such thing.' (London: Richard Cobden-Sanderson, 1922, 44). Eliot had apologized to Robertson for having inadvertently dragged him into dispute with Clutton-Brock and others through what he had said in 'Hamlet and his Problems' (*LI*, 738). Eliot notably limits (or expands) his response to Clutton-Brock by deriding his whole critical approach, alongside that of others, in his 1923 'The Function of Criticism' (*SE*, 29).

[50] See Christopher Ricks's comments on this (*IMH*, 9 and *passim*). Donald J. Childs is one of many critics who have seen Eliot's Hamlet of the 1919 essay as congruent with the speakers in the early poetry. See *T.S. Eliot: Mystic, Son and Lover* (London: Athlone Press, 1997), 150. *Hamlet*, as we shall see, figures prominently in the evolution of Eliot's drama from *The Rock* onwards.

psychological complexity in dramatic works, as also in the dramatic lyrics of Donne, is implicated in precise textual matters, and in fact actually depends upon them. All texts contain the ghosts of earlier texts, through allusion, and through the re-rendering of important stories in new (modern) contexts. It is this last which governs not only Eliot's support for the work of James Joyce, as displayed in '*Ulysses*, Order and Myth' (1923), but also his being drawn repeatedly to specific moments in and between particular Early Modern plays, as this study will later show. Such issues also inevitably influence one of Eliot's thoughts that was to evolve more fully in the early 1920s: that any poetry which aspired to metaphysics was necessarily obscure. Learnedness and allusiveness were often said, by critics at this time, to determine not just the impersonality, but the necessary obscurity, of so much Early Modern writing in drama or lyric. J.E. Spingarn, for instance, pointed to the 'classical' 'Address to the Reader' with which Ben Jonson prefaced *The Alchemist*, as evidence of the necessity to consider obscurity as central to the earlier period ('I give thee this warning, that there is a great difference between those that... utter all they can, however unfitly, and those that use election and a mean').[51] Yet, such debates at the time inevitably and ultimately led back to John Donne. Edmund Gosse was typical in associating the 'intellectual obstinacy' and 'obscureness' of Donne with recent examples of such qualities in the work of Browning. Gosse saw both 'obstinacy' and 'obscurity' as the inevitable consequence of an ambition to open poetry to the major intellectual innovations of their time.[52] Such obscurity is integral to that 'vigilance' which was earlier described in relation to Donne's (and Eliot's) sense of the language of literature, and its alertness to its own former incarnations.

Yet the overwhelming message in Gosse's writing, and in all other studies by critics of the Early Modern period at the time at which Eliot was coming to creative maturity and of whom he was aware, was the sense of the *pertinence* and immediacy of Early Modern literature for turn-of-the-century British culture. Gosse re-emphasized the paradoxical 'modernness' of Donne to an age which, in terms of taste, has 'reverted in many respects to that of the early seventeenth century'.[53] This modernity in Donne, as we have seen, raised questions for Eliot's historical sense in the early-mid-1920s, particularly in *The Varieties of Metaphysical Poetry*, as he became increasingly concerned with the incompleteness, fragmentariness, and 'dissociation' that he then saw as signifiers of Early Modern work. More directly, Gosse sought to mediate Donne's familiar unfamiliarity to 'us' in a way

[51] J.E. Spingarn, *A History of Literary Criticism in the Renaissance* (London: Macmillan 1899; 1908 second edition), 306.

[52] Edmund Gosse, *The Jacobean Poets* (London: John Murray, 1894), 66. Such views were amply confirmed in the critical apparatus presenting new editions of key Early Modern works at this time. Edward Arber's 'Prologue' to his *Tottel's Miscellany: Songes and Sonnettes*, for instance, notes the learnedness of the authors included, who wrote 'for their own delectation and for that of their friends: and not for the general public' (London: A. Constable, 1897, iii). In the essay on George Chapman which Eliot regarded as Swinburne's 'best criticism' (*SW*, 18–19), Swinburne declared Chapman to be 'gloriously obscure' in style for the same reasons, and therefore lauded him as a precursor of Browning (*The Contemporaries of Shakespeare*, 25).

[53] Gosse, *The Jacobean Poets*, 34, 64.

that found echoes also in other contemporary writing on this poet, when he related Donne's concern to expand 'the orchestral possibilities of English verse' to 'the endless experiments of the Symbolists in France'.[54]

Eliot himself dated his crucial acquaintance with the French Symbolists to his reading of Arthur Symons's *The Symbolist Movement in Literature* in 1908 as a Harvard student. As 'The Perfect Critic', Eliot's essay in which he mentions this fact, makes clear, Symons's Symbolist interests sat comfortably alongside his other critical focus, on Elizabethan literature (*SW*, 4). Such dual adherence was widespread, and could be immediately and creatively suggestive for Eliot. George Saintsbury, in his introduction to the two-volume Muses Library edition of *The Poems of John Donne*, which Eliot owned, had drawn a similar parallel to Gosse's. Saintsbury claimed that in Donne's lyric poetry:

> the peculiar quality of Donne flames through and perfumes the dusky air which is his native atmosphere in a way which, though I do not suppose that the French poet had ever heard of Donne, has always seemed to us the true antitype and fulfilment by anticipation of Baudelaire's
>
> > 'Encensoir oublié qui fume
> > En silence à travers la nuit'
>
> Everybody knows that
>
> > 'Bracelet of bright hair about the bone'[55]

Eliot's 'The Metaphysical Poets' cited this line of Donne's from 'The Relique' as emblematic of the 'brief words and sudden contrasts' that go to make up his most striking poetic effects (*SE*, 283). So, when Eliot pointed at the end of the essay to the post-Baudelairean poets Laforgue and Corbière as being closer to the school of Donne than any modern English poet had been, his implicit self-advocacy was part of a critical context that had sought to prove the contemporary significance of Early Modern writing through similar means (*SE*, 290).[56]

Moreover, the metaphorical life in the analogies made between the two traditions by such as Saintsbury was now flaming occasionally in Eliot's own verse. Looking at the women's arms 'braceleted and white and bare' under lamplight, Prufrock immediately reflects 'Is it perfume from a dress/That makes me so digress?' (*CPP*, 15). To which we might reply 'yes' and 'no', as we experience the strange sense of complex contextual and historical undertow in the lines, an undertow that is made the stronger by the kinds of concatenation established in the Early Modern criticism

---

[54] Gosse, *The Life and Letters of John Donne*, vol. II, 334.

[55] *Poems of John Donne* The Muse's Library edition, edited by E.K. Chambers with an introduction by George Saintsbury (London: Lawrence and Bullen; New York: Charles Scribners' Sons, 1896), xxviii. Theo E. Morgan has convincingly argued that Swinburne was a crucial figure in mediating the Baudelairean tradition to Eliot. See 'Influence, Intertextuality, and Tradition in Swinburne and Eliot', *The Whole Music of Passion: New Essays on Swinburne*, edited by Rikky Rooksby and Nicholas Shrimpton (Aldershot: Scholar Press, 1993), 138ff.

[56] In Eliot's Introduction to Ezra Pound's *Selected Poems* (London: Faber and Gwyer, 1928), he noted that his own 'verse' was equally influenced at its outset by Laforgue, and 'the later Elizabethan drama' (viii).

by such as Swinburne, Arthur Symons, and, in this suggestive instance, which draws Donne once more as a major influence in the panoply of Eliot's references, by Saintsbury. In his attempt to define his own mature poetics through concurrent critical thought and writing, an attempt that took on new impetus and focus towards the end of the 1910s, Eliot was also seeking to harness his reading of contemporary criticism of the Early Modern period. He was doing so in order better to understand, and to re-direct, the recourse his earlier poetry had had, in terms of its use of allusion, and its reworking of content. Eliot's argument, in 'The Beating of a Drum', that 'the *nature* of the finished product' 'is essentially present in the crude forerunner', offered a model of literary development across history that leaves the work of relating the later 'product' to its precursor texts to do. Yet that model represents Eliot's own critical method, as it is the impetus behind the referential drive of his consciously modern poetics. It is the harnessed potential of this reading that the next chapter seeks to review, in Eliot's collected poetry to *Poems, 1920*, and which this study will pursue from this point, in exploring the Early Modern texts, and the pertinent critical contexts, as Eliot's poetry and poetic dramas appeared across his career.

3

'Signs Never Come Amiss'
Early Modern Voices in Eliot's
Collected Poetry to *Poems, 1920*

EARLY MODERN ECHOES IN
ELIOT'S HARVARD POEMS

Eliot's engagement with Early Modern writers, and with the growing range of contemporary criticism emerging at the turn of the twentieth century about them, enabled him, in the later 1910s, to establish the mature keynotes of his evolving, self-conscious, modern poetic. Yet his previous references to Early Modern works in his own poetry had, until the comparative profusion of essays in 1919, carried a slightly different inflection. True to the predominant influence of Jules Laforgue upon him at this time, reference to Early Modern writing in the early poems had often served to underline the *ironic* situation of the modern speaker, rather than to characterize or authorize it. That modern speaker is characterized by an unnerved lack of selfhood which other voices, of past but related characters, persistently invade. Those past voices, then, comment upon the decentred nature of the modern speaker. Eliot's deployment of allusions to Early Modern works in his early poetry (whether it be to anonymous dramatic works such as *The Raigne of Edward III*, or Marlowe, Marston, Middleton, Webster, Shakespeare) provide jarring commentary on the poems' strategies. This is achieved through the allusions' inappropriateness to the manner and style of Eliot's declaratively modern poetic content. In 'Portrait of a Lady', for instance, the facetious reference to 'Juliet's tomb' when describing the salon's 'atmosphere', proves the distance between this *amour* and any grander significance. John Donne's 'Song' is barbed about womens' infidelity to their (male) lovers, and adds the notion that one might be taught to 'hear mermaids singing' to a list of absurd possibilities which, if realized, might prove that women could be different.[1] When the idea is transferred to Eliot's early monologue, however, Prufrock is only the more bereft, since, although he *can* actually hear the mermaids, 'I do not think that they will sing for me.' (*CPP*, 16)

In Eliot's earlier poetry, then, direct allusion to Early Modern writing serves to enliven the ironies of a speaker's emptied-out belatedness, of an *un*certain relation to tradition. Yet, what we do find in this earlier poetry, is that Eliot is already

---

[1] *The Poems of John Donne*, ed. Herbert Grierson (Oxford: Oxford University Press, 1912), 8.

establishing undercurrents and cross-currents between his various Early Modern sources, as he refers to them in the various contexts of his writing. This is a multi-vocal practice that will continue in Eliot's mature thinking about the Early Modern period, and in his generation of new poetry out of those sources. As will become clear below, these undercurrents often, further, work to provide links between various of Eliot's poems, which were actually written years apart.

'Portrait of a Lady' (1910–11), for instance, originally bore an epigraph from John Webster's *The White Devil* (V. vi). This was an epigraph made up of lines that look deliberately absurd out of context: 'I have caught/an everlasting cold.' (*IMH*, 327) This same scene from Webster's tragedy is also that from which, as the Notes tell us, Eliot was a decade later to derive line 407 of *The Waste Land*. The speech in which the idea of death, conceived as the catching of a cold, occurs, is the stop-start death speech made by Flamineo, the pander of his sister Vittoria Corombona to Brachiano. Flamineo's situation in *The White Devil* is fraught, since he has turned revenger, when he feels that he has not received proper payment for this betraying deed. In his dying speech, however, Flamineo regains something of his original nobility. The speech begins with lines that were also quoted by Eliot in 'Reflections on *Vers Libre*' (1917), where he mistakenly attributes them to Brachiano. His principal concern in 1917, however, was the lines' performative and mimetic metrical irregularity: 'I recover like a spent taper, for a flash,/And instantly go out!' (*TCC*, 186). Both Eliot's essays and poems, therefore, here as in many other instances to be discussed in this book, return repeatedly to the same moments in his source texts, and at variously related moments, across his career. In 'Portrait of a Lady' itself, the speaker's 'self-possession gutters; we are really in the dark'. (*CPP*, 21) Yet, 'This music is successful with a "dying fall"'.[2] *The White Devil* is typical Early Modern drama, in its sense that the court is a place of 'successful', if false, sentiment, and that the statements made there are duplicitous: 'Flatterers are but the shadow of princes' bodies;/the vast thick cloud makes them invisible', as Flamineo himself notes (V. iii). When creating his own version of an Early Modern court as a modern salon in 'Portrait of a Lady', and then, when contemplating the death of his own duchess, the society woman whose likeness Eliot's speaker paints in the poem, he describes himself as 'Not knowing what to feel or if I understand'.

But it is this modern speaker's typical lack of self-possession, his 'not knowing', which allows his new portrait of his Lady to be shadowed—through its knowing author's allusive contrivances—by Early Modern ghosts. It is this lack of self-possession down to *Poems, 1920* that this chapter will focus on, as it is expressive of Eliot's performative association of sources at this point. The poem's original epigraph in its context, at the moment of Flamineo's death, discovers strength in what is *irrecoverable*:

---

[2] Eliot had also deployed the phrase from Orsino's opening speech in *Twelfth Night* in 'The Love Song of J. Alfred Prufrock', in a way which uses repetition to exacerbate the original's sense of languid indulgence: 'I know the voices dying with a dying fall' (*CPP*, 14). Both uses of the allusion, however, serve to remind us of, but also to warn us against, the pretensions of the modern speakers of Eliot's sequences.

> 'Tis well yet there's some goodness in my death;
> My life was a black charnel. I have caught
> An everlasting cold; I have lost my voice
> Most irrecoverably.[3]

In that swirl of Webster's tale of lust and adultery, which chaotically leads to the principal characters' inevitable death, Flamineo's nobility at this moment looms brightly but ironically out of the endless farce and fake resolutions. Earlier, he seems to have committed suicide, to the relief of his sister Vittoria, but uses an unloaded gun, in order to test Vittoria's (and the audience's) love for him (and upon rising he speaks the lines that provide Eliot with his source for line 407 in *The Waste Land*). Eliot's final lines in 'Portrait of a Lady' catch from his source this sense of ludicrous enactment around death:

> Now that we talk of dying—
> And should I have the right to smile?

Act V, scene vi of Webster's *The White Devil*, therefore, offers a compelling back-light upon the final verse paragraphs of Eliot's 'Portrait of a Lady'.[4] The hypersensitive, equivocal, modern speaker of the poem (himself a writer) is ghosted by the voice of the pander Flamineo, one whose verbal virtuosity is carried in the play into destructive, and haphazardly violent, action. The Early Modern context makes a stark contrast to the limited and limiting emotional displays portrayed in the modern world of Eliot's poem, with its high-society teas and its 'feelings' reaching for connection 'across the gulf'. The Early Modern court setting, and tragic atmosphere, of Webster's play, lour behind what are often taken to be society frivolities in Eliot's 'Portrait', suggesting a lost potential in the modern rendition of such encounters, and providing an ironic *commentary* upon them.

When 'Portrait of a Lady' was reprinted in *Others*, 1915, however, Eliot displayed what was at this time for him a characteristic uncertainty about the appropriateness of his original epigraph. From the *Others* version of the poem onwards, the epigraph has been switched to a new one. In 1915, and himself based (and married) 'in another country', Eliot's selection of lines from Christopher Marlowe's *The Jew of Malta* to stand over the whole poem (they had originally been the epigraph for part II alone) is multiply suggestive. Yet it changes the inflection of the Early Modern 'message' latent in the work. The Marlowe lines (below) seem to underscore for its speaker an inappropriate whimsicality towards a libidinous past, and also to confirm the death of the 'lady', which had been contemplated by the speaker in the portrait's final lines:

---

[3] The source for the quotations in this chapter from *The White Devil*, and from other plays by Webster, is the edition *Webster and Tourneur* in the Mermaid Series that Eliot owned, introduced by John Addington Symonds (London: Vizetelly, 1888), 97, 123. Lines in this and the other Mermaids (as in most of the other popular editions Eliot referred to) are unnumbered; Eliot gives no line number when making his reference to the source of line 407 of *The Waste Land* (*CPP*, 80).

[4] Bernard Bergonzi makes a related, but undeveloped, general point when claiming that 'Portrait of a Lady' and 'Prufrock' are dramatic monologues where 'the drifting, invertebrate reflections of Laforgue's *Dernier Vers* are given a certain stiffening and verbal energy by the influence of late Elizabethan and Jacobean dramatic verse'. See *T.S. Eliot* (New York: Macmillan, 1972), 12.

Thou hast committed—
Fornication: but that was in another country,
And besides, the wench is dead.[5]

Once again, the scene from which these lines are taken in Eliot's source in Marlowe clearly resided deeply in Eliot's mind, in that it forms a tacit cross-current between 'Portrait of a Lady' and a poem upon which he worked six or seven years later. The scene provided him also with the epigraph for 'Mr Eliot's Sunday Morning Service'. At the original moment in *The Jew of Malta*, Marlowe's central character, Barabas, has had his riches taken from him by the governor of the island, in order to pay a tribute due to the Turk. His daughter, Abigail, has shown love towards a Gentile, and has been foolishly sent by Barabas to a nunnery. Now, on hearing that she has there become a Christian, Barabas has had all of the nuns, and his daughter, poisoned. In the lines borrowed by Eliot for his epigraph, Barabas is being confronted by two accusatory friars (the 'religious caterpillars' of the epigraph to 'Mr Eliot's Sunday Morning Service'), who suspect him of the heinous deed.

From its context, then, Eliot's use of these lines from *The Jew of Malta* seem to have an even more oblique relation to 'Portrait of a Lady' than the original lines deployed from Webster's *The White Devil*. There is something being hinted through them, about the virtuous and virginal nature of the 'Lady', but nothing more. Yet the Marlowe lines do govern, better than those in *The White Devil*, a sense of the immanent tone and of the generic nature of Eliot's poem, and thence of much of his early work. In the essay on 'The Blank Verse of Christopher Marlowe' (1919), Eliot was to claim that *The Jew of Malta* must not be taken as tragedy, but as farce. But not farce that showed the 'enfeebled' humour of the present; rather that according to 'the old English humour', which was 'terribly serious, even savage' (*SW*, 78). In this essay, Eliot quotes lines from Act II of the play, and Barabas's dying words from Act V (after he has inadvertently fallen into the heated cauldron he had intended to use as a trap for the Turk), in order to display the extraordinary caricature that Marlowe's drawing of Barabas represents.[6] The anaemic, rather than prodigious, caricature, provided by Eliot's speaker in 'Portrait of a Lady', does not escape the farcical; his meagreness is further confirmed by his lack of an avenging anger (however ludicrously carried through) about his situation, in comparison to that of Barabas (and Flamineo).[7]

Critics writing about 'Portrait of a Lady' have cast the poem as a miniature 'drama' between the society woman and the young man, a drama observed from

---

[5] The lines occur in Act IV scene I of Marlowe's play. See Marlowe's *Plays*, the Everyman edition introduced by Edward Thomas which the Extension Lectures recommend (London: Dent, 1909), 201. In accepting this punctuation for his epigraph, Eliot seems to have referred to this Everyman edition, quite recent to the time of his writing 'Portrait of a Lady', rather than to the Mermaid edited by Havelock Ellis, which has a hyphen after 'fornication' (London: Vizetelly, 1887, 241). Modern editions seem predominantly to favour a more logical question mark after the word (see, for example, *Dr Faustus and Other Plays*, edited by David Bevington and Eric Rasmussen (Oxford: Oxford University Press, 1995, 297)).

[6] The source for Eliot's quotations from the play in his essay can be found on pages 185 and 223 of the Everyman edition.

[7] In this light, Grover Smith's argument that the Marlowe epigraph signals that the young man in the poem carries out a 'psychological rape' on the Lady seems forced. See *T.S. Eliot's Poetry and Plays: A Study in Sources and Meaning* (Chicago: University of Chicago Press, second edition, 1974), 14.

outside by both poet and reader. A. David Moody has noted the way that idiom and rhythm work to create 'objective' characters here; Carol Christ, casting the poem as an early experiment by Eliot in delineating 'the relationship of gender to poetic speech', discusses also the young man's (ironic) introjection of 'false notes' into the flow of 'the Lady's lyric'.[8] Recourse to the Early Modern hinterland behind several of Eliot's gestures in the poem, however, goes further to explaining its unsettling emotional and tonal complexity, as well as the confidence, even at this stage, through which Eliot was able to draw the distinct characters in the interchange. His intent attuning to his dramatic sources brings to the modern encounter on the one hand the weight of a tragic imagination; on the other the ready descent of its potential portentousness into self-regarding farce.

What further emerges from such examples of interaction between Early Modern texts and his poetry at Harvard, is that Eliot focuses, even at this early stage of his career, on Early Modern texts in a way through which his direct allusions move outwards from themselves, to take in the full content and tone of the source text being alluded to. That content and context can then resonate differently in other of Eliot's poems, as he returns to the same speeches or scenes in Early Modern drama for further materials. Each direct quotation of an earlier text in Eliot's poetry presumes a redeemable resource and resonance. Specific words are taken over into Eliot's poetry, but each allusion also provides an implied backdrop, against which the matter of the modern poem must be viewed, and from which the ironies of the modern speaker's position are struck. Further, the reversion to particular moments in earlier texts again and again across Eliot's career establishes a set of intellectual and emotional undercurrents, as well as tonal interplay, between various of his poems and dramas. These undercurrents radiate out to include his major critical essays and ephemeral pieces in prose, which then establish another layer of suggestion and implication. The largely unacknowledged quotations from Early Modern sources deployed in Eliot's prose, quotations often made when he is discussing broader issues about poetics, work to build a fuller sense of the rhythms and human situations that Eliot was drawn to in his own poetry. Early Modern texts provided resources that he could naturally advert to, sometimes at moments over a decade apart. What emerges from recognition and understanding of this complex of allusion, context, and renewed debate, is an enhanced sense of the intensely nuanced and multiply-echoing nature of Eliot's modern poetic ambition.

THE QUATRAIN POEMS

In the early poetry under discussion in this chapter, as later, Eliot seems particularly drawn to the morbid and grotesque elements in Early Modern work. That balance soon to be heralded, in essays from 'Imperfect Critics' through to 'The Metaphysical

---

[8] A. David Moody, *Thomas Stearns Eliot: Poet* (Cambridge: Cambridge University Press, 1994), 21; Carol Christ, 'Gender, Voice, and Figuration' in Ronald Bush, ed., *T.S. Eliot: The Modernist in History* (Cambridge: Cambridge University Press, 1991), 24–5.

Poets' and beyond, a balance between thought and feeling in poetry, is at this stage given a gruesome tinge. Metaphysics are here only conceivable in proximity to the farcical or mannered contortions of life and death. 'Whispers of Immortality' is typical in that its bipartite structure directly contrasts the expansive (Early Modern) opening with Grishkin's modern maisonette existence.[9] And yet the Early Modern moment translated via statements about Webster and Donne, in 'Whispers of Immortality', is one in which 'sense' and 'the senses' are reduced to skeletal 'anguish', 'ague', and 'fever'.[10] Webster might be 'much possessed by death'; 'Whispers of Immortality' is possessed by a version of the Early Modern period in which death underwrites all earthly experience and aspiration.[11] Yet it is difficult not to see an understanding of deliberate absurdity and misplacedness as forming the basis of the resonances between the Early Modern and modern worlds, for Eliot, at this point. Grishkin's distillation of 'so rank a feline smell' 'in a drawing-room' in this poem is equated across the poem with the 'Daffodil bulbs instead of balls' said to fill the sockets of Webster's eyes. This is another reference to *The White Devil*, where Brachiano's ghost enters with a pot of lilies containing a skull, in a similar concatenation of flowers and corpses (V. iv).[12] The misogynist form of modern disgust (incompatibility between traditional associations of beauty, and sharp effects upon the senses), conjures a reversal of Webster's earlier one, in which beautiful smells contrast horrifically with the sight of the memento mori. Misogynist voices in Eliot's work find ample corroboration in his Early Modern sources. But, as we shall see, those misogynist voices exist alongside a positive concern and acknowledgement, from the early poems onwards, that women have been abused across history. Indeed, *The Waste Land* adopts its own unnerved reading of the contemporary historical malaise out of such knowledge.

At this earlier moment in his poetry, however, in 'Whispers of Immortality', Eliot, the awkward Laforguian ironist, is inevitably drawn to those moments in Early Modern drama (like those in Donne) where the inflated awfulness of the characters' situation is matched by a grotesque but revealing absurdity, and inappropriateness, in their language. It is an inappropriateness that Eliot can then take over to flavour the abstruseness of his own modern style. As in 'Portrait of a Lady', and the replacement of the original epigraph from *The White Devil* with lines from *The Jew of Malta*, Eliot's second thoughts can sometimes nervously suppress the

---

[9] 'Whispers of Immortality' therefore makes a structural principle of the debate genre, which Eliot had explored six to seven years earlier in the Marvell-indebted 'First Debate between the Body and Soul', and 'Bacchus and Ariadne: 2nd Debate between the Body and Soul' (*IMH*, 64–9).

[10] The earlier versions of this poem emphasized this mediation even more than the final one. Of Donne, for instance, we are told that 'He found no substitute for death/But toothed the sweetness of the bone', which, in the next version, became the clumsily horrible version of a Donne 'who cracked the marrow now and then' (*IMH*, 365, 368).

[11] For Pater, this was the distinguishing feature of the Italian Renaissance world, one characterized by obsession with death, with the actual experience of 'leaning' 'over the lifeless body' (*Studies in the History of the Renaissance*, London: Macmillan, 1873, 82).

[12] Correlative moments in Early Modern drama important to Eliot would be the picking up of Yorick's skull by Hamlet in the gravedigger's scene (referred to, as we shall see, in *The Rock*); or Vendice's address to the skull of his dead mistress in *The Revenger's Tragedy*—the speech which provides Eliot with the crucial notion of the 'bewildering minute', discussed in the Introduction.

implications behind his own first impulses and intensions. (This is a particular aspect of his creativity, with regard to the Early Modern period, which this study will recur to.) In Eliot's Hogarth Press *Poems* (1919), for instance, 'Sweeney Among the Nightingales' carried a second epigraph. This was later removed, but originally stood alongside those from the *Agamemnon* that have survived (*IMH*, 381). This second epigraph was derived from two phrases from the anonymous play *The Raigne of Edward III*, included in C.F. Tucker Brooke's *The Shakespeare Apocrypha* (recommended for Eliot's Extension Lectures): 'Why should I speak of the nightingale? The nightingale sings of adulterate wrong.'

These lines from *The Raigne*, which had once introduced 'Sweeney Among the Nightingales', also look forward to the unsettling image of the nightingale amid the artificial luxuries of Part II of *The Waste Land*. In the source play, the lines are spoken as Edward commissions a poet to compose something in celebration of the (married) Countess of Salisbury, with whom he is secretly in love. In order to inspire the poet, Edward musingly tries out a few similes of his own:

> Write on, while I peruse her in my thoughts—
> Her voice to musicke or the nightingale—
> To musicke every sommer leaping swaine
> Compares his sunburnt lover when she speakes.
> And why should I speake of the nightingale...[13]

Edward's words lead him into too direct an awareness of the actuality of the nature of his desire for the Countess. Mention of the nightingale is, as he acknowledges, 'to satyricall'. The words strike a further sense of generic inappropriateness, which is concomitant with the humour of Eliot's quatrain poems, including that of 'Sweeney Among the Nightingales'. Edward's passion, like the scenes of violence and torture elsewhere in the play, threatens the stability of the state. *The Raigne* is essentially a patriotic piece in which legality and honesty eventually prevail, in line with the nationalist inflection of Eliot's (and recent critics') understanding of the Early Modern—although the drama also reviews the dangers of compromise, as successive acts of clemency towards his enemies threaten to dethrone the king.

The play's theme of passion as a destabilizing force is, in its turn, further picked up in Eliot's passing allusion in 'Sweeney Among the Nightingales', as one of the promiscuous women there 'Tears at the grapes with murderous paws' (*CPP*, 56). Eliot was to quote the lines from which the allusion is taken, from Marlowe's *Dido Queen of Carthage*, in his essay on the playwright of 1919, the year after this poem was completed. Recounting the fall of Troy, Aeneas tells of the Myrmidons, 'with balls of wild-fire in their murdering paws/Which made the funeral flame that burnt fair Troy' (*SW*, 79).[14] The image, when transposed to Eliot's poem, resonates with

---

[13] *The Raigne of Edward III* in C.F. Tucker Brooke, *The Shakespeare Apocrypha* (Oxford: Clarendon Press, 1908), 75. This anonymous work remained in Eliot's mind, prompted in part by its appearance in contemporary criticism as an example of the Senecan influence on Elizabethan drama. In 1927, Eliot refers us to IV:iv of *The Raigne*, and presumably to lines such as 147ff ('whether ripe or rotten, drop we shall,/As we do drawe the lotterie of our doome'), when comparing the tone and philosophy of *The Raigne* to that of *King Lear*'s 'Ripeness is all' ('Seneca in Elizabethan Translation', *SE*, 97).

[14] The lines appear in Act II of the Edward Thomas Everyman edition (343).

bathos, as many such allusive images in early Eliot do. But it also brings forward that sense of betrayal and destructive passion that has been suggested in the original epigraph, appended from *The Raigne of Edward III*. The Myrmidons' setting of the funeral flame to Troy is, of course, an awful premonition of Dido's self-immolation on a pyre, when Aeneas deserts her to follow his destiny.[15] Eliot's removal of that original epigraph for his Sweeney poem, thereby allowing the more obvious reference to Agamemnon which recurs in the poem's final stanza to stand alone, certainly lessens to a degree the ethically, emotionally, and politically complicated prospect of unbounded desire which had once seemed central to the poem. It allows, instead, the arch and Laforguian language of Eliot's brothel scene to hold greater sway. Eliot's epigraphs, at this stage, might be taken as equivalents of 'lost' source texts for disintegrationist critics like J.M. Robertson, discussed in the previous chapter. Their suppression by Eliot, as the poems move towards their final, collected, form, creates a similar sense of unease in our feeling about the poems' completion or otherwise, to that provided by the disintegrationist urge, described in the previous chapter. It is clear that Eliot's poetry could not yet fully encounter, and so it actively suppressed, the disturbances at this point challenging it from Early Modern sources. The turning away to modern, Laforguian, irony is not yet that active integration between his two principal influences—the Early Modern and the modern French—which is signalled in 'The Metaphysical Poets', then enacted in *The Waste Land*.

The removal of some of these original epigraphs from Early Modern drama can, then, place enhanced emphasis upon the play of verbal surfaces in Eliot's work to 1920. This verbal play is most apparent in the interlocking allusions of 'Burbank with a Baedeker: Bleistein with a Cigar', a poem in which disjunctions, between the guidebook world view of the protagonists and the past (as well as those between the present and the potential depths of emotional complexity to be derived from the poem's multiple sources), are pointed up as its sole purpose. References to Marston, Shakespeare, and Chapman, alongside more contemporary ones from Browning and James, work to a single end. Here alone in Eliot's poetry, the allusions fail to gather a contextual or tonal set of resonances.[16] As Eliot's archly self-satisfied comment on the poem in a letter of 1919 to Mary Hutchinson seems to imply—'I have borrowed from half a dozen sources just as boldly as Shakespeare borrowed from North'—the exuberant effectiveness of the poem depends upon its ability to choreograph its multiple allusions, whilst sustaining at least some measure

---

[15] Eliot was later to see the encounter of Aeneas with Dido's shade in Book VI of the *Aeneid* as 'not only one of the most poignant, but one of the most civilized passages in poetry' (*OPP*, 62).

[16] A similar moment to this, in which Eliot seems to use allusion simply to enhance rhetorical effect, occurs in the earlier 'Rhapsody on a Windy Night.' 'Every street lamp that I pass/Beats like a fatalistic drum', and the mention three lines later of a 'madman' (*CPP*, 24) recall the moment in Thomas Heywood's *A Woman Killed with Kindness* when a wronged husband approaches the door behind which he expects to find his wife in bed with her lover: 'Astonishment,/Fear, and amazement play against my heart,/Even as a madman beats upon a drum' (*Thomas Heywood*, ed. A. Wilson Verity, London: T. Fisher Unwin, 1888, IV. vi, 52). Eliot's later sense that Heywood was a decent poet who lacked 'moral synthesis' and 'vision' might form a retrospective warrant for his own earlier lifting of Heywood's lines only for their verbal effect, regardless of their original emotional or dramatic purpose (*SE*, 175).

of narrative coherence (*LI* 372).[17] At this point, such borrowing does not seem to involve Eliot in the complexities—emotional, political—of the original *context* of his source quotation; complexities such as those he would later come to realize that, for example, Shakespeare had involved himself in by his bold seizing upon North to create *Coriolanus*.

Yet the references to *Antony and Cleopatra* and to *Othello* in 'Burbank with a Baedeker: Bleistein with a Cigar' simply point up the comparative mediocrity of Burbank's liaison with the promiscuous Princess Volupine. The reference to Marston's 'Entertainment for the Lord and Lady Huntingdon' amongst the epigraphs ('*so the countess passed on until she came through the little park, where Niobe presented her with a cabinet, and so departed*') simply deepens the historical irony in the poem further (*CPP*, 40). The Entertainment celebrates the goddess-like virtue of a Dowager; Niobe's handing her a cabinet, in Marston's original, seems to suggest an acknowledgement of the Countess's true-tempered motherhood, something wholly out of key with the degrading affairs in Eliot's poem. His citation of this obscure source is sympathetically showy: out of line with the other sources in his deliberately over-elaborate epigraphs, which all point Venice-wards.[18] The 'history' of literary response thereby achieved is appropriate to the setting, *yet* also seems to indicate the exhaustion of a literary tradition that constantly demands 'new' responses, and so cannot achieve the poetic fluency of the Early Modern precursors.[19]

However, 'Sweeney Erect', the poem which follows 'Burbank with a Baedeker: Bleistein with a Cigar' in *Poems, 1920*, shows that Eliot was already becoming increasingly alert to the complicating of emotion viable within seeming rhetorical exuberance. He was also alert to the aesthetic questions involved in rendering such difficult emotion, prompted by his expansive knowledge of Early Modern writing. Dated by Christopher Ricks to Summer 1919, so to a time just after the last of the Elizabethan Literature classes, in which *The Maid's Tragedy* had featured, 'Sweeney Erect' has carried its epigraph from Beaumont and Fletcher's play in all of its printings (*IMH*, xli). The hotel setting of Eliot's poem (like the salon of 'Portrait') curiously domesticates the original political scope of *The Maid's Tragedy*, but then uses that shift to create its own intense effects. Beaumont and Fletcher's king hides his

[17] A. David Moody complains that all the allusions in the epigraph do not 'mean much unless one knows the works they come from', and that this is 'true of the poem as a whole'. Yet he does see Eliot achieving a 'synthesis' between his allusions, finally (*Thomas Stearns Eliot: Poet*, 58). Eliot carried out his own extensive comparison of passages from North with several from *Coriolanus*, in a radio talk of 1929. See 'The Tudor Translators', *The Listener*, vol. 1, no. 22, 12 June 1929, 834.

[18] The other reference to Marston in Eliot's poem, to *Antonio's Revenge* (I. i, 156), has the virtue that the setting of the original play is Venice, but adds also to the melodramatic tinge of 'Burbank'. 'The dapple grey coursers of the morn/Beat up the light', echoed in Eliot's lines 9–10, is spoken in the play as Piero Sforza clasps a dagger with which he has committed his first killing, having been rejected in love (John Marston, *The Works*, vol. I, ed. A.H. Bullen, London: John C. Nimmo, 1887, 107).

[19] A. Walton Litz has argued that the allusions are so concentrated in this poem that they constitute a 'parody of the method...a critique of the paralyzed modern sensibility that can only think and feel through allusion'. 'The Allusive Poet: Eliot and his Sources', in *T.S. Eliot: The Modernist in History*, ed. Bush, 140.

adultery with Evadne by forcing her to marry Amintor, who is himself betrothed
to Aspatia—the speaker of the lines used in Eliot's epigraph:

> And the trees about me,
> Let them be dry and leafless; let the rocks
> Groan with continual surges; and behind me
> Make all a desolation. Look, look, wenches!

But the (by now typical) jarring, between Eliot's modern setting and the Early
Modern contexts called upon here, goes along with a more surprising thematic and
emotive coherence between the two historical moments captured in the relationship of this epigraph to its modern poem.

This is so because the issue of artifice is pushed immediately to the fore in Eliot's
poem. This is implicitly so through the epigraph's allusion, once its source is
known. But it also doubles its effect through the nature of the poem's opening
statement, a response to the epigraph. Aspatia's lines in Beaumont and Fletcher,
lines that enjoin her serving ladies to enter her portrait, as a figure of despair, into
the tapestry they are weaving, are picked up by the speaker of Eliot's poem, in the
opening stanza, 'Paint me.../Paint me'.[20] The first two stanzas of Eliot's poem are,
in fact, a variation on the theme signalled in the epigraph, a variation that brings
in other elements from *The Maid's Tragedy*:

> Display me Aeolus above
>   Reviewing the insurgent gales
> Which tangle Ariadne's hair...
>   (*CPP*, 42)

In the masque staged by the king in the play to 'celebrate' the marriage of Amintor
and Evadne (I. ii), Aeolus is called upon by Cynthia and Neptune to still the
threatening destructive storm of Boreas. This is a representation symbolizing several things: the true energies of desire, which the king hopes will be brought to
order, and contained by the contrived match; and also the disruptive and troubling
presence of Aspatia's consequent despair. Ariadne, symbol of such entanglement in
both *The Maid's Tragedy* and in Eliot's poem, figures later in one of the ladies' tap-
estries, in the scene containing Aspatia's injunction. But, intriguingly, the scene in
which Aspatia wants her servants to place her is not one that appears in the legends
surrounding Ariadne. She wishes to be figured deserted upon an island. It is not,
she acknowledges, what 'happened', yet: 'It should have been so'.

In Eliot's poem upon which these troubling implications play, Sweeney's sexualized
levée, and his ignoring of his distressed female intimate on the bed, is introduced,
then, through this complex network of allusion and variant. Eliot's re-writing of
Beaumont and Fletcher advertises the preciousness of such textual manoeuvres
('anfractuous'), but also the forced relation of artifice to actuality within the urge to

---

[20] Aspatia's lines appear on p. 102 of the Everyman *Select Plays by Francis Beaumont and John
Fletcher*, ed. George P. Baker, Eliot's former Harvard tutor—the edition recommended in the Extension Lectures (London: Dent, 1911).

memorialize extreme distress, such as that undergone by Aspatia in her loss.[21] *The Maid's Tragedy* is punctuated by instances of overwhelming upset amongst women, at the machinations of the neglectful king. Aspatia's tears are outdone at the end of the play when Evadne, having been encouraged to take her revenge, and having killed the king for the wrong he has done her, begs Amintor to take her now as his true wife. She is unsuccessful, since Amintor has already had his true love for Aspatia bizarrely reconfirmed by her suicidal engagement of him in a sword fight, whilst she was in disguise. These convoluted twists and alterations of perspective in *The Maid's Tragedy* perhaps provide something of the background to the constant switches from stanza to stanza in Eliot's poem. But the male response to such warranted female trauma is directly carried across from *The Maid's Tragedy* to his new version of abusive and distressed relationship. Sweeney's testing of his razor on his leg whilst his lover spasms in distress on the bed has its prolepsis in the males' response to all misunderstanding and misapprehension in *The Maid's Tragedy*, as these men draw their swords at the least incitement. Eliot's whole poem, then, enjoins us to 'look' at the suffering of women, and at its implication of all the 'ladies', as well as at their conditioned, anguished, but often prim, response ('It does the house no sort of good').

Eliot's de-gendering of the lines in his epigraph from Beaumont and Fletcher, which are given without acknowledgement of the fact that they are originally spoken by a female character, is, then, itself complicating. It draws the poem's misogynistic view of woman-as-hysteric into a larger issue of artifice, and of its relationship to abuse, which is knowingly involved with injustice and mis-speaking ('the perjured sails' which Aeolus must 'swell').[22] *The Maid's Tragedy* displays female grief as an inevitable, and therefore normal, response to male manipulation of power, a theme which, as Chapter Five will show, informs the textual undercurrents of allusion to Early Modern sources in *The Waste Land*. But, at the same time, in the masque, and the scenes of tableaux in which Aspatia, and then Evadne, reveal their despair, *The Maid's Tragedy* advertises the poised artistry that such display might become.[23] Eliot's poem, through its pastiche and surprising Jonsonian grotesquerie ('Gesture of orang-outang'), works its similar effect. At this stage of

---

[21] In his much later Foreword to Henri Fluchère's *Shakespeare*, Eliot would declare his special admiration for Fluchère's comments about Beaumont and Fletcher. Those comments in the book's main text concentrate upon the undermining of generic categories which the artifice of the collaborating playwrights achieves, with *The Maid's Tragedy* cited as signal example: 'Beaumont and Fletcher created an unreal world which tragedy rarely touched and where realism had no place' (London: Longman, 1953, vii, 59). As late as 1962, Eliot was crediting the discovery of the power of 'the cunning use of both the learned and the common word' in English poetry to Donne and Herbert. See *George Herbert* (Plymouth: Northcote House, 1994 edition, 34).

[22] Rachel Potter has argued that Eliot's quatrain poems as a whole display a 'deliberate tastelessness' where 'the female body is the site of a repulsive violence'. See 'T.S. Eliot, Women and Democracy', in Cassandra Laity and Nancy K. Gish, eds., *Gender, Desire, and Sexuality in T.S. Eliot* (Cambridge: Cambridge University Press, 2004), 225.

[23] John T. Mayer takes Aspatia as a paradigmatic model, in both Eliot's life and work. He sees her as providing Eliot with an understanding of the viewpoint of Vivien at this time, as well as with a means of self-dramatization such as that embodied by Gerontion. See *T.S. Eliot's Silent Voices* (New York: Oxford University Press, 1989), 212, 229. 'The wrong'd Aspatia' appears also in 'Elegy', part of the *Waste Land* manuscript, to be discussed in the next chapter (*WLFT*, 116–17).

his career, and later, Eliot seems fascinated, and driven in this fascination by his Early Modern tastes, by moments when (female) emotion, and the language of emotion, go astray and break out of social boundaries (as in 'Hysteria' itself). But he is equally fascinated, now as later, by the Early Modern period's alertness to artifice and to theatricality, both within human gesture and emotion, and between surface seeming and tormented actuality.[24]

'GERONTION'

It is from this established context of artifice and theatricality, and not least in its treatment of reference to Early Modern texts, that 'Gerontion' strikes out into a different kind of poetic. The poem marks a leap forward in Eliot's poetic reach, and does so typically through a renegotiation of the method through which he conducted his dialogue with Early Modern sources. This is a poetic which involves a difference in lineation and rhythm to that of the quatrain poems, obviously; but also a different kind of tonality and method of relating to its source texts and contexts. The multiple ironies of the quatrain poems, or the sharp and belittling distance between modern and original speakers in the early sequences, 'The Love Song of J. Alfred Prufrock' and 'Portrait of a Lady', give way to a more integrative approach in 'Gerontion', in which the constellation of Early Modern ur-texts is harnessed to a more circumspect and mature reflection by the poem's speaker.[25] The ironic notes can be jarringly diminishing in the quatrain verse. This is the case, for instance, when lines by 'Henry Vaughan, the Silurist', as advertised in Eliot's note on the manuscript of 'Mr Eliot's Sunday Morning Service' ('O for that night! Where I in him/Might live invisible and dim') lose their ejaculatory force in the bland context of the modern priests' approach to their church gates, 'Where the souls of the devout/Burn invisible and dim' (*IMH*, 377). In 'Gerontion' such dandyish display has been replaced by more concentrated contemplation of the potential for the modern world, as for the Early Modern period, to reach beyond the immediate and the given to some metaphysical possibility.

'Gerontion' had a long evolution, which impacted upon the experimental nature of the final work. It was begun in 1917, and not completed until after the Extension Lectures in summer 1919. This, and the close collaboration of Ezra Pound on the typescript, perhaps ensured a greater synthesis than previously within Eliot's allusive methodology.[26] The note struck by the work's epigraph from Shakespeare's

---

[24] The perspective by Canaletto in 'Burbank with a Baedeker: Bleistein with a Cigar', or 'A painter from the Umbrian school' from 'Mr Eliot's Sunday Morning Service', perform a similar effect to that in Aspatia's lines, used as epigraph here (*CPP*, 40, 54).

[25] Grover Smith has argued that in 'Gerontion', and through the imitation of Jacobean dramatists, 'Eliot recaptured the tone of the surviving past' (*T.S. Eliot's Poetry and Plays: A Study in Sources and Meaning*, 59).

[26] Interestingly, this saturation seems to have wrong-footed some of Eliot's most dependable and exemplary critics. B.C. Southam, like others, including Ronald Bush, have frustratedly sought for ur-texts from what the former calls 'Elizabethan and Jacobean dramatic verse' to describe the purpose

Measure for Measure (a note originally confirmed by a similarly dissociative quotation from Dante's *Inferno* [*IMH*, 351]) establishes a Paterian notion that consciousness is never able to escape from its self-enclosure. Consciousness can never exist in time with the life of the individual's body, or with the progression of experience across a life. Eliot's (presumably, at some level) deliberate slight misquotation of his source in the epigraph (and misquotation will become a key feature of the poem) exacerbates this distancing of self from self. His '*Thou hast nor youth nor age/But as it were an after dinner sleep/Dreaming of both*' varies Shakespeare's original text. In Shakespeare, the sleep is more connected to the communal event of eating ('an after-dinner's sleep'), and youth and age are more realized as signifieds than in Eliot's version ('Dreaming *on* both', not 'Dreaming *of* both').

As Eliot's first extended poetic response to time, timeliness, and to history, one which was begun during the years of war, and which extended into its aftermath, 'Gerontion', therefore, via misquotation in the epigraph, suggests an out-of-jointness. The Duke's famous admonition to the condemned Claudio, in Act III scene i of *Measure for Measure*, is burdened by the sense that death enforces a similar lack of consonance, and a concomitant self-unknowing, to that achieved by Eliot's slight alterations of his source:

> ... thou exist'st on many a thousand grains
> That issue out of dust. Happy thou art not;
> For what thou hast not, still thou strivest to get,
> And what thou hast, forget'st. Thou art not certain;
> For thy complexion shifts to strange effects
> After the moon.
>
> (ll. 20–5)[27]

This perpetual being other to what one seems to be, the inappropriateness of any one human state to a lived actuality, conjures to mind Donne's phrase 'I am not all Heere', as it was treated in the previous chapter. But, in this context, it underscores Gerontion's view of 'History', who:

> Gives too late
> What's not believed in, or if still believed,
> In memory only, reconsidered passion. Gives too soon
> Into weak hands...
>
> (*CPP*, 38)

The Duke's original injunction, at the start of the speech alluded to by Eliot's epigraph, makes it clear that such inappropriateness, false witness or bad faith (Eliot's

---

of ll.33–69 ('After such knowledge' onwards). See B.C. Southam, *A Student's Guide to the Selected Poems of T.S. Eliot* (London: Faber, 1994), 74; Ronald Bush, *T.S. Eliot: A Study in Character and Style* (New York: Oxford University Press, 1984), 38. Bush, in a moment of rare exasperation, agrees with A. David Moody that 'we should not pay too much attention to Eliot's sources' here. But the *actual* models, aside from the seeming reference to Middleton indicated by Eliot himself for ll. 51–3, are imprecise but at the same time resonant, as I will show.

[27] *Shakespeare's Comedy of Measure for Measure*, ed. Israel Gollancz (London: J.M. Dent Temple Edition, 1894), 55. Eliot compares this same scene from *Measure for Measure* with both that from *The Raigne of Edward III* and moments in *King Lear*, in 'Seneca in Elizabethan Translation' (*SE*, 97).

'Unnatural vices/Are fathered by our heroism'), depend upon the self's inability to 'Be absolute for death: either life or death/Shall thereby be sweeter' (ll. 5–6; the Duke, of course, delivers his words whilst living under disguise).[28] Geronion is a consciousness trapped in a purgatory without absolutes, and as such is abjected by a complex and deceitful 'History'.[29] In Eliot's witty play on words, the reader of Geronion's confession is enjoined to 'Think at last/We have not reached conclusion', when he 'stiffens' in a house that is merely rented. Thinking 'at last' that 'conclusion' is not yet arrived at carries an agony at the lack of termination in this chaotic modern circumstance. But it carries that agony forward also, into the Donne-like pun in which death and sex (presumably transient sex, with a prostitute: 'rented') are horribly combined. This pun on 'stiffens' leads us back to the previous verse-paragraph, in which 'History' is, perhaps surprisingly, gendered female, as '[She] gives too late'. The gendering of history in this way is something to which even Pound objected, in his comments on Eliot's drafts of the poem (*IMH*, 352). Yet, it is one which, as we shall see in Chapter Five, has a decisive impact upon the underlying life of allusion to Early Modern sources in *The Waste Land*.

The Versailles-shadowed version of History presented by Geronion seems to suggest that the 'forgiveness' which is available to the post-war world is impaired. Sheer complexities and confusions haunt time itself, at this moment:[30]

> Think now
> History has many cunning passages, contrived corridors
> And issues...

History is reduced to the role of whispering politico, leading 'us' astray because of the (misogynist in this view) cunning and contrivance of 'her' nature.[31] That nature, and this gendering of history, seems in part indebted to the speech of Love in Sir John Davies's *Orchestra* (1596), where, in persuading humankind to learn dancing—a central conceit of the unitary drive of the poem, as it would later be of *Four Quartets*—Love points to his goddess's participation in the art:

> Venus, the mother of that bastard Love
> Which doth usurp the world's great marshal's name,

---

[28] The Duke, and his paradoxically absolute perspective, when he speaks disguised as a monk, had a crucial effect upon Eliot's drama, as will be investigated in Chapters Seven and Eight below.

[29] Whilst otherwise persuaded by Jewel Spears Brooker's assertion of a Bradleyan coherence in the poem to be discovered through its sense that experience, however fragmentary, is 'all-inclusive', I am unsure about the way her discussion elides experience via Bradley with 'the Absolute'. Such a view fails to account for the perpetual sense of untimeliness signalled from the poem's epigraph onwards. Eliot seems to me to be taking a more critical perspective upon Bradley's formulations than allowed for by Spears Brooker's helpful reminding us of them. See Jewel Spears Brooker, 'The Structure of "Geronion"', *Mastery and Escape: T.S. Eliot and the Dialectic of Modernism* (Amherst: University of Massachusetts Press, 1994), 87.

[30] Stephen Spender has argued that Eliot wrongly allows the parallel between 'the decadence, violence, intrigues' of the Jacobean world and that of post-1918 Europe to 'take over the rest of the poem'. 'For once, Eliot has gone back to the past without discovering there an idiom which he transforms into something as modern as the present'. See *Eliot* (London: Fontana, 1975), 65.

[31] Gabrielle McIntire rightly discerns an 'erotic playfulness' here, but also a 'disturbing misogyny' in this figure, which she links to Eliot's scatological Colombo and Bolo poems (*Modernism: Memory, and Desire: T.S. Eliot and Virginia Woolf*, Cambridge: Cambridge University Press, 2008, 49).

> Just with the Sun her dainty feet doth move,
> And unto him doth all her gestures frame:
> Now after, now afore, the flattering dame
> 　　With divers cunning passages doth err,
> 　　Still him respecting that respects not her.[32]

The last line points to the fact that the Sun loves the Earth, which is rhythmically at one with it, rather than Venus, who dances out of time. 'Now after, now afore' equate to Gerontion's 'Gives too late...Gives too soon'. Venus is false ('flattering'), and prone to include her own dance-steps, in order to stray from the true pattern, or tradition, of dancing ('cunning passages doth err'). In Eliot's version of this notion, Gerontion desperately seeks to establish his own pattern and rhythm on History's cunning errancy at the end, rather than at the beginning, of his lines, through repetition and parallelism ('Think now...Think now...Think...Think at last...Think at last; Gives too late...Gives too soon; Unnatural vices...Virtues').[33]

But pattern cannot be revealed, when the signs guiding the way to achieving it cannot be absolutely understood. It is here that Eliot's other rewriting of his source texts comes to the fore. The second verse paragraph of 'Gerontion' enters into dialogue with two of Lancelot Andrewes' *Sermons on the Nativity*, those of 1618 and 1622. It is principally a dialogue with Andrewes' methods, one that Eliot was to continue in the review-article 'The Preacher as Artist', upon which he embarked not long after completing this poem.[34] The 1618 sermon, taking as its text Luke 2: 12–14 ('And this shall be a sign unto you'), is centred upon the notion that Christ, especially having chosen such a lowly place of birth, did not simply have to be born, but had to be discovered, in order for the wonder of his presence to have been realized: 'How shall they find Him without a sign? So we come from *Christus natus* to *Christus signatus*. *Natus* "born," to be found; *signatus* "signed or marked," that he may be found.'[35] The cost of not seeing a sign is therefore absolute, not simply in a religious but also a linguistic signification:

> Signs never come amiss, but are then so necessary, as we cannot miss them, when we
> should miss without them; when no sign, no *invenietis*, as here. For if a sign, if this

---

[32] Sir John Davies, *Orchestra*, 38; *Silver Poems of the Sixteenth Century*, edited by Douglas Brookes Davies (London: Dent, 1992), 363. Eliot's essay 'Sir John Davies' (1926), shows that he favoured the more philosophical *Nosce Teipsum* to *Orchestra*. But he found in the former qualities, which he translates into Gerontion's mouth. Davies is similarly dissociative to his own speaker: 'more concerned to prove that the soul is distinct from the body than to explain how such distinct entities can be united'. Davies also shares something of the vocal timbre which we might hear in Gerontion, and, as we shall see, in the speakers of Eliot's later poetry, including *Ash-Wednesday* and *Four Quartets*. His 'is the language and the tone of solitary meditation'. (*OPP*, 133, 136).

[33] Eloise Knapp Hay has read these 'linguistic reiterations' in this part of 'Gerontion' as establishing Heideggerian 'presence of absence' or 'redundancy' as the keynotes of the poem as a whole. See *T.S. Eliot's Negative Way* (Cambridge, MA: Harvard University Press, 1982), 33.

[34] Eliot, 'The Preacher as Artist', *The Athenaeum*, no. 4674, 28 November 1919, 1252.

[35] Lancelot Andrewes, *Seventeen Sermons on the Nativity* (London: Griffith, Farran, Okeden & Welsh, n.d.), 193–4. All subsequent references to this book are given in the text. In 'Lancelot Andrewes' (1926), Eliot recommends this collection as the best introduction to Andrewes' writings (*FLA*, 18).

sign had not been given, as *invenietis*; Christ had not been found. Not been found, for never had been sought in such a place. (195)

Signs are the means towards discovering truth.[36] The angels directing the shepherds, the star the magi, towards the stable, are an inevitable concomitance of the Nativity: 'And reason; for some kind of proportion there would be between *signum* and *signatum*, and if the sign be a place as here both *locus* and *locatus*.' (196)

Gerontion's is a 'decayed house', not a lowly house or stable rendered wonderful by a 'sign'. This lies behind the (laconic and ironic) reference by him, to the 1618 sermon, and in the quotation from Matthew 12: 38:

> Signs are taken for wonders. 'We would see a sign!'
> The word within a word, unable to speak a word,
> Swaddled with darkness.
>
> (*CPP*, 37)

Importantly, Andrewes' original phrase, 'Signs are taken for wonders', heads a paragraph following one in which Andrewes has been meditating upon the contemporary *relevance* of the sign ('the cratch [manger] is gone many years ago. What is our sign now? Why, what was this a sign of?'). Andrewes' answer is clear:

> Humility then: we shall find Him by that sign, where we find humility, and not fail; and where that is not, be sure we shall never find Him. This day it is not possible to keep off that theme. (200)

Gerontion is a man who recognizes his own senescence ('A dull head'), but a man not humbled before the situation of his life: 'I have lost my passion: why should I keep it/Since what is kept must be adulterated?' ('adulterate' had been an adjective in the lines stolen as the original epigraph for 'Sweeney Among the Nightingales' from *The Raigne*). Andrewes' sermon, in contrast, discovers a reasonable proportion between the terms signifying his wonder at Christ in the manger (in this sense it is a sign to wonder at):

> *Verbum infans*, the Word without a word; the eternal Word not able to speak a word; 1. a wonder sure. 2. And the...swaddled; and that a wonder too. 'He,' that (as in the thirty-eighth of Job (v. 9) He saith), 'taketh the vast body of the main sea, turns it to and fro, as a little child, and rolls it about with the swaddling bands of darkness;—He to come thus into clouts, Himself! (200–1)

There is an authority, and quotidian directness, in Andrewes' writing against which Gerontion's monologue is a stumbling effort. Gerontion's resolutely lowercase 'w's ('word within a word'),[37] and involuted sense of any potential signification, let

---

[36] The theologian Richard Hooker delineated a further propinquity between signs and the things they signify, which resonates behind Eliot's interest here, and in 'Gerontion'. When establishing the relation between the private rituals of prayer and the public worship in church, Hooker claimed that 'the duties of our religion which are seen must be such as that affection which is unseen ought to be. Signs must resemble the things they signify.' *Of the Laws of Ecclesiastical Polity*, Book V, ed. Ronald Boyce (London: J.M. Dent, 1907), 26.

[37] When introducing this as an example of Andrewes' ability with the 'flashing phrase' in the later essay, Eliot, perhaps wryly, quotes Gerontion's version of the phrase, not Andrewes' original with its capital 'W's. (*FLA*, 22)

alone wonder, are the marks of his own swaddling in his dry house '*with* darkness', not with the 'bands *of* darkness' from Job. In Andrewes, Christ as an infant is inevitably wordless, although the Word; Gerontion, in his Hamlet-like untimeliness, seems to be seeking for obscure revelations, 'cunning passages', within the language alone.[38] For the 1618 sermon is absolute in this: the sinful, through their pride or lack of humility (Gerontion's opening phrase, 'Here I am', in this context a mockery of Christ, 'Ecce Homo'), are those who are excluded, unable to read the signs.[39] Indeed, the sign is itself an attack on pride, since it 'shews us the malignity' of pride as a 'disease'. (203) As such, therefore, the sign is not 'at large indefinitely', 'But *signum vobis*, "for you", limited to some, not to all. *For*, not *to*, some others; but "to you", and such as you are a sign it is'. (202)

The relation of sign to signified is individual, a matter of virtue and election. Gerontion's other misquotation from Andrewes ('In the juvescence of the year/ Came Christ the tiger') leads only to an inevitable breaking off of this second verse paragraph of his monologue, a hiatus in the poem's syntax before re-establishment of a sense of untimeliness that, with 'In depraved May', predicts the opening phrases of *The Waste Land*. Gerontion's source for the phrase 'Christ the tiger', in Andrewes' 1622 Nativity Sermon, had itself pondered the gulf between the immediate worship enacted by the Magi, who quickly set out upon their journey towards Christ, and 'our' slowness in responding to revelation:

> But when we do it, we must be allowed leisure. Ever *veniemus*, never *venimus*; ever coming, never come. We love to make no very great haste. To other things perhaps; not to *adorare*, the place of the worship of God. Why should we? Christ is no wildcat. (254)

Andrewes concedes that the path to Christ is not 'straight'. But the quest for Him must, nonetheless, be continued. Gerontion's sudden and despairing assertion of Christ's early presence contains nothing of this historical awareness, complexity, or compensatory '*ubi est?*'

When, therefore, in a later verse paragraph, which begins with a reminder of the primary and predatory nature of Christ ('The tiger springs in the new year. Us he devours'), Gerontion switches to a different Early Modern source, he does so in a way that merely confirms the fatedness of his purgatorial situation. Beatrice-Joanna made her confessional speech in Thomas Middleton's *The Changeling* in these terms: 'I that am of your blood am taken from you,' she avers, 'Beneath yon stars, upon yon meteor/Ever hung my fate' (V. iii, 150, 154–5).[40] The echo comes back

---

[38] Eloise Knapp Hay surely misses the point when she describes the fact that the Word is speechless as a child as 'disappointing' (34).

[39] Pride and lack of humility are of course amongst the things being weighed in Eliot's other major source for 'Gerontion', *Measure for Measure*: at one point Isabella charges Angelo that he sins through pride (II. ii, 117), and the play punishes his lack of humility (*Shakespeare's Comedy of Measure for Measure*, 38).

[40] Eliot quotes from this speech twice in his essay 'Thomas Middleton', the first time to show Beatrice-Joanna's acceptance of her fallen state, the second to acclaim Middleton's mastery of versification (*SE*, 164, 169). Eliot was evidently quoting here from his Mermaid Edition of *The Changeling*, which gives Beatrice-Joanna's words as 'I that am of your blood', rather than the commonly-accepted and differently meaning 'I am that …' (*Thomas Middleton*, edited by Havelock Ellis, Volume I (London: Vizetelly, 1887), 164).

from Gerontion: 'I that was near your heart was removed therefrom/To lose beauty in terror'. Once he has killed a detested suitor for her, Beatrice-Joanna becomes (in Eliot's later view in his essay on Middleton) uncontrollably habituated to sex with the man she loathes, Deflores. Eventually, she dies for her obsession. Gerontion's loss of 'beauty' is correlative with this ur-text in that he also, in old age, has lost 'my passion'. His 'honesty', like Beatrice-Joanna's belated truthfulness, amounts merely, at this point, to a sense of what has inevitably gone astray.

Gerontion's lack of consonance with the rhythms of his experience, at this out-of-joint historical moment (which is also the moment of the poem's creation), leads him, not to a tragic consummation, but to a final scattering of exotic names ('Mr Silvero', 'Hakagawa', through to 'De Bailhache', 'Fresca', 'Mrs Cammel'). Such names are 'signs' that signify little, beyond a random collection of aesthetes encountered across Europe.[41] This scattering of course becomes literal in the late moments of Gerontion's speech, as we find these names 'whirled/Beyond the circuit of the shuddering Bear/In fractured atoms' (*CPP*, 39). Lack of signification, pondered through a post-Rutherford vision, returns us, at the end of the poem, to the ironic mode of Eliot's early allusions to Early Modern texts. In his dying speech, as we saw in the Introduction, George Chapman's Bussy d'Ambois, a vindictive self-server at the French court, achieves a kind of transfiguration. He envisages his fame preceding him to heaven, in a passage whose key images are derived (as Eliot was well aware) from Seneca:

> Fly, where the evening from th'Iberean vales,
> Takes on her swarthy shoulders *Heccate*
> Crown'd with a grove of oakes! flie where men feele
> The burning axletree: and those that suffer
> Beneath the chariot of the Snowy Beare:
> And tell them all that D'Ambois now is hasting
> To the eternall dwellers...
>
>   (V. 3. 138–51)[42]

In Gerontion's late 1910s universe, signs, names, become ultimately and unrevealingly 'whirled' at large.[43] Through Eliot's setting of Gerontion's monologue in conscious negotiation with its principal Early Modern sources, however, there is the register of an evolving and complex, multivocal, poetic alertness to the involving complications and liberations in that earlier period. His references to those Early Modern sources can be precise and direct—allusive—but they can also draw upon a more diffuse context established by the earlier text and its atmosphere. Yet it is that aversion to the context of the earlier text that most enables Eliot to remake his

---

[41] Bergonzi, in *T.S. Eliot*, 54, finds Gerontion's use of names reminiscent of Dante's, 'with the crucial difference that for Dante the people he met had histories and identities as well as names, and were part, in both life and in death, of an ordered, hierarchised world'.

[42] Frederick S. Boas's edition of Chapman's *Bussy d'Ambois and the Revenge* (Boston: D.C. Heath, 1905), 137.

[43] As later chapters will show, 'whirled', and homophonic puns upon it, feature in work ranging from *Ash-Wednesday* to *Four Quartets*. These are puns which again derive from Sir John Davies' *Orchestra*.

source into something different and new. 'Burbank with a Baedeker: Bleistein with a Cigar' had taken the allusive charge of Eliot's poetry to a situation of exhaustion and futility. From 'Gerontion' onwards, however, Eliot would actually make the poetry out of the significant cross-currents that he read out of Early Modern sources. Each new poem became a new context that revisited and reinvented those sources as a way of generating its own energies. His readings of the Early Modern canon which he had evolved, and which was more or less established by him, as the next chapters demonstrate, by the early 1920s, mean that he consistently (and sometimes contradictorily) reinflects or refocuses his sense of the earlier texts, and of the links between them. But it is those refocusings which become Eliot's new poetry, and which, in their turn, establish the links between the poetry in Eliot's mature oeuvre.

4

'Ideas, and the Sensibility of Thought'
The Quest for a Metaphysical Poetry, 1920–2

DEAD VOICES AND NEW COMBINATIONS

The materials gathered together in *The Waste Land: a facsimile and transcript* show the extent to which, in terms of its negotiation with texts from the Early Modern period, Eliot's 1922 poem continued the reference points and scope that he had established in the 1910s. Works that had constituted crucial foci, for Eliot, through to *Poems, 1920*, here form presences behind the new sequence of poems. Some Early Modern works, by now familiar in the Eliot canon, such as John Webster's *The Duchess of Malfi* and *The White Devil*, are again alluded to directly. But these works also appear cryptogrammatically, beneath the play of allusions in *The Waste Land*. As Eliot, at this period, began to experiment more ambitiously with the cross-currents to be inferred between those Early Modern texts which he deployed in his new poetic context, he suggested, and particularly with regard to such texts, that the process of reading is partly one of decoding.[1] In *The Waste Land*, and Eliot's later work, that decoding involves coming to an understanding of the interconnections between the earlier texts evoked and, implicitly, their further relation to the critical tradition within which they have been established. This chapter will consider the means Eliot evolved to orchestrate those interconnections, as he strove more intently to make, out of his now defined Early Modern landscape, a metaphysical poetry for the early twentieth century. This chapter, and the next, therefore stand at the methodological centre of this book.

In the drafts of *The Waste Land*, it is possible to see some familiar interconnections evolving which then reside beneath the surface of the final published work. For example, Valerie Eliot has noted that Eliot pencilled a plot summary of *The Duchess of Malfi* on the verso of a typescript of the rejected section, 'The Death of

---

[1] Cryptogram: anything written in such a form 'that a key is required to know how to understand and put together the letters' (*OED*). Eliot was taken with the notion of the cryptogram when referring to the critical work written at the time he was drafting *The Waste Land*. In his Preface to *Homage to John Dryden: Three Essays on Poetry of the Seventeenth Century*, which brought together the reflections on Dryden, Marvell, and the Metaphysical Poets he had published in 1921, Eliot refers to his long-held ambition to write a survey of the poetry of the seventeenth and eighteenth centuries. Since he could not undertake that project, however, he hopes that 'these three papers may in spite of and partly because of their defects preserve in cryptogram certain notions which, if expressed directly, would be destined to immediate obloquy' (London: Hogarth Press, 1924), 9. In the facsimile of *The Waste Land*, London's people are sarcastically described as striving to 'trace the cryptogram' (*WLFT*, 43).

the Duchess'. 'Elegy' makes horrified lament for 'the wrong'd Aspatia', heroine of Beaumont and Fletcher's *The Maid's Tragedy*, and main instigator of the clash between artifice and harsh modern reality in 'Sweeney Erect'. Aspatia is, now, literally coming alive before the speaker's eyes, in the draft poem, also eventually rejected from the final version of *The Waste Land*.

But the inclusion, in *The Waste Land: a facsimile and transcript*, of drafts of sections, or of whole poems, which did not get included in the final work demonstrates, also, the ways in which Eliot was responding almost immediately to various prompts from outside his immediate writing of his new poem. These were prompts provided by (as ever) his reviewing activity, or by editions of Early Modern writing that were appearing, across the time Eliot was working on the poem, which began at some point in 1919.[2] The inclusion of work like 'Exequy' amongst the materials, with its references to Bishop Henry King's elegy, marks the impact upon Eliot of two important anthologies of Early Modern poetry, which both appeared in 1921. These were George Saintsbury's long-delayed *Minor Poets of the Caroline Period*, Volume III, which included a large selection of King's work; and Herbert J.C. Grierson's *Metaphysical Lyrics and Poems of the Seventeenth Century* (the subject of Eliot's 'The Metaphysical Poets'), which reprinted three King poems, including 'The Exequy'. Eliot was clearly partly reminded about an enduring, early enthusiasm, and partly brought into a fuller engagement with King's work by this means. His poetry sounded an elegiac tenor for several years after.[3] Grierson also reprinted ten poems by Andrew Marvell, the subject of discussion by Eliot in a tercentenary essay of 1921. 'To His Coy Mistress' provides matter for prolonged reflection in Eliot's essay, and then is echoed at several points in *The Waste Land*. This was the first time Marvell's poem had been directly included amongst the panoply of Eliot's sources since its occurrence in 'The Love Song of J. Alfred Prufrock' (1911). As with the metaphysical lyrics, the critical task of commemorating Marvell, and perhaps that poet's prominence in the Grierson anthology, prompted Eliot creatively, in the poetry he was then writing.

What we find in Eliot's critical and creative engagement with Early Modern writing at this point is his use of a continuing constellation of imagery, and of unresolved and irresolvable questions about poetry's nature and signification. The Early Modern texts enabled Eliot to develop, beneath the episodic surface of his text, with its constant changes of voice and direction, a structural thread of

---

[2] The dates of composition of the various papers in *The Waste Land* transcript have not been resolved by the manifold tables concluding Lawrence Rainey's *Revisiting The Waste Land* (New Haven and London: Yale University Press, 2005). I accept fully Jim McCue's rebuttal of many of the premises of Rainey's attempt ('Editing Eliot', *Essays in Criticism*, vol. LVI, no. 1, January 2006, 1–27). For the purposes of my argument in this chapter, I follow Rainey in presuming that 'The Death of the Duchess' was the first substantial piece drafted towards the complete poem (200–1). This is agreed by Christopher Ricks (*IMH*, xlii) and by Lyndall Gordon (*T.S. Eliot: An Imperfect Life*, New York: W.W. Norton, 1998, 540). Both Ricks and Gordon see 'Dirge' and 'Elegy' as part of this early drafting also; Rainey disagrees.

[3] In November 1922, Eliot enquired whether Richard Aldington had read the King poems in the Saintsbury volume, and recommended them to him as being amongst the 'finest'. Eliot thought that he might write a short essay on King at this point (*LI*, 787). In 1924 he could use the phrase 'hollow vale' from 'The Exequy' as though it were obviously synonymous with a slough of despond (*LII*, 393).

instances, images, and themes, which run through *The Waste Land* from beginning to end. He was, thereby, enabled to manage an architecture founded upon hidden cryptogrammatic echoes, on a scale beyond any that he had attempted hitherto. Without those buried cross-currents, and centring preoccupations, *The Waste Land* would lack shape and variety, in its consideration of the cultural and historic situation of 'the mind of Europe' after World War I. Those cross-currents also raise, more openly, several issues that have underscored the earlier work: issues including generic complication; the treatment of women by males, as emblematic of historical malaise in modernity; and the nature of the elegiac in the modern world.

The early 1920s saw Eliot directly extending the central notion of 'Tradition and the Individual Talent', although it is a particular extension of ideas on this topic that had begun with the article 'Reflections on Contemporary Poetry' (1919), an article that predates the more famous essay by three months. In 'Reflections on Contemporary Poetry' Eliot had celebrated 'the secret knowledge' that young poets share with some precursor figure. But he laments that such 'knowledge' is often absent from the experiments of contemporary writing, which is 'deficient in tradition':

> No dead voices speak through the living voice, no reincarnation, no re-creation. Not even the *saturation* that sometimes combusts spontaneously into originality:

> > fly where men feel
> > The cunning axletree: and those that suffer
> > Beneath the chariot of the snowy Bear

> is beautiful, and the beauty only appears more substantial if we conjecture that Chapman may have absorbed the recurring phrase of Seneca in:

> > signum celsi glaciale poli
> > septem stellis Arcados ursae
> > lucem vero termine vocat [...]
> > > sub cardine
> > glacialis ursae [...].[4]

Instead of the 'monuments' seen to constitute 'tradition', or 'the mind of Europe', in the iconic 'Tradition and the Individual Talent' (*SE*, 15), tradition here is formed by allusive echoes, which can be perceived or created by the later writer, between texts across the centuries. Here, the main character's dying speech in George Chapman's *Bussy d'Ambois* (1607) is, as elsewhere by Eliot, referred back to its precursor text in Seneca's tragedies.[5]

---

[4] T.S. Eliot, 'Reflections on Contemporary Poetry', *The Egoist*, vol. VI, no. 3, July 1919, 39.

[5] Eliot makes a mistake, however, when presenting these lines from Seneca as lying behind *Bussy d'Ambois*, V. iii, 145–51. In meaning to cite Chapman's version of the chorus's commentary on Hercules' agony in *Hercules Oetaeus* (ll. 1519–24), Eliot here actually gives as the source lines from Seneca's *other* Hercules play, *Hercules Furens*: 'signum celsi...vocat' ('the icy constellation at the high pole,/ Arcas' bear with its seven stars,/turns its wain and calls down the light') comes from the choral ode, 129–31; 'sub cardine' ('under the turning-point of the icy bear') comes from the line, following that in Hercules' speech beginning 'Quis hic locus?', which provides 'Marina' with its epigraph (1138–40).

Eliot's point about how such reference in poetry is received is crucial for his mature practice. We respond immediately to the 'beauty' of such allusive moments, but that response becomes greater if we recognize the prior (*traditional*) element behind, or ghosting and ventriloquizing ('speaking through'), those moments. The new work literally becomes a re-embodiment of the old, or a re-making of it; the gamut of Eliot's terminology when describing this phenomenon is inclusive, rather than vague. And Eliot, as noted at the end of the previous chapter, makes this suggestion from the situation of a practitioner who deliberately seeks for this kind of beauty. 'Gerontion', completed in the same month as the appearance of 'Reflections on Contemporary Poetry', contains, as we have seen, its own echo of Chapman's (and thence Seneca's) lines in its own concluding paragraph.

What the example of Early Modern writing was providing Eliot with at this point, in the years when he was pondering and drafting *The Waste Land*, is the re-confirmation that 'dead voices' must directly and unaltered 'speak through the living voice' of the true contemporary poet. The modern poet must select from them, and orchestrate them into new meanings. This is particularly so when the contemporary poet is seeking to perceive order within a devastated world, in which dissociation, and incoherence, is to be read everywhere. Further evidence of Eliot's thought in this respect is provided by the two review articles he wrote in response to A.H. Cruickshank's *Philip Massinger* in 1920, articles he later combined to form the essay on this late Early Modern writer, in *Selected Essays* onwards.[6] In line with his championing of the critic J.M. Robertson's 'disintegrationist' work (discussed in Chapter Two), Eliot's 'Philip Massinger' opened by lauding the 'scholarship' of Cruickshank's approach to his subject, one which, he claimed, contrasted with the vague criticism, founded upon 'good taste', used when discussing Massinger across the nineteenth century. The two aspects of Cruickshank's approach had been given early in his book:

> It was the custom in those days, as in the time of Plautus at Rome, for playwrights to revise old plays; and still more was it usual for them to collaborate.[7]

Eliot advocated, then, Cruickshank's scholarly attempts to discover which parts of Massinger were re-workings of plots and passages from earlier work, and which parts are not his alone, but the result of collaboration with such as Field, Daborne, Dekker, Tourneur, and (mostly) Fletcher. According to Eliot, Cruickshank offered 'facts', 'method', over mere 'judgment' (*SE*, 205–6).[8] Cruickshank applied that 'method' most consistently, as Eliot thence enthused, when he delineated the indebtedness of Massinger to Shakespeare:

> Massinger was a devoted admirer and imitator of Shakespeare in thought, device, and expression. It is not strange, therefore, that he should copy his metre, or rather, develop his own on the same lines.

---

[6] T.S. Eliot, 'Philip Massinger', *TLS*, no. 958, 27 May 1926, 325–6; 'The Old Comedy', *Athenaeum*, no. 4702, 11 June 1920, 760–1.

[7] A.H. Cruickshank, *Philip Massinger* (Oxford: Basil Blackwell, 1920), 2.

[8] The terms of Eliot's advocacy here again recall those of his review article 'The Beating of a Drum' (1923)—also discussed in Chapter Two.

In the service of exploring this admiration, Cruickshank included a lengthy Appendix 'On the influence of Shakespeare', and another to the 'Common Causes of Metrical Variety' in Elizabethan verse writing.[9] It is the former of these appendices that provided Eliot with much of his matter in the first part of 'Philip Massinger', where he seized upon several of Cruickshank's exempla as proving Massinger's direct verbal indebtednesses to Shakespeare. The drift of Eliot's argument is that, in every example passage, Massinger's language lacked 'colour', 'particularity', 'feeling', compared to his master. Hence, he was unable to create 'living' characters whose psychological motives were consistent with the coherent progression of the drama.

However, the critical instigation provided by Cruickshank's book sparked Eliot to discover related passages in Massinger's plays, which he could add to the debate. In other words, Cruickshank sent him back to Massinger's work, from which he spotlighted two passages then alluded to at moments far apart in his subsequent poetry. As so often in his critical writing, Eliot was spurred to develop a deeper appreciation for the Early Modern writer in question than the author under review; but it is an appreciation that is then translated into his poetry, even at a distance from the original impulse. In this instance, when Eliot adds, to prove his argument about indebtedness over that made by Cruickshank, 'two more passages, not given by our commentator', those passages are in their turn telling for his own poetry (*SE*, 208). The phrases 'Here he comes,/His nose held up; he hath something in the wind'—a sneering allusion to Aretinus in Massinger's *The Roman Actor* (IV. i, 51–3)—seem to lie behind the voices in the crowd waiting for the 'Ego' who is Eliot's 'Coriolan' ('Here they come') (*SE*, 208; *CPP*, 127). The second passage contributed by Eliot to the debate with Cruickshank comes from a taunt by Aretinus in the same scene. Eliot's fascination with an Early Modern source typically takes a very specific and local focus within the play in question. Aretinus has discovered two lovers' betrayal of other loves, and offers to help them escape in exchange for payment: 'As tann'd galley-slaves/Pay such as do redeem them from the oar' (IV. i, 75–9).[10] As so often, Eliot is fascinated by moments where discovered secrets are met by brutally unexpected response, as he is redrawn in the essay on Massinger to this same scene in *The Roman Actor* for another poetic touchstone. Eliot cross-refers the oar image to Massinger's other play of hidden passion (this time with positive outcome), *The Bondman* (IV. iii, 75ff). In these lines, Leosthanes hymns his presumed love. This latter source, then, immediately is made to resound in Eliot's poetry, which seems an end point in the chain of Early Modern echoes

---

[9] Cruickshank, 57; Appendices IV and VI. The 'common causes' identified in the latter appendix might have given pause to Eliot, meditator about *vers libre*: rhyme; the occasional use of an eleven-syllable line; free use of trisyllabic feet; occasional interjection of short lines; skilful variation of pauses and caesuras; 'metrical variation', or the use of short syllables at line-endings. Many of these qualities were early identified as integral to Eliot's 'Auditory Imagination', from 'Gerontion' onwards, by Helen Gardner (*The Art of T.S. Eliot*, London: Faber, 1949, 19ff).

[10] 'I am acquainted with sad misery/As the tanned galley-slave is with his oar', as *The Duchess of Malfi* reflects in the horrific last scene of her life. As we shall see in the next chapter, Webster's play has marked formative influence on *The Waste Land*. See *Webster and Tourneur*, ed. John Addington Symonds (London: Vizetelly, 1888), 203.

originally pondered in the essay. After the thunder has 'said' '*Damyata*' in *The Waste Land*, V, we have a description of loving echo. The boat responds 'Gaily, to the hand expert with sail and oar/[...] your heart would have responded/Gaily' (*CPP*, 74). 'Oar' occurs at the end of Eliot's line, as it does in his two Massinger 'examples' not from Cruickshank. 'Beating oars' are heard from Elizabeth and Leicester's barge in 'The Fire Sermon' (70).

Overall, however, Eliot's argument in 'Philip Massinger' was aimed to resist Cruickshank's assertion that Massinger's 'imitation' of Shakespeare should win him critical consideration as a writer *second only to* Shakespeare. Eliot's rebuttal was icy, as it deftly pounced upon Cruickshank's term of high approbation for Massinger's ambition ('imitator'), whilst silently denying its justice. In Eliot's famous dictum: 'Immature poets imitate; mature poets steal.' For Eliot, Massinger's indebtedness does not prove his worth per se, since he does not, to take the terms of 'Reflections on Contemporary Poetry' again, 're-create' (however much he 'reincarnates') Shakespearean imagery (*SE*, 206).[11] On these grounds, Eliot's remarks, particularly in the first part of 'Philip Massinger', mount a defence of the playwrights he favours, over what he sees as Cruickshank's overweening claims for Massinger. He quoted counter-examples from Tourneur and Middleton, who, together with Webster, 'exhibit that perpetual slight alteration of language, words perpetually juxtaposed in new and sudden combinations'. For Eliot, such alteration and juxta-position evidenced highly developed perceptual and intellectual sensibility. Eliot claimed, further, in a suggestion which looked forward to that formulation 'a dis-sociation of sensibility', which 'The Metaphysical Poets' describes as having occurred in England, that, with the deaths of these playwrights (and of Donne and Chapman), this combination of sensibility receded forever (*SE*, 209–10). His own poetry of re-creation sought to recover that loss, by re-evoking the voices of the time of the original historical rupture.

Eliot's 'Philip Massinger', therefore, plays upon the terms Eliot evolved also in 'Swinburne as Critic' from this same year, 1920. In Early Modern writing there exists 'a quality of sensuous thought, or of thinking through the senses, or of the senses thinking' (*SW*, 19). But Eliot, in 'Philip Massinger', also evolved his histori-cal sense beyond its definition in 'Tradition and the Individual Talent', by consider-ing the issue of textual citation between literary generations. In this, Eliot's thinking seems to have been positively aided by his disagreement with Cruickshank, whom he quoted on the fact that Massinger was 'typical of an age which had much culture, but which, without being exactly corrupt, lacked moral fibre'.[12]

Against Canon Cruickshank's dated 'moral fibre', Eliot posited the more vivid 'sensuous thought', effected through 'words perpetually juxtaposed in new and sudden combinations', as counters to the lack that he perceived in his own age.[13]

---

[11] Cruickshank lays out Massinger's 'imitation' on 77ff, via plot summaries and displays of similar imagery between his work and Shakespeare's. He makes his claim for Massinger's superiority to all other contenders to Shakespeare's place on p. 142.

[12] Cruickshank's phrase appears on *Philip Massinger*, 19.

[13] Eliot was shortly to begin comparing the Early Modern period to the modern age, in 'The Metaphysical Poets', and, in a more questioning way, in 'John Donne' (1923). This latter notes

More particularly, Eliot was shortly to present his own antidote to Massinger's 'imitation' of Shakespeare in his textual negotiations in *The Waste Land*, which 'steal' more of Shakespeare's lines than any of his previous works. This is even more so when the associated drafts are taken into account. 'Philip Massinger' seems to have confirmed Eliot in the growing view, as displayed by 'Reflections on Contemporary Poetry' of the previous year, that 'imitation' was a danger for a poet living in less culturally unified times than the Early Modern heights of achievement, and that this was particularly proven when considering Shakespeare's work as potential precursor. Alongside the more opaque references demonstrated by Cruickshank to have been Massinger's response to Shakespeare, what was needed was directly and allusively to hear the 'dead voices' in the 'living' work. In *The Waste Land*, then, Eliot directly confronted Shakespeare, and reworked his words, as he had previously, in shorter lyrics, those of Middleton, Beaumont and Fletcher, Webster and Tourneur. Shakespeare now formed the crucial role amongst the inter-involved Early Modern 'voices' in the poem. He had become pivotal to the various forms of dialogue with the past that *The Waste Land* makes.[14]

In seeking to achieve this necessary vividness of 'words perpetually juxtaposed', Eliot continued, in the early 1920s, to consider the practice and language of the Elizabethan playhouse. As he developed the notion of 'impersonality' from 'Tradition and the Individual Talent', in 'The Possibility of a Poetic Drama' (1920), Eliot rounded against a literature of 'reflection' upon experience, in favour of what he called 'presentation'. A play must, after all, convince as a plausible world view, a re-creation of a world for the audience (*SW*, 54, 57). Plato's dialogues, Greek drama, Flaubert, are to be favoured for their presentational qualities above Thackeray and Goethe, or contemporary prose drama. Elizabethan drama is to be favoured above all.[15] Eliot was a few years away from *Sweeney Agonistes*, however, and his essays on poetry of the early 1920s involved him in a sense of how complex the act of poetic 'presentation' could be, of how intransigent is the ambition to create 'words perpetually juxtaposed in new and sudden combinations' in a culture as severely 'dissociated' as the 'age' following World War I. 'John Dryden', 'The Metaphysical Poets', 'Andrew Marvell', and Eliot's contemporary magazine articles and London Letters of this period, reveal him pondering a method through which

the 'sympathetic' nature of the earlier age to 'us', but frets that this seeming relation might have evolved on a 'local' or temporary basis (*The Nation and the Athenaeum*, XXXIII 10 9 June 1923, 332). As Chapter Six will show, this comparison became more complex and fraught at the time of the Clark Lectures, *The Varieties of Metaphysical Poetry* (1926).

[14] Under Lawrence Rainey's system of dating the papers of *The Waste Land* manuscript, the fragment re-imagining the passage from *The Tempest*, 'Those are pearls that were his eyes', was one of the earliest parts composed (Rainey, *Revisiting the Waste Land*, 200–1). Valerie Eliot describes it as a 'First Draft', dates it to 1921, and sees in the piece a combination of an expansion upon the lines from *The Tempest*, together with reference to lines from *Othello* (*WLFT*, 123, 131). In its cross-cutting between plays, the fragment might be seen as an experiment towards the method which the sequence as a whole would deploy.

[15] When reflecting upon the contemporary productions by The Phoenix Society theatre group, who were concerned to present authentic productions of Early Modern works, Eliot reaffirmed that the continuing popularity of Shakespeare's work amounted to a confirmation of the unbroken appeal of poetic drama ('London Letter', the *Dial*, 70, no. 6, June 1921, 687).

to exact such 'combinations'. But it was a method which was attuned to the fact that, as he put it in 'Philip Massinger', 'new and sudden combinations' effected in language by a poet must both reflect enhanced feeling and thought but also transmit them with immediacy to readers (*SE*, 210). The 'development' that Eliot evolved through his reading in the Early Modern period, at the same time as he wrote *The Waste Land*, was partly to discover, and partly to create, a notion of what a realistic but metaphysical poetry might amount to for 'our age'.

'WIT': A METAPHYSICAL METHOD

The 'metaphysical' becomes in Eliot's writing at this period partly a *method*, derived from his recent sharpened understanding of allusive and recreative key facets of Early Modern writing, and partly *content*. This content emerged in *The Waste Land*, and the poetry to 1925, from Eliot's response to his contemporary situation, but also from the way he read that response through moments in favoured Early Modern texts. My comments on the content of *The Waste Land* will be reserved for the next chapter, since it shadows the work Eliot wrote *after* the sequence itself—*Sweeney Agonistes* and 'The Hollow Men'. For the remainder of this chapter, I will concentrate upon the sources for the specific poetic *method* that Eliot evolved to combine the many voices of the past in his new poem.

As we have seen, in evolving a *method* for developing his poetic beyond the deployment of a persona to mediate the experience of 'Gerontion', Eliot was exercised by the criticism of Early Modern work with which he was circumstantially engaged. To this extent, the substantial review articles that appeared in the *TLS* in the first half of 1921, 'Andrew Marvell' and 'John Dryden', are as significant as the more familiar 'The Metaphysical Poets' of later that year, in determining some of the parameters of Eliot's discussion, with himself, about method and technique at that moment. Eliot seems to have acknowledged as much, when grouping these three essays together as *Homage to John Dryden* in 1924: the title's suggestion that the three works stand in tribute to the *later* poet, rather than the two Early Modern writers, is itself significant for the *timbre* that Eliot hoped the trilogy of essays might achieve.[16]

Eliot's classic formulation of 'wit', in 'Andrew Marvell', as 'a recognition, implicit in the expression of every experience, of other kinds of experience which are possible', is correlative with the notion of poetry as embedding 'secret knowledge' or 'keys' from other past contexts of writing. But it, to an extent, builds upon the notion of poetic myriad-mindedness, which had become a feature of popular editions of Marvell, in the last decade of the nineteenth century (*SE*, 303). In the Introduction to the Muses' Library edition, which the Bodleian inventory shows

---

[16] 'Andrew Marvell', *TLS*, no. 1002, 31 March 1921, 201–2; 'John Dryden', *TLS* no. 1012, 9 June 1921, 361–2; 'The Metaphysical Poets', *TLS* no. 1031, 20 October 1921, 669–70. At the time of publication, Eliot declared of *Homage to John Dryden*, that the essay on Dryden himself was 'the best' (*LII*, 484).

that Eliot owned, G.A. Aitken compared Marvell's mind to the garden figured in his own poem of that title:

> where he found Quiet and Innocence, and where every fruit of form pressed itself upon him as he walked. But the mind, retiring into its own happiness, created other worlds and seas, transcending those of the natural world.[17]

Aitken's sense that Marvell achieved a 'graceful form, simplicity combined with depth of thought', is not unallied to Eliot's definition of 'wit', with regard to Marvell's writing, which similarly indicates a depth of intellect behind a graceful surface lyricism (*SE*, 293).

Where Eliot, in 'Andrew Marvell', carries his sense of 'wit' further than such as Aitken's definition of the poet's mind, however, is in presenting 'wit' as a structuring principle, at both a local and larger level in a metaphysical poem. Taking 'To His Coy Mistress' as prime example, Eliot notes the almost syllogistic relation between the three strophes of Marvell's poem, as well as the 'wit' deployed to create the procession of imagery (*SE*, 296). As an example of the syllogistic, Eliot gives a passage from the second strophe of 'To His Coy Mistress' ('the worms shall try/ That long-preserved virginity'), alongside lines from the third, which he had echoed already in 'The Love Song of J. Alfred Prufrock' ('Let us roll our strength and all/ Our sweetness up into one ball'). Eliot comments on the Donne-like mood of the former passage here. It is, notably, that 'mood', rather than the cathartic effort enjoined in the second passage, which determines Eliot's echo of the start of Marvell's second strophe in 'The Fire Sermon' from *The Waste Land*:

> But at my back in a cold blast I hear
> The rattle of the bones, and chuckle spread from ear to ear...
> But at my back from time to time I hear
> The sound of horns and motors.
>
> (*CPP*, 67)[18]

Eliot's re-creation of Marvell's lines 'But at my back I always hear/Time's wingèd chariot hurrying near' preserves, in the first instance, the original imagining of the lover's skeleton 'in thy marble vault'. The 'cold blast' presumably contains something of the biblical resonance of punishment, which B.C. Southam hears in Eliot's version. But it is also, literally, the frigid air escaping at the opening of a grave.[19] In the second instance here of 'But at my back', Eliot creates something of a literal rendition of that high speed of rhythm and imagery, which his essay mentions in relation to Marvell's poem (*SE*, 295). Eliot's new lines, in the wake of Marvell's,

---

[17] *The Poems of Andrew Marvell, Sometime Member of Parliament for Hull*, ed. G.A. Aitken (London: Lawrence & Bullen: New York: Charles Scribner's Sons, 1892), lxiv. Eliot's essay opens, rather oddly, by repeating Marvell's parliamentary situation from this title (*SE*, 292).

[18] The lines quoted in 'Andrew Marvell' from the second strophe of 'To His Coy Mistress' later take on a chilling presence at the end of Eliot's 'Lines to a Duck in the Park', where bread, with cognizance taken of its significance in the communion rite, is seen as more congenial food for the 'Duck' than an 'enquiring worm', 'That soon...shall try/Our well-preserved complacency' (*CPP*, 136).

[19] B.C. Southam, *A Student's Guide to the Selected Poems of T.S. Eliot* (London: Faber, 1994, sixth edition), 167.

retain the 'marked caesura' which he felt characterized the original's (albeit shorter) lines, and which presumably ensured their rapid pace (*SE*, 298). Yet, given the interest in 'speed' or 'hurry', which is enhanced in 'To His Coy Mistress' and elsewhere in Marvell by such technique, Eliot's replacement of 'always hear' by the diffident 'from time to time I hear' is striking. It marks his belated sense that such 'dead voices' can only sporadically break through the surface depredations of the opening of 'The Fire Sermon'.

What Eliot's successive variations upon Marvell's theme further manage to enforce is that 'element of *surprise*', for which Eliot praises his predecessor's adaptation of traditional form and imagery to his own purpose.[20] This is a 'surprise' that, for the reader, makes 'the familiar strange, the strange familiar' (*SE*, 300–1).[21] Such is the effect of Eliot's use of quotation in *The Waste Land* as a whole, an effect achieved by taking 'familiar' rhythms and images from past texts, and making them 'strange', when setting them within their modern context. Eliot's appropriation of Marvell's *carpe diem* address to his reluctant lover, to this degree, picks up from the scarred relationships of the end of 'A Game of Chess' ('HURRY UP PLEASE ITS TIME'), and looks forward to the depressing encounter, in 'The Fire Sermon', between the typist and the house agent's clerk ('The time is now propitious, as he guesses') (*CPP*, 66, 68). As in other cases, Eliot's appropriation of lines from Marvell rests in a relationship, not just to the images near it, but within the larger structure of the poem, as Eliot felt that Marvell's use of wit succeeded in doing.

What is notable in Eliot's consideration of 'wit' in this essay, and in 'John Dryden' and 'The Metaphysical Poets' also, is that it seems to derive from direct encounter with critical tradition around 'metaphysical' poetry, as it had developed from Dryden himself, and was then given fuller expression by Dr Johnson in his *Life of Cowley*.[22] 'Andrew Marvell' cites Johnson's *Life*, with its succession of examples of outlandish images from Cowley, to suggest that Marvell's imagery could become of the same order sometimes. It could be 'distracting', and draw

---

[20] Surprise, of course, links Eliot's Early Modern interests to that fascination he also had for Edgar Allan Poe. As he acknowledges here, Poe also made surprise a necessary factor in poetry's effect.

[21] 'Surprise' immediately formed a crucial factor in the early promotion of Eliot's poetry itself, and in the promotion of his understanding of Early Modern literature as being fundamentally the correct one for his time. In discussing 'T.S. Eliot's Theory of Poetry', Hugh Ross Williamson noted the element of 'surprise' in Eliot's use of imagery, citing specifically the opening lines of 'The Love Song of J. Alfred Prufrock'. The technique of 'surprise', as Williamson saw it, was not something Eliot originated, but 'something which he found in the work of the Metaphysical poets'. Williamson had earlier thanked Eliot in a note for his 'kindness' in 'supplying certain facts of which I have made use', in *The Poetry of T.S. Eliot* (London: Hodder and Stoughton, 1932), 56–7. George Williamson, in tracing *The Donne Tradition*, notes in early remarks the importance of 'the close relation of...three things in Donne, wit, surprise, conceit', things he discusses across the book. George Williamson thanks Eliot in his Preface for reading part of his book in manuscript (George Williamson, *The Donne Tradition: A Study in English Poetry from Donne to the Death of Cowley*, Cambridge, MA: Harvard University Press, 1930, 28).

[22] In this emphasis, Eliot was departing from the contemporary criticism of the earlier period with which he was familiar. Neither Aitken, nor Grierson in his Introduction to *Metaphysical Lyrics and Poems*, nor the more general survey books discussing the poetry of the Early Modern period, such as George Saintsbury's *A History of Elizabethan Literature* (London: Macmillan, 1907 edition), perceive 'wit' to have been crucial to metaphysical poetry, as Eliot did.

attention merely to itself, rather than continuing the 'witty' evolution of the imagery in the poem (*SE*, 297–8).[23] Johnson, who saw Cowley's 'Ode on Wit' as unrivalled, famously defined 'wit' as the governing characteristic of the 'metaphysical' in poetry:

> But wit, abstracted from its effects upon the hearer, may be more rigorously and philosophically considered as a kind of *discordia concors*; a combination of dissimilar images, or discovery of occult resemblances in things apparently unlike.... The most heterogeneous ideas are yoked by violence together; nature and art are ransacked for illustrations, comparisons, and allusions; their learning instructs, and their subtlety surprises.[24]

For Johnson, of course, the achievement of such metaphysical poetry was too 'dearly bought'.

In his classic formulation about the necessary *difficulty* of a poetry adequate to 'our civilization', Eliot, in 'The Metaphysical Poets', also portrayed this kind of writing as carrying an inevitable price. It is a high price, given the circumstances out of which, and against which, the poet must create new work:

> Our civilization comprehends great variety and complexity, and this variety and complexity, playing upon a refined sensibility, must produce various and complex results. The poet must become more and more comprehensive, more allusive, more indirect, in order to force, to dislocate if necessary, language into his meaning. (*SE*, 289)

Eliot's definition retained the sense of scope ('nature and art are ransacked'), the allusiveness, but also the *violence* of Johnson's definition of what metaphysical poetry must achieve and promote, in order to contain its images ('force', 'dislocate'). All of these qualities are absent from what (to adopt a title, which the editor of the volume of Dryden's *Essays* owned by Eliot, imposed on the original text) Dryden had seen as the threefold derivation of 'The Proper Wit of Poetry': 'finding the thought...the variation, deriving, or moulding, of that thought...clothing and adorning of that thought'.[25] Johnson's definition lacks the clarity of Dryden's. Yet Eliot seems to have favoured Johnson's definition, and seen the necessary forcing of heterogeneous qualities together ('comprehensive, allusive, indirect') as, in

[23] Eliot displayed a similarly discriminatory eye with regard to Marvell's conceits, in a review article of 1923. In 'Andrew Marvell' the *essay*, Eliot had early showed an awareness of historically changing taste with regard to wit (*SE*, 293). In 1923 this becomes a pivot upon which his judgement rests: 'Our conceits cannot be those of Marvell; they will spring, equally genuine, from a different impulse, from a different level of feeling.//Marvell is, without doubt, a very conceited poet.' Eliot, 'Andrew Marvell', *The Nation and Athenaeum*, vol. xxxiii, no. 26, 29 September 1923, 809.

[24] Dr Johnson, *Lives of the Most Eminent English Poets* (London: Frederick Warne & Co: New York: Scribner, Welford and Armstrong, 1872), 9. This is the 'Chandos Edition' which Ronald Schuchard has identified as the edition Eliot possessed (*VMP*, 64). Eliot was to compare 'wit' in Johnson, Dryden, and Cowley in Lecture VII of *The Varieties of Metaphysical Poetry* to illustrate its changing (and increasingly less potent) meaning (191–4). He later wrote that 'wit' was so important to him that it contained 'more than anything I could enclose in a definition', but that the technique characterized the period from Donne to Vaughan more than any other. 'A Note on Two Odes of Cowley', *Seventeenth-Century Studies Presented to Sir Herbert Grierson*, ed. John Dover Wilson (Oxford: Clarendon Press, 1938), 241.

[25] John Dryden, *Essays*, ed. W.H. Hudson (London: Dent, 1912), 192. Schuchard identifies this as Eliot's edition, *VMP*, 64; Eliot quotes Dryden on wit from this essay on p. 192 of the lectures.

1921, symptomatic of the poet's situation 'at present'. It was also the only means to describe, critically, the poetry which must result from that situation.

Eliot's engagement with Dryden, in the year before *The Waste Land* was published, served further to clarify historically the *nature* of a belated metaphysical writing, and the angle from which such writing must approach its contemporary subject matter. Mark Van Doren's *John Dryden: A Study of His Poetry*, the impulse for Eliot's long review article 'John Dryden', traced the hinterland of the meaning of 'wit' between the first generation of metaphysical poets and that of his book's subject. It is that hinterland, specifically, that Van Doren considered the foundation for the long poem on 1666, *Annus Mirabilis*, which Dryden called his 'wit-writing'.[26] Van Doren noted the classical allusion underpinning Dryden's poem, but, more broadly (and in terms that clearly struck the author of 'Philip Massinger') he considered Dryden's way with earlier writers, whom 'he visits', then 'takes from them whatever he can carry away' (34, 105). Eliot's 'John Dryden' tacitly seized upon this aspect of Van Doren's study, when noting that Dryden's poetry is particularly striking in the way it absorbs earlier writing, in order to broaden its own scope of possibility (*SE*, 312). For Eliot, such capacity enhanced Dryden's ability to create 'surprise', which is (as in the Marvell essay), considered the essence of poetry (*SE*, 308). Once more, then, in line with the effect he was seeking in *The Waste Land* at this same time, allusion is linked through wit to bring presentational directness to the writing.

But Eliot seems also to have responded to the general tone of Van Doren's critical evaluation of Dryden. For Van Doren's emphasis saw Dryden as having continued the metaphysical tradition (Donne forms the constant point of comparison) by sustaining 'a speaking voice' in all of his writing. In other words, Van Doren found in Dryden that quality which turn-of-the-century critics had associated specifically with Donne, and which Eliot was later to see as linking the achievements of Donne and Dryden, as was indicated in Chapter Two. To define the speaking voice, Van Doren perceived in Dryden's work a relaxed approach to metrics:

> he succeeded in manipulating his measures so that he could speak directly and easily yet with dignity.... Dryden was a believer in significant variety of accent... within the heroic line... the freedom of blank verse seems to have been in his thoughts. His pauses come anywhere. (76)

Van Doren's emphasis upon 'wit-writing', as conceived by Dryden, as a form of contemporary speech, aligns Dryden closely with the tradition in which he had situated him in the opening chapters of his book. He saw Dryden there as a graduate of the 'school of Hobbes', a writer who, in his concept of the imagination, 'ignored the transforming power in favour of the recording power'. For Van Doren, then, Dryden's poetry 'was a poetry of statement. At his best he wrote without figures, without transforming passion.' (25) To this extent, Dryden's poetry promotes certain generic choices, since 'Dryden was speaking in his most communicative cadences in the satires and the epistles.' (66–7)

---

[26] Mark Van Doren, *John Dryden: A Study of His Poetry* (New York: Harcourt, Brace and Howe, 1920), 32. Subsequent references to this book are given in the text.

Eliot's 'John Dryden' takes the generic implications of his subject's outlook seriously, to effect a potent implication out of Van Doren's key terms: Dryden can make 'the prosaic into the poetic', and by so doing make a 'trivial' occurrence into something more directly, even satirically, significant (*SE*, 310). The drafts of *The Waste Land* reveal a considerable satiric drive impelling several of its subsequently deleted passages (a drive only taken up later by Eliot in the unfinished 'Coriolan'). If, as Lyndall Gordon maintains, the 'Fresca couplets', which had stood at the start of 'The Fire Sermon' across Pound's various readings of the drafts, were the last part of the manuscript to be removed and replaced by the current opening, it is indicative of Eliot's own uncertainty of generic choice regarding his poem.[27] In the various drafts of 'The Fire Sermon', 'Phantasmal' 'goblins' (or variously 'gnomes') 'burrow' through the fabric of London (*WLFT*, 31, 43). Adapting the terms of Eliot's meditation on Dryden's achievement, it is notable that both the Fresca passage, and the other more clearly satiric moments in *The Waste Land* drafts, serve to *diminish* rather than to 'transform' their poetic objects.[28]

METAPHYSICAL CONCEITS AND POETIC 'OBSCURITY'

The tone *The Waste Land* adopts, in both draft and finished form, remains closer to that *'recording'*, rather than 'transforming', power, which Van Doren traced as characteristic of 'metaphysical' 'wit-writing' as it had survived from the Early Modern period through to the end of the seventeenth century. Even with the access to a more religious potential in Part V of Eliot's poem, the writing *records* 'What the Thunder said'. It does not seek a syllogistic synthesis of elements that have been laid down in earlier parts of the sequence.[29] When he described what manages the process of 'recording' across the poetic space, however, Eliot's formulations during the period of work on *The Waste Land* consistently suggest the importance for him of earlier notions of poetic development alongside Dryden's. Collectively, these influences work as a way to contain the 'complexity' of what it is that poetry seeks coherently to record. 'Andrew Marvell' describes the wit-derived movement and structuring of poetry via its images; 'The Metaphysical Poets', after delineating the necessary violence which the poet must enact upon, and through, the language, to make 'meaning', concedes that 'we get something which looks very much like the conceit' (*SE*, 289). *The Waste Land*, then, can be taken from this context, to deploy

---

[27] Gordon, *T.S. Eliot: An Imperfect Life*, 544.

[28] William H. Pritchard, when considering the satiric potential in the poem, links back to the 1919 essay 'Ben Jonson' in deciding that Eliot's characters are versions of Jonson's 'humours' ('Reading *The Waste Land* Today', *Essays in Criticism*, vol. XIX, no. 2, April 1969, 180–6).

[29] Others have noted the biblical reference of the thunder in Part V of the poem. But, in another of Eliot's sources for the work, Middleton's *Women Beware Women*, Bianca, responding to the threat from the Duke, notes that 'Should thunder speak/And none regard it, it had lost the name' (II. ii; *Thomas Middleton*, ed. Havelock Ellis (London: T. Fisher Unwin, 1895, 302). *The Tempest*, that other key text for Eliot's poem, has the thunder speak 'the name of Prosper' (III. iii, 99; *Shakespeare's Comedy of The Tempest*, ed. Israel Gollancz (London: J.M. Dent, 1894, 74)).

wit as a way of linking a series of conceits, which, in turn, record, without transforming poetically, the devastations of modern history.

But Eliot's conception of the conceit was also complicit with his engagement with the criticism that mediated this version of the Early Modern to him. Herbert J.C. Grierson's Introduction to *Metaphysical Lyrics and Poems of the Seventeenth Century* (which set Donne as the instigating and overarching presence, with his 'new psychological curiosity')[30] felt the necessity to tackle the 'still audible criticism' of the 'metaphysicals' from such as Dr Johnson, by asserting that 'even the fantastic thoughts, the conceits of these courtly love poets and devout singers are not to be dismissed'. The 'conceit' enabled the passionate, original, but also the religious, petition of these lyric poets:

> they succeed in stumbling upon some conceit which reveals a fresh intuition into the heart, or states an old plea with new and prevailing force. And the divine poets express with the same blend of argument and imagination the deep and complex currents of religious feeling which were flowing in England.... In the metaphysical subtleties of conceit they found something that is more than conceit, symbols in which to express and adumbrate their apprehensions of the infinite.[31]

Grierson's understanding of the revelation that the 'conceit' could make to individual feeling, to 'the heart', and also to 'thought' (and thence into the theological 'infinite'), entered into the historical discriminations of Eliot's 'The Metaphysical Poets'. Yet something like it is present earlier also, in 'Swinburne as Critic'.

'Swinburne as Critic', however, had been important in other senses, since it suggested models for that concatenation, found in 'The Metaphysical Poets', between poetic 'conceits' and '*difficulty*'. Eliot agreed with Swinburne that Chapman was a 'difficult poet', and that that difficulty goes beyond the obvious obscurity of Chapman's contorted conceits. But, crucially, Eliot pointed to a *purpose* in difficulty, a purpose intricate with the technical deployment of poetic conceit (*SW*, 18–9). For Swinburne's essay on Chapman, included in *Contemporaries of Shakespeare*, the 1919 collection under review by Eliot, perceived Chapman's poems to be 'full of earnest thought, of passionate energy', and to be written by 'a man of genius'. But Swinburne also saw Chapman as having an 'encrusted mind'. Chapman's 'vigorous but unfixed and chaotic intellect', his being 'overcharged with over-flowing thoughts', led him to create work which was the 'most gloriously obscure in style' that Swinburne says he has ever written on. Chapman is 'not sufficiently possessed by any one leading idea, or attracted towards any one central point'. Looking for recent analogies (in a vein that would have appealed to the Eliot of *The Varieties of Metaphysical Poetry*, as Chapter Six demonstrates), Swinburne found comparison between Chapman and Browning.[32]

---

[30] The shift to, as he sees it, a more 'psychological' poetic in the Early Modern period, earns Eliot's dismay, from at least the time of the Clark Lectures onward (*VMP*, 130). See Chapter Six below.

[31] Herbert J.C. Grierson, ed., 'Introduction', *Metaphysical Lyrics and Poems of the Seventeenth Century*, Oxford: Clarendon Press, 1921, xiv, xxxii–xxxiii.

[32] A.C. Swinburne, *Contemporaries of Shakespeare*, ed. Edmund Gosse and Thomas James Wise (London: Heinemann, 1919), 25. Charles Larson has noted the importance of *Donne* also in this nineteenth-century debate. The only *Complete Poems* of Donne which appeared during that century

Chapman wrote perhaps the most famous Early Modern defence of 'obscurity' in poetry, alongside Jonson's 'Address to the Reader' from *The Alchemist*. 'Obscuritie' was the essence of what Chapman was fascinated by. As the dedicatory epistle to Chapman's long poem 'Ovid's Banquet of Sense' has it:

> Obscuritie in affection of words, & indigested concets, is pedanticall and childish; but where it shroudeth it selfe in the hart of his subject, uttered with fitness of figure, and expressive Epethites; with that darknes wil I still labour to be shadowed: rich Minerals are digd out of the bowels of the earth, not in the superficies and dust of it.[33]

This association of obscurity with 'concets', 'fitness of figure', 'expressive Epethites', is not dissimilar from Eliot's sense of the prescription upon 'poets in our civilization' in 'The Metaphysical Poets'. It was Chapman's assertion that obscurity is 'in the hart' of the necessary subject for poetry, and thence of its 'concets'. Similar contentions would seem to have generated the epistolary exchange that the article 'The Metaphysical Poets' brought about, between Eliot and the previous generation's leading critic on Early Modern literature, George Saintsbury. In the issue of the *TLS* that appeared after Eliot's article, Saintsbury contested Eliot's understanding of 'metaphysical' as it derived from Dryden. Saintsbury claimed that the word merely meant the poet's 'second thoughts' about any subject, and that it was not inter-involved with poetic technique per se. Swinburne was to that extent as 'metaphysical' as Donne.[34] Eliot's reply, in the next issue of the *TLS*, is appropriately deferential to Saintsbury (he would shortly dedicate *Homage to John Dryden* to the older critic), and seems positively to entertain the notion of 'second thoughts' ('I have mentioned Chapman'). What he resisted, however, is the notion that Swinburne had thought, 'even *once*', about his use of imagery. In this way, Eliot sought to sustain his own (and the seventeenth-century's) sense of the power of the conceit, and the nature and purpose of his historical understanding in 'The Metaphysical Poets' (*LI*, 600). Conceits, in the tradition as Eliot understood it from Chapman and Donne, and now put into practice in his present work on *The Waste Land*, are consciously originated attempts to articulate the difficult matter of the world, and hence articulate the use of wit throughout the poem.

As evidenced in this exchange with George Saintsbury, Eliot displayed a renewed assurance, derived from his various reconsiderations of Early Modern writing in the early 1920s, an assurance about the necessary nature of the modern metaphysical poetry, which he was striving for as he drafted *The Waste Land*. This understanding led, in turn, towards clearer awareness of the importance for him that the inherently episodic nature of poetry, as described in relation to his knowledge of

---

was Alexander Grossart's two-volume edition of 1872–3, and it was dedicated to Browning, 'the poet of the century for thinkers'. See 'Alexander Grossart's Donne and Marvell', *Reinventing the Middle Ages and the Renaissance*, ed. William F. Gentrup (Arizona: Brepolis, 1998), 190.

[33] Jonathan Hudston, ed., *George Chapman: Plays and Poems*, Harmondsworth: Penguin, 1998, 239–40. George Williamson sees Chapman's epistle to 'Ovid's Banquet of Sense' as a 'literary manifesto' for 'metaphysical poetry' on a par with the Imagist manifesto for modern poets (*The Donne Tradition*, 61). Following Eliot, Williamson includes a section in his study on 'The Conceit', as the characterizing factor in metaphysical poetry.

[34] George Saintsbury, letter on 'The Metaphysical Poets', *TLS*, no. 1032, 27 October 1921, 698.

Early Modern poetry and drama in the opening chapters of this book, be reconsidered as a series of conceits. 'Metaphysical poetry' is writing governed by 'wit', by a hidden or 'implicit' connection between its phases and images, and by a 'cryptogrammatic', yet 'recording', perspective. All of these facets enabled Eliot to structure the materials that were generated for the poem out of his response to the post-war world. Eliot's interest in dramatic 'presentation', at this period, also seems to consider the text of longer poems to be best conceived as a series of dramatic monologues, or soliloquies. These speeches are, variously, proximate to the 'recording' voice of the poetry at any one moment. It is such 'presentation', in the gaps between, or the re-starting of, various voices in the poem, which ensure the work's continuing freshness and surprise. Although traces of it remain (as in the typist episode, which is roughly a sequence of run-together quatrains),[35] Eliot's definitive movement away from lyric form in *The Waste Land* continues the scripting of his poetry more closely to the idiom of Early Modern drama, which had first become truly conscious with 'Gerontion'.

Given the direct allusion to *Paradise Lost* in 'A Game of Chess' ('sylvan scene'), it is possible that, in his construction of his verse paragraphs in *The Waste Land*, Eliot might have had one further, and perhaps unlikely, model at the back of his mind. In *A History of Elizabethan Literature*, Saintsbury, who seems to have felt he was coining the phrase 'verse paragraph' with regard to Milton, praised the way *Paradise Lost* escapes the potential 'monotony' of its blank verse, by thinking in terms of larger units:

> by arranging the divisions of his sense in divisions of verse [and] attaining almost protean variety by availing himself of the infinite permutations of cadence, syllabic sound, variety of feet.[36]

Having earlier dismissed the Latinate rhetoric of Milton, Eliot was in 'Milton II' (1947) to acknowledge the same strength in that poet, his ability 'to give a perfect and unique pattern to every paragraph' (*OPP*, 157). *The Waste Land* thinks in terms of building up its presented moments into blocks of subject or reference, and then of linking those blocks, without a narrative or discursive bridge, and into larger phases. The Miltonic verse paragraph, which includes a range of subject matter grouped under one theme, would seem, alongside the notion of the successive dramatic soliloquy, and the 'specimens' of Early Modern drama excerpted by Charles Lamb, to proffer one further pertinent model for this revolutionary structure. In this exploration of a more wit-led, cryptogrammatic, musicality, Eliot was evolving a metaphysical poetic that carried him across *The Waste Land* to the works he wrote up to 1925.

---

[35] The drafts of 'The Fire Sermon' show the passage to have originally been scored in quatrains, the identifiable form from *Poems, 1920* (*WLFT*, 31–5).
[36] Saintsbury, *A History of Elizabethan Literature*, 327.

5

Cryptograms

The Waste Land, Sweeney Agonistes,
and 'The Hollow Men'

'THE DEATH OF THE DUCHESS'
AND *THE WASTE LAND*

The engagement with the Early Modern period, which Eliot made in the late 1910s and early 1920s, underwrote much of his new concentration, in terms of *method*, when writing *The Waste Land*. It is true, also, that much of this Early Modern writing, and not just in terms of the allusive ambition of Eliot's sequence, but also the cross-currents the chosen allusions instigate, underwrote the *content* of the poetry, and the perspective taken upon that content from within the sequence. The threads of connection between precursor Early Modern texts, and the ways they had been perceived by other critics, unearth the cryptogrammatic undercurrents that helped generate, and then link together, using a metaphysical wit, the various parts of Eliot's sequence. If, in other words, we accept the common dating of 'The Death of the Duchess', with its reference to John Webster's *The Duchess of Malfi*, as an early fragment of the poem, and begin to constellate around it those Early Modern texts which Eliot and his contemporaries associated with that play, we begin to see further into the underlying conceits that shape the final poem. Many sources Eliot cites in imbricated ways; it is therefore only possible to emphasize key points here, beginning with 'The Death of the Duchess', the kernel for much in the final poem. The crucial themes derived from the Webster play, such as that of a declared love which misses its desired auditor, then feature in 'The Hollow Men' (1925), as will be demonstrated below. The discussion also takes in *Sweeney Agonistes*, begun between *The Waste Land* and 'The Hollow Men', Eliot's first drama which, as its drafts indicate, bears a surprising Early Modern connection to 'The Hollow Men', a connection that thence becomes vital in Eliot's mature poetic dramas of the 1930s and 1940s.

The cryptogrammatic connections between the *secular* Early Modern texts averted to in *The Waste Land* underwrite two of the central preoccupations of the poem. These are preoccupations familiar to all readers of Early Modern work: love or desire, the misapprehensions and tragic failures resulting from them, and the memorial or elegiac. These preoccupations are blended with an inconstant appearance of what Herbert Grierson calls, with regard to metaphysical poetry, 'religious feeling', often through direct or generic allusion to biblical sources.

The suggestiveness of that kind of allusion has been well covered by earlier critics and annotators, including Grover Smith and B.C. Southam. It is also an intermittent suggestiveness in Eliot's career at this stage, and does not yet present the structural possibilities, for a poetic sequence (as it would do later in the 1920s), of his reading in secular sources. The emphasis, in this chapter, which deploys Eliot's readings in the Early Modern period to uncover some of the structural, and cryptogrammatic, relations between the various moments of *The Waste Land*—and thence into his immediately subsequent work—means that the readings will largely be directed to the secular strand in the poem. This is the case except where the secular directly intersects with Eliot's biblical echoes. Eliot originally had his bird, in 'A Game of Chess', sing 'into the dirty ear of death; lust'—words which presumably were deleted because they spelt out too clearly the brutally secular, Early Modern, foci of his attention at this point (*WLFT*, 11).

Particularly in Parts II and III of *The Waste Land*, the treatment of women as objects of love or lust is the modern aspect of the allusive underwriting of the whole poem, with its glimpsed mythic narrative about sterility and fertility. The predominant lament for the lost or fallen, elsewhere in the sequence, fits into this seasonal patterning, and it fits also with the historical context out of which *The Waste Land* was written. But, as will become clear, Eliot's echoes, and appropriation, of Early Modern texts for his sequence cast this lament in directly intimate and familial terms, regardless of the courtly or political situation from which such lament originally derived. The nature of that intimacy is what Eliot's recourse to Early Modern sources enables him to build his large poetic structure upon. To this extent, close consideration of the sequence's own imaginative beginnings, in Eliot's considered encounter with Webster's *The Duchess of Malfi*, does much to establish the underlying idiom and emphases of the complete published work.

The suppressed draft of 'The Death of the Duchess' translates, as Pound's marginalia about 'cadence repetition' signals, something of the social world of Boston, as earlier delineated in 'Prufrock' and 'Portrait of a Lady', to London's Hampstead. The draft resonates behind both the finalized versions of 'A Game of Chess', and 'The Fire Sermon', to both of which sections, as Valerie Eliot notes, lines from 'The Death of the Duchess' were eventually transferred (*WLFT*, 105, 107). This draft, however, would also seem to have had wider applicability to Eliot's final text. In its repeated mention of 'thoughts' assuming (albeit in these circumstances a short) life independent of their thinker, the draft arguably picks up something of the force of Eliot's argument about the specific quality of Early Modern poetry, as he expounded it, in his contemporary criticism. (Christopher Ricks dates 'The Death of the Duchess' to 1919, which is the same year as 'Swinburne as Critic', with its notion of 'sensuous thought'.)[1] The completed *The Waste Land*, at obvious and at 'shrouded' levels (to adopt Chapman's cogent metaphor for the power of conceits), continues Eliot's specific quest for that elusive, and uniquely metaphysical, potential.

---

[1] Christopher Ricks, *IMH*, xlii. In deleted lines from 'The Fire Sermon', the people of London are lamented for not knowing either how to think or to feel (*WLFT*, 31, 37).

As Valerie Eliot also notes, the draft 'The Death of the Duchess' is centred upon Act III scene ii of Webster's *The Duchess of Malfi*. There, the Duchess, who has been secretly married to her steward, Antonio, inadvertently betrays herself to her (incestuous?) brother Ferdinand (*WLFT*, 130). Seated at a mirror applying make-up, the Duchess does not realize that Antonio has left the room, and that Ferdinand has entered, when she says:

> Doth not the colour of my hair 'gin to change?
> When I wax gray, I shall have all the court
> Powder their hair with arras, to be like me.
> You have cause to love me; I entered you into my heart
> Before you could vouchsafe to call for the keys.
> *Enter* FERDINAND *behind.*
> We shall one day have my brothers take you napping;
> Methinks his presence, being now in court,
> Should make you keep your own bed; but you'll say
> Love mixed with fear is sweetest. I'll assure you,
> You shall get no more children till my brothers
> Consent to be your gossips. Have you lost your tongue?
> 'Tis welcome:
> For know, whether I am doomed to live or die,
> I can do both like a prince.
> *Ferd.* Die then, quickly![2]

'The Death of the Duchess' scatteredly (mis)quotes the first four lines of this speech, which captures the mixture of vanity, and tragic dignity, displayed by the Duchess in her doomed, hopeless, passion.[3] She will eventually be strangled onstage at her brothers' command. Eliot's scene, at the opening of 'A Game of Chess' in *The Waste Land*, is also this one, alongside the more obvious derivation from Shakespeare's *Antony and Cleopatra*, a derivation to be discussed further below. A woman, in front of a mirror in the firelight, is anxious about the love that she has won, and feels the need to protect it. More significantly, the Duchess's speech in Webster adds to the feared misdirection of words, and the anxiety that they prove a barrier to reciprocity between lovers, which carries over to the final version of Eliot's poem, and thence into 'The Hollow Men'.[4] This underscores Eliot's polemical sense elsewhere of the violence necessary to the modern poet's use of language.

---

[2] *Webster and Tourneur*, with an Introduction and Notes by John Addington Symonds (London: Vizetelly, The Mermaid Edition, 1888), 177. As Valerie Eliot also notes (*WLFT*, 130), Eliot was enthusiastically pointing to the exemplary drama of this speech as late as 1941 ('The Duchess of Malfy' [sic], *The Listener*, vol. xxvi, no. 675, 18 December 1941, 826). But he had quoted the lines 'You have cause to love me' correctly in 'Reflections on *Vers Libre*' (1917): a further instance of Eliot recurring to Early Modern texts crucial to him, across his writing life (*TCC*, 186).

[3] The Mermaid Edition carries at this point a long footnote referencing comments by Charles Lamb, in his *Specimens of English Dramatic Poets*, on the horror of the play and the dignity of the Duchess (London: Routledge, 1927 edition), 210.

[4] Intriguingly, two deleted lines at the end of 'The Death of the Duchess' suggest that Eliot might have intended to continue the poem in the steward, Antonio's, voice. The deleted words 'I am steward of her revenue' show the intricacy of the interconnections made by Eliot when reading between, and writing out of, his favourite Early Modern texts. These are words which might be spoken by Antonio,

'Have you lost your tongue?' predicts the increasingly fraught words of the woman in 'A Game of Chess' ('Speak to me'), and reference to the Philomel passage just before it (*CPP*, 65). To this end, the original Duchess's image of the heart as a kind of locked box, demanding keys (which it is appropriate for Antonio, as a steward, to carry), seems to play into the potentially solipsistic aloneness shared by many in *The Waste Land*. Eliot slightly misquotes the line as 'Before ever you vouchsafed to ask for the key' (*WLFT*, 105). The quoted lines in 'The Death of the Duchess', therefore, look forward to the eventual lines 412–3 of the final sequence, 'We think of the key, each in his prison/Thinking of the key' (*CPP*, 74).[5] The image from the Duchess's speech, therefore, survives to interconnect the various allusions and images of Eliot's poem, and to translate between the various preoccupations of its content.

The 'mixing' of love and fear in the Duchess's speech seems particularly appropriate to this translation in the final version of *The Waste Land*. It is a 'mixing' (a word used close to the start of 'The Burial of the Dead') that all too horribly underwrites the action of *The Duchess of Malfi*. More immediately, the mixture forms a part of the frantic poetic interruptions in the opening of the final version of 'A Game of Chess' (*CPP*, 65). The series of questions aimed by the woman in that section of Eliot's poem might derive from a variety of sources. The scene in *The Duchess of Malfi* that will conclude with the actual 'death of the Duchess', Act V scene ii,[6] opens with the Duchess and her companion Cariola plagued by the riot of madmen hired by her brother ('What hideous noise was that?...What noise is that?'). This seems more dramatically related to the version of Webster's play re-rendered in this draft of *The Waste Land*, especially as it serves to establish links with images from other sections of the final version of the poem:[7]

but are in fact Maffe's in Chapman's *Bussy d'Ambois*, when he has been sent from court to seek to buy Bussy's attendance there ('Will my Lord have me be so ill a steward/Of his revenue, to dispose a summe/So great, with so small cause?' (I. i, *Chapman's Bussy d'Ambois and the Revenge*, ed. Frederick S. Boas, Boston: D.C. Heath, 1905, 12). Maffe's words confirm the misevaluation of the trappings of wealth which also goes to the heart of the tragic issue regarding the Duchess of Malfi's marrying of her steward: Eliot briefly makes clever play here of this theme (and perhaps of its significance for contemporary Hampstead), before dropping it in the final version.

[5] Eliot's reference in the 'Notes' to Dante and to F.H. Bradley as explication for this passage might be supplemented by one from Walter Pater's 'Conclusion' to *The Renaissance*: 'Experience...is ringed round for each one of us by a thick wall of personality....Every one of those impressions is the impression of the individual in his isolation, each mind keeping as a solitary prisoner its own dream of a world' (Walter Pater, *Studies in the History of The Renaissance*, London: Macmillan, 1873, 209).

[6] Southam notes Eliot's own concurrence with the suggestion that they derive from Webster's other masterpiece, *The White Devil*, but also notes the relevance of Act V scene iii (B.C. Southam, *A Student's Guide to the Selected Poems of T.S. Eliot*, London: Faber, 1994, 161–2).

[7] Eliot's reference to another Webster play, *The Devil's Law-Case*, in order for his 'Notes' to 'explain' the 'noise' in 'A Game at Chess' as the wind 'under the door', adds a note of farcicality to the desperate outbursts from the woman. In Webster's play Romelio has just tried to kill his rival in love Contarino, who everyone thinks is dying anyhow. Contarino miraculously revives, but some quack doctors mistake his coming-back-to-life as 'the wind in that door still' (III. ii, 147). Valerie Eliot's comment that Eliot later admitted that the source alluded to in the 'Notes' had no significance, since he had altered the phrase's original meaning, adds a further layer of irony to that ironic note which the allusion *does* enter (*WLFT*, 126). The context of the phrase in *The Devil's Law-Case* retains that fraught

DUCH. The robin red-breast and the nightingale
Never live long in cages.
CARI. Pray, dry your eyes.
What think you of, madam?
DUCH. Of nothing;
When I muse thus, I sleep.
CARI. Like a madman, with your eyes open?
DUCH. Dost think we shall know one another
In the other world?[8]

Thinking of the passage from Petronius that would eventually become the epigraph to *The Waste Land*, Eliot had originally called Part II of his poem 'In the Cage' (*WLFT*, 17). The sense here, that the Duchess exists in a limbo, between life and death, musing and reality, waking and sleep, is confirmed in Eliot's reference to 'pressing lidless eyes'. This is an image that will be translated from 'The Death of the Duchess' directly into 'A Game of Chess' (*WLFT*, 107).

The issue of eyes and sight in *The Waste Land* seems to have been generated from a panoply of sources. But, again, further reading in the original source outside of the immediate allusion provides something of the implicit links through the Early Modern text that make for the intricate and 'wit-writing' architecture of the final poem. The source referred to for the 'A Game of Chess' passage in Eliot's 'Notes', to the game from Thomas Middleton's *Women Beware Women*, provides several other references to eyes. In Act II scene iii a mother is duped into playing chess to distract her, whilst her daughter-in-law is seduced by a duke on the balcony above the stage. Using the word that appears in connection to eyes in *The Waste Land* Part I, the mother says as excuse for her errors in the game 'My eyes begin to fail'. Soon thereafter her daughter-in-law, Bianca, shocked and self-disgusted at her seduction, ('Fearful for any woman's eye to look on'), shivers at the 'infectious mists and mildews' of the Duke's eyes. Crabs eat the lids of Bleistein's eyes in the drafts of 'Dirge', which echo the passages that eventually make their way from Shakespeare's *The Tempest* into the poem (*WLFT*, 119, 121). Eliot's compounding of the 'lidless eyes', with a fateful knock on the door, might derive from Act III scene i, 173, of *Women Beware Women*, when the enthusiasm of the unknowing cuckold son at his rejoining with Bianca is rudely interrupted by the knocking of the Duke's servant, come to demand her presence at the Duke's palace.[9]

More broadly, however, images of eyes resonate across the inexpressive, purgatorial situation of the speaker with 'failed' eyes, from the opening section of *The*

(and sometimes comic) interchange between life and death which runs through *The Waste Land* and much of Eliot's poetry. More remote seems the allusion to *The White Devil* signalled by Eliot for line 407 of the poem, which takes away the sneering misogyny of Flamineo's original (*Webster and Tourneur*, 119).

[8] *Webster and Tourneur*, 203. 'The Death of the Duchess' also includes a poignant quotation from Webster's *The White Devil*, in which a child whose mother has been killed asks a similar question about life in death: 'What do the dead do, uncle? Do they eat,/Hear music?' (*WLFT*, 107; *Webster and Tourneur*, 55–6).

[9] *Thomas Middleton*, ed. Havelock Ellis, Mermaid Edition, vol. I (London: Vizetelly, 1887), 303, 304, 312. The knock in its turn looks forward to the fearful ending of *Sweeney Agonistes*.

Waste Land, which signals (as it would do again in 'The Hollow Men') the state of being, like Webster's Duchess, 'neither/Living nor dead', knowing 'nothing', and 'looking' into 'the heart of light, the silence' (the Duchess in Eliot's own discarded draft sits before 'the silence').[10] (*CPP*, 62)

The Act V situation of the Duchess in Webster's play is that of someone clinging to sanity in the midst of (literal) 'madness':

> The Heaven o'er my head seems made of molten brass,
> The earth of flaming sulphur, yet I am not mad.
> I am acquainted with sad misery
> As the tanned galley-slave is with his oar;
> Necessity makes me suffer constantly,
> And custom makes it easy.

Eliot was familiar enough with this passage to quote it ('the great lines') against similar uses of 'oar' images by Massinger, in the contemporary essay on him discussed in the previous chapter (*SE*, 209). Yet the harrowed situation of the Duchess, her struggle to retain her sanity in a maddened world, forms an undercurrent of connection with other works behind *The Waste Land*, such as Thomas Kyd's *The Spanish Tragedy* or Shakespeare's *Hamlet*. If the Duchess yearns for some 'conference with the dead', as suggested at the start of her speech quoted just above, she remains trapped upon 'the wheel' of life.[11] This entrapment is something Eliot projects upon 'the inhabitants of Hampstead' in 'The Death of the Duchess', as he had the people of London, in deleted lines from 'The Fire Sermon' (*WLFT*, 43, 105).

What 'The Death of the Duchess', Eliot's re-rendition of *The Duchess of Malfi*, in the early draft towards *The Waste Land*, does to 'A Game of Chess'—and thence into the rest of the finished work—is to establish, once more in Eliot's writing, the theme of illicit desire. It also establishes the vulnerability, particularly of women in sexual relationships, to corruption or abuse in a sinister and cynical world. These are the themes of those Early Modern dramas to which he was frequently drawn, dramas of which Webster's play here is a primary instance. The cloying version of sexuality that the opening of 'A Game of Chess' delivers, by adapting Enobarbus's speech about Cleopatra from Shakespeare's play, drives home further the sense that love and desire are purposeless. This is a theme then reiterated, in the pub scene at

---

[10] The word 'nothing' of course connects 'A Game of Chess' with the situation on Margate Sands at the end of 'The Fire Sermon'. It is a word which vitally resonates across another source that looms in the drafts. *King Lear* is flippantly evoked (in Eliot's earlier mode with allusion from the Sweeney poems) to describe a Fresca 'more sinned against than sinning' (*WLFT*, 41). *King Lear*, like the quotations in *The Waste Land* from *The Tempest*, and more circumstantial allusions such as those to *The Duchess of Malfi*, of course makes much horrible play on eyes/seeing.

[11] *Webster and Tourneur*, 200. The Wheel is introduced via the tarot pack in Part I of *The Waste Land*. The Duchess describes herself as being 'broke upon' the wheel; *The Waste Land* Part V describes Coriolanus as 'broken' like 'the river's tent' in Part III. In a draft of 'The Fire Sermon', the typist returns home to find her 'broken breakfast' (*CPP*, 67, 74; *WLFT*, 31). *Ezekiel* VI, as a source for the phrase 'broken images', reporting God's vengeance upon Israel, is suggestive more broadly: 'your dwelling places the cities shall be laid waste...your altars may be laid waste and made desolate, and your idols may be broken and cease'. So is set in train the prophetic strand of the poem which leads to Tiresias. The wheel, as we shall see, becomes a prominent image in Eliot's later poetry and drama; 'broken' is applied to the desolate Charles I arriving at Little Gidding (*CPP*, 191).

the end of 'A Game of Chess'. Like the tableau of the Duchess, this is a scene about a woman altering her appearance to attract her lover, which then leads into the typist's encounter in 'The Fire Sermon'. The theme at the opening of 'A Game of Chess' touches nearly upon the issue of nature, natural process, and artifice—the Early Modern theme that Eliot had explored through the fate of Aspatia in 'Sweeney Erect'. Enobarbus recounts Cleopatra in her pavilion on her barge—in a passage previously echoed by Eliot in 'Burbank with a Baedeker: Bleistein with a Cigar'— as 'O'er-picturing that Venus where we see/The fancy outwork nature' (II. ii, 200–1).[12] The over-richness of the opening of 'A Game of Chess' takes its cue from these words. But, more broadly (as in its allusion to *The Duchess of Malfi*), this opening marks an unworldly resistance to time, and an acceptance of deception, as the tragic basis upon which to sustain love and desire.[13] The concatenation of these sources also plays into the many other moments in the finished poem, where women are shown to be (often brutalized or violated) subjects of male desire, moments where the Early Modern sources, or their connection to Eliot's passages, serve to underwrite the perception of the dissolution of relations between the sexes in the world of the poem. The violence on display, in Eliot's definition of metaphysical poets in his essay on Grierson's anthology, seems directly manifest in the poem's view of the treatment, across history, of women. Eliot, the so-called misogynist, is in fact dramatizing through the adaptation of Early Modern sources, as he had in *Poems, 1920*, how women have been brutalized in history. The contemporary cataclysm, in other words, is repeatedly figured through the violation of women by males. History, that surprisingly female presence in 'Gerontion', is repeatedly brutalized and abused in Eliot's next work, *The Waste Land*.

Eliot's Early Modern dramatic sources here, like Marvell's 'To His Coy Mistress', are (often unhealthily) focused by female chastity, and by the prurient threat to it exerted by male aggressors. The mythic dependence of the poem's 'structure' upon

---

[12] Enobarbus forms a tacit 'recording' presence in the sequence, precursor to Tiresias in 'The Fire Sermon'. That is how he was perceived by Arthur Symons in his *Studies in the Elizabethan Drama*, the book Eliot had reviewed in 1920: 'Enobarbus acts the part of the chorus. He is neither for nor against virtue; and by seeming to confound moral judgements he serves the part of artistic equity.' (London: William Heinemann, 1920), 6. Against this background, the response of Donald Childs to the opening of 'A Game of Chess' seems inexplicable—'the man is the victim and the woman is the potential murderer; she drowns the senses' (*T.S. Eliot: Mystic, Son and Lover*, London: Athlone Press, 1997, 115). Eliot's 'Hamlet and His Problems' (1919) had seen *Antony and Cleopatra* and *Coriolanus* as Shakespeare's most 'assured' successes (*SW*, 84).

[13] Eliot's alteration of Enobarbus's 'The barge she sat in' to the (oddly capitalized) 'Chair' is intriguing. It seems to signal a modernization of the situation, whilst also, through that capital letter, resisting it. Notably, when Shakespeare's Antony and Cleopatra are said to sit in chairs, they are 'enthron'd' in 'chairs of gold' in the marketplace of Alexandria (III. vi, 4). Eliot's 'glowing' 'throne' suggests that he had both Shakespeare moments in mind. When introducing Elizabeth on the Thames at the end of 'The Fire Sermon', Eliot originally placed her in a 'barge', which was then crossed out (*WLFT*, 49). This is historically accurate, according to Eliot's source in J.A. Froude (see Lawrence Rainey, *Revisiting The Waste Land*, New Haven and London: Yale University Press, 2005, 111). But it clashes with the line about the modern Thames from the previous stanza, retained through all drafts and into the final poem, where barges 'drift'. It also, perhaps, made the connection between Eliot's various moments in the sequence too obvious, again. The reference to the *Aeneid* via the 'laqueria' in this opening passage from 'A Game of Chess' suggests that Dido might be another model for the 'wrong'd' woman here, as she was earlier in 'Sweeney Among the Nightingales'.

sterility and fertility here takes on a more alarming tone. Eliot would later claim, in 'Thomas Middleton' (1927), that his subject understood women better than any of the other playwrights of the age (*SE*, 166). Yet the allusions to *Women Beware Women*, and to *A Game at Chess*, in Eliot's 'A Game of Chess', both underwrite this understanding through alertness to female vulnerability, in brutalizing male circumstance.[14] In the political allegory of *A Game at Chess*, the White Queen's Pawn is as vulnerable as Bianca had been in *Women Beware Women*. The Pawn is under threat from the aggressiveness of the black pieces in the 'game', and especially that of the knight: 'Is it not my fortune/To match with a pure mind?' she asks, 'all chaste loving winged creatures/Have their pairs fit, their desires justly mated;/Is woman more unfortunate?' (IV. i, 1121ff).[15] The game of chess that Miranda and Ferdinand are discovered playing in *The Tempest*, of course, is set to ensure her chastity until her wedding day, and enables the lovers to mimic their disagreements and tensions over the board: 'for a score of kingdoms you should wrangle,/And I would call it fair play', as Miranda says (V. i, 174).[16] In Eliot's 'Game', this has all adopted both a sinister and an aimless overtone. But the relation between the sexes across *The Waste Land* remains overshadowed by the potential for violation.[17] The 'change' of Philomel has become a picture over the woman's fireplace. The bird's song resonates in 'The Fire Sermon', and is echoed by the hermit thrush in Part V. In another possible filament to the network of allusion, Eliot's vocabulary about Philomel's trauma closely mirrors some of the vivid elements of Arthur Golding's Elizabethan translation of Ovid's *Metamorphoses*, the book that Pound thought to be 'the most beautiful in the language'.[18]

As Tereus seizes Philomel on the ship, in Golding's version, we are told that:

> So barbarous and beastly was his thought
> That scarce even there he could forebear his pleasure to have wrought
> ...so by force, because she was a maid
> And all alone, he vanquished her.

---

[14] In a later review of a new edition of Middleton's *A Game at Chesse*, Eliot instead noted the 'variousness' of Middleton's work, and that Swinburne had offered a 'deafening eulogy' to it in his Introduction to the Mermaid edition of Middleton's Plays (*TLS*, 23 January 1930, no. 1460, 56).

[15] A similarly threatened chastity occurs as a frisson in Thomas Heywood's *The English Traveller*, where the character enjoined to remain chaste is male, Young Geraldine. That chastity is betrayed, however. Eliot admired, he wrote in 1931, the scene where chastity is discussed (II. i), and he quoted lengthily from it (*SE*, 178–9). Intriguingly, Heywood includes the phrase 'undone so many', when a character reflects on trouble caused by property (Mermaid edition, ed. A. Wilson Verity, London: T. Fisher Unwin, 1888, 204).

[16] *Shakespeare's Comedy of The Tempest*, ed. Israel Gollancz (London: J.M. Dent, 1894), 98. Page numbers for subsequent references to this edition appear in the text.

[17] This is true also of one of the sources for the shadow imagery in ll. 28–30, Part I, of *The Waste Land*. In Beaumont and Fletcher's *Philaster*, princess Arethusa's chastity is constantly under suspicion (although she is blameless)—suspicion not least from Philaster himself, who she genuinely loves. He becomes maddened by his doubt over her, and, at one point, rants against women's inconstancy, saying he will preach to the birds and beasts 'how that foolish man,/That reads the story of a woman's face/And does believe it, is lost for ever;/How all the good you have is but a shadow,/I'the morning with you, and at night behind you,/Past and forgotten' (III. ii) (*The Best Plays of Beaumont and Fletcher*, ed. J. St. Loe Strachey, London: T. Fisher Unwin, 1893, vol. I, 150–1). Some of this tone comes through in the sinister threat of Eliot's lines.

[18] Ezra Pound, *ABC of Reading* (London: Faber, 1951), 58.

Later, Tereus takes Philomel 'rudely' by the hair; when she cries out for help, he cuts out her tongue with his sword, yet 'the stump whereon it hung/Did patter too'.[19] The most striking words here are all words that Eliot deploys in his description of the picture over the fireplace. (Golding's 'stump' conjures awful associations with Shakespeare's Lavinia, from *Titus Andronicus*, who suffers a similar torture.)[20] *The Waste Land* as a whole is shadowed by an inability to speak, or to make oneself understood. Pertinently, given the close of Eliot's poem, the literal loss of a tongue is something suffered by Hieronymo in Kyd's *The Spanish Tragedy*, as it had been by Lavinia: threatened with torture, Hieronymo bites out his tongue to defy his assailants (IV. iv).[21] And, in line with the vulnerability of the female characters in and behind Eliot's poem, Caliban has been banished from Prospero's cave because he tried to rape Miranda (I. ii, 346–51).[22]

The theme of violation and punishment inheres also, although with different gender inflection, in the reference to John Day's *The Parliament of Bees*, which rather strangely gets set against the 'white bodies naked', the skeletons, in the second verse paragraph of 'The Fire Sermon': 'the sound of horns and motors' as Sweeney comes to visit Mrs Porter and her daughter (*CPP*, 67). Day's allegorical poem, about the calming of an insurrection in a beehive through discussion in its parliament, and through the mediation of 'Prorex, the master bee', plays to some of the fears of degeneration and miscegenation louring over *The Waste Land*.[23] The particular passage Eliot alludes to is spoken by 'the plush bee', Polypragmus—a

---

[19] *Ovid's Metamorphoses*, trans. Arthur Golding, ed. Madeleine Forey (Penguin: Harmondsworth, 2002), Book Six, ll. 655–710, 193–5. It is important that Tereus is Philomel's brother-in-law, just as Lavinia is raped by her stepbrothers: Eliot's being drawn to these moments is, as will become clear when considering the issue of mourning in *The Waste Land*, horrifically predicated upon family proximity.

[20] A stage direction in IV. i sees her turn over some books 'with her stumps'. George P. Baker, one of Eliot's Harvard tutors, in a book recommended on the Extension Lectures Reading List, re-narrates this scene. He pictures Lavinia writing in the sand 'with a staff in her mouth which she guides by the stumps of her arms' (*The Development of Shakespeare as a Dramatist*, New York: Macmillan, 1907, 130–1).

[21] *The Minor Elizabethan Drama*, vol. I: *Pre-Shakespearean Tragedies*, ed. Ashley Thorndike (London: J.M. Dent, 1910), 269. This is the edition of *The Spanish Tragedy* recommended for the Extension Lectures.

[22] In the fragments of the poem discovered by John Haffenden in the Bodleian Library, the levée of Fresca is ushered in (ungrammatically and with horrible double-entendre) by 'When the rude entrance of Tarquin'. In further confirmation of the significance of such images behind the finished work, the ravisher of Lucrece is introduced here, as most famously recalled in Shakespeare's poem about her rape (John Haffenden, 'Vivien Eliot and *The Waste Land*: The Forgotten Fragments', *PN Review*, 175, vol. 33 no. 5, May–June 2007, 20).

[23] The late nineteenth-century critics with whose opinion Eliot was familiar were divided over the generic nature of Day's poem. Swinburne sees it as 'a direct and obvious presentation, satirical or panegyrical, of contemporary and characteristic types of men and women' (*Contemporaries of Shakespeare*, ed. Edmund Gosse and Thomas James Wise, London: Heinemann, 1919, 303). George Saintsbury, in *A History of Elizabethan Literature*, saw it as 'a sort of dramatic allegory, touched with a singularly graceful and fanciful spirit' (London: Macmillan, 1907 edition, 286). Arthur Symons, editor of the volume in which Eliot came across Day's poem, casts it in formal terms that would have appealed to Eliot's own project: 'There is not even an attempt at anything like a plot; what we have is a sequence of scenes, sketching, and lightly satirising, the "humours" of the age' (*Studies in the Elizabethan Drama*, 206).

figure like Jonson's Mammon, or Coriolanus (or Eliot's own Sir Alfred Mond). Polypragmus rants against those bees who misunderstand his ambition: 'illegitimate scum,/And bastard flies, taking adulterate shape/From reeking dunghills'. His is a vision close to the satiric picture of London's people as 'gnomes burrowing' in deleted sections of 'The Fire Sermon' (*WLFT*, 31). Polypragmus's ambition is to build his own beautiful hive apart from such 'scum', an artificial heaven not remote from the Early Modern court, or from the woman's room as described at the outset of 'A Game of Chess':

> Overhead
> A roof of woods and forests I'll have spread,
> Trees growing downwards, full of fallow-deer;
> When, of the sudden, listening, you shall hear
> A noise of horns and hunting, which shall bring
> Actaeon to Diana in the spring;
> When all shall see her naked skin; and there
> Actaeon's hounds shall their own master tear,
> As emblem of his folly that will keep
> Hounds to devour and eat him up asleep.
> All this I'll do that men with praise may crown
> My fame for turning the world upside-down.[24]

Polypragmus displays a Mammon-like, complacent voyeurism (Gerontion's 'wilderness of mirrors'), which plays down the fatal cost of Actaeon's tragic mischance as mere 'folly'. Eliot's appropriation of the passage, in narrating the visit of Sweeney, bears something of that salacious frisson and jingle ('keep', 'eat him up asleep'). But it also carries forward the sense of the dubious relation between (female) beauty and artifice, which troubles the relationships cast in 'A Game of Chess'. Diana's 'naked skin', revealed by Eliot in the last line he quotes as his source from John Day in his 'Notes' to *The Waste Land*, rests queasily alongside the battlefield-like strew of skeletons we have just been given sight of. The artifice of the sudden switch of emphasis, of which Eliot makes us aware through the chiming '-er' rhymes of his rewriting, suggests once again, via another complex dialogue with an Early Modern source, the disturbing nature of the heterosexual relations cast by Eliot in *The Waste Land*. This passage is succeeded by a reminder of Philomel's plight, ironically archaized ('So rudely forc'd/Tereu').

Love and lust rest uncomfortably close here, as they always did in Early Modern texts, to the body-as-corpse. The connections that the poem makes between earlier texts, highlighting the artifice involved in all creation of beauty, only exacerbates our sense of this '*difficulty*' within the various conceits in each verse paragraph. Unlike Eliot's earlier work, where Early Modern texts had stood in stark, often satiric, *contrast* with the modern scene described, Eliot's dialogue with the Early Modern period now casts it as premonitory of many aspects of his 'recording' of

[24] *Nero and Other Plays*, ed. Herbert P. Horne, Havelock Ellis, Arthur Symons, and A. Wilson Verity (London: Vizetelly, 1888, Mermaid edition), 226.

modernity. There has been a conflating and compacting of Early Modern modes of perception with modern ones, in response to the mass deaths in the trenches of the French and Belgian battlefields.

The Early Modern period is one of the many subjects conversed with, or unearthed, by Eliot's poem, but only because it is necessarily a part of the world into which it emerged in 1922: 'The nymphs have departed'. But the original Thames of Spenser's 'Prothalamion' could seem already 'foule' and tainting, in comparison to the swans upon it. 'Lawyers' have already taken the place of the Templar Knights who used to grace the city; time threatens all, since the 'Brydale day...is not long'. And the river must only 'run softly' (in Spenser as in Eliot) 'til I end my song'.[25] Once again, reference to the moment at which true relation might be established through marriage is circumscribed, in Spenser's original, as in Eliot's later text, by suspicion that detritus might clog or corrupt the union. That love's consummation, in other words, is haunted by its ready passing, even as the 'Brydale day' is being celebrated.

The 'Death of the Duchess', and its dialogue with its precursor text and correlatives, therefore, does much to establish the figuration of history via betrayal, and mischance—but also via violence in gender and sexual relations—which underscore Eliot's conscious ambition in *The Waste Land*. Yet Webster's original text, as presented in the edition with which Eliot at this point was most familiar, also suggests a broader connection between his major sources, and over the tonality of his final poem, which will now be discussed.

THE WASTE LAND AND 'ELEGY'

The Waste Land and its drafts notoriously read the relation between the living and the dead from both perspectives, death and life: 'doomed to live or die', as Webster's Duchess puts it. It is aided in doing so by the Early Modern texts behind it, both cryptogrammatically so and in those sections editorially suppressed. In Eliot's suppressed 'Elegy', the dead Aspatia, in Poe-like fashion, threatens to become a living one (*WLFT*, 116). The two, in this realm, are not easily separated. The nightmare in *The Duchess of Malfi*, after the death of the Duchess, is that the dead are not left to rest: Ferdinand, in remorse at being the cause of his sister's death, runs mad, and is diagnosed with 'lycanthropia':

> In those that are possessed with't there o'erflows
> Such melancholy humour they imagine
> Themselves to be transformed into wolves:
> Steal forth to churchyards in the dead of night,
> And dig dead bodies up.[26]

---

[25] Edmund Spenser, *Poetical Works*, ed. E. de Selincourt (Oxford: Oxford University Press, 1912), 601–2. This is the edition recommended by Eliot for his Extension Lectures.
[26] *Webster and Tourneur*, 219.

The image binds *The Duchess of Malfi* to Webster's other masterpiece, *The White Devil*, and thence to the end of Eliot's 'The Burial of the Dead'. Addressing Stetson, the speaker enjoins him to 'O keep the Dog far hence, that's friend to men,/ Or with his nails he'll dig it up again!' (*CPP*, 63) Eliot's passage directly paraphrases the dirge uttered by Cornelia in *The White Devil*. This is a dirge sung by a mother over the body of her young son, Marcello, who has been killed in a fit of anger during a dispute with his brother over a woman: 'But keep the wolf far thence, that's foe to men,/For with his nails he'll dig him up again.' Typically, Eliot domesticates his original source, making 'wolf' into 'dog'. He initially wavered when drafting the poem, and kept Webster's original 'foe', before finally changing it to 'friend' (*WLFT*, 9).[27]

Cornelia's speech carries echoes of Ophelia's last speech onstage in *Hamlet*. Ophelia: 'There's fennel for you, and columbines' (IV. v); Cornelia: 'There's rosemary for you—and rue for you' (V. iv).[28] Ophelia's plangent words at parting from her court servants will, of course, appear at the end of 'A Game of Chess'. But Eliot, in citing Cornelia's Dirge from *The White Devil* at the end of 'Burial of the Dead', is already setting a potential further chain of connection uniting his poem with its sources, a chain that dictates the tone and wit-derived relation between further aspects of the content of *The Waste Land*.[29] Indeed, if we turn to the Mermaid 'Best Plays' of *Webster and Tourneur* which Eliot owned and used, we find that the lines about the wolf from Cornelia's Dirge carry a footnote, directing us to Charles Lamb's commentary in *Specimens of English Dramatic Poets*:

> I never saw anything like this dirge, except the ditty which reminds Ferdinand of his drowned father in the Tempest. As that is of the water, watery; so this is of the earth, earthy. Both have that intenseness of feeling, which seems to resolve itself into the elements it contemplates.[30]

As well as being a useful description of the nature of an Early Modern poetic conceit, Lamb's connection suggests also a structuring principle for Eliot's poem, its evocation of the elements of earth and water when considering 'burial'.[31] What seems vital in picking up upon this link is that the 'intenseness of feeling' which

---

[27] Once again, Eliot is drawing upon a moment in Early Modern literature which haunted him— the 'Dirge' had also been cited in 'Reflections on *Vers Libre*' (*TCC*, 187).

[28] *Shakespeare's Tragedy of Hamlet*, ed. Israel Gollancz (London: J.M. Dent, Temple Edition, 1895), 137; *Webster and Tourneur*, 110.

[29] Ophelia's closing speech comes at Act IV scene v, 178; her address to the 'Sweet ladies' slightly earlier at line 72 of the scene. This last might set up a further thread of connection between the texts shadowing Eliot's writing: when describing the beauty of his desired Duchess in *The Duchess of Malfi*, Antonio brags 'Let all sweet ladies break their flattering glasses/And dress themselves in her'—a gesture which looks forward to the later scene of the Duchess at her dressing table. Awfully, in the scene in which the Duchess is strangled, Act IV scene ii, Cariola bursts out in pity: 'O my sweet lady!' (*Webster and Tourneur*, 140, 208).

[30] *Webster and Tourneur*, 111. Hugh Ross Williamson in 1932 strangely mentions the Lamb passage in his discussion of *The Waste Land*, but ignores it in favour of an unfolding of the mythic significance of the Dog (*The Poetry of T.S. Eliot*, London: Hodder and Stoughton, 1932, 104).

[31] 'Full fathom five' both versions of the 'Dirge' attached to *The Waste Land* transcripts begin (*WLFT*, 118, 120).

Eliot draws upon here, as in his recovery of sources for thinking about love and sexual relations, gains from the intimate and familial aspects of the laments engaged by his poetry. Cornelia laments her young son; in the connected (via Lamb) play, *The Tempest*, the son (mistakenly) laments his father. Whatever the historical sweep engaged by 'The Burial of the Dead' as post-war writing, its intensity and unexpectedness is derived, in Eliot's structuring of his poem, from this family proximity, rendered as a vital setting within which Early Modern drama principally operates.

Later, in the reference to Hieronymo from *The Spanish Tragedy*—a play that all contemporary critical sources relate textually to *Hamlet*, as we saw in Chapter Two—we find Eliot again pointing up loss and recuperation. 'Why then Ile fit you' (*CPP*, 75). Hieronymo's son Horatio has been hung by his rival in love for the hand of Bellimperia. Hieronymo has delayed his revenge upon the murderer, but now, having feigned madness to glean more information about the killing, and having been urged to put on a play-within-the-play to catch his man, Hieronymo seizes a similar chance to Hamlet's, publicly to expose the murderer. He has been a poet in his youth—hence his 'fitness' to this task of staging the play.[32] It is as though the speaker of the end of *The Waste Land* is 'fitting' its audience to what they wish to hear, as madness encroaches 'againe'.[33] Yet that speaker also reminds us of the strain of familial lament that has accompanied the losses in the sequence as a whole, just as it has reminded us of Philomel a few lines previously, as the two themes of violation and loss are touched upon by Eliot for one last time.

The references to *The Tempest* (a play itself focused on delusion and dreaming, those major themes of Eliot's here and elsewhere, as we shall see) set music as a mediator between the various experiences or elements recouped in *The Waste Land*.[34] Ferdinand, interjecting into Ariel's song just before the line 'Full fathom five thy father lies', asks 'where should this music be? i' th' air or the earth?:[35]

> Sitting on a bank,
> Weeping again the king my father's wreck,
> This music crept by me upon the waters,
> Allaying both their fury and my passion
> With its sweet air: thence I have follow'd it,
> Or it hath drawn me rather.
>
> (I. ii, 389–94) (24–5)

---

[32] Thomas Kyd, *The Spanish Tragedy*, in *Minor Elizabethan Tragedy*, IV. i, 67, 258. Intriguingly (and oddly) from the perspective of *The Waste Land*, Hieronymo suggests that his play might be acted in 'unknown languages', Latin, Greek, Italian, and French, 'that it might breed more variety' (170). This polylingualism infects *The Waste Land* also.

[33] This meaning had currency in the Early Modern period—in the comedy by Middleton (and Dekker), *The Roaring Girl*, admired by Eliot in his 1927 essay on 'Thomas Middleton', Sebastian thinks he will reveal his father's scorn for Sebastian's supposed love for Moll Cutpurse: 'I think I shall fit you' (II. i, 140). See also Middleton and Rowley's *A Trick to Catch the Old One* (II. i, 72).

[34] Martin Scofield has seen the tempest itself, which includes its aftermath, 'the sky clear for eventual forgiveness', as Prospero's attempt to 'transcend tragedy', just as Eliot has to 'transcend despair and disillusion' in his poem. 'Poetry's Sea-Changes: T.S. Eliot and *The Tempest*', *Shakespeare Survey*, 43, ed. Stanley Wells, 1990, 123.

[35] These songs from *The Tempest* open Edward Arber's selections in his *Shakespeare Anthology* (London: Henry Froude, 1899), a book on Eliot's Extension Lectures Reading List.

It is strange that "'This music crept by me on the waters'" is the only line of quoted text in *The Waste Land* which appears in speech marks (as it does through all the drafts). It is as though, after the crucial depredations of the typist's encounter with the house agent's clerk, and via the foresight of Tiresias, the governing authority of literary tradition is reasserted, and must typographically be seen to be so.[36] Readers, after all, are made to 'follow' the music, as it leads to the 'splendour' of Magnus Martyr.

What readers of *The Waste Land* are actually following, though, is a lament that reminds us of loss; of the dead; of pointed interplay between memory and forgetting, which are encountered from the start of the poem. Ferdinand notes of Ariel's Song that 'the ditty does remember my drowned father'. In another text on the burial of the dead, with which Eliot was also engaged, whilst working on *The Waste Land*, Sir Thomas Browne's *Hydriotaphia: Urne Buriall*, this question of memory and watery oblivion is to the fore.[37] Browne weighs the virtues of burial in earth with that in water, noting that 'the old Heroes in *Homer*, dreaded nothing more than water or drowning'. He also considers the virtues of pagan, as against Christian, funeral rites, finding little consolation in any of these possibilities:

> Darkness and light divide the course of time, and oblivion shares with memory, a great part even of our living beings; we slightly remember our felicities, and the smartest stroaks of affliction leave but short smart upon us. Sense endureth no extremities, and sorrows destroy us or themselves. To weep into stones are fables. Afflictions induce callosities, miseries are slippery, or fall like snow upon us, which notwithstanding is no unhappy stupidity. To be ignorant of evils to come, and forgetfull of evils past, is a merciful provision in nature, whereby we digest the mixture of our few and evil dayes, and our delivered senses not relapsing into cutting remembrances, our sorrows are not kept raw by the edge of repetitions.[38]

This is an ignorance and a forgetfulness willed in the opening passage of *The Waste Land*. Browne recognizes that his ideal goes against human and cultural urges to memorialize the dead. But for him, as for Eliot, with his poem's multiple 'raw' 'repetitions', 'oblivion' is not something to be controlled by any one individual. To raise, in memory, only the frantic questions of another of Eliot's source texts in this opening phase of his poem, John Donne's *Devotions Upon Emergent Occasions*:

> what's become of man's great extent and proportion, when he himself shrinks himself and consumes himself to a handful of dust; what's become of his soaring thoughts,

---

[36] The lines had been entered in a weirdly mangled version, one which redoubles the sense of family loss, without quotation marks at l. 192. Caliban's later famous lines 'The isle is full of noises/Sounds and sweet airs' (III. ii, 132–3) perhaps lurk behind the urgent questionings about 'noise' at the start of 'A Game of Chess', and behind the many noises averted to in the poem as a whole.

[37] Browne's work is discussed and cited in Eliot's 'Prose and Verse', *Chapbook*, 22 (April 1921), 3–10, where he finds Browne's writing too rhetorical, but does not comment on the content (although he quotes from it).

[38] *The Religio Medici and Other Writings of Sir Thomas Browne*, ed. C.H. Herford (London: Dent, 1912), 99, 136. Subsequent references appear in the text.

his compassing thoughts, when he himself brings himself to the ignorance, to the thoughtlessness, of the grave?'[39]

Browne also admits to many questions unresolved by the oblivion of death (and even imagines resurrection as a form of 'living death'), amongst which are 'Why the *Psyche* or soul of *Tiresias* is of the masculine gender, who being blinde on earth, sees more than all the rest in hell?' (127)[40] The drafts of *The Waste Land* are more anxious than the final version to assert, as the 'Notes' continue to do, the all-seeingness of Tiresias-like figures. The drafts reiterate or vary phrases such as 'I have seen and sometimes see' (*WLFT*, 9, 31, 37). The process of editing and excision that the manuscript underwent removed much of this unitary dominance; as Browne recognized about modernity, 'The great mutations of the world are acted, or time may be too short for our designes.' (132)

Mark Van Doren made as a key theme of his reading of Dryden the fact that that poet 'seems always to have been moved by the idea of universal dissolution'. Appealingly, to the poet of the last sentences of 'Gerontion', Van Doren points to the importance in Dryden's work of the notion of 'scattered atoms', into which the world and its contents might suddenly dissolve.[41] It was a fear that Dryden exerted all of his poetic potential to resist. Similar forces seem to be at play in, and behind, *The Waste Land*. Critics have consistently perceived *The Waste Land* as integrative of Eliot's personal trauma in the early 1920s with the breakdown of the European world all around him. Stephen Spender claimed that in the sequence 'everything private is exposed as symptoms of the neurosis which is that of civilisation itself'. Alan Williamson has written of the 'almost seamless unification' here, 'of the inner psychic journey with the history of myth and religion'.[42] Consideration of the Early Modern instigations and context for Eliot's masterpiece, however, reveal further the reach of the elegiac intonation of the poem, opening up more broadly A. David Moody's contention that what is enacted here is 'a rite...for the dying and the dead'.[43] These instigations also broaden our intimations about the emphasis upon gender, in Eliot, as one ground upon which the various violence of history is enacted, in the present, as it always has been—they expand our sense of the complex hinterland of the trauma that the sequence seeks to bring into order, be it mythic, historic, or, ultimately, literary.

[39] John Donne's *Devotions Upon Emergent Occasions, together with Death's Duell* (Michigan: Ann Arbor, 1959), 24–5. B.C. Southam gives three other potential sources for the phrase 'handful of dust', from Conrad and Tennyson (*A Student's Guide*, 144–5). 'Exequy' amongst the drafts of *The Waste Land* takes a strange turn in this vein. Bishop King's poem of 'The Exequy' is praised in both 'Prose and Verse' and 'The Metaphysical Poets' (as we saw in the Introduction) for its fineness; Eliot's poem, however, bizarrely imagines a posthumous existence for its speaker, as a local deity adored by lovers (*WLFT*, 101).

[40] In the rejected night-out scene from the start of 'The Burial of the Dead', 'Tom', in a pun on his drunken condition, is described as 'blind', as though he is an ur-Tiresias (*WLFT*, 5).

[41] Mark Van Doren, *John Dryden*, pp. 106, 203.

[42] Stephen Spender, *Eliot* (London: Fontana, 1975), 91; Alan Williamson, 'Simultaneity in *The Waste Land* and *Burnt Norton*', in Ronald Bush, ed., *T.S. Eliot: The Modernist in History* (Cambridge: Cambridge University Press, 1991), 158.

[43] A. David Moody, *Thomas Stearns Eliot: Poet* (Cambridge: Cambridge University Press, 1994), 111.

Eliot's resistance to dissolution seems to derive from his ability to hear, through the language, and through linked images that draw together Early Modern texts, the possibilities of wit-written relation that will allow him to structure his sensibility's response to such dissolution amongst contemporary conditions. All of this is contained within the notion of 'presentation', of the poetry as a drama of unexpected but successive conceits, rapid scenes, which repeat and vary the central themes of violation, and of loss, within the purgatorial realm of the poem.

AFTERMATHS OF *THE WASTE LAND*

The dramatic possibilities of that presented response to contemporary history were increasingly emphasized, as Eliot moved beyond the poetics of *The Waste Land* in order further to consider the notion of what a metaphysical poetry might achieve. To this end, as he was completing his sequence, Eliot was already evolving a dialogue that would help him more intensively to identify the *poetic* characteristics within drama, that favoured genre amidst his Early Modern preoccupations. It is an identification conducted in ways that have both immediate relevance to the content of *The Waste Land* and thence Eliot's move beyond it, into work on *Sweeney Agonistes* and 'The Hollow Men'. In this context, the Early Modern period continues to provide Eliot with a method for his poetry. But the disturbing nature of that connection between form and content in the Early Modern texts he was fascinated by also obtains an increasingly important role, in Eliot's newly concerted attempts, across the 1920s, to centre his poetry around a Dantean conception of grace and purpose.

At this period of work on *The Waste Land* and beyond, the drama critic of the London *Daily News*, William Archer, clearly riled Eliot. Archer's dislike for some of the more sensational elements of Early Modern plays, and what Eliot saw as his failure to recognize the dramatic potency of poetic drama per se, led Eliot to make agitated responses to various of Archer's proclamations. Eliot's 'London Letter' for the *Dial*, June 1921, took issue with Archer's somewhat scandal-mongering objections to the work of the Phoenix Society, a theatre club established to present Early Modern and Restoration work unedited, and in a form as close to original performing practices as possible.[44] When, in 1923, Archer published his thoughts at length, in *The Old Drama and the New: An Essay in Re-Valuation*, Eliot clearly considered the attack that Archer made upon Early Modern work as worthy of more concerted response. Archer's criticism seems to have been, almost, a

[44] Eliot, 'London Letter', the *Dial*, 70, no. 6, June 1921, 686–91. Eliot was a subscriber to the Phoenix Society, and wrote a letter to the *Athenaeum* in February 1920, seeking further support for its projects. In that letter he mentions having recently (and pertinently) seen *The Duchess of Malfi* and Dryden's *Marriage À la Mode* at the Society. He takes a first swipe at Archer there too. He also attended productions of Congreve's *Love for Love* and Rowley, Dekker and Ford's *The Witch of Edmonton* in April 1921 (*LI*, 448). 'Dramatis Personae' records him having recently seen the Society's production of Ford's *'Tis Pity She's a Whore* (*The Criterion*, vol. I, no. 3, April 1923, 304–5). He accompanied Virginia Woolf to see *King Lear* there in March 1924 (*LII*, 342).

touchstone for the kind of opinion regarding drama to which Eliot was most opposed, at a moment when he sought to formulate the new governing ideas behind the major shifts in his poetry after *The Waste Land*. From 1923 to 1924, Eliot's attention swung openly towards the drama, which had been a prevalent but subdued part of his poetics hitherto. *Sweeney Agonistes* was begun, according to Lyndall Gordon, in September 1923, although not first published until 1926–7.[45] A little later, in a letter to Ottoline Morrell of 30 November 1924, Eliot responded to her delight at reading in manuscript 'We are the hollow men' and 'Eyes that last I saw in tears'; he called the lyrics an 'avocation to a much more revolutionary thing I am experimenting on' (*LII*, 545–6). The lyrics, which were soon to be assembled as 'The Hollow Men' and related work, in other words, were congruent in Eliot's mind, in terms of their writing, with the work on the new drama of *Sweeney Agonistes*.

Against this revisionary backdrop in Eliot's work, from 1923 to 1928, Archer's *The Old Drama and the New* acted as a point of departure for Eliot's prose regarding the Early Modern period. Now, in contradistinction to the essays upon individual Early Modern dramatists, he again weighed the value of poetic drama as a *form*. Archer's book was considered in 'Four Elizabethan Dramatists' (1924); in a review of a new edition of Webster's works; and, again, in 'A Dialogue on Dramatic Poetry' (both 1928).[46] *The Old Drama and the New* provided a way for Eliot, initially, to orient the shift that occurred in the formal character of his poetry, after the publication of *The Waste Land*. It was a shift towards more directly articulating the key question that will define his later career—a question put by one of the participants in his 'A Dialogue on Dramatic Poetry': 'what great poetry is not dramatic?' (*SE*, 51)

Archer adopted a Darwinian approach to his understanding of dramatic development since classical times. He attacked what he clearly saw as a vogue for 'minor' Elizabethan work (he mentions Eliot), and foregrounds 'imitation' (what we would call realism or naturalism) as the 'indispensable substratum of drama'. Modern drama in prose, in other words, has, for Archer, finally succeeded in 'liberating' itself from constrictive 'convention'. Elizabethan drama was not truthfully, or usefully, poetic, for him. The poetry was not allied to action, but instead provided moments of lyricism, within a 'semi-barbarous' yet 'unnatural' plot structure.[47] Archer attacked, therefore, what he saw as the inconsistencies in a string of Elizabethan works, including some of Eliot's favourite source plays. Beaumont and Fletcher's *The Maid's Tragedy* and *Philaster*, Webster's *The Duchess of Malfi*, Jonson's *Volpone*, Ford's *The Broken Heart*: all came in for scorn, from Archer, for showing a

[45] Lyndall Gordon, *T.S. Eliot: An Imperfect Life* (New York: W.W. Norton, 1998), 91.

[46] Review of *The Complete Works of John Webster*, ed. F.L. Lucas, *The Criterion*, vol. VII, no. IV, June 1928, 156; *Of Dramatick Poesie An Essay 1668* by John Dryden. Preceded by a Dialogue on Poetic Drama by T.S. Eliot, London: Frederick Etchells and Hugh MacDonald, 1928.

[47] Eliot's comments criticizing Archer, made across three pages in 'A Dialogue on Dramatic Poetry', are largely restricted to a repeated assertion that the critic knows little about poetry, and therefore cannot understand that poetry and drama in Early Modern work are not separate, but are the same activity (*SE*, 50–3).

'largeness of conception', but 'loose, ill-jointed, haphazard' plotting and rhetorical style. The fragmenting of narrative 'logic', that quality noted by critics from the late nineteenth century, in relation to Early Modern plays, was overridden for many by the poetry of the speeches. Now, for the prosaic Archer, this 'haphazard' became cause for the dismissal of these plays. Eliot, bred up by the early 1920s through the earlier critical consensus, was well placed to contradict him. Yet in doing so, typically, he developed a means of moving his own practice forwards.

Archer was dismissed by Eliot, in a public forum, for displaying a lack of intelligence (*LI*, 448). But actually (and this presumably is why Eliot was provoked into responding to him across a four-year period) the closing pages of *The Old Drama and the New* show Archer to have been a shrewd respondent to many of the already-established emphases of the contemporary intelligentsia's agenda, when promoting Elizabethan writing as a model for modern practice, which saw rhetoric as a necessary component of work written for the bare Elizabethan picture stage, where the creation of credible worlds using scenery was impossible. In his historical reading of dramatic evolution in England, the modern platform stage had removed that temptation. More specifically, Archer went to the heart of the *metaphysical* appeal of Elizabethan drama to modern critics and writers, and rejected it wholly:

> the theatre of all ages is a machine devised, or rather developed, for the purpose of presenting to an assemblage of human beings imitations of human life, and thereby awakening a certain order of emotions which cannot be aroused in an equal degree by any other means.... It is a merit in an imitation to resemble the thing imitated, and [for this] to be achieved by what may be called consistent and homogeneous methods, not by a confusion of planes, a jumbling of conventions. [Elizabethan drama has been] praised by its eulogists mainly on the ground of its impurity... the recitatives and arias which break the continuity of its texture and keep it shifting from plane to plane.[48]

Presumably 'homogeneous' is meant to resonate against Dr Johnson's description of metaphysical poetry as 'heterogeneous'. Yet Archer's conception of the drama as a 'machine' rests uneasily with his primary, essentially organic and evolutionary, notion of its historical development. The metaphor seems aimed to declare the modernity of Archer's sense of drama's particular generic construction. Archer's critical terms, at this level, might seem to have given Eliot particular pause in relation to his own evolving—and often contradictory—notions of the relation between the 'new' and the 'old' (or the traditional) in Early Modern drama at this moment. Archer's antagonism toward Elizabethan drama, and toward poetic drama more broadly (he mentions Tennyson's *Becket* specifically—the work later to

---

[48] Archer, *The Old Drama and the New: A Re-Valuation*, 16, 59, 62ff, 128, 133–4. The notion of planes in relation would become increasingly important to Eliot when describing dramatic pattern in the 1930s. As the next chapter will show, it was also integral to critical discussion of Early Modern texts with which Eliot became familiar in the 1920s. He had used the phrase 'different planes' to describe 'life' in the early 'Mandarins', 3, when mocking a fat and 'stoic' seeming industrialist (*IMH*, 21, 136–7).

become a point of dialogue for *Murder in the Cathedral*),[49] seems not just to rebuke Eliot's position in essays like 'The Possibility of a Poetic Drama' (1920) but also to trouble his more recent critical stance.[50] Eliot's riposte, in this sense, was telling, since he turned, in 'Four Elizabethan Dramatists', Archer's own criticism against him. Based upon his more favourable experiences of watching productions at the Phoenix Society, Eliot argued that Elizabethan drama shared, with the modern drama favoured by Archer, a 'lack of convention', one which is allied to, and confirms, the 'faults' that riddle dramatic construction: faults involving a lack of consistency or coherence (*SE*, 111–112).[51] For Eliot, what these 'faults' confirm is not that positive evolutionary development from Early Modern work to the contemporary which Archer finds, but rather a *continuity* between the two, a continuity founded upon 'a general philosophy of life', or 'general attitude toward life', which the Early Modern writers 'based on Seneca and other influences'. Strikingly, for Eliot's next reconfiguration of his response to Early Modern writing, to be discussed in the next chapter, this is the 'general attitude' of Romantic anarchy and 'dissolution', which has culminated both in Sir Arthur Pinero and in 'the present regiment of Europe' (*SE*, 116–17).

SWEENEY AGONISTES AND 'THE HOLLOW MEN'

Eliot's immediate expression of these perceptions, *contra* Archer, of the continuity between Early Modern and contemporary drama, were fed into the work begun in later 1923, and eventually published as *Sweeney Agonistes: Fragments of an Aristophanic Melodrama*. Eliot declared himself a 'classicist' as understood by T.E. Hulme, in the 1923 essay 'The Function of Criticism' (*SE*, 26). He was beginning to feel deep unease with a contemporary 'attitude towards life' that bore similarities, for him, with the Early Modern period. Yet, in his work after *The Waste Land*, these are correlatives that continue to perform a consistently positive function *within the poetry*. Eliot's generic subtitle to *Sweeney Agonistes* suggests that he was searching to derive his work from a sense of 'convention'. However, it is a convention that he

---

[49] William Archer, *The Old Drama and the New*, 52. Tennyson's play about the city's sainted martyr formed the production given at the Canterbury Festival in 1932 and 33, preceding Eliot's *Murder in the Cathedral*, written for the Festival and first produced there in 1935. See E. Martin Browne, *The Making of T.S. Eliot's Plays* (Cambridge: Cambridge University Press, 1969), 34.

[50] Eliot's 'The Possibility of a Poetic Drama', his first essay hinting at the 'possibility' which would absorb much of the second half of his poetic career, notes the 'Elizabethan age in England' to have been one able to 'absorb a great quantity of new thoughts and new images,' and hence to have almost split from tradition. But it was also, as a result of this absorption, the age which produced blank verse of 'a subtlety and consciousness, even an intellectual power' that has not been repeated. The modern drama's failure to present a similar 'world' of possibility is, Eliot says, what raises the possibility of adapting such poetry to the modern world (*SW*, 51–2).

[51] The full title of this key 1924 essay by Eliot is 'Four Elizabethan Dramatists: A Preface to an Unwritten Book'. There is evidence in its closing pages that the 'unwritten book' was to be constituted by a point-by-point, dramatist-by-dramatist, refutation of Archer's argument (*SE*, 116). This was an extraordinary project for Eliot even to have contemplated, but one that further reveals the seriousness with which he viewed Archer's challenge, and its usefulness when formulating his own thoughts at this period.

synthesized from ancient and more recent models, and one he felt to be lacking from modern drama.[52] *Sweeney Agonistes*, like the plays from *The Family Reunion* (1939) onwards, finds classical models to work its new variations upon. But, as with *The Waste Land*, *Sweeney Agonistes* also derives impetus and shape from the Early Modern models that Eliot had explored in the 1910s. The revivification of not only Sweeney, but also of Doris, in *Sweeney Agonistes*, takes us back to 'Sweeney Erect', with its epigraph to, and origin in, Beaumont and Fletcher's *The Maid's Tragedy*. It also takes us forward to 'The Hollow Men', several sections of which appeared as 'Doris's Dream Songs' in *Chapbook*, November 1924.

In the passage from Beaumont and Fletcher's play cited in the epigraph to 'Sweeney Erect', Aspatia, who has been jilted by the man she was to marry, Amintor, speaks about her maidservants making a tapestry, which skews the myth of Ariadne better to reflect emblematically her psychological situation. The tapestry will alter the myth, in that it will portray Ariadne/Aspatia deserted and abandoned by Theseus upon an island, as she orders the servants:

> Do it again by me, the lost Aspatia,
> And you shall find all true but the wild island.
> Suppose I stand upon the sea-beach now,
> Mine arms thus, and mine hair blown with the wind,
> Wild as that desart; and let all about me
> Be teachers of my story.[53]

In 'Fragment of a Prologue', the first part of *Sweeney Agonistes*, we see Doris involved in an activity like that in Part I of *The Waste Land*, drawing cards to foretell her future. She draws several with ambiguous import, but also the two of spades, 'THE COFFIN!'. As a consequence of this prediction, the doomed nature of Aspatia's story seems part of the louring atmosphere of threat and violence that hovers over the latter pages of *Sweeney Agonistes*. But the parallels between Doris and Aspatia are confirmed there also. At the opening of the second section, called 'Fragment of an Agon', Sweeney offers (or threatens) to carry Doris to a 'cannibal isle' (compare Aspatia's 'wild island'), which leads to two jazz 'numbers' by the assorted characters in the 'melodrama', but also to sinister assertions by Sweeney.

As though in confirmation of the link back to the poems of the late 1910s, but also of Eliot's continuing preoccupations with death and out-of-jointedness, the surviving typescript of *Sweeney Agonistes* originally carried an epigraph from that opening of the Duke's speech in *Measure for Measure* which had given the tenor to 'Gerontion': 'Be absolute for death, either death or life/Shall thereby seem the sweeter: reason thus with life—'.[54] Doris's response to the second jazz number, in

---

[52] As Chapter Eight notes, Eliot's drama *The Cocktail Party* was originally also denominated by him 'a melodrama', but displays a similar awkwardness with the genre.

[53] *Select Plays by Francis Beaumont and John Fletcher* edited by George P. Baker, (London: Dent, 1911), 102.

[54] Israel Gollancz, ed., *Shakespeare's Comedy of Measure for Measure* (London: J.M. Dent, Temple Edition, 1894), 54. The Duke's lines are at Act III scene I, 4–5. The *Sweeney* typescript is at Kings College, Cambridge. Hayward Bequest, V7A.

'Fragment of an Agon', leads to an exchange with Sweeney which reveals the presence of the now-removed epigraph behind the complexity of thought that troubles the melodramatic surface of Eliot's play. Doris's 'That's not life, that's no life' sparks the reply from Sweeney which includes:

> That's what life is. Just is.
> *DORIS*: What is?
> What's that life is?
> *SWEENEY*: Life is death.
> (*CPP*, 123–4)

Sweeney's sardonic presence in the second part of the play derives much from the reasonable, but extra-human, utterance of Shakespeare's Duke: 'That's all the facts when you come to brass tacks:/Birth, and copulation, and death'. (122) His seemingly interchangeable identity with that of the prostitutes' landlord, Pereira, at least in Doris's eyes, hints, as the Duchess of Malfi had, at an unresolved debate between the two states of death and life. For the Duke, the between-state is echoed in his dual role in *Measure for Measure*, as both authority over his 'kingdom' and disguised interloper who delivers speeches of higher wisdom. This is, perhaps, the purport of the also metaphysical implications of the title of the scenario for *Sweeney Agonistes* that Eliot, at some point later, drew up to expand the completed fragments: *The Superior Landlord*.[55]

The sharp note of 'reality', which Sweeney interjects into the otherwise comic and frothy surface of *Sweeney Agonistes*, marks him, even at this outset of Eliot's play-writing career, as a central figure of a piece with later heroes in his drama, most particularly Harry in *The Family Reunion* (the use of the citation from Orestes as an epigraph in the published book version to *Sweeney Agonistes* confirms the link). But the link back to *Measure for Measure*, in the typescript's original epigraph, also points towards the generic and rhythmic complexities that *Sweeney Agonistes* displays. In the review 'The Beating of a Drum', which appeared in *The Nation and the Athenaeum* in October 1923 (the month after Gordon's dating of Eliot's starting work on his play), Eliot thought through the role of the truth-telling Fool in Shakespeare. He read Lear's Fool, the Porter in *Macbeth*, and Antony in the scene on Pompey's galley, back to the origins of all drama, as it had been conceived at the time in F.M. Cornford's *The Origins of Attic Comedy* (1922).[56]

---

[55] Michael J. Sidnell discusses Eliot's scenario for expansion of the fragments in *Dances of Death: The Group Theatre of London in the Thirties* (London: Faber, 1984), 90–2, and Appendix A. Sweeney's sinister expansion of the death/life paradigm here into Sweeney Todd territory, through his narration of the story of the man (himself?) who 'did a girl in' ('He didn't know if he was alive/and the girl was dead', *CPP*, 125), links back to Eliot's 1917 prose 'Eeldrop and Appleplex'. Eeldrop tells of the man 'in Gopsum Street' who murdered his mistress: 'for the man the act is eternal . . . for the brief space he has to live, he is already dead'. Eeldrop's interest in the ambiguous defining moment here is linked to the comic interchange between Eeldrop and Appleplex around Pater's notion of living to full intensity, in the 'Conclusion' to *Studies in the History of the Renaissance*. Appleplex sees the whole idea as 'pre-Raphaelite' (*Little Review*, 4, May 1917, 8, 10).

[56] In many ways, the book which Eliot was reviewing in his article, Olive Mary Busby's *Studies in the Development of the Fool in the Elizabethan Drama*, would seem to be at odds with Eliot's anthropological approach. She resists seeing the Elizabethan clown as related to the 'folk fools' of the Mummers plays, as Eliot does. Intriguingly, however, she links the 'frankness' and satirical qualities of Fools'

Following Cornford, Eliot emphasized the ritualistic origin of the drama, its 'rhythmic form', but also the generic choices that discovery of those origins entail. The salving possibilities of the Fools' stark and 'comic' truths are best found 'in tragedy, or in some form which is neither comedy nor tragedy'. *Measure for Measure*, and other plays to which Eliot was continually drawn, such as *Timon of Athens*, and Shakespeare's late plays (sometimes called the Romances), are clearly, for him, examples of this mixed form.[57] As we shall see in Chapters Six and Eight, the late plays by Shakespeare then have great importance for Eliot's poetry, and mature dramas; but this sense of 'mixed' generic possibilities had been something in which Eliot had been interested from early in his career. J. Alfred Prufrock is not, in his own view, Hamlet. He may be an attendant lord, but is, also, 'almost' a Fool (*CPP*, 16).

That the 'rhythmic form' of *Sweeney Agonistes* is also a mixture, of jazz-influenced cadences and classical dramatic speech, is something that has been observed most recently by David Chinitz, who points to the way in which the Fragments' 'back chat' also depends upon Senecan stichomythia.[58] Yet Eliot's 1927 introduction to 'Seneca in Elizabethan Translation' alerts us to 'a trick of Seneca of repeating one word of a phrase in the next phrase' (*SE*, 88). The jazzy rhythmic liveliness of *Sweeney Agonistes*, therefore, is also founded upon verbal repetition. Eliot's assertion in his essay is that Elizabethan dramatists, including Marlowe and Shakespeare, cannot have failed to learn something from the new rhythms becoming available to English through contemporary translations of Seneca.[59] But in *Sweeney Agonistes*, the interchange between Doris and Sweeney cited above demonstrates that Eliot had already previously 'learnt something' from either one or both sources—the

comments to the function of the chorus in 'ancient classic drama', which would 'throw into sharp relief the folly of men'. This comment carries something of the quality of Sweeney, and of Harry later. Busby sees such frankness as childlike and 'the most striking characteristic of the primitive being', introducing something of the issue as discussed in 'The Beating of a Drum'. In this 'primitiveness', the Fool is apposite for the Elizabethan age, which, according to Busby, was 'not...highly sophisticated' (London: Oxford University Press, 1923, 19, 38, 86).

[57] T.S. Eliot, 'The Beating of a Drum', *The Nation and the Athenaeum*, vol. XXXIV, no. 1, 6 October 1923, 11. The link of *Sweeney Agonistes* to Cornford, and to this 1923 review, is confirmed by the 1933 letter to Hallie Flanagan about the play, to be found in the Hayward Bequest along with the typescript. Eliot recommends that Flanagan read Cornford before she considers staging the play as she has suggested she might. He also tells her that he originally conceived the speeches as being 'accompanied by light drum taps to accentuate the beats'—pointing her literally to the 'primitive' rhythms which the review considers the basis of all theatre and dance. The knocks on the door that close the second part of *Sweeney Agonistes* perhaps offer a modern (if ominous) equivalent: although in this letter Eliot surprisingly compares them to the angelus.

[58] David Chinitz, *T.S. Eliot and the Cultural Divide* (Chicago: University of Chicago Press, 2003), 110.

[59] The recent scholarship upon which Eliot drew for 'Shakespeare in Elizabethan Translation', as for his related essay 'Shakespeare and the Stoicism of Seneca' of this same year, 1927, makes similar associations. John W. Cunliffe's *The Influence of Seneca on Elizabethan Tragedy, An Essay*, for example, links Seneca's stichomythia to the opening scene of *Hamlet*: 'The appearance of artificiality is removed by occasional irregularity, which has the semblance of carelessness, but is really the outcome of highest art; and to the majesty of verse is added the naturalness of ordinary conversation.' (New York: G.E. Stechert & Co., 1925 edition, 22). Eliot holds up the opening scene of *Hamlet* as a model of dramatic writing in his unpublished lectures 'The Development of Shakespeare's Verse' (1937), and thence as a model for his own dramatic ambition. He used not dissimilar terms to Cunliffe's about these topics, in 'Poetry and Drama' (1951) (*OPP*, 75–6).

stoic Roman and the Early Modern.[60] The staccato to-ing and fro-ing of the voices, the repetitions, give a simultaneous impression of a changing, but patterned, and lively, vocal 'action' to the writing. It is an action that is, nonetheless, underpinned by the immoveable stasis of the 'reality' of the world, as voiced abruptly by Sweeney once he arrives.

Most immediately in Eliot's career, the limbo horror of the interchangeable situation between life and death, viewed in the Duke's classic speech in *Measure for Measure*, and thence in Sweeney's speeches in *Sweeney Agonistes*, finds its stichomythic and rhythmic equivalent in the *lyric* writing of the brief poems, which Eliot put together in 1925 to form 'The Hollow Men':

> We are the hollow men
> We are the stuffed men...
> (*CPP*, 83)

The Hayward typescript of *Sweeney Agonistes*, however, also bears a second epigraph alongside that speech from the Duke's, one that displays the dichotomies underlying the change that Eliot's preoccupations underwent, during his writing of *The Waste Land*. The Duke's 'Be absolute for death' shows Eliot's continuing reflection on the antithetical combination of opposing states—'*either* death *or* life/Shall thereby seem the sweeter' (my italics). But the inclusion, on the front page of the *Sweeney Agonistes* typescript, beneath the play's original alternative title ('PEREIRA/ OR/THE MARRIAGE OF LIFE AND DEATH/A Dream'), of a *second* epigraph, introduces a further element of possibility within such moments of opposition:

> Between the acting of a dreadful thing
> And the first motion, all the interim is
> Like a miasma, or a hideous dream.
> (II. i, 63–5)

Eliot's misremembering is instructive, as so often. All editions of *Julius Caesar*, including the Temple Edition that he owned, have 'Like a phantasma' in the last line here. Brutus's actual words, therefore, carry the potential implication of the spectral or ghostly, which is vital to the play, and to Eliot's appropriation of it in 'The Hollow Men' ('phantasmal' goblins had burrowed in the Hampstead-set drafts of 'The Fire Sermon'). The first *OED* date for 'miasma' is 1665; Eliot's misapprehension of Brutus's situation as analogous to 'infectious or noxious exhalations from putrescent organic matter' vivifies it sensually, but is reminiscent of the 'miasmal mist' that had shrouded the True Church in his earlier poem, 'The Hippopotamus'.

This second epigraph on the *Sweeney Agonistes* typescript, in Eliot's version, takes Brutus's characteristic hesitation before the prospect of the conspirators' plan to

---

[60] Eliot's 'Seneca in Elizabethan Translation' was originally the Introduction to *Seneca His Tenne Tragedies Translated into English Edited by Thomas Newton Anno 1581* (London: Constable 1927). Interestingly, though, Eliot had thought about taking on this task since August, 1923, when he first put down some thoughts about Seneca in a letter to the series editor in which the volume appeared, Charles Whibley (*LII*, 198). According to Gordon, as we have seen, Eliot began *Sweeney Agonistes* in the month after this letter was written, as though his thoughts more immediately in this instance took a creative course with the material.

kill Caesar, and gives it pungent reality. It forcefully implies that the new drama of *Sweeney Agonistes* takes place in such an interim; between the fated 'motion' (the drawing of the Tarot card signifying 'THE COFFIN') and the violent enactment of its portent (the 1933 Group Theatre production of the play, and the scenario *The Superior Landlord*, both ended with Sweeney stabbing Doris).[61] What occurs in 'the interim', then, is ('hideous') 'dream', this last the only repeated word on the Hayward title page.[62] 'Dream' is related not just to the ritualized interchanges of *Sweeney Agonistes* itself, its sudden alternations between stichomythic speech and song, but is also congruent to the new short lyrics published as 'Doris's Dream Songs' in 1924, which evolved into the sequence 'The Hollow Men' in 1925.[63]

That the passage from *Julius Caesar* was much on Eliot's mind during this period and beyond, and that it played a crucial part in his own personal reflections across his life, is variously evidenced.[64] Eliot's previous engagement with Early Modern drama had, of course, paid significant attention to several plays that are centred upon the notion of an 'interim' between intention and action—most notably *Hamlet* and Kyd's *The Spanish Tragedy*. In a talk given at Cambridge University, on 8 November 1924, on 'A Neglected Aspect of Chapman', one which includes that other amongst his favoured playwrights from the constellation of Early Modern sources for 'The Hollow Men', Eliot deployed the word 'Kingdom' to describe that realm outside of the everyday world in which true understanding might reside (*LII*, 546). But the immediate purgatorial situation of 'The Hollow Men' suggests that Eliot's engagement with the specifics of Shakespearean tropology was at this point more to the purpose for him. (Chapter Six will take up the increasing importance of George Chapman in the mid to late 1920s.)

The contemporary criticism with which Eliot was familiar paralleled Brutus with Hamlet. For instance, the preface by Israel Gollancz to the Temple Edition of *Shakespeare's Tragedy of Julius Caesar*, also owned by Eliot, has a section headed '*Julius Caesar* and *Hamlet*' in which the characters of Brutus and Hamlet are described as 'twin brothers', 'idealists forced to take a prominent part in the world

---

[61] Michael Sidnell, *Dances of Death: The Group Theatre of London in the Thirties*, 92.

[62] In Ben Jonson's *Catiline, his Conspiracy*, Caesar himself utters a similar sentiment: 'The more/ Actions of depth and danger are consider'd,/The less assuredly they are perform'd', in *The Complete Plays*, ed. Felix Schelling, vol. II (London: J.M. Dent, 1910), 129.

[63] 'Eyes that last I saw in tears', poem I of 'Doris's Dream Songs' from *The Chapbook* of November 1924, eventually appeared outside *The Hollow Men*, as the first of the 'Minor Poems' in Eliot's *Collected Poems*. 'The wind sprang up at four o'clock', originally II of 'Doris', appeared as the second 'Minor Poem'. Some of *its* lines derived from 'Song to the Opherian', included amongst *The Waste Land* manuscript pages, and published by Eliot under the pseudonym 'Gus Krutzsch' in *The Tyro*, no. 1, Spring 1921.

[64] Eliot quotes these same three lines when writing about a similar locution in Valéry's 'Le Cimetière Marin' in 'A Brief Introduction to the Method of Paul Valéry', *Le Serpent par Paul Valéry*, trans. Mark Wardle, 'Published for the *Criterion* by R. Cobden-Sanderson' (London 1924), 10. Eliot's familiar point is that such echoes, although accidental, between languages, illustrate the balance between tradition and originality which the modern poet must make. Eliot later told Robert Sencourt that, at the moment in February 1933 when he dropped the letter in the postbox to his solicitor in London, instructing him to draw up a deed of separation from Vivien, the lines from *Julius Caesar* ran through his mind (*T.S. Eliot: A Memoir*, ed. Donald Adamson, London: Garnstone Press, 1971, 122).

of action'.[65] Gollancz even takes this similarity as evidence that Shakespeare was working on the two plays at the same time. Eliot's preoccupation with the relation between tragic action and individual misapprehension would culminate in the two major contemplations of Senecan ideas in Early Modern work, both from 1927, 'Seneca in Elizabethan Translation' and 'Shakespeare and the Stoicism of Seneca'. More immediately, however, the concatenation of the 'interim', between 'motion' or 'acting', and 'dream', formed the complicating element that Eliot set within the provisionally Dantean apparatus of 'The Hollow Men'.

The 'Between the' locution, from Brutus's delimitation of that 'interim', emphatically forms the incantatory structure of Part V of 'The Hollow Men'. The sense of that temporal space (or vacancy) as a 'miasma, or a hideous dream', is exacerbated by the Shadow, which falls between possibilities of action and their realization. The Shadow eventually brings interruption to the very syntax of the sequence, its concluding prayer, 'For Thine is/Life is/For Thine is the' (*CPP*, 86). Sweeney had been vehement about 'what life is'; Shakespeare's Duke averred that, by being 'absolute for death', 'life/Shall be...sweeter'. Various interruptions have come to such assurance, in Eliot's project. They had characterized the early personae, and Prufrock most particularly. But, in the poetry and plays written after *The Waste Land* the 'interim' becomes the location for poetry itself.

Chronicles, xxix, 15 ('our days on earth are as a shadow'), and the Book of Job, seem the most evident precursors of Eliot's 'Shadow'. Yet Edgar Allan Poe's prose-poem 'Shadow—A Parable' seems a likely further source for Eliot's imagery here. Poe's brief piece carries as its epigraph another familiar formulation, in *Psalms*: 'Yea! Though I walk through the valley of the Shadow of Death'.[66] Poe's mythical ancient speaker is a participant at what seems a funeral feast with the corpse present: 'But although I, Oinos, felt that the eyes of the departed were upon me, still I forced myself not to perceive the bitterness of the expression.' When the Shadow moves through the banquet room, what creates horror amongst the feasters is, though, derived from the fact that 'the tones in the voice of the shadow were not the tones of any one being, but of a multitude of beings... the well-remembered and familiar accents of many thousand departed friends'.[67] The Poe resonance behind 'The Hollow Men', therefore, would seem to emphasize the fearfulness of

---

[65] Israel Gollancz, *Shakespeare's Tragedy of Julius Caesar* (London: J.M. Dent, 1896, ix). Subsequent references to this edition appear in the text. Gollancz also compares the relationship between Brutus and Cassius to that between Amintor and Melantius, in that other vital play for Eliot, Beaumont and Fletcher's *The Maid's Tragedy* (xiii).

[66] In the 1957 radio broadcast mentioned at the start of my Introduction, Eliot included Henry Vaughan's 'Death: A Dialogue' amongst his favourite poems. Besides involving the familiar 'debate' between Soul and Body which, as we shall see in the next chapter, involved Eliot's thoughts about the Metaphysicals, Vaughan's poem is always printed with a quotation from the Book of Job, v. 21–2, after its last stanza: 'Before I go whence I shall not return, even to the land of darkness, and the shadow of death....See *The Poems of Henry Vaughan, Silurist*, ed. Canon Beeching (London: George Routledge, 1905), 24.

[67] Edgar Allan Poe, *The Complete Tales and Poems* (Harmondsworth: Penguin, 1982, 458). Herbert Read, who read 'The Hollow Men' in manuscript, claimed that the sequence represents Eliot's most confessional work, showing Eliot's 'agony' before 'the shadow of moral judgement, the Tables of the Law, the Commandments' (*T.S.E.—A Memoir*, Wesleyan University Press, 1971, 28).

the unveiling of many voices within one voice, that haunted and horrified polyvocalism behind Eliot's continuing poetic practice. What the Poe reference, like the
Dantean moments within the sequence, do not bring to the fore, however, are the
precise tensions of 'interim' and 'hideous dream', which the references to *Julius
Caesar* in 'The Hollow Men' signal.

In fact, the language of 'The Hollow Men' seems more steeped in the dilemmas
of *Julius Caesar* than in those of Dante or Poe. The true conflict at the centre of
Shakespeare's play is between the blunt pragmatism and assured selfhood of Caesar,
which have dangerous consequences for Rome, and the equally dangerous, sleepful
doubting, of Brutus. As Antony remarks of Caesar admiringly, 'When Caesar says
"Do this", it is perform'd.' (I. ii, 10); as Caesar says of himself, 'I rather tell thee
what is to be fear'd/Than what I fear; for always I am Caesar' (I. ii, 212–13). There
is no gap between intention and action here. No need for Caesar, as Eliot felt there
to be for the modern poet, to 'dislocate' words into performative meaning.

By contrast, Brutus's perturbation at the prospect of killing Caesar leads to Cassius's seeking to steel his courage, by assuring him of his worth, through a typical
Early Modern conceit:

> CASSIUS: Tell me, good Brutus, can you see your face?
> BRUTUS: No, Cassius; for the eye sees not itself
>   But by reflection, by some other things.
> CASSIUS: 'Tis just;
>   And it is very much lamented, Brutus,
>   That you have no such mirrors as will turn
>   Your hidden worthiness into your eye,
>   That you might see your shadow.
>
> (I. ii, 51–7)

The inability of Brutus to find such a confirming reflection echoes behind 'The
Hollow Men', which, through a web of allusions, draws in Dante also, and explores
the same conceit. Brutus's failure to confirm himself by seeing his 'shadow' leaves
him vulnerable to the harrowing intervention of unknown forces, and to misapprehension. This is the 'miasma' under which he lives, and which disables him
from decisions that might reverse his drift towards a tragic fate, upon the killing of
Caesar. Eliot's mini-sequence explores a similarly incoherent situation.

In Part I of 'The Hollow Men' only those who have crossed into death with 'direct
eyes' see truly that what seem like 'violent souls' (the conspirators against Caesar, for
instance, or the Gunpowder plotters) are 'hollow men'. But, in the uncertain world
of these poems, this does not yield a 'directness' correlative to the worldly pragmatism of Caesar. Instead, eyes 'do not appear' in the sequence's Part II; they 'are not
here' in Part IV. Lack of mutual gazing, like that in Donne's 'The Extasie', means lack
of love's reciprocity. The Duchess did not turn her eyes from her mirror, and so fell.
So the 'shadow', which might confirm the self, is rendered truly 'hollow', malevolent,
and disruptive, *unless* the vision of Beatrice's eyes in the *Paradiso* miraculously 'reap-
pear' (*CPP*, 83–5). Therefore, the Shadow of Part V does appear, a fearful entity that
prevents desired action, or any univocal completion and resolution. The Shadow
appears independently of an originating or perceiving 'you'. There is a lack, in other

words, of that creative watchfulness towards the self with which Eliot's recognition of the dramatic force of Donne's phrase 'I am not all Heere' imbued him. There is also no salving love, mutual desire, as previously also in *The Waste Land.*

Brutus confirms, in the lines immediately before Eliot's haunting main source for his sequence in *Julius Caesar*, that 'Since Cassius first did whet me against Caesar/I have not slept./Between the acting...'. 'The state of man' in him, 'Like to a little kingdom' (the word Eliot deploys to denominate the dream realm of death), has suffered 'insurrection' (II. i., 61ff). As the play progresses, Brutus's self-identification becomes closer to the ghost of Caesar, interrupter of his final carrying-through of that action begun with Caesar's murder, and seemingly to be ceased at the Battle of Philippi. The ghost describes itself as:

> Thy evil spirit, Brutus.
> BRUTUS: Why coms't thou?
> GHOST: To tell thee thou shalt see me at Philippi.
> BRUTUS: Well; then I shall see thee again.
> GHOST: Ay, at Philippi.
>
> (IV. iii, 332–5)

The speaker of Poe's Tale feels 'the eyes of the departed' on him. The shocked iteration by Brutus of the ghost's verb 'see' echoes back to Cassius's earlier 'that you might see your shadow'. As G. Wilson Knight, the Shakespeare critic sponsored and favoured by Eliot from the late 1920s onwards, would congenially put it, '"Eyes"' are, indeed, especially frequent' in *Julius Caesar*, and these seemingly noble Romans seem 'excessively given to tears'.[68]

Both eyes and tears are prevalent in *The Waste Land*, and now recur in 'The Hollow Men', as in the related 'Eyes That Last I Saw in Tears'. Such references set Early Modern sources as integral to this poetry in ways equal to, and consonant with, the familiar Dantean recursion. They give 'hideous' reality to the knowledge that *both* Brutus and Cassius are 'hollow men', as Brutus describes the notion, in the lines which give Eliot's sequence its title:

> [H]ollow men, like horses hot at hand,
> Make gallant show and promise of their mettle
> But when they should endure the bloody spur,
> They fall their crests...
>
> (IV. ii, 23–6)

The use of 'fall' as an unexpected transitive verb here, perhaps underwrites the indeterminate agency forced by the inversion of Eliot's repeated verb 'Falls' in Part V of 'The Hollow Men'. It is an inversion that imparts unnerving ambiguity to the motivation and provenance of the Shadow's intervention.

'The Hollow Men' enacts a compelling engagement with Dante's progressive journey towards vision in *The Divine Comedy*, and with an irruptive Shakespearean

---

[68] G. Wilson Knight, *The Imperial Theme: Further Interpretations of Shakespeare's Tragedies including the Roman Plays* (London: Oxford University Press, 1931), 37, 43. For a possible further source for the imagery of eyes and tears in Eliot's sequence, see my 'T.S. Eliot and Chapman: "Metaphysical" Poetry and Beyond', *Journal of Modern Literature*, vol. 29, no. 4 (Summer 2006), 36.

tragic division. This is one that splits reciprocal and recognitional action into other courses, as 'Lips that would kiss/Form prayers to broken stone.'[69] By the end of Eliot's sequence, it is prayer that is typographically and epistemologically 'broken', as, Brutus-like (or Hamlet-like), the integrative speaking voice of the poem is lost literally 'between' possibilities, sinking, as Brutus says 'hollow men do', 'in the trial'.[70] The Gunpowder Plot, therefore, presents a key intimation here in Eliot's mini-sequence, of that 'dissociation' in English history which 'The Metaphysical Poets' had seen fully to have arrived with the English Civil War. Figures in Eliot have previously existed in the 'interim', or void, 'between'. Tiresias in *The Waste Land* is 'between' his two worlds, the living and the dead. But this situation, as we shall see in later chapters, becomes the natural one for Eliot's poetry, up to, for instance, the place 'Between un-being and being' of 'Burnt Norton', or 'Between melting and freezing' in 'Little Gidding' (*CPP*, 175, 191).

Yet the slimmed-down form of 'The Hollow Men', its incantatory stichomythic-formed rhythms and reiteration, intensifies the complication of the Dantean machinery of the sequence, both with the tragic waverings of Shakespearean heroes and with the analogous historical failure of the Gunpowder Plot conspira-tors.[71] The battle for a transitive language of recognition, one that will confirm a univocal selfhood for the poems' spectral speaker, is enacted *against* the Dantean pattern that informs it, yet *within* a dynamics shared with Shakespeare's *Julius Caesar*.

'The Hollow Men' is perhaps the one of Eliot's poems that has most divided critics; it is a difficult poem to construe. In what is the most persuasive commen-tary on the poem, Robert Crawford emphasized that the 'romanticism and anthro-pology' which typically underpins the sequence is also imbued deliberately with 'confusion', 'confused' identity.[72] A. David Moody, in contrast, notes that Eliot follows here 'the very modes of Dante's sensibility'; despite the complexities of the sequence, and its lapsing into fragmentation, for Moody it enacts 'a more intelligi-ble structure' than its monumental precursor, *The Waste Land*.[73] The involved con-sideration of the Shakespearean context for the poem here, however, suggests the degree to which Eliot typically involved his various sources in a process of juxtapo-sition and dialogue when evolving 'The Hollow Men'. Out of that dialogue, the

---

[69] There has been some questioning, however, as to the fastness of the Dantean progression, in Eliot's understanding of it. David Spurr, for instance, has perceived a 'division in [Eliot's] poetic conscious-ness', since he 'borrows images from Dante's Earthly and Celestial Paradises as if they were diametrically opposed states of being instead of intermediate and final stages on the way to beatitude' (*Conflicts in Consciousness: T.S. Eliot's Poetry and Criticism*, Chicago: University of Illinois Press, 1994, 56).

[70] The enduring pressure of the trial of his first marriage upon Eliot is proven by a postcard sent to him by Virginia Woolf, after he had had tea with her in February 1938. On the postcard, Woolf has simply written out Brutus's lines about 'hollow men' from *Julius Caesar*. See 'Some New Woolf Let-ters', ed. Joanne Trantmann Banks, *Modern Fiction Studies*, vol. 30, no. 2 (Summer 1984), 123.

[71] Hugh Kenner's reading of the sequence instates Guy Fawkes as the emblematic figure: 'This reduction of Early Modern individualism to a theme of lugubrious festivals...provides an historic perspective on modern England' (*The Invisible Poet: T.S. Eliot*, London: Methuen, 1960, 160).

[72] Robert Crawford, *The Savage and the City in the Work of T.S. Eliot* (Oxford: Clarendon Press, 1987), 158.

[73] Moody, *Thomas Stearns Eliot: Poet*, 127.

historical purpose of the sequence emerges more clearly, as does the instigation for the emotional hinterland of the gestural and pared-down writing.

The Early Modern context, in other words, forms an interruptive commentary on the poetry's newly concerted religious or visionary aspiration, as it will throughout Eliot's later verse and plays. In the brief period from 1922 to 1925, Eliot had succeeded in recasting the Early Modern model of the poetic of *The Waste Land* into the more determinedly stichomythic rhythms of *Sweeney Agonistes* and 'The Hollow Men'—rhythms mediated by different Early Modern sources to those he had deployed across the later 1910s and into the 1920s. The issue of reconciling the many conflicting voices forcing themselves into the poetry, within a coherent whole, however, was to grow in importance across his career. By re-inflecting Early Modern originals, the process, the ontology, and hermeneutics of those later works evolved from the content of these early 1920s poems. Such complications come under increasing pressure in the succeeding years, as Eliot moved closer to acceptance of the authority of Christianity into his life. Yet his continuing reassessments of Early Modern works, and the allegory he found within them for the difficult issue of sustaining belief in the modern world, gather intensity in the mid to late 1920s.

6

'The Pattern Behind the Pattern'
Ash-Wednesday, the Ariel Poems, and 'Coriolan'

THE VARIETIES OF METAPHYSICAL POETRY

The years leading up to Eliot's acceptance into the Church of England, in 1927, were marked by an increasing ambivalence in his thinking about those Early Modern figures who had proved a constant recourse for him to that point. The crucial tension, evident in 'The Hollow Men', between a glimpsed, Dantean, visionary order or possibility, and a consuming and countering human actuality ('hideous dream'), gradually became integral, at this stage, within Eliot's judgements about familiar Early Modern figures and contexts. The question broached in Eliot's 1923 review 'John Donne', as to the nature of Donne's appeal for the modern age, became symptomatic, as Eliot extensively reconsidered his early opinions, between 1925 and the early 1930s. This chapter will review this strong reconsideration through the ways in which Eliot sought solutions to this tension, by evolving more flexible metaphors for what he felt to be the integrative possibilities within poetic form, metaphors that might include his religious and anthropological propensities. It considers the critical background to the synthesis that he sought to achieve between Christianity and Roman stoicism at the time of his conversion, as a means to holding together the dual strands of his preoccupation with both Dante and Early Modern theologians and playwrights. Close discussion of the poems he wrote in the wake of his confirmation demonstrate, then, the practical impact of this new thinking in the later 1920s and at the start of the next decade.

Eliot's wry remarks, in the opening pages of his 1926 Clark Lectures on *The Varieties of Metaphysical Poetry*, spelt out the reflective 'affinity' that he perceived, between the poetry of the seventeenth century and that of 'our own age' (*VMP*, 43). It is an 'affinity' that Eliot sustained as a point of motivation across the subsequent lectures. Paradoxically, such 'affinity', Eliot averred, explains the extreme 'difficulty', which the modern age experiences, when it seeks 'to understand' the earlier century. The seventeenth century, he claimed, in an echo of other contemporary critics' views (as described in Chapter Two above), 'experienced the acute crisis of the transition from the old to the new Europe (to the Europe, we might say, of 1914)...' (*VMP*, 74).

The quest of the Clark Lectures satisfactorily 'to define' the nature of the original Metaphysical poetry in English bore directly, then, upon the posited near-contemporary moment, just before the literally horrendous, recent 'transition' in World

War I. The Early Modern period provided a way of signifying that now lost world, one itself born of earlier 'crisis'. As previously for Eliot, his 'historical sense' is keyed as the means to diagnose the present malaise. Through a similar juxtaposition to that in 'The Hollow Men' between *Julius Caesar* and Dante, the various critiques of seventeenth-century writing in *The Varieties of Metaphysical Poetry* work to articulate the contemporary drift, as Eliot saw it, into obscurity, incoherence, and a lack of performative articulation. As much as he is promoted, in the Lectures, as an antidote to Eliot's list of perceived 'wrongs' in the Early Modern period, so Dante is offered, also, as a means to anatomize the faults in recent poetry, including, presumably, those felt by Eliot to blight his own work to date.

The latter pages of *The Varieties of Metaphysical Poetry* are, however, freighted by acknowledgement that the thirteenth century was sealed in remote history: there could be no 'return', 'whatever that may mean', to its original 'conditions and beliefs'. Eliot felt that he had demonstrated in his Lectures 'only the eternal utility, in a world of change, of any achievement of perfection'. The comparison and challenge offered to the modern poet, by Dante's '*range, intensity,* and *completeness* of emotion', is aimed to promote 'conscious control over the quality of our poetry' (*VMP*, 222, 228). Eliot's comparison in the Lectures of two historical periods, the medieval European and the English Early Modern, in other words, allowed him to establish the grounds for a critical approach to, and within, his own potential new poems. Eliot is again, as he had in previous essays, including 'The Metaphysical Poets', entering a measurement of lets and balances into the reading of 'Tradition' itself.[1]

Central to this enterprise in the Clark Lectures was what seems, at first, to be a dry scholarly debate; one appropriate, perhaps, to his occasion, speaking to a Cambridge audience. But it is a debate that proved to have vital importance for Eliot's poetic development, at this time, and subsequently. This debate was formed by Eliot's consideration of the proportion of medieval to Early Modern elements in the reading, and thence the poetry, of John Donne. Eliot's named interlocutor, in this regard, was Mary Paton Ramsay, whose *Les Doctrines médiévales chez Donne, le poète metaphysicien de l'Angleterre (1573–1631)* had gone into a second edition in 1924. Ramsay's book offered Eliot something of a motivation to clarify his own opinions regarding Donne's relation to modernity. He had crucially mentioned Ramsay's book in a review of Mario Praz's *Secentismo e Marianismo in Inghilterra*, a review of 1925 that is an important precursor of the Clark Lectures.[2] But Ramsay's arguments clearly necessitated further reflection, as they contested some of Eliot's previously established presumptions. For Ramsay was adamant about the historical significance of her argument. Considering the span of years covered by Donne's life, she asserted that:

---

[1] Similar comparison and sentiments were shortly to find their way into Wyndham Lewis's *The Lion and the Fox: The Role of the Hero in the Plays of Shakespeare*: 'For to-day we are in the midst of a "transitional" period, on a vast scale' (London: Grant Richards, 1927), 85. Lewis's book was shortly to influence Eliot's re-focusing of his views on these matters, as will become clear below.

[2] *TLS*, no. 1248, 17 December 1925, 878.

C'est une période que les historiens de tout genre sont d'accord à considérer comme capitale pour la formation des temps modernes.[3]

Ramsay's comparative reading of Dante with Donne is consonant with that in Eliot's Clark Lectures (and across his later admiration for both figures). Yet it is also consonant with the Lectures' valuation of Donne:

> Lucrèce et Dante, appartiennent à vrai dire, à un ordre poétique plus élevé que celui de Donne. Ils exposent une philosophie reçue par chacun d'eux de ses prédécesseurs. Dante en particulier accepte un système philosophique qui embrasse le monde materiel et le monde intelligible, système élaboré et synthétisé par un genie philosophique de premier ordre.... Pour cette philosophie, le monde de la nature matérielle n'est point séparé du monde métaphysique.[4]

Ramsay emphasized, however (and this is where Eliot's understanding diverged from hers), the close resemblances between Dante and Donne's philosophy, 'grace probablement au système identique de philosophie qui leur est commun' ('thanks perhaps to the identical system of philosophy which they share'). This is a system that includes their shared knowledge of Saints Augustine and Aquinas, and of the Pseudo-Dionysus. But it extends to the notion that both Dante and Donne saw God as having revealed himself in and through Christ. Ramsay admitted 'une certaine difficulté' in her final view of Donne's relation to his precursors, a difficulty:

> à reconstruire la doctrine exacte de Donne en matière philosophique ou théologique. Il n'en a nulle part fait une exposition complète. Il n'est en réalité un systématique.[5]

As a result, Ramsay asserted what Eliot would later maintain, with regard to the work of George Herbert and Shakespeare, that 'il faut lire son oeuvre en entier' ('it is necessary to read the complete work').[6] When the ambition is ventured, to establish Donne's 'medieval doctrine', and to promote his thinking as equivalent to Dante's, Donne's sermons and letters become as relevant as his poetry—a view that had been promoted earlier by Edmund Gosse, as Eliot would have been aware.

To Eliot, in contrast, it was the *lack* of system in Donne that underwrites his view of Donne's *post*-medieval situation. The Clark Lectures develop the view Eliot also

---

[3] Mary Paton Ramsay, *Les Doctrines médiévales chez Donne, le poète metaphysicien de l'Angleterre (1573–1631)* (London: Oxford University Press, 1917, 1924 second edition), 10: 'Historians of all kinds are agreed in considering that period crucial in forming the modern age.'

[4] Ibid., 15: 'Lucretius and Dante belong, truthfully, to a more elevated poetic order than Donne's. They reveal a philosophy received through each one of their predecessors. Dante in particular accepts a philosophical system which embraces the material and intelligible worlds, a system elaborated and synthesized by philosophical genius of the highest order.... For that philosophy, the world of material nature is not at all separate from the metaphysical world.'

[5] Ibid., 15, 180–1, 136: '... in reconstructing the exact doctrine of Donne in philosophical or theological matters. Nowhere has he made a full exposition. There is not really a systematic one.'

[6] Eliot's position on Shakespeare's career will be discussed below. As late as 1962, Eliot was making the argument for considering all of Herbert's work together: '*The Temple* is, in fact, a structure, and one which may have been worked over and elaborated, perhaps at intervals of time, before it reached its final form. We cannot judge Herbert, or savour fully his genius and his art, by any selection to be found in an anthology; we must study *The Temple* as a whole' (*George Herbert*, Pymouth: Northcote House, 1994 edition, 22).

promulgated, in the review of Mario Praz's book, that the 'very indiscriminate variety of Donne's reading is evidence of his modernity'—a view that is expanded upon at the outset of the second Lecture (*VMP*, 67ff). The Lectures then sought to trace the further 'disintegration of the intellect', which followed, in Eliot's (and Praz's) opinion, from similar lack of discrimination in the later English Metaphysicals, Richard Crashaw and Abraham Cowley. The term that both review and Lectures discovered, to contrast with the achieved metaphysics of Dante's medievalism, is 'psychological'.[7] The 'ontology' to which Dante had ready recourse, the Aquinean Catholicism of the Italy of his time, had been diverted and distracted, so Eliot maintained, across the succeeding centuries, and through the translation of such thought into England (*VMP*, 79). Eliot foregrounded, more urgently now, what had been pivotal in his earlier responses to John Donne, such as 'Preacher and Artist': the failure to adhere to an established philosophy or system of belief is taken as a demonstration of limitation in Donne's metaphysics. This was encapsulated by Eliot as 'the fraction of *thought* into innumerable *thoughts*' (a phrase proximate to the 'scattering' Gerontion derived, as we have seen, from George Chapman and John Dryden). Donne's greatness is closely, and darkly, allied to the 'chaos' within his thinking—a chaos immediately linked by Eliot to that of 'modernity' (*VMP*, 155).[8]

Such remarks established the challenge of Eliot's own ideas and poetry from this point on. It was a challenge founded upon the need to redirect his critical stance *against* Donne and the 'modern' into an achieved creative expression (which is also a critical one) that sustained the countervailing, or Dantean, possibilities. Eliot's position, through reconsidering the Early Modern period, and recent writing about it, shifted from seeing in 'the metaphysical poets' a spur to the poetic presentation of a necessarily 'difficult' response in, and to, a 'complex' contemporary time, to an almost Yeatsian stance, in which the poet must take a stand against the drift of the age. This is not to say, however, that Eliot's new resistance amounted to a wholesale rejection of the Early Modern period, which had prompted so much in his earlier perceptions and poetry. The Clark Lectures, and his subsequent critical writing, find Eliot determinedly renegotiating those aspects of the earlier literature that had become integral to his poetic.

---

[7] Eliot became somewhat rooted in this reading of Donne's 'inconsistency', repeating it on various later occasions, including 'Rhyme and Reason: The Poetry of John Donne' (*The Listener*, vol. III, no. 62, 19 March 1930, 503), and 'Donne in our Time', *A Garland for John Donne 1631–1931*, ed. Theodore Spencer (Cambridge, MA: Harvard University Press, 1931, 11).

[8] In a direct reprise of the issues considered in 'Preacher as Artist', Eliot's 1926 essay 'Lancelot Andrewes' repeats this charge. Eliot cites again the selection from Pearsall Smith 'I am Not all Here' to demonstrate the comparative virtue of Andrewes' contemplative nature, compared to Donne's 'self-expressive' one. In an indication that Eliot's valuation of such matters remained fluid and uncertain, however, 'Lancelot Andrewes' is notably more equivocal in its judgement upon Donne than the Clark Lectures are. Andrewes is 'medieval', Donne 'modern' and so more 'sympathetic'; 'dangerous' to those fascinated by personality, not as 'spiritual' as Andrewes, but 'valuable' nonetheless (*FLA*, 24–7). Elsewhere, Eliot at this time could be more relaxed about the related quality, 'personality'. In a review of Herford and Simpson's vast Jonson edition, he claimed that Jonson had, through his 'immensely impressive personality', had more effect upon subsequent writing than any one man. Compared to Swift, however, he was less successful at including that personality completely in the work ('The Oxford Jonson', *The Dial*, vol. LXXXV, July 1928, 66, 68).

As Eliot's 'historical' inquiry across the Clark Lectures developed, into a consideration of the 'disintegration of the intellect' perceptible in later Metaphysical poetry in English, he turned again to the technical, but also integrative, element of poetry, upon which his understanding of Early Modern writing had fixed for the previous five years (*VMP* 76).[9] He focuses once more upon the conceit. In Donne, Eliot claimed, 'disintegration' of his thought produced 'the extravagant development of a simile or metaphor to emphasise an idea'. The pleasure in reading Donne, then, is now presented as lying in consideration of the 'exactness' with which that 'extravagant development' is 'carried out' in the poem. For the later Metaphysical writers, of whom Crashaw proves the major example, here and elsewhere, the conceit for Eliot seemed to have become detached from any originating or shaping thought. Ideally, a conceit that provides a way to capture the various ontological implications within a single thought might be set as a corrective, but also as an integrative possibility, within a new work. 'Wit' seemed to have failed as a way of sustaining coherence within, and between, conceits. Crashaw in particular, Eliot claimed, displayed 'perversity of feeling', one that was 'briefer...more violent' than Donne's conceits, but also incapable of being 'carried further', and so of being (theologically) led further astray (*VMP*, 180–1).

CONCEITS, STOICISM, AND GEORGE CHAPMAN

The years of the mid to late 1920s find Eliot casting himself, via his concentrated reconsiderations of Early Modern work, in an historical dilemma, in that the formerly integrative possibility which 'wit' and 'conceit' had, at the start of the decade, overarchingly provided to the question of poetic structure, no longer held. The absence of a guiding philosophy behind the poetry, along with a perceived modern (which mirrored the seventeenth-century) loss of intellectual force, meant that the poetry had become detached from any connection to that syllogistic possibility which Eliot had formerly read out of the earlier period. However, his recognition of the formal benefits for Dante's poetry, to be found in the accommodation of Catholic ontology into *La Vita Nuova* or the *Commedia*, did not provide available correlative possibilities for the modern European writer. Rather, the Early Modern period and its aftermath transmitted a more accurate set of perceptual, philosophical, and technical means for the modern poet—but means which only dramatized further the shared 'disintegration'. This is so, even for a writer such as Eliot, who was more consistently seeking his own spiritual reconciliations at this period, in *Ash-Wednesday*, and in the 'Ariel' poems written across the last three years of the 1920s. As will become clear below, in a further revision of his perspective, as, in

[9] As the 'Author's Preface' to the Clark Lectures indicates, 'The Disintegration of the Intellect' was the proposed title of a trilogy of books on the Early Modern period, which Eliot was planning at this stage (*VMP*, 41). Arguably, Eliot's later essays on Elizabethan Dramatists, 'Thomas Heywood', 'John Ford', and 'John Marston', were each engaged with mapping such 'disintegration'—a significant redefinition of the word from Eliot's earlier embracing of 'disintegration', practised most noticeably by J.M. Robertson, as the proper methodology for resolving textual issues in the Early Modern period.

1927, such tensions within his own thought led Eliot back to the Early Modern period, and to consideration of the Stoic inheritance that it derived from Seneca. He mounted, at the moment of his confirmation, a renewed attempt to cite the earlier period as an historical example for considering his own philosophical and religious difficulties.

Eliot's disagreement with Ramsay about Donne's 'philosophy', and consequent modernity, and his encounter with Mario Praz's criticism, particularly about Crashaw, gave him a sharp sense of the 'dangers' in seeking several kinds of resolution to these dilemmas.[10] Eliot's rendering of Crashaw in *The Varieties of Metaphysical Poetry*, as in the later 'Note on Richard Crashaw' included in *For Lancelot Andrewes*, was virtually interchangeable with Praz's in *Secentismo e Marianismo in Inghilterra*. He quoted the same stanzas as Praz, in fact, to demonstrate that, in poems such as 'The Weeper', as Praz put it, the conceits lack 'a central point round which the poems should gravitate in a harmonious coordination of its parts' (an interesting figural and critical anticipation of Eliot's 'still point' in *Ash-Wednesday*).[11] For Crashaw, tears and weeping were guiding conceits. He deployed them, most notably, as figures for the suffering undergone by Mary Magdalene and St Theresa (Crashaw's 'The Weeper' on the former, and 'Hymn' to the latter, both appeared in Grierson's *Metaphysical Poetry* anthology). These figures, therefore, extended the Early Modern contextual reference, in Eliot's own constellation of poems around 'The Hollow Men', beyond Shakespeare. The unlikely envisaging of a 'blackened river' as a face that 'sweats' with tears in Eliot's poem 'The wind sprang up at four o'clock' (*CPP*, 134), for example, displays a disturbed and disturbing dawn-time confusion. Yet the image recalls Crashaw's 'The Teare', with its dewy rose just 'slipt from Aurora's dewy Brest':

> such the Rose its selfe when vext
> With ungentle flames, does shed,
> Sweating in too warme a Bed.[12]

---

[10] Praz's and Eliot's critique of the Early Modern poetic conceit, and the aberration to be discovered in Crashaw's late version of it, had a certain critical currency at the time. In his survey of the earlier period, for instance, George Saintsbury noted that 'The very maddest and most methodless of the "Metaphysicals" cannot touch Crashaw in his tasteless use of conceits', and pointed particularly to Crashaw's 'The Weeper' (*A History of Elizabethan Literature*, London: Macmillan, 1887; 1907 edition, 369).

[11] The quotation derives from Praz's own translation of his essay as 'Richard Crashaw and the Baroque' which appears in *The Flaming Heart* (New York: Norton, 1958, 226). Praz quotes the stanza from 'The Teare' central for Eliot's argument on p. 223; those from 'The Weeper' (including reference to the 'lilies reek') and the Golden Tagus on the same page (see in comparison *VMP* 172–3; *FLA* 95–6). The conversation between Praz and Eliot over such matters clearly continued for some time: a later essay in *The Flaming Heart*, on Eliot himself, reveals in a footnote that Praz had been granted sight of the then unpublished Clark Lectures (355).

[12] Richard Crashaw, 'The Teare', *The Poems English Latin and Greek*, ed. L.C. Martin (Oxford: Clarendon Press, 1927), 84. This is the edition reviewed by Eliot in 'A Note on Richard Crashaw'. Martin's Introduction notably discusses at length Crashaw's links to Nicholas Ferrar's community at Little Gidding. Martin makes the suggestion that Crashaw retreated there after Puritan attacks on the chapel in Cambridge's Peterhouse College, where he was resident (xxiiiff). Crashaw so joins the 'common genius' 'united in strife' in Eliot's later poem (*CPP*, 195). Praz discussed the connection between George Herbert and Little Gidding in *Secentismo e Marianismo in Inghilterra*.

Similarly, in an image that might have struck Eliot as disintegrative, John Donne, in 'Love's Diet', has eyes that 'weepe not, but sweat'.[13]

If the later 1920s found Eliot seeking a solution to the 'extravagance' and 'vagrancy' of such uses of conceit, and failure of 'wit', that solution emerged through two interconnected concepts which, for him, *also* underpinned his engagement with Early Modern work at this period, and thence across the latter part of his career. These concepts were what he called 'doubleness' and 'planes in relation'. This latter was a formulation seemingly first broached by Eliot during his talk to the University of Cambridge Literary Society on 8 November 1924—at the point he was completing some of the poems later included in 'The Hollow Men'. Speaking on 'A Neglected Aspect of Chapman', and drawing analogies from Fyodor Dostoevsky, Eliot had pondered the relation between the purposelessness of peoples' everyday lives and some other realm in which some meaning might be rendered (*LII*, 546). A 1925 review by Eliot described the thinking of George Chapman as proto-metaphysical, in that:

> Chapman himself is mixed; his classical stoicism is crossed with a strain…of other-worldliness; resulting, here and there in the tragedies, in a sense of double significance which gives him here and there a curious resemblance to Dostoevsky.[14]

As Ronald Schuchard, the editor of *The Varieties of Metaphysical Poetry*, notes, this concept regarding Chapman, and the analogy to Dostoevsky, was repeated directly when Eliot sought to describe the 'double meaning' in Donne's 'The First Anniversarie. An Anatomie of the World' (*VMP*, 152–3).[15] Eliot's classic formulation of the notion of 'doubleness' perhaps only was made, however, in 'John Marston' (1934). In that essay, Eliot saw 'doubleness' as a characteristic feature of poetic drama per se. This is a 'doubleness' that might manifest in a 'certain apparent irrelevance' in the dramatic action. It is an 'irrelevance' that reveals instead 'an under-pattern', 'as if it took place on two planes at once', and operated 'in conformity with the laws of some world that we cannot perceive' (*SE*, 229). This 'doubleness' is a quality which, as we shall see, Eliot would pursue in his discussion of 'The Development of Shakespeare's Verse', in the unpublished lectures given at Edinburgh in 1937, and at Bristol in 1941, and elsewhere: both it and 'planes in relation' became the presiding metaphors of the ambition and critical stance to modernity in his later poetry and drama.

Once again, this shift of ground by Eliot, the derivation of new metaphors to encapsulate a shift in his commitment and sensibility, was rooted in his negotiation with Early Modern writing, and with its mediators, critical and editorial.

---

[13] *The Poems of John Donne*, Volume I, 55.

[14] Eliot, 'Wanley and Chapman', unsigned review of *Essays and Studies by members of the English Association*, vol. XI, collected by Oliver Elton, *TLS*, no. 1250, 31 December 1925, 907. Eliot gave the talk in Cambridge on Chapman, Dostoevsky, and Dante (*LII*, 531).

[15] Eliot's consideration of Donne's longer poems in Lecture V of the Clark Lectures raises the spectre of episodic versus 'organic' poetic organisation, which, as we saw in Chapter One, had figured in his earlier engagements with criticism of Early Modern work, especially the drama. Eliot in this lecture proclaims the long poems as Donne's 'most successful', but, on the other hand, as displaying the 'floating' aspect of his poetic thought most strikingly (*VMP*, 133, 152–3).

A tradition has grown up that regularly dates Eliot's interest in 'under-pattern' to his encounter, in 1929, with the work on Shakespeare's later plays by G. Wilson Knight, work that exhaustively unknotted the underlying 'musical' relations between the recurrent images in those works.[16] This 'influence' is then read into Eliot's own direct encounter with Shakespeare's later plays in the Ariel poem 'Marina', and in 'Coriolan'—a view that Wilson Knight was himself instrumental in promulgating, and for substantial reasons.[17] However, reference to Eliot's reiterated writing on Chapman, plus his broader engagements with the Early Modern period across the 1920s, suggests that the ideas of 'planes in relation' and 'doubleness' were for him more slowly evolving. Moreover, they were rooted earlier in his thought than the simple common acceptance of definitive revelations, through the encounter with Wilson Knight's work, holds to be the case. Eliot's treatment of both concepts was more variously complex than this standard critical judgement implies.

Certainly, the critical work on the Early Modern period to which Eliot was responding *across* this decade carried more of the anthropological and religious (Christian) implications typical in his way, later, of thinking about 'doubleness'. These implications were, further, in stark contrast to the more strictly textual literary engagements of Wilson Knight. It is these more expansive resonances of 'doubleness' that then entered into Eliot's poetry over the last three years of the decade, as they had, in less formulated ways, from *The Waste Land* onwards. (Lyndall Gordon has dated 'Journey of the Magi' to August 1927, and work on *Ash-Wednesday* as running from December 1927 to April 1930.)[18] Contrary to accepted critical opinion, there was continuity, in other words, in this engagement of Eliot's, continuity that carried him across the time of his confirmation, and the religious poetry he worked on in its aftermath. And that engagement began with his completion of *The Waste Land*. Indeed, it is a continuity which complicates the notion of the nature of the religious poem that Eliot was developing at this crucial stage.

Eliot's poetry of the last three years of the 1920s manifests the complexities and obscurities involved in moving between 'planes' of meaning, once previously assured models of mythological progress, including progress beyond penitence and expiation to forgiveness, are rendered uncertain. This uncertainty (like Brutus's) is the 'brief transit', the 'place', of *Ash-Wednesday* (*CPP*, 98). Eliot's newly sustained engagement with the work of George Chapman in the mid-1920s led him towards alternative analogies for the relations between such levels of consciousness, or spiritual possibility, within the broader notion of 'doubleness'.[19] Eliot's 1925 review 'Wanley and Chapman', for instance, found him concentrated upon one particular essay in the volume under his discussion, an essay by Janet Spens, 'Chapman's

---

[16] This is a claim repeated, for instance, in Neil Corcoran's *Shakespeare and the Modern Poet*, which notes the 'harmony' between the Edinburgh lectures and Wilson Knight's ideas that 'probably influenced' Eliot (Cambridge: Cambridge University Press, 2010), 116.

[17] See G. Wilson Knight, 'T.S. Eliot: Some Literary Impressions', in *T.S. Eliot: The Man and His Work*, ed. Allen Tate (London: Penguin, 1971), 247–9.

[18] Lyndall Gordon, *Eliot's New Life* (Oxford: Oxford University Press, 1988), 37.

[19] As the next chapter of this study will indicate, Eliot's encounter with the work of the scholar W.J. Lawrence in 1927 would bring a practical theatrical slant to this metaphysical focus in his work.

Ethical Thought'. Eliot especially commended Spens's comments on Chapman's two 'long, obscure and very beautiful poems', 'The Banquet of Ovid' and 'The Shadow of Night'. Spens, who noted the many parallels between Chapman's time and her own, had also, in her chapter, foregrounded the rendition of 'inner experience' in the two poems of 'The Shadow of Night', for their breaking with the established order of our symbolic expectation. Chapman had found new conceits for the 'inner' life, and that impacted upon the technical nature of his work, upon the imaginative coherence of his writing. According to Spens, 'Now, in the expression of that inner life, association takes the place of design. Such a poem as *The Shadow of Night* is a colour-scheme, a dream- fugue.' For her, once the narrative order of perception and association was broken in this way, the poems in 'The Shadow of Night' 'are best understood as a sort of musical composition.'[20] Spens's 'sort of' properly respected the difficulty in making this kind of analogy between words and music. But her 'musical' was at least correlative to that '*new* organisation of many poetic elements', which Eliot had recovered from the recent translation of major poems by the French poet Paul Valéry in 1924.[21] Spens's assertion also looked forward to Eliot's own compositional methods in the later 1920s and beyond. Her perception about Chapman lingered behind the heralding of a 'logic of the imagination' alongside a 'logic of concepts' in Eliot's Preface to his translation of St John Perse, *Anabasis*: and *Anabasis* then prefigures 'Journey of the Magi'.[22] The notion of poetry as 'musical composition' might apply also to the ordering of *Ash-Wednesday* and the Ariel poems, obviously, as much as to some of Eliot's drama and to *Four Quartets*.

That Eliot, in 'Wanley and Chapman', saw such methods of composition as definitive of the 'period of transition' which he there took the Elizabethan age to have been, and that he figured it via George Chapman specifically, raises further ontological issues. These are issues that both picked up strains in his earlier writing, and, again, looked forward to the centring foci of the poetry he was shortly to begin writing. In 1925, Eliot's finding in Chapman a crossing of 'stoicism' with 'otherworldliness' instigated a critical inquiry that lasted for several years in his essays, and which, in turn, fed into his poetry and drama for much longer. 'Doubleness' here takes on specific metaphysical, philosophical, and religious potential, which was absolutely central to Eliot's later thought and poetry.

The complex presence of a stoical attitude, derived for the Elizabethan dramatists from Seneca, had been a staple of the criticism of the earlier period for quite a time, before Eliot took it up in the mid-1920s. John W. Cunliffe's *The Influence of Seneca on Elizabethan Tragedy* (1893), for instance, is referred to several times in one of Eliot's major contributions to this discussion from 1927, 'Seneca in Elizabethan Translation'. Cunliffe promoted Seneca's modernity in his book, and

---

[20] Janet Spens, 'Chapman's Ethical Thought', *Essays and Studies by Members of the English Association*, vol. XI, ed. Oliver Elton (Oxford: Clarendon Press, 1925), 161, 163.
[21] T.S. Eliot, 'A Brief Introduction to the Method of Paul Valéry', *Le Serpent par Paul Valéry*, trans. Mark Wardle (London: R.Cobden-Sanderson, 1924), 11.
[22] T.S. Eliot, 'Preface', *Anabasis* (London: Faber, 1931, 1959 edition), 10.

the 'cosmopolitan' nature of his stoical ideas, alongside the technical features for which Seneca is purported to have been responsible, in the development of Early Modern drama: its five-act structure, elaborate rhetorical figuration, reflective psychology, and the inclusion of a chorus of ghosts and supernatural figures to comment upon the travails of the living characters.[23] F.L. Lucas, whose *Seneca and Elizabethan Tragedy* (1922) was another important source for Eliot's 'Seneca in Elizabethan Translation', was sceptical about the number of direct borrowings from Seneca in those tragedies (something with which Eliot disagreed; *SE*, 97). But Lucas put forward the vital role of classical, particularly Latin, literatures in galvanizing Early Modern drama, and rehearsed the same list of technical features which Seneca donated to that drama as Cunliffe had.

However, Lucas made several reflections upon the argument about Seneca, which were suggestively crucial for Eliot. They were crucial not just to Eliot's sense of the impact of Seneca upon the drama he was most influenced by, but also to the categories of choice and possibility involved in thinking through the presence and purpose of philosophical and religious ideas in his later work. Lucas's phrases here, indeed, looked forward to the static, and verbally dependent, 'action' of Eliot's own dramas. Lucas considered the ways in which the fact that Seneca's plays were written for recitation, not performance, threw 'the whole burden' of their creation, and of audience response, 'upon the language', which therefore 'had to be violently rhetorical' and 'variegated'. For Lucas, this was a key impact of Seneca upon the English drama—a drama whose extravagant rhetorical qualities had preoccupied Eliot since at least '"Rhetoric" and Poetic Drama' (1919). Lucas pursued, however, the philosophical significance of this 'burden' in the plays: 'the Stoic, however altruistic, remained an egotist'. 'It is not his "ego" that the Stoic hates, it is the emotions that make personality.' Lucas saw such egotism as correlative to the aesthetics and resultant religious impetus of the plays:

> The Renaissance had rediscovered in the Classics first the worship of earthly and human beauty for its own sake, whereas Medievalism had typically reserved nudity to the damned in Hell; secondly and still more, the worship of Strength and the Superman. With Nietzsche, its creed was 'Was ist gut fragt Ihr? Tapfer sein ist gut.' ['What is good you ask? To be brave is good.'][24]

'Shakespeare and the Stoicism of Seneca', Eliot's other major contribution to the tradition of this criticism, published in 1927, sought to describe the 'new attitude' that he intuited in Shakespeare. It was an 'attitude' 'derived' from Seneca, as a 'modern' attitude, in that it 'culminates' 'in the attitude of Nietzsche'. For Eliot, this was an 'attitude of self-dramatization', which various of Shakespeare's heroes reach at the moments of most intense tragedy, usually their deaths. Eliot again discovers this 'attitude', which is correlative, on different ground now, to that he had earlier relished in Donne, in the dying speeches of Chapman's Bussy

---

[23] John W. Cunliffe, *The Influence of Seneca on Elizabethan Tragedy: An Essay* (New York: G.E. Stechert & Co., 1925 edition), 14–5.
[24] F.L. Lucas, *Seneca and Elizabethan Tragedy* (Cambridge: Cambridge University Press, 1922), 56, 59, 108.

and Biron, as well as those of the heroes of John Marston (*SE*, 129).[25] Chapman and Marston are integral to Eliot's understanding of the 'doubleness' perceptible in some Early Modern drama. Yet in 'Shakespeare and the Stoicism of Seneca', Eliot's discussion of the last words of Othello found him, in an echo of Lucas's contention, exploring an 'egotism' 'however altruistic': 'He is endeavouring to escape reality.... He takes in the spectator, but the human motive is primarily to take in himself.' Othello dramatizes himself 'against his environment'. (*SE*, 130–1)

Eliot's critical attitude here is an extension of his earlier reflections upon the self-divisions, and compensatory watchfulness, to be perceived in Donne's rhetoric, and upon the allure of Donne's 'modern' personality. More immediately, the self-reflexiveness, and '*cheering himself up*' that Eliot perceives in Othello's last speech, infects the speaker of his own 'Journey of the Magi', begun in August 1927. The Magus of Eliot's poem is a speaker 'absolute' for death, in the Duke's sense from *Measure for Measure*; 'glad' of it, but nonetheless, and relatedly, perturbed across his lifetime by the sign he saw in Bethlehem. His 'environment'—to deploy the term in 'Shakespeare and the Stoicism of Seneca'—is rendered devastatingly uncertain for him, in other words, by the sight of the baby Christ. But, Othello-like, this Magus asserts his experience against that 'new' situation. Othello's late demand, that his auditors 'Speak of me as I am; nothing extenuate,/Nor set down aught in malice' is translated by Eliot as the Magus's:

> And I would do it again, but set down
> This set down
> This:
>
> (*CPP*, 104)

The repetitions here, the fractured lineation and enjambments, recalling those of 'The Hollow Men', reflect the bewilderment of Eliot's speaker, in contrast to the restored riches of Othello's final self-assertion. Eliot's Magus is droll and resigned. His comment upon the eventual discovery of Christ's birthplace is 'it was (you may say) satisfactory'. Nothing is revealed in 'Journey of the Magi', beyond an unease at former ways, now interrupted by the Nativity, which induces a *Sweeney Agonistes*-like confusion of former categories of understanding. Was what the Magi saw a 'Birth' or a 'Death'? The answer is, of course, both: so, 'I should be glad of another death' stands as the poem's final line.

In what is, for Eliot, a comparatively rare piece of social observation relating to Early Modern writing and its origins, 'Shakespeare and the Stoicism of Seneca' noted the appeal of Roman stoicism to the slaves, who were relegated within, or

---

[25] Wyndham Lewis makes a similar equation between Chapman's thought and Shakespeare several times in *The Lion and the Fox* (London: Grant Richards, 1927, 179, 284–5). He isolates Othello's last speech for discussion of its rare qualities even in Shakespeare's oeuvre on pp. 191–2. Eliot had been making similar points about Shakespeare's heroes since 1919, and '"Rhetoric" and Poetic Drama', but without making the Nietzsche parallel. He had cited a further instance of this trend from Beaumont and Fletcher's *King and No King*, Act III, where Arbaces, 'King' of Iberia, thinks that he will be talked about in future, on account of his 'incestuous' feelings for his 'sister' (she is revealed not to be so, and all's well). See 'Ben Jonson' (*SW*, 98) The scene Eliot cites appears on p. 191 of the Everyman edition of the play (edited by George P. Baker, London: J.M. Dent, 1911).

cast outside, the workings of the state.[26] This accounts, he claimed, for the ready accommodation of stoicism within early Christianity: 'Stoicism is the refuge of the individual in an indifferent and hostile world too big for him.' (*SE*, 131)[27] Yet the disturbance in 'Journey of the Magi' transcends class and becomes existential. It crosses, in fact, with those religious uncertainties that were detected, by Eliot, at the heart of the relationship between a stoic world view and a Christian one. This is 'doubleness' as a kind of bifurcation of the self, under pressure of historical and miraculous event. The Magus finds himself in such a Christian world now, a world predicted also by the 'environment' created for his 'journey' by Eliot's appropriation of Lancelot Andrewes' Christmas Day sermon of 1620—that vital source also for the earlier 'Gerontion', and soon to be so again for the fine distinctions of *Ash-Wednesday*.

To this extent, it is important to the imaginative negotiation enacted in 'Journey of the Magi', the negotiation between Stoicism and Christianity, that its speaker is, like those of 'Gerontion', *Ash-Wednesday*, and 'A Song for Simeon', an old man. Andrewes' Christmas Day sermon, when imagining the Magi's quest, repeats the 'unseasonable' nature of its particular 'difficulties': 'It was no summer progress.' Perhaps, when mixed with the other key influence upon 'Journey of the Magi', St John Perse's *Anabase*, which Eliot was translating at this time, such pithy reflections in Andrewes spark the Magus's recall of 'summer palaces' there. (Unlike Eliot's speaker, though, Andrewes' magi retain something of that positive, summer spirit, out of season, given the purpose of their quest: they 'came cheerfully and quickly' to their goal.) Andrewes was notably eager to point up the contemporary pertinence of the magi's journey, for his audience at James's court:

Set down this; that to find where He is, we must learn of these to ask where He is, which we full little set ourselves to do.[28]

Andrewes' typical wordplay,[29] 'set down...full little set', further, in its authority and pedagogic ecclesiastical purpose, underscores the dramatic and damaged

---

[26] C.D. Blanton has some telling remarks about Eliot's identification of himself with the *metics* of Athenian Greece, the immigrants, slaves, and small businessmen who upheld religious value in an alien context. See 'London', in *T.S. Eliot in Context*, ed. Jason Harding (Cambridge: Cambridge University Press, 2011), 35.

[27] Another essay of 1927, 'Thomas Middleton', reveals a similar social engagement when considering literary texts. The essay reprints as its second part Eliot's review of Kathleen M. Lynch's *The Social Mode of Restoration Comedy*. Lynch's book links the unique 'absolute' realism of Middleton's comedies directly to the 'social unrest of contemporary London life...class barriers are breaking down' (London: Macmillan, 1926, 24, 26). Eliot uses the same quotations deployed by Lynch—such as those from Middleton's *Michaelmas Term*—to pursue similar ends, reflecting again upon the 'transitions' of Middleton's time as exemplified in class terms (*SE*, 168–9). These reflections underlying his critical and historical stance, of course, bear directly upon what Eliot sought to achieve in *The Waste Land*, II, and *Sweeney Agonistes*.

[28] Lancelot Andrewes, *Seventeen Sermons on the Nativity* (London: Griffith, Farran, Okeden & Welsh, n.d.), 153, 155. Relevant to the tone, both of the speaker of 'Journey of the Magi' and also previously 'Gerontion', is the opening of the next Nativity Sermon, that of 1623 in *Seventeen Sermons*: 'Seeing the text is of seasons, it would not be out of season with itself'. (260)

[29] The Introduction to *Seventeen Sermons* points to the 'puns and quips' which typify Andrewes' style, and which were so objectionable to the Puritans (viii).

equivocation of Eliot's speaker in 'Journey of the Magi'.[30] 'Shakespeare and the Stoicism of Seneca' quoted Clermont's speech on 'the great Necessity' from Chapman's 1613 tragedy, *The Revenge of Bussy d'Ambois* (IV. i), to describe precisely this state of mind, and the broader 'absorption' of stoic ideas into Christianity:

> A man to join himself with the universe
> In his main sway, and make all things fit.
> (quoted *SE*, 131)

This is clearly one of the passages from Early Modern drama that most resonated in Eliot's mind; he had cited it in 1921, in 'The Metaphysical Poets', when noting how 'erudition' altered the sensibility of writers like Donne and Chapman, and how, for both, it allowed a 'sensuous' apprehension to their thought (*SE*, 286).[31] But, what is most notable in Eliot's critical writing of the mid-1920s and beyond is the intensified sense, already implied in 1921 but not developed then, that 'thought', the allusiveness of Chapman's writing ('A man to join' translated Epictetus), is *necessarily* 'stoical'. This is a sense that, of course, has important implication for the religious nature of Eliot's own writing from this point. 'Shakespeare and the Stoicism of Seneca' also shows that Eliot's renewed engagement with these matters had been partly vivified by his encounter with 'Professor Schoell's' recent book on Chapman's sources. Schoell had demonstrated, according to Eliot, that the 'dark' thinking of Chapman resulted from his lifting of his stoicism direct from a range of intermediate writers, such as Marcelo Ficino. It is a 'lifting', according to Eliot, which involved Chapman in translating long passages from those sources, and putting them down in his own writings 'out of context'.[32]

Schoell's Chapman, therefore, is a familiarly traditional figure; commenting on Chapman's use of intermediary scholars to render his stoicism, we are told that 'en vrai homme de la Renaissance, il confound l'oeuvre originale et la commentaire'.[33] The view of Chapman that Schoell created, in fact, resonated with Eliot's recent scepticism about Donne. His sources are 'mal digéré' (poorly digested or integrated), and what makes works like the *Hymns to the Night* so 'difficult', according to Schoell, is that 'il n'y regne aucun ordre' ('there is no order there'). Chapman

---

[30] The aged speaker of Eliot's 'A Song for Simeon' to an extent rehearses that damage from the opposite direction, in an inverse of the Magus's apprehension. *His* agitation is that he has not yet witnessed Christ's advent, and that he might not do so, warranting the subjunctive and imploring nature of his 'Song'.

[31] Eliot would cite the passage again in 'Thinking in Verse: A Survey of Early Seventeenth Century Poetry' (*The Listener*, vol. III, no. 61, March 1930, 441). Herbert Read, in 'The Nature of Metaphysical Poetry', an essay which Eliot had originally included in *The Criterion*, also cites Clermont's passage as a key example of such metaphysics. This is one that Read sees shared by Chapman, and Donne, but which he felt derived for both from Dante (reprinted in *Reason and Romanticism: Essays in Literary Criticism*, London: Faber and Gwyer, 1926, 44). Eliot, although he abetted publication of both the essay and the book which eventually included it, queried, in a review of the book, Read's presumptions. He does so in a way that chimes with his own doubts about Donne and Chapman: 'Mr Read stating that the empirical plane matters little [i.e. in metaphysical writing] and that the psychological matters much, is throwing away a trick' (*The New Criterion*, vol. IV, no. iv, October 1926, 756).

[32] Franck L. Schoell, *Études sur l'Humanisme Continental en Angleterre à la Fin de la Renaissance* (Paris: Librarie Ancienne Honoré Champion, 1926). Schoell notes the Latin origin of Clermont's speech on Necessity on p. 101. Subsequent references to Schoell appear in the text.

[33] 'Like a true Renaissance man, he confuses original work with commentary [upon it].'

simply added example to example, source to source, so that 'la pensée reste amorphe et ne progresse selon aucun règle'.[34] In this context, Schoell noted that it is often impossible to distinguish the basis of the beliefs uttered, or commented upon, in Early Modern texts. Citing Hamlet's remarks upon Fortune (III. ii, 70ff), Schoell concludes that:

> Le stoicisme, à vrai dire, est parfois si fort teinté de Christianisme qu'on ne sait trop si c'est une voix Chrétienne ou une voix franchement Stoïcienne qui se fait entendre.[35]

That haunted question of origination, which had played behind Eliot's determinedly modern poetics from the outset, here takes on a vital resonance, and is one the Ariel Poems and *Ash-Wednesday* set out immediately to capture.

It is clear that Eliot's poetry, in the wake of his confirmation into the Church of England in 1927, displays a Christianity 'teinté' with Stoicism. It is a poetry derived, as with a similar crossing of influence in 'The Hollow Men', from his understanding of Early Modern texts as mediated by recent commentaries.[36] 'Journey of the Magi' and 'A Song for Simeon' add ontological enquiry to this, through their being set at the historical moment of encounter between the Stoic Roman world and the new Christian one—that moment, with its own 'Renaissance' connotations, which was captured in Pater's *Marius the Epicurean*, the work that Eliot had quoted from as early as 1917.

LANCELOT ANDREWES AND *ASH-WEDNESDAY*

Eliot's more expansive critical engagement with Lancelot Andrewes at this moment in his career, taken with his subsequent essay on the Restoration archbishop, John Bramhall, offered further potential for understanding *Ash-Wednesday* and the 'Ariel' poems of the later 1920s. 'Lancelot Andrewes' (1926), whilst gathering up the qualities of Andrewes' sermons that had pressed behind the allusions to him in 'Gerontion', also expanded Eliot's meditations on this crucial Early Modern figure for him. Under this aegis, for instance, the essay carried a long quotation from Canon F.E. Brightman's introduction to his translation of Andrewes' devotional prayers, the *Preces Privatae* (*FLA*, 17–18). Eliot's selection of Brightman's words typically harps upon the prevalence of allusiveness across Andrewes' writings; it was a notion that ran across Brightman's introduction ('His imagination was

---

[34] 'The thinking is unformed and does not progress according to any rule.' Eliot's version of this view of Chapman in his review of Schoell, 'The Sources of Chapman', is to claim that Chapman was a 'man of emotional', rather than 'intellectual', power, a man who did not take 'the trouble to do much thinking himself' (*TLS*, no. 1306, 10 February 1927, 88). The remarks chime in with the view of Shakespeare and Dante given in 'Shakespeare and the Stoicism of Seneca', and 'Dante' (1930).

[35] 'Truly, Stoicism is throughout tainted with Christianity to the extent that it is not easy to say whether it is the voice of a Christian or a committedly Stoical voice which is being heard.'

[36] This is not to say that it is necessary to take the issue as far as John J. Soldo does, and claim that 'Eliot's Stoicism' can be used 'as a convenient tag for his wider sensibility' (*The Tempering of T.S. Eliot* (Epping: Bowker, 1983), 85). The Christian inheritance, as mediated partly by Early Modern sources, is equally vital within Eliot's work, as this chapter maintains.

collective and organising, as it were, rather than speculative and creative').[37] So far, so sympathetic, to one whose poetic method was like Eliot's. But the *nature* of Eliot's quotation from Brightman in 'Lancelot Andrewes' was also telling, since it related to what was, for Brightman, the formal 'poetic' consequence of Andrewes' habit of arranging his prayers 'in a measure to mark the inner structure and the steps and stages of the movement' (L). Andrewes' practice of creating what Brightman called 'new combinations of existing material' took on, as his commentary saw it, a pleasing typography on the page. The ontological consequence of this radical arrangement of the *Preces* became clearer, when Brightman returned to it at the end of his Introduction:

> And again the forms of prayer sometimes consist of lists of words, phrases, synonyms, topics, and this sometimes without context or any external connection with what goes before or follows. Consequently the *Preces* challenge reflexion... and sometimes, if they are to be used at all, must be treated as germs left to us to develop, rather than as prayers which can be recited as they stand. And the external arrangement, isolating as it does, by the use of lines, the several steps which go to make up the movement, at once suggests and encourages the use of devotions. (lvii)

As Brightman pointed out, the 'steps' of the *Preces* are illustrated and demonstrated through their appearance on the page. What such spatial arrangements allow is a range of mediating moments or spaces, in which the devotional reader can 'develop' the intimations provided by the text at each stage. (Eliot seems to use the word 'steps' to the same purpose in *Ash-Wednesday* III, *CPP*, 93.) The 'organisation' that Andrewes brings to this 'solid matter', the materials it provides towards a reader's private prayer, enables at once progression—the climb upwards—and also pause. This is a submission of self to external direction, but also to liberation into personal reflection. It is that dual perspective again, familiar from Eliot's early response to Donne's sermons. Unlike Eliot's fretting at this time about Donne's and Chapman's arbitrary imposition of themselves ('personality', 'psychology') upon their alluded-to texts, and thence upon their readers, Brightman promoted for him a model of adjustment in the Andrewes of the *Preces* (a model which Eliot in his essay noted might be applied also to Andrewes' Sermons [18]):

> To one to whom knowledge is so large an element in life and is itself so living a thing; whose learning is so assimilated as to be identified with his spontaneous self, and has become as available as language itself, originality and reminiscence become in a measure identical. (xxix)

For the self-consciously modern Eliot, 'language itself' was never so readily handy of access or deployment. But the model of 'assimilation' demanded by the *Preces* rested close to his own words for communion with earlier texts, 'saturation' and 'absorption'. As a metaphor for the formal and typographic aspects of the *Preces*, Brightman's repeated 'steps' obviously summons *Ash-Wednesday* III more broadly, a section itself derived from a key moment in Dante's *Purgatorio*, and originally

---

[37] F.E. Brightman, Introduction, *The Preces Privatae of Lancelot Andrewes* (London: Methuen, 1903), xxix. Subsequent references to this book are given in the text.

printed as a separate poem with the Dantean title 'Som de L'Escalina' ('to the topmost of the stair').[38] More loosely, alongside the obvious references to Dante, the metaphor might be applied to the English devotional aspiration of the whole *Ash-Wednesday* sequence, signalled by the five verse paragraphs beginning with 'Because' in the first four lines. Each repetition provides a stage in 'explanation' of the speaker's motivation to progress.

In order for the poem to attune its readership to such aspiration, however, much depended for Eliot upon the nature of the speaker in *Ash-Wednesday*. This is a speaker who, in many ways, after the polyvocalism of *The Waste Land* and the dream-like mixing of voices in 'The Hollow Men', emerges again here as a more meditative dramatic persona comparable to 'Gerontion'. But this meditative voice has other origins as well. Writing about 'Sir John Davies' in 1926, Eliot concentrated upon his subject's long poem on the soul's relation to the body, 'Nosce Teipsum'. Eliot noted that although Davies's 'philosophy' was not original, his style was, since it avoided typical Elizabethan 'flowers of conceit', and achieved a language 'of remarkable clarity and austerity'. *Unlike* the Senecans, with their 'orotund and oratorical' style, Davies's work was praised as 'the language and the tone of solitary mediation; he speaks like a man reasoning with himself in solitude' (*OPP*, 134, 136). Davies's speaker, like that of Donne's poem 'The Extasie', performs a 'dialogue of one', in other words, but more intensely so, in his 'solitude'.[39] Whilst it is tempting to discover, in the iterative structure of Davies's much-anthologized stanzas, quoted by Eliot at the start of his essay, incitement to his own iterations at the start of *Ash-Wednesday*,[40] Eliot did adopt something correlative to the tonal range, and linguistic tenor, of 'Nosce Teipsum' to his poem. He took over, as well, from Davies, the sense that the meditative voice across a long poem must now work 'cumulatively', rather than within the more fractured moments of the verse paragraphs in his earlier work (*OPP*, 135).

Crucial to that meditative process was Eliot's reversion, at the opening of Part V of *Ash-Wednesday*, to those passages on the 'Verbum Infans' in Lancelot Andrewes' Nativity Sermons; these were also passages that had preoccupied Gerontion. The references to the Sermon of 1618 that had fuelled Gerontion's reflections on 'the Word', had, in fact, been given cumulative effect by the Griffin, Farran, Okeden and Welsh edition of Andrewes' *Sermons on the Nativity*, recommended by Eliot in his anniversary essay. Andrewes had reflected in 1606:

> For Him to condescend to be born, as children are born, to become a child—great humility; great *ut Verbum infans, ut tonans vagiens, ut immensus parvullus*; 'that the Word be not able to speak a word, He that thundereth in Heaven cry in a cradle'.[41]

---

[38] Compare the suffering of those who follow Christ envisaged by Simeon, 'Light upon light, mounting the saints' stair' (*CPP*, 105).

[39] Herbert Grierson, *The Poems of John Donne*, vol. I (Oxford: Oxford University Press, 1912), 53.

[40] 'I know my life's a pain and but a span;/I know my sense is mock'd in everything;/And, to conclude, I know myself a Man—' (quoted, *OPP*, 132).

[41] *Seventeen Sermons on the Nativity*, 29. Andrewes returns to his point in Sermons VI (91) and VIII (114) of this selection. 'A Song for Simeon' adopts a similar allusion to Andrewes in its old man's desire for release (*CPP*, 105).

Eliot imagines a possibility in *Ash-Wednesday*, however, that the Word might remain (and not simply because of the child's pre-articulacy) 'unspoken', but also 'unheard'. This is a tragic possibility that the Star might not have directed the Magi to Bethlehem at all, a possibility envisaged by Andrewes: 'For if a sign, if this sign had not been given, no *invenietis*; Christ had not been found.' (195) In Andrewes it amounts to a fear, in his current world of James's court, that the sign might be ignored, a fear inherent in Andrewes' repeated insistence that 'hoc erit signum. But signum vobis, "for you"' ('here shall be a sign, but a sign for you'). (202) Eliot's anxiety that, amid the noise of his contemporary world, the Word might not be registered, carries something of this original burden from Andrewes, and is part of the crucial context out of which *Ash-Wednesday* is derived.

Eliot's insistence that, despite this lack of audition, discovery, or recognition, 'Still is the unspoken word, the Word unheard', to an extent both mirrors and makes a counter-assertion to those Andrewes-like anxieties. In his phrases 'the unstilled world still whirled/About the centre of the silent Word', Eliot drew Sir John Davies's other major work, *Orchestra* (also a source for 'Gerontion'), into his nexus of pieces (*CPP*, 96). In stanza 34 of *Orchestra*, Love is speaking to a 'wild disordered rout'. She seeks to divert their wayward energies towards some more productive activity:

> Behold the world how it is whirled round:
> And for it is so whirled, is named so;
> In whose large volume many rules are found
> Of this new art, which it doth fairly show:
> For your quick eyes, in wandering to and fro
> From east to west, on no one thing can glance
> But, if you mark it well, it seems to dance.[42]

Against 'Chance', a few stanzas later, Love asserts a vision of order, one that resonates within Eliot's vocabulary for those glimpses of underlying 'pattern' in his later work:

> The gods a solemn measure do it deem
> And see a just proportion everywhere,
> And know the points whence first their movings were,
> To which first points when all return again,
> The axle-tree of heaven shall break in twain.[43]

Davies projected a time when the universe should revert to its origin in 'the gods', through terms picked up by Eliot in *Burnt Norton* II.[44] If we grant that the buried

---

[42] Sir John Davies, *Silver Poets of the Sixteenth Century* (London: Dent, 1994), 362. In a letter dated only '25 May' in the Brotherton Library, University of Leeds, G. Wilson Knight Collection, Eliot misremembers the 'world/whirled' 'pun' as being by Donne—but says self-mockingly that his line is an improvement 'rhythmically' on its original (MS20cKnight [K]).

[43] *Orchestra*, stanza 36. Eliot seems to have been drawn particularly to this phase of *Orchestra*—stanza 38 provided the 'cunning passages' analogy for 'History' in 'Gerontion'.

[44] Helen Gardner long ago noted the similarity between Davies' inclusion of the four elements in his 'dance' and Eliot's structuring of each of the *Four Quartets* around a single element in turn. See *The Art of T.S. Eliot* (London: Faber, 1949) 45.

(or partly revealed) metaphor of the dance ('the dance along the artery') echoes behind these moments in Eliot's poetry, from *Ash-Wednesday*, through *Coriolan* I, to *Burnt Norton* V, the word 'still' ('Still is the unspoken word') takes on powerful suggestive force.[45] Florizel's yearning for Perdita, in Shakespeare's *The Winter's Tale*, begins the thought:

> ...when you do dance, I wish you
> A wave o'th'sea, that you might ever do
> Nothing but that, move still, still so,
> And own no other function.
>
> (IV. Iv, 140–3)[46]

Burnt Norton V translated the paradox as 'a Chinese jar still/Moves perpetually in its stillness' (*CPP*, 175). *East Coker* V demanded that we be 'still and still moving' (*CPP*, 183). But when Eliot made the original version of such wordplay in *Ash-Wednesday*, the poetry gathered a different force. As *Ash-Wednesday* I enjoins, in a phrase which draws also on the Psalms and Pascal: 'Teach us to sit still.' 'Still is the unspoken word', in Part V, adds strength to this, through its resonating, not only with the theological contemplation of signs that Eliot had derived from Andrewes, but, further, with the emotional world of the first four Ariel Poems, which were written alongside *Ash-Wednesday*.

As the opening of *Ash-Wednesday* V posits, 'If the lost word is lost' (compare the 'lost heart', 'lost lilac', 'lost sea voices' of VI): Perdita is literally the 'lost word', the word for that which is lost, which is to be redeemed, as Marina (named for the sea upon which she was born), was, crucially, for Eliot, to be redeemed in *Pericles*. In Davies's terms, and in Eliot's variation and meditation, 'if you mark it well', the dance will be revealed everywhere. It will be revelatory, or speaking, of truths normally 'unheard'; but it will also centre upon that paradox, drawn from Shakespeare and from Davies, that it is the point of 'stillness' which will bring order, or 'pattern', to the seemingly 'lost', or aberrant, energies of the universe, as also of human society.

To this extent, the prophetic strain in *Ash-Wednesday* derived from both Andrewes and Shakespeare, regathers its 'knowledge' of aberrance and untimeliness from 'Gerontion'. The parenthetical self-description by the poem's speaker near the beginning as an 'agèd eagle' (the stress marking on the second syllable ensures and advertises its precious archaism) 'explains' the loss of hope towards any redemption ('still' as inertia) in the poem. Andrewes' Nativity sermon of 1606 draws upon Deuteronomy 31, to remind us of an aspect of Christ's relation to his people, which had been prophesied by Moses, is provided via the 'simile, stretch forth His wings "as the eagle over her young ones", and take them ... bear them, and bear them through' (26).[47] The Nativity sermon of 1611 opens with a page upon the eagle revealed by the prophets, and especially St John:

[45] Terence Hawkes structures his response, to Eliot's response, to Shakespeare around the metaphor of the dance in *Meaning By Shakespeare* (London: Routledge, 1992), 90–120. My interpretation here does not tread upon his toes in any way.

[46] *Shakespeare's Comedy of A Winter's Tale*, ed. Israel Gollancz (London: J.M. Dent, Temple Edition, 1894), 86.

[47] The passage from *Coriolanus* in which the title character compares himself to 'an eagle in a dovecote' had been cited by Eliot as early as 1919, in '"Rhetoric" and Poetic Drama' (*SW*, 68).

As an eagle in the clouds he first mounteth wonderfully high beyond Moses and his *in principio*, with a higher in principio than it; beyond Genesis and the world's creation...and 'the Word was then with God, and was God'. (84)[48]

Our 'agèd eagle' has wings that are 'no longer wings to fly' (*CPP*, 90). Like Gerontion, his age makes him both out of step with the activities and progression of his times, but also all the more sensitive to them. The speaker of *Ash-Wednesday*'s reversal of fresh, original associations and ascents ('mounteth'), the tiredness and frustration in the voice ('Why should'?), is inherent in the repeated reversions across the sequence to invocation of the redemptive female figure, the Lady. As Part V again has it, the word/Word will *not* 'be found' (read aloud, the capital letter is 'unheard'). Not found, and not here, and not now ('The right time and the right place are not here' [96]). That unseasonableness, which runs from Andrewes through 'Journey of the Magi', as it had through 'Gerontion' previously, continues setting the tone of Eliot's poetry.

The speaker of *Ash-Wednesday* cannot utter the repentance that had governed the poem's central and original metaphor of 'turning'—that is, a turning (back) towards God. Guido Cavalcanti's *Ballata XI*, given new currency for Eliot and others by Ezra Pound's several re-translations of it, casts the *Ballata* itself as a missive to a Lady literally remote, and so feared 'lost', from the poet-lover. 'Perch'io non spero di tornar già mai': 'Because no hope is left to me, Ballatetta,/Of return to Tuscany,/Light-foot go thou some fleet way/Unto my Lady straightway.'[49] It is as though the confirmed distance between poet and object of desire, in the poem recovered by Pound, encouraged, in *Ash-Wednesday*, that reversal of the impetus towards repentance in Eliot's other source, Andrewes' Ash-Wednesday sermon of 1619. That sermon re-presents Andrewes' variations upon Joel II, 12, 13 ('Turn you unto me with all your heart'). Andrewes is clear about the twofold nature of repentance, its doubleness in time:

> First, a 'turn', wherein we look forward to God, and with our 'whole heart' Resolve to turn to Him. Then a turn again, wherein we look backward to our sins wherein we have turned from God, and with beholding them our very heart breaketh. These two are distinct, both in nature and names; one, conversion from sin; the other, contrition for sin.[50]

In Andrewes' *Preces Privatiae*, 'Time' and 'Place' are given as the first two of the 'Circumstances for Prayer' ('Accompaniments' being the third).[51] The 'right' time and place are not available for Eliot's modern and agèd speaker, leaving a lamented absence that haunts *Ash-Wednesday*.

This induces here, as across Eliot's later poetry, such as *Burnt Norton* I, a sense of regret, mourning for lost possibilities. 'Mourning' is linked in Joel, together with 'weeping', 'fasting', as part of the contrition necessary to complete repentance.

---

[48] Logan Pearsall Smith calls one passage in *Donne's Sermons: Selected Passages* 'Eagle's Wings', in which a preacher is compared to an eagle, 'that every soul in the congregation might see as he sees' (Oxford: Clarendon Press, 1919, 17).

[49] *The Translations of Ezra Pound* (London: Faber, 1943), 121.

[50] Lancelot Andrewes, *Selected Writings*, ed. P.E. Hewison (Manchester, Carcanet, 1995), 70. Subsequent references to this selection appear in the text.

[51] Andrewes, *Preces Privatiae*, 9.

'Mourning' is thence reflected upon by Andrewes, in this Ash-Wednesday sermon, as 'the affection of sorrow... the sorrow which reason itself can yield'. (71) This is sorrow at 'our sins past', which we must 'set before us and look at sadly'. 'But we seek no place, we allow no time for it. Our other affairs take up so much as we can spare'. However, such mourning 'will become' 'the weightiest affair of all'. (81–2) The speaker in Eliot's *Ash-Wednesday*, lamenting 'Why should I mourn', and his wearied acceptance of former wonders as 'usual', reveals the measure of his Baudelairean *aboulie*, but also the lack of purchase upon salvation or redemption allowed him, in 'one time... one place', where there is 'not enough silence', 'No place of grace', 'No time', as Part V has it (*CPP*, 96). He has no hope to 'turn', or yet to 'turn again', in the adoption of Andrewes' gestural iconography, since neither place nor time is allowed in these 'circumstances'. The poem resides in that unlocatedness to the end, imploring 'Pray for us... will the veiled sister pray.' A. David Moody's reading of *Ash-Wednesday* is compelling in that, despite its acceptance of an established critical view that the achievement of the sequence lies in its 'deliberate and effective entering upon "the way of penance" which means dying into the New Life', Eliot's poetry here remains perplexing, and also unlikeable.[52] Close attention to the Early Modern contexts of the poem suggests that such unease is more a 'deliberate' aspect of Eliot's purpose in *Ash-Wednesday* than has previously been considered, however. The religious and literary bases to which the sequence recurs instil an understanding that, whatever the metaphoric and structural value of progressive climbing or verbal consonance, 'circumstance'—historical or personal—inevitably prevents the achievement of a state of 'stillness' or 'grace'.

'MARINA'

Similar imprecations to those in *Ash-Wednesday*, and their connection with 'Time' and 'place', mark out the Ariel poems Eliot was working on at this time in the late 1920s. These ideas find their fullest expression in 'Marina', which appropriates various Shakespearean redemption narratives towards its own quest for a situation of visionary comfort. *Ash-Wednesday* stands in a very complex and difficult relation to the theological tradition coming down from the Early Modern period, to which it seeks to align itself. 'Marina' tunes into similarly multivalent historical implication, in order to foster a correlative sense of relief, and exhaustion, from its unresolved context. In order to do so, it draws upon several crucial mediating critical sources, as Eliot in the later 1920s moved forward his understanding of what a 'religious', as opposed to a 'devotional', version of a metaphysical poetic might become.[53]

---

[52] A. David Moody, *Thomas Stearns Eliot: Poet* (Cambridge: Cambridge University Press, 1994), 152–4.

[53] In 1930, Eliot made clear that what he meant by 'religious' is 'what is inspired by religious feeling of some kind'; by 'devotional' that which is 'directly about some subject connected with revealed religion.' Surprisingly, the work of Henry Vaughan is, therefore, 'religious'; that of Herbert and Crashaw 'devotional'. See 'The Devotional Poets of the Seventeenth Century: Donne, Herbert, Crashaw', *The Listener*, Vol. III no. 63, 26th March 1930, 552.

In his Introduction promoting G. Wilson Knight's *The Wheel of Fire* (1930), Eliot linked Knight's work to Colin Still's 'interesting book' *Shakespeare's Mystery Play*. Both critics' approach to Shakespeare, in Eliot's view, revealed how the 'appearances' visible through language and imagery, manifest on the writing's surface, present a hidden 'reality' inhering within it.[54] Eliot takes up here again the notion of the cryptogram, in a more anthropological and religious context. Still's 1921 study of *The Tempest* spoke to many of Eliot's preoccupations, from *The Waste Land*, through *Ash-Wednesday*, to the Ariel and later poems. Still's method resonated both with Eliot's anthropological knowledge, and with his evolving interest in Christian tropology. For Still, Shakespeare's last play presented a 'sustained allegory', founded upon ancient initiation ceremonies; ceremonies that are interchangeable, in Still's rendering, with the rituals of the Christian Church. That 'sea-change' undergone in Ariel's vital song 'Full fathom five' ('Those are pearls that were his eyes'), for instance, is elided by Still into a re-echo of 'baptism in the Christian church and the "washings" in the pagan rites, it is represented as a physical occurrence'.[55] That important source for *The Waste Land* is given a double significance in Still's book, which appeared while Eliot was working on his poem. Still defined *The Tempest* as a 'pilgrimage from Purgatory to Paradise', one for which his constant analogy came from Dante: Miranda is cast as a later Beatrice, representative of purity, but also of Wisdom. (62) Premonitory of Eliot's elemental symbolism in *Four Quartets*, Still insisted that earth, water, fire, and air give allegorical and figural significance to this 'pilgrimage', which, in consequence, derived what we might now conceive of as an Eliotic doubleness:

> They are allegorical figures which represent not only states of existence after death but also *states of consciousness to which we can attain during life*. Thus a crossing of the River Styx (WATER) to Elysium (AIR) represents not only the shedding of the EARTHLY and WATERLY bodies at death, but also the ascent of the consciousness through the plane of sensuous emotion to the plane of reason. In other words, a purely subjective experience may be depicted as a journey of the living through the mythical abodes of the dead. (92)

The last chapter investigated the tropological significance given (via Lamb) to the structure of *The Waste Land* by such 'crossing' from 'EARTHLY' and 'WATERLY' states or stages. In a rhetorical and conceptual turn, relevant to Eliot's reconsideration of John Donne in the mid-1920s, Still saw the ascent through 'successive stages or planes of consciousness' as symbolic of 'psychological changes': *The Tempest* represents a religious, physical, *and* 'psychological pilgrimage'. (105, 118) Such integrative understanding might be used, by an Eliot, to question a writer like Donne, for his lack of a similarly progressive symbolism towards what Still called

---

[54] T.S. Eliot, 'Introduction' to G. Wilson Knight, *The Wheel of Fire* (London: Oxford University Press, 1930), p. xix. Wilson Knight signalled his own debt to Still's 'too little recognised landmark in Shakespearian Studies' in his 'Prefatory Note' to the 1951 edition of his 1931 book *The Imperial Theme* (London: Methuen), vii.

[55] Colin Still, *Shakespeare's Mystery Play: A Study of The Tempest* (London: Cecil Palmer, 1921), 19, 42. Subsequent page references to this book are given in the text.

'the psychology of salvation.' (118) Having elaborated *The Tempest*'s symbolism through its multiple sources and resonances, as he saw them, Still concluded by finding analogies between Miranda/Beatrice and Princesses from fairy-tales, but also with Shakespeare's Perdita from *The Winter's Tale*. Still's description of these perceived analogies, though, conjured Shakespeare's Marina from *Pericles*, shortly to be re-figured by Eliot. Still quoted Prospero's asseveration several times:

> I have done nothing but in care of thee,
> Of thee, my dear one, thee, my daughter, who
> Art ignorant of what thou art...
>
> (I. ii, 16ff)[56]

In Shakespeare's late plays, the conception of a miraculous daughterly redemption, discovered as miraculous final consequence of a repeatedly aberrant fatherhood, links Prospero to Pericles and Leontes, and to the speaker of the final line of Eliot's 'Marina' ('My daughter'). But Still related the specific imagery of *The Tempest*—including Miranda's sleep on being told her life story by Prospero, and the gathering of logs by Ferdinand—to the forest in the Sleeping Beauty myth. These are a set of images which come together in 'Marina' also. Eliot's ocean scene echoes with 'woodsong', a singing 'woodthrush', and laughter heard amidst leaves (looking forward to *Four Quartets*), in a scene set 'Under sleep, where all the waters meet' (*CPP*, 109). For Still, such meeting points, transitional phases in his concept of elemental 'ascent', took on special significance. Mist, the interstitial phase between water and air, formed the link between 'the plane of sensuous emotion' and 'the plane of reason'—that space where, for Eliot, metaphysical poetry truly resided. (92) Yet, 'mythologically', for Still, mist also represented Purgatory, the place of expiation of sins, before progression towards salvation. (108) The 'fog' obscuring the Maine coast in 'Marina' is potentially another such place of progression through ambivalence to 'grace'. Yet the poem remains notably unresolved: the lone bird, calling through the fog at the end, is the only sign of Dantean 'hope'.[57]

Such symbolic potential in Eliot's poem comes along with a precise form of metrical experimentation, one that mimics the progression towards liberation and recovery which 'Marina' effects. If 'Marina' bears the marks of the religious anthropology of Still, and the thoughts upon the 'music' and symbolism of poetry in Wilson Knight, it also shares with other of the Ariel poems a sense of the benefits gained in the development of Shakespeare's late verse *technique*. This is an insight that sees Shakespeare's versification moving ever towards a more intense poetic

---

[56] *Shakespeare's Comedy of The Tempest*, ed. Israel Gollancz (London: J.M. Dent, 1896), 5–6.
[57] Eliot's (and Still's) paradigm of the voyage to salvation would have received reinforcement from other conceits with which he was engaged from the mid-1920s. For example, the biographical introduction by Christobel M. Hood to a printing of the shorter poems of the poet and martyr Robert Southwell quotes passages which deploy similarly cryptogrammatic, but foreboding metaphors, as in Southwell's letter of 16 January 1590: 'We sail in the midst of these stormy waves with no small danger, from which, nevertheless, it has pleased Our Lord hitherto to deliver us.' (*The Book of Robert Southwell, Priest, Poet, Prisoner*, Oxford: Basil Blackwell, 1926, 28). Eliot's review of Hood's work, 'The Author of the "Burning Babe"', notes the 'great interest' of her introduction, but links Southwell's poetry to the 'concettismo' of Crashaw, its 'fusion or confusion' of the human and divine, in contrast to the clarities of Donne's work (*TLS*, no. 1278, 29 July 1926, 508).

freedom. Eliot allowed J.M. Robertson to publish two reflections in *The Criterion*, 'The Evolution of English Blank Verse' (1924) and 'The Scansion of Shakespeare' (1929), which chimed in with his own earlier 'Reflections on *Vers Libre*', but which gave further literary-historical underpinning to such ideas. In 1924, Robertson noted that Shakespeare's 'advance' in metrical terms was dependent upon an 'unshackled variety of stress *within* the line' and 'interfluent sense', whereby the line-units are 'felt only as pulsation in a movement that may pause anywhere'. Across his career, Robertson claimed, Shakespeare had become 'ever more untrammelled' in this direction.[58] The flexibility of metre in later Shakespeare, then, was equivalent to the expansion of dramatic possibility in his work. Robertson's 'The Scansion of Shakespeare' in 1929 took these points ever further. Robertson dismissed, in criticism of these plays, any metrical analysis as 'mere ways of counting syllables'. In his view, such analysis was an irrelevance, in comparison with Shakespeare's increasing understanding that 'true metre is the rhythmic time value of the total line'.[59]

'Marina', written under the aegis of the late play *Pericles, Prince of Tyre*, upon which Shakespeare collaborated with George Wilkins, was Eliot's most orchestrated exploitation of such metrical possibility so far in his career. The poem's speaker is notoriously cast in what Eliot called a 'crisscross' role, 'interfluent', in that he draws his voice both from Pericles and from another father (one who actually destroys his offspring rather than, like Pericles, thinking that he has), the Hercules of Seneca's *Hercules Furens*.[60] But, although 'Marina' sustains a sense of the dramatic continuities possible within its largely unpunctuated movement, it shares also another feature of the musical and syntactical freedoms of late Shakespearian style. *Pericles* contains passages that, in their rendering of extreme emotion, are notoriously elliptical. An early example occurs when Pericles narrates his discovery of the incest between Antiochus and the daughter whom he, Pericles, had been set to marry. The speech is to his councillor and friend, Helicanus, who has sought to assuage Pericles' disturbance, once he finds the incest out:

> Thou speak'st like a physician, Helicanus,
> That minister'st a potion unto me
> That thou wouldst tremble to receive thyself.
> Attend me then: I went to Antioch,
> Where, as thou knowst, against the face of death,
> I sought the purchase of a glorious beauty
> From whence an issue I might propagate,

[58] J.M. Robertson, 'The Evolution of Blank Verse', *The Criterion*, vol. II, no. 6, February 1924, 184. This issue also contains Eliot's 'Four Elizabethan Dramatists'. Robertson's remarks are reminiscent of Ezra Pound's 'principle' that poetic rhythm should be composed 'in the sequence of the musical phrase, not in the sequence of a metronome' (*Literary Essays of Ezra Pound*, ed. T.S. Eliot, London: Faber, 1954, 3).

[59] J.M. Robertson, 'The Scansion of Shakespeare', *The Criterion*, vol. VIII, no. xxxiii, July 1929, 640.

[60] Eliot noted the 'crisscross' nature of his poem in the letter accompanying his donation of the manuscript of 'Marina' to the Bodleian Library, Oxford (MS Don C 23/1–3 [x.ii.100]). Eliot added Seneca's original line as the poem's epigraph when he typed up his first draft ('Quis hic locus, quae region, quae mundi plaga?').

> Are arms to princes and bring joys to subjects.
> Her face was to mine eye beyond all wonder;
> The rest—hark in thine ear—as black as incest.
> (I. ii, 65–72)[61]

The ellipses and elisions here largely depend upon the connectives, which form a major structural role in the sentence, and also sustain the inclusion of subordinate detail—'That minister'st...That thou', or 'From whence...[Which] Are arms'. 'Marina' has 'what...what...what' structuring its opening verse paragraph, and, more proximately to Pericles' speech above, 'Those...those...those...Those...// Are become unsubstantial', so elliptically 'linking' the second and third verse paragraphs. The poem also puts 'Made' at the start of a sentence, eliding the personal pronoun 'I', which had been established as the subject in a previous sentence (*CPP*, 109, 110). Norman Dugdale Sykes noted, in 1919, that this last form of 'omission of the relative pronoun in the nominative case', alongside 'verbal antithesis', such as 'life and death', formed the 'peculiarities' of the Wilkins style, as it is exemplified in *Pericles*.[62] Eliot, who was familiar with Dugdale Sykes' work, displayed a similar liking for such antitheses, from *Sweeney Agonistes* onwards. Eliot's early poetry had manifested some of its *vers libre* surprise through occasional use of ellipsis, as in 'The Love Song of J. Alfred Prufrock', 'I am not Prince Hamlet.../Am an attendant lord' (*CPP*, 16). But 'Marina', written under the aegis of the rhythms of *Pericles*, performs his starkest use of ellipsis, and omission of subject, from its sentence construction.[63]

Robertson, and other contemporary critics, pointed frequently to the effect of similar rhythmic innovation in the work of John Donne. They saw the increasing rhythmic experiment by Shakespeare, across his career, as evolving towards ever more complex and sophisticated rendering of spoken character as '*dramatic*'. As such, Shakespeare's technical innovations are linked to a version of selfhood in his work that is familiar to Eliot's modern(ist) conception. Writing on *The Problem of the Shakespeare Sonnets* in 1926, in a book that garnered the last supportive review about his critical method from Eliot, J.M. Robertson emphasized that Shakespeare 'is the dramatist of human interaction, absorbed in the spectacle, not in himself'. The Sonnets, in this view, are the expression of an invented character, not of Shakespeare personally.[64] Eliot could recover this sort of tonal implication: his absorption of an adapted line from Shakespeare's sonnet XXIX (line 7) into *Ash-Wednesday* ('Desiring this man's gift and that man's scope') immediately cast the seemingly confessional mode of the sequence's opening ('Because I do not

---

[61] *Shakespeare's Tragedy of Pericles*, ed. Israel Gollancz (London, J.M. Dent, 1896), 14. Subsequent references to this edition are given in the text. Modern editors continue to attribute such ellipses to the work of Wilkins, whose style was characterized by such features. See, for example, the Arden Shakespeare version of the play, edited by Suzanne Gossett (London: Thomson, 2004), 200.

[62] Norman Dugdale Sykes, *Sidelights on Shakespeare: Studies of Two Noble Kinsmen and Other Plays* (Stratford-upon-Avon: The Shakespeare Head Press, 1919), 150, 165.

[63] Eliot exchanged letters with Dugdale Sykes about Tourneur's plays in 1922 (*LI*, 635–6); he later recommended Sykes' work on Tourneur and Middleton (*SE*, 186).

[64] J.M. Robertson, *The Problem of the Shakespeare Sonnets* (London: Routledge, 1926), 212–3. Eliot's review, in which he says that he agrees with Robertson's method in this book, as he always had done, appeared in *The Nation and Athenaeum*, vol. XL, no. 19 (12 February 1927), 664.

hope') within a more theatrical modality.[65] This is confirmed, as mentioned above, by the ready self-description of the speaker as an 'agèd eagle', a persona consistent with the contemporary Magus, Simeon, and with the world-weary speaker of 'Animula' (who also shares much of the life view of J. Alfred Prufrock).[66]

The cumulative idea that self is achieved through paradoxically theatrical methods, visible from Eliot's recent reading and writing, has direct consequences for the address and purpose of 'Marina'. The rhetorical questioning of the piece is interestingly a matter of tone, or pacing, which is enforced on the poem's readers. Like Yeats in some of his most famous later work, Eliot minimally deploys question marks here. The reader is, in this sense, made to choose how to perform the piece, and so to perform the uncertain progress towards redemption that the poem presents. In 'Marina' such questions are directly derived from the Senecan reference of the poem's epigraph. And they also share much of the baffled statements of amazement from Shakespeare's *Pericles*, when he understands, in Act V scene i, that it is true that Marina, whom he had thought drowned, has been returned to him: 'At sea: What mother?' (105); 'What was thy mother's name?' (107); 'Tell me…what this maid is' (106). When Pericles begins to lose his senses under the pressure of this miracle, he hears music (or does he?):[67] 'But hark, what music?' (108); 'But what music?' (108). There is a link between hearing and comprehension, which reminds us of *Ash-Wednesday*'s 'unheard', but which is most tellingly transmuted by Eliot in 'A Song for Simeon' as the 'unspeaking and unspoken' Word of God, or again, in 'Marina' as the 'unspoken'.[68]

The need to decipher people's nature, and even their living or dead state, from physical signs, runs through *Pericles*, from that early speech about the 'face' of Antiochus' daughter cited above, a face which is ambiguously 'read' by Pericles as a 'book of praises, where is read/Nothing but curious pleasures' (I. i, 15–16). Such disturbance around the identification of life, beauty, wonder, and also corruption, in *Pericles* leads the father, upon rediscovery of his daughter, Marina, to enquire:

[65] A very early draft of the opening of *Ash-Wednesday* had the speaker asking why he should 'emulate' such 'things' as the Shakespeare line, as though aware of the inescapability, but also of the need to kick back against, the tradition. Hayward Bequest, King's College, Cambridge, ms V6.

[66] 'Animula' traces the development of a child through a rapidly sketched set of incidents. In this, it (along with the final Ariel poem, 'The Cultivation of Christmas Trees') forms a comment on the religious poetry of Henry Vaughan. Eliot responded with impatience to an edition of Vaughan's work edited by Edmund Blunden in 1927. He asserted that Vaughan's poems indulged 'in the luxury of reminiscence of childhood', and criticized Blunden for his 'delight' in this. Such 'reminiscence' is 'weak'; such scenes are 'something to be buried and done with'. The spiritual purpose of 'Animula' is, presumably, partly offered as a corrective ('The Silurist', *The Dial*, September 1927, 261).

[67] The Arden editor, Suzanne Gossett, queries whether the music should really be played (390).

[68] Chapter IX of Percy Allen's *Shakespeare, Jonson, and Wilkins as Borrowers: A Study in Elizabethan Dramatic Origins and Imitations* considers the authorship of *Pericles* (London: Cecil Palmer, 1928). Eliot reviewed the book favourably, singling out Allen's raising of the issue that poets borrow as much from themselves, and their own earlier work, as they do from others (something amply proven in Eliot's practice in the current book; *TLS*, no. 1366, 5 April 1928, 255). Allen's point had been that Shakespeare, such is his greatness, *never* borrowed from himself. Those passages in *Pericles* which look as though he had are poor imitations by Wilkins of renowned Shakespeare originals. (211) Allen's preliminary remarks trace his interest in Elizabethan borrowing to his seeing a production of *Pericles* at the Phoenix Society in the Old Vic season 1923–4. I have not been able to substantiate whether Eliot attended the production of a play so important to him, although he attended performances of other plays in this season (*LII*, 360–2, 432–3).

But are you flesh and blood?
Have you a working pulse? and are no fairy?
(V. i, 143–4)

Pericles declares himself to be within 'the rarest dream', unable to dissociate from the swarming delusions of his brain the hoped-for relief that his daughter is not lost. Eliot compacts these various issues of reading, from his source, into a few phrases ('What is this face, less clear and clearer/The pulse in the arm'). But the crucial questions, the doubt and uncertainty of identification, remain as markers of his modern sensibility.[69]

At the heart of Shakespeare's and Wilkins' *Pericles*, and instilled in its elliptical metrics, as in Eliot's, are multiple disconnections, losses, and dislocations: the action moves bewilderingly between Antioch, Tyre, Tarsus, Pentapolis, Ephesus, and Mytilene, and the dangerous seas between them.[70] Pericles' 'loss' of his wife, Thaisa, and of his daughter, in a shipwreck, finds multiple metaphorical resonances across the rest of the play, as does the projection of these qualities in Eliot's poem.[71] Tarsus suffers famine, and its king, Creon, laments that 'So sharp are hunger's teeth that man and wife/Draw lots who first shall die to lengthen life' (I. iv, 45–6). Marina, lamenting her dull life after her resurrection from the sea, rants that:

> most ungentle fortune
> Have placed me in this sty, where, since I came,
> Diseases have been sold dearer than physic,
> O, that the gods
> Would set me free from this unhallow'd place,
> Though they did change me to the meanest bird
> That flies i' the purer air!
> (IV. vi, 102–8) (90–1)

Eliot's 'sty of contentment' is here, but also perhaps the dangerous thrill of the 'glory of the hummingbird'. The ejaculated 'O' in line 5 of 'Marina' is true to the high-wrought tension of Shakespeare's play, and is to be heard from many characters: from Pericles in the storm ('O, still/Thy deafening dreadful thunders', III. i, 4); from Thaisa on being restored to Pericles ('O royal Pericles' 'O let me look!' 'O my lord', V. iii, 14, 27, 30); most notably, for Eliot, from Thaisa's father, calling her attention to the duty of nobility towards women ('O, attend, my daughter', II. iii, 57) (39).[72]

---

[69] Pericles had earlier surprisingly reassured Antiochus that, despite the latter's incest, he would come to some contentment, since 'sore eyes see clear' (I. i, 100).

[70] Eliot first encountered the work of G. Wilson Knight when Knight sent Faber a putative book on Shakespeare's Late Plays, *Thaisa* (Tate, ed., *T.S. Eliot: The Man and his Work*, 247). Although not published in this form, Knight's ideas about *Pericles* did appear in *The Shakespearean Tempest* (London: Oxford University Press, 1932). Knight's pages on the play make this point about the significance of the sea to the play's themes: 'Love, marriage, birth—all are here opposed by tempests, a whirl of sweet things rocked, lost, yet saved amid tempestuous adventure. So Pericles welcomes the new-born babe [Marina], "this fresh-new sea-farer".' (222)

[71] In 'John Ford' (1932), Eliot links Marina to the fate of Ercola, who is reconciled to her aged father Meleander only at the end of Ford's *The Lover's Melancholy* (*SE*, 195). Meleander's own words about the loss of Ercola play an important role, as we shall see, in Eliot's thinking about *The Rock* and *Little Gidding*.

[72] The first draft of 'Marina' saw Eliot repeating 'O my daughter' (in all versions of line 5 of the poem) in the final line also—he dropped the 'O' in his second draft. Bodleian Library, Oxford, MS. Don. *c.*23/1–3 (x.ii.100).

What is striking about Eliot's rhetorically gestural and largely unpunctuated 'Marina', of course, is that this panoply of allusive pressure behind the poem, the direct questions about provenance and identity, are curiously located for readers within its aural texture. The question mark in its Senecan epigraph is echoed only once in the poem ('Given or lent?'), although questions are being incanted throughout. 'Marina' hovers between a curious presence and absence, therefore. It presents an ultimate rendition of that ghostly interplay of, and between, source texts, and the new invention of them, in the 'circumstances' of the modern poem. The stoical here is muted within the Romance, the regenerative symbolism of the rebirth out of the baptismal waters—to adopt the anthropological approach of G. Wilson Knight and Colin Still. But Stoicism remains a part of the pressure behind Eliot's text, and questions its Romance ambition. The boat, after all, needs 'caulking'.

It is true of course that the Chapman-like interweaving of the Senecan/Herculean with Christian reconciliation is integral to the 'crisscross' nature of the poem.[73] The Shakespearean motifs in 'Marina' suggest humility, before the recognition and redemption of the living child. The Senecan motifs suggest a murderous denial of such possibility. What this implies is that the poem's journey towards the scarce-conceived hope of yielding the self to something beyond (the 'new world'— in every sense—mentioned in the poem's first draft) is crossed by its immediate thwarting, at least in Eliot's own mind.[74] The possibility that the rhetoric thinly veils a vaingloriousness on the part of its speaker, a ridiculous and hollow form of 'self-dramatisation', is everywhere present in Eliot's belated work. What the Chapman echo of Seneca might urge us towards is a further understanding of the ways in which Eliot was aware that 'hope', proclaimed at the end of 'Marina', might become corrupted into sham rhetoric. It might become implicated in a quotidian, or political, expediency that undermined the work's otherwise mythic or Christian purpose, as a true balance between these tendencies is virtually impossible to sustain.

'CORIOLAN'

After the religious determinations of the symbolism in 'Marina', sham and political expediency then became foregrounded in Eliot's unfinished sequence of the first years of the 1930s, 'Coriolan'. That the religious and the political were implicated had been acknowledged by him in the notorious preface to *For Lancelot Andrewes*, and in the book's discussion of religious 'order' and 'style'. Such troubled implication

---

[73] Raymond B. Waddington has demonstrated that Chapman, by making this link in plays such as *Bussy d'Ambois*, is drawing upon an association familiar to Early Modern mythographers, including Francis Bacon, whereby Hercules, through his voyage to free Prometheus, was associated with the Christian Word's quest to free the flesh into spirit (*The Mind's Empire: Myth and Form in George Chapman's Narrative Poems*, Baltimore: Johns Hopkins U.P., 1974, 33–4).

[74] Denis Donoghue has admired the perfect 'closure' of 'Marina', moving as it does 'from the present tense to the past to the future and back to the present'. But he also recognizes that, in another sense, the poem is not at all closed, but continually moving forward. See 'Eliot's "Marina" and Closure', *The Hudson Review*, vol. 49, no. 3 (Autumn 1996), 365.

exercised Eliot more importunately in the later 1920s, and into the 1930s, than hitherto. Writing of the (to him) ideal, balanced, Anglo-Catholic theology of John Bramhall, a bishop of the Restoration period whom he casts as a successor to Andrewes, Eliot claims that:

> [Bramhall's] thinking is a perfect example of the pursuit of the *via media*, and the *via media* is of all ways the most difficult to follow. It requires discipline and self-control, it requires both imagination and hold on reality. In a period of debility like our own, few men have the energy to follow the middle way in government; for lazy or tired minds there is only extremity or apathy: dictatorship or communism, with enthusiasm or with indifference. (*FLA*, 34)

Bramhall's major work, his *Just Vindication of the English Church*, had in fact demanded:

> obedience entire to the universal Church from the communicant, who disbelieves nothing in Holy Scripture, and if he hold any errors unwittingly and unwillingly, doth implicitly renounce them by his fuller and more firm adherence to infallible rule.

Bramhall married such 'obedience entire' to the Church to an absolute monarchism, on the lines declared by Eliot in his famous *credo*, which formed the Preface to *For Lancelot Andrewes*.

In his book on Bramhall that instigated Eliot's review-essay in 1927, W.J. Sparrow-Simpson included this last citation, from Bramhall's *Just Vindication*, as part of his summary of the bishop's beliefs. Yet Sparrow-Simpson made it clear that, for him, Bramhall's 'political conception' was absolutely 'contrary' to that 'prevailing in the twentieth-century. Bramhall represents the rights of despotism.'[75] Eliot, in his 'John Bramhall', made no such demurral. He spent much time, instead, offering his own extension of Bramhall's ideas, by attacking the 'chaotic' mind, and the 'psychological analysis', of Bramhall's contemporary, the anti-monarchist Thomas Hobbes—an echo of his recent remarks about Donne (*FLA*, 29, 33).[76] But Eliot's own work of the later 1920s had continued to explore the 'apathy' of 'tired' minds struggling to sustain belief. The cross-currents of *Ash-Wednesday* mount a dramatization, after all, of a stranded speaker close to *aboulie* ('Why should...?'). This is someone who seems abject before the voices of the past. Paradoxically, however, this is also a speaker lacking that 'historical sense' which Eliot saw as a glowing quality of Bramhall (*FLA*, 34)—'historical sense', of course, which in 1919 had promoted 'Tradition' and its relation to new works.[77]

---

[75] W.J. Sparrow-Simpson, *Archbishop Bramhall* (London: Society for Promoting Christian Knowledge, 1927), 107. The quotations from the *Just Vindication* are given on p. 151.

[76] Eliot's derision at Hobbes in this essay is surprising. Its dismissive tone exceeds anything he reserves for other critics or philosophers, outside of *After Strange Gods* (1934). But it perhaps discovered its impetus from F.L. Woodward's essay, 'Thomas Hobbes', in *Social and Political Ideas of the Sixteenth and Seventeenth Centuries*, edited by F.J.C. Hearnshaw (reviewed by Eliot in the *TLS*, 11 November 1926). Woodward scorns the presumption behind Hobbes's anti-monarchist atheism: 'Where then is Leviathan? How are the mighty fallen!' (London: George Harrap, 1926, 170).

[77] Eliot had recently quoted at length from a contemporary French study of Elizabethan literary collaboration which reflected on 'l'inertie mentale', as a force that might be countered by collaboration: 'l'inertie mentale nous fait répéter nos actes, nos pensées, nos attitudes, nos paroles', Maurice

The difficulties of sustaining, like Bramhall, a disciplined faith in a hostile political context would, of course, form the dramatic impetus of Eliot's first play, *Murder in the Cathedral*. More immediately, what Sparrow-Simpson identifies as an absolutist belief, which carries political resonance, would receive displaced consideration in the two parts of Eliot's abandoned 'Coriolan'. That *Coriolanus* formed one of the compelling Shakespeare plays for Eliot has been well attested by Neil Corcoran in his *Shakespeare and the Modern Poet*.[78] '"Rhetoric" and Poetic Drama' (1919) had held up Coriolanus' late speech, 'If you have writ your annals true', alongside Othello's and Timon's last words, as examples of those 'really fine' moments where a character '*sees himself* in a dramatic light' (*SW*, 68): Donne's vigilance, *in extremis*. Eliot's striking early formulation is precursor to the conclusions about Othello in the 1927 'Shakespeare and the Stoicism of Seneca'. 'Hamlet and his Problems' acclaims *Coriolanus* as Shakespeare's 'most assured artistic success' (*SW*, 84). The suppressed 'Ode', from *Ara Vos Prec* (1920), carried a fragment of Coriolanus' words of aggression towards the Volscians (IV. v, 67)[79] as its epigraph (*IMH*, 383). A Coriolanus appears in 'A Cooking Egg', then appears 'broken' in the last part of *The Waste Land*. *Coriolanus* forms, then, another instance of Eliot's consistent empathies. Yet his 'Coriolan' poems display Eliot's recasting of multiple mediatory voices about *Coriolanus* into a new context, voices that establish the emotional centre, and the perspective taken upon it, in Eliot's poems. His obvious early enthusiasm for Shakespeare's play, as evidenced by these multiple references, does reflect, as Corcoran suggests, a surprising tendency at the time. But, by the early 1920s and into the 1930s, *Coriolanus* was garnering a level and quality of critical attention overlooked by Corcoran. This was critical attention of which Eliot was aware, and which, in its turn, formed a set of issues that are instructive about Eliot's ambitions in 'Coriolan'.

Eliot's interlocutor John Middleton Murry made several attempts to counter what he perceived as a British antipathy to *Coriolanus*, one that he said contrasted to current French interest in it. In his first essay on the play, from 1922, Murry claimed that Coriolanus is 'a martyr to the aristocratic idea…an alien'. Therefore, and oddly, he sought to make the play more appealing, by 'rescuing' the character of Virgilia, Coriolanus' wife, as a key counterweight to such unsympathetic traits in the 'hero'. Intriguingly, Murry saw the contempt for the mob uttered by Coriolanus as reflecting a 'prejudice' of Shakespeare's own: 'The greatest writers strive to be impersonal, and on the whole they achieve impersonality', but 'prejudice will out'.[80] Murry's words here

---

Chelli asserts ('mental inertia makes us repeat our actions, thoughts, attitudes, and words'). Eliot quoted these words in his 'Massinger', unsigned review of *Etude sur la Collaboration de Massinger avec Fletcher et son Groupe*, par Maurice Chelli, and Massinger's *A New Way to Pay Old Debts*, ed. A.H. Cruickshank (*TLS*, no. 1294, 18 November 1926, 814). The phrases appear on p. 271 of Chelli's book (*Etude sur la Collaboration de Massinger avec Fletcher et son Groupe* (Paris: Les Presses Universitaires de France, 1926).

[78] Corcoran, *Shakespeare and the Modern Poet*, 102–10.
[79] *Shakespeare's Tragedy of Coriolanus*, ed. Israel Gollancz (London: J.M. Dent, 1896), 85. Subsequent page numbers for this edition appear in the text.
[80] John Middleton Murry, *Countries of the Mind: Essays in Literary Criticism* (London: Collins, 1922), 32, 48.

seem an indirect answer, via Shakespeare, to Eliot's central doctrine from 'Tradition and the Individual Talent'. In another essay on *Coriolanus*, Murry displayed a sentimentalism similar to his first comments. But he now placed the emotional heart of the play somewhere between the characters of Coriolanus and his mother. His perception struck a note that would trouble the second of Eliot's 'Coriolan' poems, 'Difficulties of a Statesman': 'His consciousness, his memory, his purpose—these are all in the keeping of his mother, Volumnia…Coriolanus and Volumnia together are one being—Volumnia the mind and purpose, Coriolanus the body and strength.' In terms surely distasteful to Eliot, yet pertinent to that aspect of *Hamlet* that fascinated him, Murry noted the 'Oedipal' nature of their relationship.[81]

But other contemporary critics, more favoured by Eliot, were concerned to take the discussion of Shakespeare's play away from the kind of emotional concentration posited by Murry, and into consideration of its politics. In a review of 1925, Eliot seemed to accede to the arguments of the critic Charles Whibley who had claimed that Shakespeare probably was a 'Conservative'. Yet Eliot disagreed with the conclusion that Whibley then made about *Coriolanus*, when looked at from this point of view. Eliot favoured an approach that sustained the open-ended nature of drama:

> Is the lesson to be drawn from such a play as *Coriolanus* the lesson that democracy leads to anarchy, the lesson of the perfect type of aristocrat? We might like to believe that Shakespeare had in mind anything so positive. But it is possible to draw another conclusion: the conclusion that Shakespeare was as conscious of the faults and vices of the 'aristocrat' as he was of those of the plebs…[82]

This 'conclusion' has a vital impact upon the perspective taken in 'Coriolan'. As Corcoran acknowledged, the two critics who seem most to have affected Eliot's understanding of the play were Wyndham Lewis and G. Wilson Knight. My point, though, would be that the obvious influence of these readings, in fact, draws upon, or reflects, earlier commentary with which Eliot was also familiar. We can witness the *gradual* development of crucial elements in Eliot's opinion about *Coriolanus*, elements that then yield their eventual bounty, in his mature creative output. Corcoran fails to note that Wyndham Lewis finds an equation for the character of Coriolanus that takes his reading of Shakespeare's hero close to Eliot's own immediate concerns of the later 1920s, as encapsulated initially in 'Shakespeare and the Stoicism of Seneca'. Wyndham Lewis saw in the play both 'the distinguished intonation of "the aristocrat"' and 'nietzschean invective'. These facets are held up as part of Wyndham Lewis's case that, in Shakespeare's writing, there are opposing 'forces' which, despite our cultural inclination, we must not seek to see as 'reconciled' in any way.[83]

---

[81] John Middleton Murry, *Discoveries: Essays in Literary Criticism* (London: Collins, 1924), 269, 279. Murry opens this essay on the play by adverting to the recent controversy about its 'success' or otherwise compared to that of *Hamlet*, and quotes Eliot as having made a definitive statement of the issues (265).

[82] T.S. Eliot, 'A Popular Shakespeare', unsigned review of *The Works of Shakespeare: Chronologically Arranged*. With Introductions by Charles Whibley, *TLS*, no. 1255, 4 February 1925, 76.

[83] Wyndham Lewis, *The Lion and the Fox*, 23. Eliot saw Lewis's reading of *Coriolanus* as 'revelatory' and 'peculiarly pertinent' when he revisited Lewis's work on its tenth anniversary ('The Lion and the Fox', *Twentieth-Century Verse*, 6–7, November/December 1937, unnumbered pages).

Eliot's pre-publication sighting of Wilson Knight's 'An Essay on *Coriolanus*', before it appeared in *The Imperial Theme*, would seem, in this context, to have reoriented his alertness to the symbolic basis of the play as he moved towards writing 'Coriolan'.[84] The suppressed 'Ode' from *Ara Vos Prec*, with its cursing and cursed tone, had seemed, in its eviscerated account of a marriage night in the middle stanza, to derive from the violent and wounded nature and consequence of Coriolanus' savagery. That savagery culminated in the report about him at Corioli (the triumph which gives him his honorific name): 'From face to foot/He was a thing of blood, whose every motion/Was timed with dying cries' (II. ii, 106–8). Wilson Knight's 'Essay' shows how such natural, if excessive, imagery in the play is always blended with the sheerly material—'The imagery is often metallic.... This metal suggestion blends naturally elsewhere with the town setting.' At the end of Eliot's 'Difficulties of a Statesman', we note, the small creatures of the natural world erupt oddly into the 'dust' of the townscape, only to be ignored by the ironic and sterile metropolitan bureaucratic call made for more committees to administer life. The 'natural' is over-written by the machinations of human social and political pettiness (*CPP*, 130).

As Wilson Knight contends, this metal 'suggestion' in the imagery of *Coriolanus* seems eventually to become the nature of Coriolanus himself, who is described, late in the play, as a 'kind of nothing'. He is a 'nothing' who needs to discover a new existence for himself through wreaking revenge upon his native Rome (V. i, 12). Eventually, 'he moves like an engine, and the ground shrinks before his treading' (V. iv, 18).[85] Eliot's 'Triumphal March' opens with, and repeats, such materiality ('Stone, bronze, stone, steel') (*CPP*, 127–8). It is notable, however, in the light of Eliot's comment on Whibley's popular Shakespeare, that his *poem* 'Coriolan' has been set for a collective voice, that of the plebs ('We hardly knew ourselves'). The perspective taken is not that of the aristocracy who so dominate Shakespeare's play, but that of a voice in, and of, the crowd, 'waiting' for the arrival of the 'hero'. There is talk of a holiday-like atmosphere ('our stool and our sausages') that is notably absent from the 'triumph' described in *Coriolanus*. In Shakespeare the victorious general is greeted by the tribunes, after Corioli, and scorns the crowd. Eliot's 'Triumphal March', to that extent, seems closer to the crowd-setting of the first scene of *Julius Caesar* (source for 'The Hollow Men') rather than to the later tragedy— *Julius Caesar*, after all, is another play about an 'Ego', whose relation to the people is one of fateful and tragic difficulty. When he does appear, the eyes of Eliot's hero share something of the activity of the crowd, since those eyes are 'waiting' also. Presumably, in his case, they show him waiting for the celebration of his triumph, through a sacrifice at the temple. But those eyes are also 'watchful... perceiving, indifferent', almost tautologically bored in their expression as they look upon the crowd, whose comparative liveliness has been conveyed in the swift-speaking voice of the poem (*CPP*, 127). That issue of (self-)vigilance, of seeing, which had formed a key conceit for Eliot, and a modern poetic possibility, from the 'Eyes' of *The Waste*

[84] Wilson Knight, 'T.S. Eliot: Some Literary Impressions', 248–9.
[85] Wilson Knight, *The Imperial Theme*, 155, 190.

Land and 'The Hollow Men', here takes on rebarbative political force. It now suggests the irreconcilable between political dichotomies—democratic, Communist, and Nietzschean/Fascist.

Part of the jarring effect of the poems, in Eliot's uncompleted 'Coriolan', is caused by their anachronistic insertion of references, to modern armaments and also to a modern-day boy, then man, 'Cyril'. These are anachronisms, in this Roman setting, on a par with those struck by Ezra Pound in his *Homage to Sextus Propertius*. Further seeming jarring is caused by the link forced in 'Triumphal March' (and thence by the intrusive biblical reference at the opening of 'Difficulties of a Statesman') between a pagan and a Christian viewpoint, at this 'still point of the turning world'. We are in the realm of the Ariel poems once more. As though in mind of Murry's labelling of Coriolanus as a 'martyr', the temple scene in 'Triumphal March' sparks a facetious, but striking, reference to Cyril being taken to church on Easter Day.

But this sense of martyrdom raises a theological and aesthetic perplexity, which will become hugely significant in Eliot's drama. The commentators upon Coriolanus' faults in Shakespeare's play are unanimous in attributing to him the very Christian sin of pride:

> Caius Martius was
> A worthy officer i'th' war, but insolent,
> O'ercome with pride, ambitious past all thinking,
> Self-loving.
>
> (IV. vi, 32–5)

Even his arch-enemy, Aufidius, notes that 'He bears himself more proudlier,/Even to my person, than I thought he would' (IV. vii, 8). The 'eyes' of the hero in Eliot's 'Triumphal March' are both 'perceiving' and 'indifferent'; he chooses to separate himself from the crowd that he watches, perhaps sensing their threat to his triumph. The plebeian perspective of 'Triumphal March' and 'Difficulties of a Statesman' offsets the human drama, encapsulated in the second of these poems by a version of the original hero's fraught relationship to his mother, Volumnia, against the rising militarism of contemporary Europe. By maintaining, in line with Eliot's review in response to Whibley's 'Popular Shakespeare', an even-handedness of emphasis between the crowd and the hero, Eliot does not play down the faults of either—the chaotic anticipation of the one, the pride of the other.[86] But the nature of Coriolanus's sin, that pride derived from Eliot's source text, will form part of the sceptical questioning which underwrites the drama beginning to emerge in Eliot's writing of the 1930s.

Eliot's confirmation in 1927 released a reconfiguration of his attitude towards his Early Modern preoccupations. That integrative potential which he had previously seen established in the conceits and wit of the Metaphysical poets no longer held true in his concern to maintain in one form disintegrative modern tendencies

---

[86] Northrop Frye, commenting on Eliot's recourse to Seneca, asserted that 'The ancestor of Romantic egoism is Seneca the Stoic, whose conception of the hero seems like a cult of spiritual pride.' (*T.S. Eliot*, Edinburgh: Oliver and Boyd, 1963, 19).

with salving religious ones. His poetry, in consequence, was drawn to those moments at which a Christian sensibility could be perceived in tension with a Stoic one, and where a former world might illuminate the travails of a recognizably more uncertain modern one. 'Lostness' became compensated by 'stillness', as Eliot exploited multiple literary and critical voices to new ends, and further dilemmas, which would be confronted in the early dramas he now began to write.

7

Towards a New Dramatic Articulation
The Rock and *Murder in the Cathedral*

THE EARLY MODERN AND TEXTUAL 'PATTERN'

Eliot's discussions about the nature of what he variously called 'doubleness', 'planes in relation', 'otherworldliness', 'under-pattern', or 'pattern'—qualities to be perceived, he claimed, in poetic drama especially—intensified across the years that he himself began working in this medium. His 1928 response, in the form of 'A Dialogue on Dramatic Poetry', to Dryden's 1668 essay 'Of Dramatick Poesie', had shown him openly expressing, in this non-personal context, what had been buried within the reviews and passing references in lectures and essays for several years already. This was the issue of what he had one speaker in 'A Dialogue' call 'the relation of drama to religion'. Eliot's Preface to the original publication of his dialogue declared that 'I have no clear opinions on this subject' and, hence, his 'theories' are distributed amongst the characters set by him to debate the genre.

Yet the primary focus of the extended piece he created, in response to Dryden, is about the need for a literary form that can assume something, in the secular world, of the nature and epistemology of religious ritual.[1] As Eliot's character 'B' states, in a contention that raises again the notion of personality as divided between 'planes' of perception, 'we' are both aware of the divine realm *and* of the human one. The relationship between the two perspectives is vital, for 'us'. Therefore, 'we' desire a modern version of 'liturgy', to salve the secular grounding of our lives. This desire might then be supplied by poetic drama, which mimics liturgical rhythm in its typical movement of its main character towards expiation. 'B's sense of what constitutes the 'dramatic' is remarkably flexible, and is in line with the generic complexity that we have discovered Eliot explore, for instance, in his readings of John Donne,. 'What great poetry is not dramatic?' he asks, enlisting Dante and Homer to the cause (*SE*, 49). In this context, significantly left open is the possibility that 'drama' is as available to the private reader of lyric verse as it is to the 'spectator' of the public 'liturgy' that full poetic drama might mount on the stage. This chapter will review the practical aspects of Eliot's knowledge of Early Modern theatre, as they developed across the later 1920s, and then fed into his first attempts at

---

[1] *Of Dramatick Poesie An Essay 1668* by John Dryden. Preceded by a Dialogue on Poetic Drama by T.S. Eliot (London: Frederick Etchells and Hugh MacDonald, 1928), x. Eliot's Preface is not reprinted in the *Selected Essays* version of his essay; subsequent references in this chapter are, however, for conformity with other references, to that later one.

drama, *The Rock* and *Murder in the Cathedral*. It will consider how, in his thinking and subsequently in his practice, historical features of the Early Modern theatre, such as what one critic called the 'doubling' of parts, bear precise philosophical and religious resonance, as Eliot again redirects some of his established conceits to new creative ends. He understood the *practice* of drama as a form of epistemology, and one that both complicates and enhances those 'liturgical' aspects Eliot hoped that his own work might display.

Eliot's engagement with the criticism of G. Wilson Knight, on the later plays of Shakespeare, undoubtedly clarified his understanding of some of these possibilities. Wilson Knight's 'spatial' and 'musical' reading of the plays suggested that Shakespeare's deployment of a set and definitive range of imagery, in each work, offered an illuminating counterpoint to the action being carried forward on the stage.[2] The implication was (although Wilson Knight did not develop the theoretical aspects of his critical approach very clearly) that Shakespeare's constant pressing upon a set of images produced, within the audience's imagination, a deeper understanding of the intricacies and implications of each drama. Wilson Knight's own theoretical terminology, in fact, remained weak and unilluminating. In the grandly titled chapter 'On the Principles of Shakespeare Interpretation', which opens *The Wheel of Fire* (1930), he gestured vaguely to a poet's choosing 'a series of tales to whose life-rhythm he is spontaneously attracted', and thence giving that 'life-rhythm' a 'spatial' structure within the work—presumably with the sense that that 'life-rhythm' will be felt somehow by the audience.[3]

What the advocacy of such 'interpretation' enabled, in Eliot, was the final laying aside of an issue that had been troubling him from the mid-1920s onwards at least: the relation of his own academic discipline, philosophy, to his creative career in poetry. In a 1925 review about 'Shakespeare and Montaigne', for instance, Eliot had asserted that 'The attitude of the *craftsman* like Shakespeare—whose business was to write plays, not to think—is very different from that of the philosopher or even the literary critic.'[4] Yet the Clark Lectures, and later essays like 'Shakespeare and the Stoicism of Seneca', had advocated, for dramatists, and for poets following Donne, the value of a settled 'system' of philosophy or belief, which a writer could deploy to provide structure to their work. Eliot's Introduction to *The Wheel of Fire* reasserted this point, although it recognized the personal nature of his preference: 'I like a definite and dogmatic philosophy,' Eliot said, a philosophy such as that to be found most eloquently in Dante. The consistent playing upon the notion of 'pattern', as something which Eliot felt that Wilson Knight's 'interpretation' had revealed, saw

---

[2] That Eliot found both 'spatial' and 'musical' formal elements essential to achieved drama is evidenced by his article 'Audiences, Producers, Plays, Poets', in which he claims that form and musical pattern are *both* necessary to sustaining 'interest' in a play (*New Verse*, no. 18, December 1935, 4).

[3] G. Wilson Knight, *The Wheel of Fire: Interpretations of Shakespearean Tragedy* (London: Oxford University Press, 1930), 9.

[4] T.S. Eliot, 'Shakespeare and Montaigne', unsigned review of *Shakespeare's Debt to Montaigne* by George Coffin Taylor, *TLS*, 24 December 1925, no. 1249, 895.

him contrarily reflecting upon the *poetic* and *practical* implications of art that did not consistently look for authority to, or imaginatively present, 'dogma'[5]:

> Shakespeare's pattern was more complex, and his problem more difficult, than Dante's. The genuine poetic drama must, at its best, observe all the regulations of the plain drama, but will weave them *organically* (to mix a metaphor and to borrow for the occasion a modern word) into a much richer design.[6]

Eliot's self-conscious falling back upon an essentially nineteenth-century conception of creativity—one given, as we have seen, renewed energy at the turn of the twentieth century by critics of the Early Modern period, such as Symonds and J.M. Robertson—was telling, about the difficulties he was faced with when trying to articulate 'the whole design' of a drama. Eliot's Introduction to *The Wheel of Fire* notably talked about the need, not just to see Shakespeare's dramas singly, but to understand the 'design' and 'development' of his whole career.

We are granted only glimmerings of what Wilson Knight or Eliot might mean by terms such as 'pattern' or 'design'. Writing of what he saw as the rapidly created *Macbeth*, Wilson Knight talked of the 'one swift act of the poet's mind...the technique confronts us not with the separated integers of "character" or incident...there is an interpenetrating quality'. Again, on the moments in *Measure for Measure* (Angelo), or *Macbeth*, when a character seems to speak out of a wider understanding: 'they utter, not those things of which humanity is normally aware, but the springs of action'.[7] Wilson Knight's subsequent book, *The Imperial Theme*, in its exhaustive engagement with nearly every use of any particular kind of imagery, in some of Shakespeare's later tragedies seemed to come closer to some moments in Eliot's poetry and dramas.[8] Particularly when writing about *Antony and Cleopatra*, which for Eliot also was an important play, Wilson Knight described a dramatic organization that seamlessly united the action to its perceived significance; one that is 'aware of all significances and relations, mapped out below, juxtaposed, understood'. Or, describing Enobarbus' rapturous vision of Cleopatra on her barge, that essential passage for *The Waste Land* II: 'There is motion in this description; but, as in a picture, it is motion within stillness. There is mystery and something "beyond nature".'[9] Stillness and motion, 'motion within stillness', have formed, as we have seen, the reconciled anthitheses of Eliot's mature verse from 1927 onwards.

---

[5] Lewis Freed has noted that error is implicit in literary interpretation and metaphysics, as Eliot derived them from Bradley: 'every interpretation of a poem is a partial formulation of one thing' (*T.S. Eliot: The Critic as Philosopher*, Indiana: Purdue University Press, 1979, 168).

[6] T.S. Eliot, Introduction to *The Wheel of Fire*, xv, xviii.

[7] G. Wilson Knight, *The Wheel of Fire*, 155, 285.

[8] Without making contrasts to Knight's practice, David Gervais has perceived a paradox at the heart of Eliot's critical practice regarding Shakespeare. Although he constantly 'stresses Shakespeare's "art"', Eliot 'avoids talking about the plays as artistic wholes'. This, Gervais suggests, is because Eliot could not cope with tragedy as a form—'It was through Dante, and Dante's religion, that he found a context for tragedy'. See 'Eliot's Shakespeare and Eliot's Dante', *T.S. Eliot and Our Turning World*, edited by Jewel Spears Brooker (Basingstoke: Macmillan, 2001), 118. My suggestion would be, though, that Eliot had been trained up to see only the 'moment' in Shakespeare, as in other 'art'—see Chapters One and Two above.

[9] G. Wilson Knight, *The Imperial Theme: Further Interpretations of Shakespeare's Tragedies including the Roman Plays* (London: Oxford University Press, 1931), 225, 257.

Most notable is the way in which Wilson Knight's delineation of the paradigms within the imagery of Shakespeare's mature work led him towards conceptions that impinge upon the territory of Eliot's imagination. Describing the bereavement of Hamlet, not just because of his father's death but also because of his loss of love for Ophelia, we hear that 'Between the sick soul and the knowledge of love there are all the interstellar spaces that divide Hell from Heaven.' This is the limbo world of *East Coker* III, the 'dark' 'vacant interstellar spaces' which 'they' all go into, the idling of the underground train 'too long' between stations, or the waiting in the darkness between scenes in a theatre (*CPP*, 180). On the last scenes of *Timon of Athens*, a play that again had long-standing significance for Eliot, Wilson Knight wrote: 'As Timon severs all contact with the finite world and, like some majestic liner, cleaves the dark seas of infinity, we voyage too...leave safe coasts and plough forward into the unknown'.[10] Wilson Knight's consistent interest in ships and voyaging—most tellingly displayed for Eliot, perhaps, in the essay on *Pericles*, discussed in the last chapter—is shifted here into a metaphysical realm, the 'faring forward' which will carry Eliot's later *Quartets*, and which is most explicit in *The Dry Salvages* III (*CPP*, 188).

Eliot's last four set-piece essays on single Early Modern dramatic authors, written between 1930 and 1934, saw him strive to apply the recent insights, gained from this encounter with an 'interpretation' such as Wilson Knight's, to a range of post-Shakespearean work. 'Cyril Tourneur' (1930) found again in *The Revenger's Tragedy*, that major work for the younger Eliot, 'a horror of life, singular in his own or any age, [which] finds exactly the right words and the right rhythms' (*SE*, 192). But the other essays struggle largely to find what 'Thomas Heywood' (1931) calls the 'inchoate pattern', which this generation of dramatists, according to Eliot, shared (*SE*, 175). 'John Ford' (1932) even brings in Wilson Knight as a standard of comparison for his subject. But this essay finds in Ford, as opposed to Shakespeare, 'no symbolic value' (*SE*, 195).

'John Marston' (1934) is the final of such essays by Eliot, and stands apart in its more sustained consideration of the organizational and ontological issues derived from the Early Modern period as they had shaped Eliot's poetry from the mid-1920s. 'John Marston' was written when work on the pageant-play, *The Rock*, was complete, and that on *Murder in the Cathedral* was soon to begin. 'John Marston' is, perhaps as a result of this recent drama writing, the most intriguing of Eliot's meditations on 'doubleness', as he derived it from his knowledge of Early Modern poetic drama. The fact that, as he acknowledged in his essay's opening pages, Marston is a less familiar figure amongst the Early Modern dramatists, seems to galvanize Eliot the more strongly towards proclaiming Marston's 'poetic genius'.[11] 'John Marston' ranges widely across the playwright's writing, as Eliot sought to define what that intuited 'genius' entails. The main book under review by Eliot in

[10] G. Wilson Knight, *The Wheel of Fire*, 27, 246–7. Eliot had quoted Timon's last speech as an example of a hero dramatising himself, alongside the speeches of Othello, Coriolanus, and Antony, in '"Rhetoric" and Poetic Drama' (*SW*, 68).

[11] Eliot's essay on Marston originally appeared in the *TLS* on 23 July 1934. At the beginning of that month, Eliot had printed an article by Theodore Spencer in *The Criterion*, which similarly notes Marston's comparative neglect (there was no Mermaid volume of his plays), his 'repellent personality'— but also his 'pertinence' and originality (vol. III, no. LIII, July 1934, 582).

the essay, H. Harvey Wood's first volume of a collected *The Plays of John Marston*, contains only three works, *Antonio and Mellida*, *Antonio's Revenge*, and *The Malcontent*. But, like many of his pieces on the Early Modern dramatists particularly, Eliot's review characteristically covered Marston's full career. Indeed, throughout his essay, Eliot drew, rather, upon the earlier edition of Marston's *Works*, edited by J.H. Bullen (1887), than upon the new edition he was meant to be commenting on. In fact, he quotes Marston from the Bullen text, which he had used to quote from as far back as 'Burbank with a Baedeker: Bleistein with a Cigar', even when covering the plays given in Harvey Wood's (original spelling) volume. Once more, the practice of reviewing led Eliot to revisit texts familiar to him, and that revisiting galvanizes something of his new creative thought.

Eliot's discussion of Marston was notable, since it reversed the terms of H. Harvey Wood's Introduction to his edition. Harvey Wood complained, for instance, about the 'deliberate contortions of speech and affectations of style' in Marston, contortions that derived from 'too intensive study of the sententious manner of Senecan tragedy, [which] has resulted in a congested, tortuous, obscurity'. Harvey Wood compared these negative qualities of Marston's style to those in Chapman, and also to the more 'sophisticated' Shakespeare. He did so, to the credit of Shakespeare and Chapman, over Marston himself. Eliot, contrastingly, saw Marston's versification as having 'no poetic merit' particularly, but, in fact, 'a peculiar jerkiness and irritability'.[12] Marston was, for him, a poet 'wrought to the pitch of exasperation' (*SE*, 224). Marston's characterization was uninteresting, the personages in the plays 'lifeless', but Eliot found that there was an odd, compensatory, 'significant lifelessness in this shadow-show' (*SE*, 225). That paradoxical 'jerkiness' and 'lifelessness' actually seemed to spark Eliot's curiosity (see 'The Hollow Men'), and his sense of the 'peculiar' nature of Marston's achievement.[13] It is this that launched him upon his famous definition of the 'doubleness' or 'under-patterning' in Marston, one he also compared to that in Chapman's two plays about Bussy d'Ambois. This was a patterning, Eliot claimed, which was perceptible rarely, like 'drowsing in sunlight. It is the pattern drawn by what the ancient world called Fate; subtilized by Christianity into delicate mazes of theology'. (232)

It is worth dwelling, for a moment, upon the play of Marston's that sparked this most exuberant and expansive commentary from Eliot, upon his theme of 'pattern' in drama to this point in his career (the unpublished 1937 lectures on 'The Development of Shakespeare's Verse' would expand it further). *Sophonisba; Or, the Wonder of Women* was Marston's attempt, in 1606, to answer those critics who had argued that he could not write a focused serious work. It is a classical

---

[12] *The Plays of John Marston in Three Volumes*, ed. H. Harvey Wood, vol. I (Edinburgh: Oliver and Boyd, 1934), xxxi. In his Introduction to *The Malcontent* (the other new edition of Marston that Eliot had under review in his essay), G.B. Harrison compares the main character, Malevole, to Hamlet, Jacques (from *As You Like It*), and Thersites (from *Troilus and Cressida*)—so setting him as a further precedent for Eliot's truth-telling Sweeney, and, as we shall in the next chapter, for Eliot's later dramatic heroes (London: J.M. Dent, 1933, x).

[13] In 1923, in a letter to Alfred Kreymborg, author of *Puppet Plays*, Eliot had elided discussion of the several planes of rhythm he was seeking in what was to become *Sweeney Agonistes* ('a dominant rythm [sic] and subordinated rythms' [sic]) with comments on the puppet theatre. The letter suggests that he wanted to build his own puppet theatre 'and preordain every move and gesture and grouping' (*LII*, 192–3).

tragedy, self-consciously rivalling, as its prefatory address makes clear, Ben Jonson's success in *Sejanus*. Unlike Marston's other work in this medium, there are no 'comic' passages, or other distractions. Sophonisba's fate is fought over, along with that of her city, Carthage. In a complicated plot, the just-married Sophonisba remains a virgin across the play, as her new husband, Massinissa, is called away on their wedding night, to fight his rival (and Sophonisba's jilted lover) Syphax. Syphax is a dissenter, who has vengefully allied himself, and his forces, with the invading Roman army. At one point, Sophonisba is saved from a (temporarily) triumphant Syphax, only by the use of the standard Early Modern 'bed trick'.

But this time we witness a version of the trick with a sinister undertone. For Syphax is tricked into having sex with a person other than the one he desires, Sophonisba, by a grotesque enchantress, Erictho. Then, becoming increasingly Cleopatra-like, Sophonisba fears being enslaved by the victorious Romans, and poisons herself, even though Massinissa has been restored to her. A.H. Bullen, in his Introduction to Marston's *Works*, dismissed the result of this hectic plotting and characterization in *Sophonisba* as 'stiff and crude, wanting in energy and dramatic movement, too rhetorical, "climbing to the height of Seneca in his style"'. The one aspect of the play that clearly disturbed him is the 'recital of Erictho's atrocities', which he feared, when staged in the theatre, would threaten the well-being of 'women of delicate health'. But, more significantly, given Eliot's interest in the particularities of 'Fate' later in the 1930s, in *The Family Reunion*, Bullen compares the effect of Erictho's incantations, at moments in Marston's play, to those in the *Eumenides*: the vengeful figures that Eliot would soon, awkwardly, put onstage.[14]

Eliot's reaction to all of this was strikingly strong: he over-read Bullen's objections to Erictho, as though Bullen had claimed that the character was introduced merely to add 'gratuitous horror'. Instead, Eliot asserted, Erictho is 'integral' to the plot, part of that 'double reality' which evidences Marston's 'poetic genius' (*SE*, 230). It is notable that the passage from Erictho, cited by Eliot in 'John Marston' to display the distinctive qualities of that 'genius', is from a long speech, given as the enchantress prepares to play her trick on Syphax. She assumes the bodily shape of Sophonisba, in order to sleep with him, and so save the abject heroine from rape, in a scene reminiscent of passages from other Early Modern playwrights and poets we have seen Eliot drawing upon in *The Waste Land* and elsewhere. The passage celebrates the overgrowth by nature of the 'once glorious temple rear'd to Jove' on this spot, where now boys write obscene graffiti and shepherds defecate on ancient tombs. This, to quote words later from the same passage given by Eliot, is where Erictho lives:

> There once a charnel house, now a vast cave...
> Within rests barren darkness; fruitless droughte
> Pines in eternal night; the steam of helle
> Yields not so lazy air; there, that's my cell.[15]

---

[14] *The Works of John Marston*, ed. A.H. Bullen (London: John C. Nimmo, 1887), vol. I, xlv.

[15] Act IV.i, 162 ff. The passage appears on p. 293 of vol. II of Bullen's edition of the *Works*; Eliot's quotation 'Where statues and Jove's acts' begins at l. 154. The passage is given as one of Charles Lamb's *Specimens of English Dramatic Poets* (London: Routledge, 1927 edition), 67.

The 'double reality' that Erictho encapsulates is, then, conveyed through a strikingly modern (graffiti, shit) inversion of the qualities of purity and innocence that Sophonisba, who is in many ways like Isabella in Shakespeare's *Measure for Measure*, or Marina or Miranda, represents. Erictho's hideous cave at the site of the ruined classical temple is reached through dark tunnels running from the palace. It is as though the trauma in the play's surface political world, underwritten as it is by rivalry over love for Sophonisba, only further reveals the corruption that comes to all established higher, even religious, aspiration in the play. Eliot's other quotations in his essay, attesting to the 'double reality' that he felt Marston uniquely to have delineated, are strikingly Senecan, culminating in the lines he cited from Sophonisba's final speech. There, she proclaims her freedom as a woman, as she is handed the poison by Massinissa (Eliot quotes only the last two lines of these four):

> How near was I unto the curse of man. Joy!
> How like was I yet once to have been glad!
> He that ne'er laughed may with a constant face
> Contemn Jove's frown: happiness makes us base.
>
> (V. iii, 89–92)

The fated misery of humanity, and the distance between gods and people, is the constant theme. The only relief is in escape. Further on in her last speech, in a passage not quoted by Eliot, Sophonisba makes statements correlative to those dying words he had been haunted by in other dramas, most notably in *Bussy d'Ambois*, *Othello*, *Antony and Cleopatra*, or *Coriolanus*:

> And I do thank thee, heaven! O my stars,
> I bless your goodness, that with breast unstain'd,
> Faith pure, a virgin wife, tried to my glory,
> I die, of female faith the long-liv'd story...
>
> (101–4)

This equivalent of Othello's 'Set this down', or Coriolanus' 'If you have writ your annals true', is surely one of the qualities that led Eliot to his disproportionate praise of Marston's rather muddled work. The 'doubleness' here seems notably stoical, again, as though the 'pattern' in Marston is a (albeit bleakly expressed) traditional and uncomplicated one. It is significant that Eliot did cite the passage where, in a bantering exchange about her situation with some Libyan senators, Sophonisba reflects upon the different perspectives of gods from humans (although, Eliot typically omits again the gender-inflection in her views, this time mockingly delivered, when he leaves out the final two lines given here). One senator laments that the fall of Carthage is foreseen by the gods; Sophonisba ripostes:

> Gods naught foresee, but see, for to their eyes
> Naught is to come or past; nor are you vile
> Because the gods foresee; for gods, not we
> See as things are; things are not as we see.
> But since affected wisdom in us women
> Is our sex' highest folly, I am silent...
>
> (II. i, 134–9)

This is a nice play upon words and sounds, one that conjures a sense of the 'eternally present' perspective towards which Eliot's *Quartets* will yearn, from the opening passage of *Burnt Norton* onwards. *Sophonisba* was suggestive for Eliot, in that it engages many of the themes with which we are more familiar, from Eliot's favouring them amongst better-known work, such as those aspects of Shakespeare's plays that he foregrounded throughout. These are the themes of purity and corruption; former religious meaning (the temple) defiled (the cave); self and fate; self and otherness.

Eliot strikingly quoted here the phrase from *The Revenger's Tragedy* IV. i: 'I think man's happiest when he forgets himself', as correlative, in his mind, to Sophonisba's last speech.[16] In a subtext, which clearly fascinated Eliot, the pure Sophonisba and the degraded witch Erictho are curiously linked ('doubled') in the perverse psychology of Marston's play. This is so, literally, through its bed-trick. The border between innocence and corruption is very narrow. Related antitheses are translated into Eliot's own dramas, which engage his later career. In *The Family Reunion*, and in *The Cocktail Party*, fragile borders between seemingly opposed qualities of good and evil, the innocent and the daemonic, are near to the surface of the text. But those dramas also show after-images of the Early Modern influences that had long affected Eliot, and which were perhaps, again, re-sparked in him by his recent encounter with the criticism of Wilson Knight.

Knight's chapter in *The Wheel of Fire* on '*Measure for Measure* and the Gospels' conjured a picture of the Duke in Shakespeare's play that intriguingly takes the issue of 'pattern' into further questions about metaphysical presence, and its relationship with character. Knight argued this in ways that would resonate with Eliot's broader interests. By the end of *Measure for Measure*, Knight asserted:

> We have ceased altogether to think of the Duke as merely a studious and unpractical governor, incapable of office. Rather he holds, within the dramatic universe, the dignity and power of a Prospero, to whom he is strangely similar. With both, their plot and plan is the plot and plan of the play; they make and forge the play, and thus are automatically to be equated in a unique sense with the poet himself...[17]

As an example of the Duke's 'philosophy' in the play, Knight pointed us to his final soliloquy, about the hidden vice that can reside within 'virtuous' characters, at the end of Act III. That speech begins with the blessing with which the Duke dismisses his interlocutors, 'Peace be with you' (III. ii, 254). The dismissal reminds us of the

---

[16] The ironies of this are, typically, manifold—the line is spoken mockingly by the revenger, Vendice, as he is being sent on his way to perform further killings by his brother: 'Hip. O brother, you forget our business./Ven. And well remembered; joy's a subtle elf,/I think man's happiest when he forgets himself.' (*Webster and Tourneur*, ed. John Addington Symonds, London: Ernest Benn, 1888, 416).

[17] G. Wilson Knight, *The Wheel of Fire*, 79. Quomodo in Middleton's *Michaelmas Terme* (discussed briefly by Eliot in his essay on the playwright) tries a similar manoeuvre to the Duke in *Measure for Measure*. Quomodo fakes his own death in order to see how his wife and son deal with his land acquisitions. However, given the chance, his wife runs immediately into marriage with another man she has been desiring from afar.

same one which will be used, by the similarly disguised Riley/Harcourt-Reilly, in Eliot's *The Cocktail Party* ('Go in peace').[18] It also reminds us of the way that Harcourt-Reilly and the mysterious Guardians (Knight harps on the 'supernatural authority' of the Duke) control that play.

The Rock

Those Prospero-like qualities, the figuration of authorial characters within Early Modern works and thence in Eliot's dramas, will form a recurrent theme across these last chapters of this book. More immediately, however, Shakespeare's Duke seems to hold a vestigial presence within Eliot's first experiment in drama, the pageant play *The Rock*, commissioned for performance in 1934. This was a pageant play that aimed to raise money for the building of new churches in the diocese of London, but it displays some aspects of Eliot's response to Early Modern work from his nearly contemporary reviews and preface. Having lamented the lack of a sense of the purpose of the Church in the modern world, the Chorus Leader of the opening chorus of Eliot's work perceives the approach of the pivotal character, also (and oddly) named 'The Rock'. Like the Gods as conceived by Sophonisba, in their distance from humanity, The Rock is 'He who sees what has happened/And who sees what is to happen'.[19] The Rock combines, therefore, a Tiresias-like with a Duke-like role. But he seems increasingly to merge with the latter, as at one point he appears, as Shakespeare's disguised Duke does, wearing a monk-like habit. Halfway through, in the published full text of Eliot's pageant, he comes on stage *'with his cowl flung back'* (51): we are reminded not only of Shakespeare's charismatic author figure but also the 'hooded' 'third' figure, in brown mantle, who walks alongside in *The Waste Land* (*CPP*, 73).

The Rock pronounces in terms that bear the authority of the Duke's 'Be absolute for death' speech in *Measure for Measure* (III. i), the speech that had provided the epigraph for 'Gerontion', and which underpins much of Eliot's subsequent work and thought. The Rock, with cowl flung back, acknowledges the 'blinding movement' of time, in which human achievement is 'lost'. He, however, utters a perspective upon that loss which prefigures much in Eliot's later poetry:

> Remember, all you who are numbered for GOD,
> In every moment of time you live where two worlds cross,
> In every moment you live at a point of intersection,
> Remember, living in time, you must live also now in Eternity. (52)

[18] T.S. Eliot, *The Cocktail Party* (London: Faber, 1950), 114. Subsequent references are to this edition. Harcourt-Reilly's extension of his phrase as 'Go in peace, my daughter', when he dismisses Celia who has just committed herself to a path of spiritual redemption, carries echoes of 'Marina' and, behind it, of Shakespeare's *Pericles* as discussed previously. (128)

[19] T.S. Eliot, *The Rock: Book of Words* (New York, Harcourt Brace and Company, 1934), 8. Subsequent page references for this edition are given in the text.

The 'point of intersection' looks forward, for instance, to the place of meeting with the 'familiar compound ghost' in section II of *Little Gidding* (*CPP*, 193).[20] E. Martin Browne, the 'intimate narrator' of the process of development behind all of Eliot's plays, has pointed out that, although the printed text of the pageant sees The Rock eventually revealed (through translation of the Latin origin of his name, *Petrus*) to be St Peter, Eliot himself wanted his identity 'undefined for as long as possible', and he conceived him as a more abstract mediator of eternal possibilities.[21] This shrouding of identity is something integral of course to Early Modern drama, as it will be to the pivotal action of Eliot's developed dramas, which will be discussed in the final chapter. Here, the undefined nature of the central 'character' reflects upon the feeling Eliot later recorded, regarding the pageant, in 'The Three Voices of Poetry', that *The Rock* inherently displays 'not a dramatic voice' (*OPP*, 91). That proximity between poet and character, which Wilson Knight described in relation to the Duke and Prospero, is literally enacted in Eliot's first attempt at presenting a dramatic piece.

The Rock, like Lancelot Andrewes' sermons, and *Ash-Wednesday*, is haunted by the possibility that such 'points of intersection' are not recognizable in the modern world, where, as the Chorus Leader puts it, for the first time 'Men have left GOD...for no god'. (51) The displays of Communist and Fascist rallies, which the pageant presents, as also the chorus of the contemporary unemployed, further emphasize the feeling of untimeliness, that major facet of the Duke's insights in *Measure for Measure* and of Gerontion. The untimeliness is that of The Rock's confidence in the continuing Church, at this contested and dangerous historical moment. As the Chorus Leader puts it, 'Not for ourselves we mourn, O Rock, but for the unborn.' The possibility of living 'in Eternity', a possibility opened by the building of a new church, which provides the main stage 'action' of the pageant, seems increasingly in doubt. Indeed, the building of the church itself comes under threat, as the labourers struggle with the foundations, until The Rock produces a long-dead, ghostly, former Bishop of London, Blomfield, an earlier builder of churches in the capital, to 'encourage' the workers. Typically, for Eliot, the 'miracle' as those workers see it, which enables the completion of the new church building, only occurs when the past literally, as here, comes in, to underwrite the creation of something in the present. The historical sense is put into active use to redeem the action of the pageant from threatened stalling or breakdown, to lift it out of that interim in which the drama occurs, here, as in all of Eliot's plays.[22]

Reflecting on a rousing speech by an earlier builder of London churches, Rahere, after the church building has been completed, Edwin, one of the three main

---

[20] Carol H. Smith sees the speech as alluding also to 'the still point of the turning world' in *Ash-Wednesday*, as part of her survey of the issue of Time in the play: *T.S. Eliot's Dramatic Theory and Practice* (Princeton: Princeton University Press, 1963), 88.

[21] E. Martin Browne, *The Making of T.S. Eliot's Plays* (Cambridge: Cambridge University Press, 1969), 26. Browne is an 'intimate narrator', since he directed the first productions of all of Eliot's plays, as well as later interpretations upon which he engaged in conversation with Eliot himself.

[22] Arthur Waugh, in the Introduction to the World's Classics *The Poems of George Herbert*—the edition Eliot owned—noted that Herbert had rebuilt the church at Leighton Bromswold during his stewardship there (London: Oxford University Press, 1907, xii).

builders Eliot created to mediate the action in a suitable style to the audience, reflects to his companions that:

'is meanin' was this: 'e said, 'e and 'is mates was a-goin' to work with us. 'Visible and invisible,' that's what 'e said. We only saw 'em for a moment, to be sure, in some queer kind o' ancient garb; but if you remember rightly it was from that time things begun to come to rights. (65)

The creation of the builders, as characters who put the religious point of the pageant into an immediate idiom, and who have their own vernacular philosophy around it (one of them even gives a demotic rendition of Dunne's theory of time [15–6]), is a telling instance of Eliot's own drawing upon his Early Modern models to establish the framing of the enterprise in his pageant.

As E. Martin Browne notes, drafts of the play conceived Ethelbert, Alfred, and Edwin, the three builders given speeches, as 'Anglo-Saxon labourers': hence their names. They were initially, and literally, embodiments of the continuities between ancient past and present conveyed by the meaning of the drama, which presents the necessity for the physical presence of the church in the city. Such direct reference, though, was obviously thought too explicit for the final version. The opening of the builders' interplay and knockabout survives across Eliot's drafts, though, albeit in an abbreviated version. The foreman, Ethelbert, sings ' "A pick-axe and a spade, a spade/For and a shrouding-sheet..." ' and comments 'I 'eard that at the Old Vic once.' (11) The reference is slightly more obvious in some earlier drafts, where Bert (as he is called by his companions) continues 'That's Shakespeare, that is. He wrote some good songs, Shakespeare.'[23]

Eliot's own predilection for Shakespeare's songs was long-running, particularly for the Ariel songs from *The Tempest*. Yet here, the mock-Cockney of Eliot's foreman points us not only to the stock accents of Shakespeare's comic characters (these speak prose too) but to the gravediggers of *Hamlet* (V. i, 102)[24] as his prime model for these modern labourers. Shakespeare's gravediggers share the vernacular philosophic understanding of life and death of Eliot's men, as they do of the workings of time upon humanity, and of the comparative futility of human action. The aforementioned Rahere, conjured in Eliot's pageant as though in tribute to the lamented Yorick, was the 'King's Jester' at Henry VIII's court, before he had a vision and became a monk who undertook a pilgrimage to Rome and built churches. (25) Similar conversions from worldly to spiritual dedication will overtake Harry, in Eliot's play *The Family Reunion*, and Celia, in *The Cocktail Party*. In a crucial exchange in *The Rock*, that worldly experience serves usefully to challenge the typical (if un-Shakespearean) weariness and hopelessness of Eliot's men, as they encounter the dampness of the soil they are trying to build upon:

---

[23] Bodleian Library, Oxford, MS don. d. 44, 99. Browne quotes the passage without comment on p. 15 of *The Making of T.S. Eliot's Plays*.
[24] *Shakespeare's Tragedy of Hamlet*, ed. Israel Gollancz (London: J.M. Dent, 1895), 154. Subsequent references given in the text.

EDWIN: ...why try to build a church in this place? It's only fit for allotments for
          growin' whelks and cockles in, this is.
ALFRED: Why do they need a church 'ere?
RAHERE: Because God needs a church here. (24)

The ghostly help that Rahere's men offer the modern workmen is dependent upon
their, as he puts it, having faith. (28) The idea is another of the jarring elements in
the play, since the faith the modern characters might have in their building ability
is not necessarily proven, as it was for Rahere, to be exemplary of their Christian
belief. What the printed text of the play calls the 'Builder's Song', a song repeated
several times across the piece, ends by proclaiming 'a Church for us all'. But that
assertion again rests uncertainly with the persistent questions previously in this
'song', which signal continuing unemployment and poverty, capitalist misappro-
priation, and grudging passivity: 'How late shall we wait?' (28–9) Shakespeare's
gravediggers, of course, also consider themselves to be builders for eternity. To the
question 'Who builds stronger than a mason, a shipwright, or a carpenter?', the
answer given is ' "A grave-maker". The houses he makes last till doomsday.' (V. i,
45, 65) (152–3) Hamlet, coming upon the gravedigger as he sings, comments
upon the inappropriateness of such an activity, given this employment. But Hamlet
learns that singing is in fact the most apposite response to a gravedigger's proximate
awareness of the futility of the human situation, and confirms his insight through
his address to Yorick's skull. (65ff) Eliot's builders, aware of the void beneath the
human show, raise similar questions to those in *Hamlet*, and indulge similar
knockabout and farce to Shakespeare's comedians (Rahere is comically compared
by Edwin to the contemporary music-hall performer George Robey).

The manuscript materials relating to *The Rock* in the Bodleian Library, Oxford,
show Eliot, in notes to himself, ask whether the seemingly positive trajectory to
human history provided by the Church had halted, as men might now be seen to
be 'failing Xianity', and so the world to be falling into 'decay'.[25] That hiatus in the
finished version, which is only bridged by the literal appearance of support from
the past upon the modern stage, carried potentially apocalyptic potential in Eliot's
initial conception of the drama. But the drafts also show him to have been assiduous in tracking down materials to give authenticity to the Early Modern religious
figures which intervene in his pageant at one point, into the debate between a
Major, Millicent, and Mrs Poultridge, about the appropriateness of church decora-
tion, and the role of the clergy, in the modern Church. Several sheets in the archive
contain his copyings-out of passages from 'Latimer's Sermon' ('O London, London,
repent, repent'), and from the 'father of Congregationalism', Robert Browne
('Their stinted service is a Papish beadroll'), which are in their turn put directly
into the play's final text.[26]

Concurrent with the mediation provided for the framework of *The Rock*, via the
demotic of the gravediggers in *Hamlet*, contemporary editors of these two Early
Modern preachers, who are then made to speak anonymously through Eliot's text,

[25] Bodleian Library, Oxford, MS don. d. 44, 85.
[26] Bodleian Library, Oxford, MS don. d. 44, 61, 63–4.

emphasized the populist nature of their preaching. Latimer is praised by Canon Beeching, in contrast to Andrewes and Donne, for the fact that he goes against their appeals to 'the trained intelligence':

> Whether he is preaching in a country town or before the king at Westminster, [he] always speaks so that the servants and handmaids shall carry away as much as the gentler sort.

This is because, it is asserted, Latimer's sole subject is 'righteousness', a matter of 'conscience', and not of 'the intellect'.[27] The book from which Eliot drew his passages from Robert Browne, notes that preacher's appeal to a non-conformist 'companie' through his 'harsh and spicy' rhetoric.[28] At this stage of his preparations towards writing *The Rock*, Eliot was in America; his transcriptions from Champlin Burrage's book about the preacher Robert Browne were made on notepaper headed 'Eliot House'. Doubleness, like that figured in Marston's *Sophonisba*, is conveyed by Eliot into unlikely territory.

To this extent, *The Rock* manifests what the title character calls in his opening address, and 'however you disguise it', a worldly version of 'The perpetual struggle of Good and Evil'. (9) Another of the Builder's Songs recasts this, with metropolitan fervour, as 'Ill done and undone,/London so fair./We will build London/Bright in dark air'. (19) Like the comparable passage from *Little Gidding*, this encapsulates the swaying equivocation of the 'ill done' and/or 'undone' that hover threateningly in *The Rock*, until we arrive at the 'miracle' of the church's completion at its end. Eliot seems to be nodding here to a passage from John Ford's play *The Lover's Melancholy*, in which an old man, Meleander, reflects upon the sins and errors that he (wrongly) presumes led to his having his life's joy, his daughter Ercola, snatched away from him:

> Sigh out a lamentable tale of things
> Done long ago, and ill done; and, when sighs
> Are wearied, piece up what remains behind
> With weeping eyes, and hearts that bleed to death...
> (IV. ii, 119–22)[29]

Meleander's is one of those reflective moments in Early Modern drama when a character perceives their tragic situation as a story not wholly their own. As with

---

[27] Introduction by Canon Beeching to *Sermons by Hugh Latimer Sometime Bishop of Worcester* (London: J.M. Dent, 1906), vii. Eliot transcribed passages from Latimer's 1548 so-called 'Sermon of the Plough' on p. 58 of this edition; the transcription appears on p. 72 of the printed text of *The Rock*.

[28] Champlin Burrage, *The True Story of Robert Browne (1550?-1633) Father of Congregationalism* (London: Henry Froude, 1906), 13. The passages Eliot transcribed appear on pp. 23–4 of the Burrage, and on pp. 73–4 of *The Rock*.

[29] *John Ford*, ed. Havelock Ellis (Mermaid Edition, London: Vizetelly, 1888), 67. Contrary to Meleander's (and our) fears, Ercola had in fact been spirited away because she is threatened with rape. She has to live disguised as a boy in Athens. The experience leaves her with anger at life like her father's—and like Eliot's—as, for example, in 'the span of time/Doth waste us to our graves, and we look on it./An age of pleasures, revelled out, comes home/At last and ends in sorrow' (IV. iii, 57–60). (72)

the sources for *The Waste Land*, familial lament in his Early Modern source text is again recast by Eliot into a statement of social, and historical, significance.

The 'dark air' does not disappear because the new world, or church, is built within it. Eliot's sense of the complexities behind the Early Modern framework, and the resonances that he gives to *The Rock*, underpin an unease that the difficulties of identification, in this pageant play, transmits. The generic instabilities of this work, which combine the comic-philosophic Cockney banter of the builders with the biblical rhetoric of the choruses and The Rock's pronouncements, are of a piece with the nature of a pageant play, commissioned as it was to raise money for building new churches in the City of London. But similar rhetorical and generic instabilities persist across Eliot's other plays, as they do in Shakespeare's 'problem plays', including *Measure for Measure* and *Troilus and Cressida* (a source, as we shall see, for *The Cocktail Party*), and in Shakespeare's late plays or Romances.

EARLY MODERN STAGECRAFT, CHARACTERIZATION, AND ELIOT'S DRAMAS

Eliot's mature verse dramas display, then, traits that carry them beyond allusion into variation, or repetition in different form, of some of his set themes. These are traits that, at least partly, derive from Eliot's attention to the Early Modern dramas he was most familiar with, and to the critical context in which they were being perceived at the time. As he moved closer to achieving what now seems his long-signalled interest in writing his own plays, certain strands within that persistent attention (although strands reflected, as often before, through his occasional commissions, such as reviews for the *TLS*) seem to have become more vivid in Eliot's thinking. These strands, in their turn, fed into his own distinctive theatre business, from the time of his response to the suggestion that he write *Murder in the Cathedral* onwards.

Part of that critical context, although one to which Eliot had not until the later 1920s been openly alert, was the question of the actual staging of Early Modern drama, both originally and in the modern theatre. Some work had taken place, from the end of the nineteenth century, to consider the actual conditions of dramatic production as they influenced the writing of those Early Modern plays highlighted (albeit equivocally, in Eliot's view) in Lamb's *Specimens*. Whilst it had formed a facet of the critical surveys of the Early Modern drama in the later nineteenth century (witness John Addington Symonds's General Introduction to the original Mermaid Series, discussed in Chapter One), Eliot's concern about overemphasizing the textual aspects of these plays, without sufficiently considering their performance practice, had been pre-empted, at a theoretical level, by various essays of the actor-manager William Poel.[30] Poel's 1893 essay 'The Stage of Shakespeare' had lamented that:

---

[30] As late as 1936, Eliot was paying tribute to Poel's transformative effect in turning the study of Shakespeare's plays towards this practical necessity. See 'The Need for Poetic Drama: A Schools Broadcast to Sixth Forms', *The Listener*, vol. XVI, no. 411 (25 November 1936), 994.

The interdependence of Shakespeare's dramatic art with the form of the theatre for which Shakespeare wrote his plays is seldom emphasised. The ordinary reader and the everyday critic have no historic knowledge of the Elizabethan playhouse; and however full the Elizabethan dramas may be of allusions to the contemporary stage, the bias of modern dramatic students is so opposed to any belief in the superiority of past methods of acting Shakespeare over modern ones, as to effectively bar any serious enquiry.[31]

Poel's various similar contentions bring to the fore, again, that sense of historical difference within familiarity which underwrote Pater's and Eliot's interest in the Early Modern period. In a later polemical essay, Poel pointed to the 'citizens' playhouses' that existed, in Elizabethan times, 'in close proximity to both palace and warehouse, there all classes of the community sat within sight of each other'. Such unity he contrasts to the 'wrong' practice in contemporary theatre of the early twentieth century, plagued as it was by 'theatre capitalists', 'traders', and, in consequence, a theatre that had become an 'industry' at odds with artistic purpose.[32]

These issues of historical accuracy and dramatic performance seem particularly to have engaged Eliot anew, though, in 1927, when he excitedly reviewed two books by the American scholar W.J. Lawrence, *The Physical Conditions of the Elizabethan Public Playhouse* and *Pre-Restoration Stage Studies*.[33] Like Poel, and other recent critics such as Symonds or the combative William Archer, W.J. Lawrence's starting point was the bareness of the Elizabethan theatre, when compared to modern playhouses. The original platform stage (as opposed to the later one framed by a proscenium arch) was a stage surrounded, and partly occupied, by the audience. It lacked the presentational facilities modern audiences had come to depend on, and wonder at, such as scenery.[34] As *The Physical Conditions* saw it, in those original plays, as a result, 'The appeal was largely to the imagination, and to that appeal there was a vivid response.'[35] Lawrence did not show himself to be particularly concerned to develop the relation between the plays' texts and the imagination, however. This reticence is probably what, in his theories, most appealed to Eliot. Instead, Lawrence concentrated upon the practicalities of the plays in their original theatre settings, and saw the imagination as something that is, in fact,

[31] William Poel, *Shakespeare in the Theatre* (London: Sidgwick and Jackson, 1913), 3.

[32] William Poel, *What is Wrong with the Stage* (London: George Allen, 1920), 5.

[33] Eliot had earlier, however, displayed impatience with the prolonged argument of a piece by W.J. Lawrence, which considered the presence of cornets in the stage directions regarding music in Early Modern drama, a piece that he felt obliged to print in *The Criterion* in 1923 (*LII*, 227–8).

[34] One of the Early Modern plays which derives most comic energy from the audience's partial positioning onstage in the original theatre was Beaumont and Fletcher's *The Knight of the Burning Pestle* (1613)—a play which Eliot included on his Reading List for his Extension Lectures in Elizabethan Literature, 1919–20. Similar stage business then opens Jonson's *Bartholomew Fair* (1614)— also on Eliot's lecture list.

[35] W.J. Lawrence, *The Physical Conditions of the Elizabethan Public Playhouse* (Cambridge, MA: Harvard University Press, 1927), 3. Arthur Melville Clark's *Thomas Heywood: Playwright and Miscellanist*—the book notionally under review in Eliot's essay 'Thomas Heywood'—points to the effect of 'no scenery, and the crudest machinery and lighting' in the original theatres, when accounting for the 'degree of artificiality and exaggeration and heightening, declamation and eloquence and peculiarities of style' commonly found in Early Modern dramatic verse, and particularly in that of his subject, Heywood (Oxford: Basil Blackwell, 1931, 232).

carefully governed and directed through the stage presentation. As *The Physical Conditions* concluded, in a statement that remained in creative tension with this kind of earlier assertion in his book:

> What we have…to bear in mind is that no permanent appurtenance of the Elizabethan stage had existence in the eyes of the audience until it was actually pressed into the service of the scene…. Nothing was imagined on the Elizabethan stage that could conveniently be shown.[36]

As a result of this approach, W.J. Lawrence's paired book, *Pre-Restoration Stage Studies*, emphasized the necessary 'realism' of effects in the Early Modern theatre. If the end of the first scene of *The Tempest* called for 'drenched' players, 'that is what was seen'; if the 'Illusion of Sounds' called for a representation of birdsong at a moment in a play, that was what was heard.[37]

Eliot's enthusiastic review of W.J. Lawrence's linked books of 1927 lamented only that there were not enough diagrams of the Elizabethan playhouses provided in them for the reader to keep up with the author's analysis (he gripes at having to draw his own!).[38] Eliot praises particularly, however, Lawrence's chapters on 'realism', which included (amongst much else) discussion of the use of animal blood on the original stage, to convey the effects of violence and manifold killings; ways of pretending to cut out tongues (useful knowledge for staging *Titus Andronicus* and Kyd's *The Spanish Tragedy*—both plays alluded to in *The Waste Land*); how to perform 'hangings' or 'beheadings'; as well as the relish created in the Early Modern audience by the playwrights' seizing the opportunity to 'intensify' the 'horror' 'by every possible stage artifice':

> Torture scenes in which the rack, the strappado, and burning with hot irons figured were carried out with rigorous exactitude. (235–6)

Eliot's own theatre works allow themselves only two such moments of 'horror'. There is the killing onstage of Thomas Becket in *Murder in the Cathedral*, but, in the other instance, Eliot sticks to the Greek conventions of the shaping model for his play, and the horror is conveyed only by report. Celia Coplestone's crucifixion, as narrated in *The Cocktail Party*, caused a suitably outraged response in the theatre, from its first rendition in Edinburgh onwards.[39]

Eliot's interest in the terrifying and horrific realism of the Elizabethan stage, as presented (or re-confirmed) by W.J. Lawrence, then underpinned his fascination with two other chapters in *Pre-Restoration Stage Studies*, as evidenced in his review. These were the chapters on the use of trapdoors in original productions and

---

[36] W.J. Lawrence, *The Physical Conditions of the Elizabethan Public Playhouse*, 70.

[37] W.J. Lawrence, *Pre-Restoration Stage Studies* (Cambridge, Massachusetts: Harvard University Press, 1927), 222. Subsequent references are given in the text.

[38] 'Stage Studies', unsigned review of *Pre-Restoration Stage Studies* by William J. Lawrence; *The Physical Conditions of the Elizabethan Public Playhouse* by William J. Lawrence, *TLS* 8th December 1927, no. 1,349, 927.

[39] E. Martin Browne charts the shock caused by this crucifixion, from Eliot's drafts for the play, through rehearsals to production, and Eliot's modification (his toning down) of the passage in the published text. See *The Making of T.S. Eliot's Plays*, 225–9.

(relatedly, as it turns out) that on '"Hamlet" As Shakespeare Staged It'. Lawrence worries away at the issue of where on the stage the trapdoor was placed, through which the ghost of Hamlet's father arose. Eliot, whose own considerations of this opening scene of *Hamlet* characterized his discussions of poetic drama from the 1930s through to 1951, pointed out, in his review, that Lawrence's argument proved, in contradistinction to tendencies in modern psychological interpretations of the play, that the ghost *did* appear physically on Shakespeare's stage at the Globe. The presence of the trapdoor on early stages not only made such ghostly presences possible, but an expected feature of a play for an Early Modern audience. Eliot's own *The Family Reunion* somewhat awkwardly stages its own actual appearance of ghostly, godlike figures, when the Eumenides chasing Harry appear outside his family home. E. Martin Browne has charted Eliot's input to conversations regarding the difficulties of staging that the revelation of the actual figures created in production, conversations similar to those reflected in W.J. Lawrence's worrying away at the placing of the trapdoor for *Hamlet*.[40] There is an interesting concatenation between Eliot's experience, as reader, of such problems on the Elizabethan stage as raised by W.J. Lawrence, and his own interest in confronting such things, when writing plays in the later 1930s. The practical and philosophical relation between the objective experience as something shown, and the subjective experience as it is narrated, will form one pivot of my discussion of Eliot's mature dramas in the next chapter.

The other practical issue raised by W.J. Lawrence, which had a considerable impact on Eliot's theatre, but which also resonates out into his established poetics and metaphysics, as they have hitherto been delineated across this book, is what Lawrence called 'doubling' on the Early Modern stage. Eliot mused beyond the scope of Lawrence's own speculations, in his *TLS* review, only on this matter. The issues raised across Early Modern drama, by the limited number of players in each theatre company, a limited number that yet had to deliver complex and populous plots, involved considerable thought for Early Modern dramatists, as Lawrence contended. They had to allow for the necessity that actors must adopt several characters within any one play, and that those characters must remain separate, and immediately identifiable, in their distinct roles, to the audience. Intriguingly, with relation to 'Marina' and other of his poems, and in his musing over Lawrence's review, Eliot was notably fascinated by the prospect that the actor playing Perdita in Shakespeare's *The Winter's Tale* might also take on the part of her mother, Hermione. Lawrence in fact briefly raised this, only strongly to dismiss it. (62) Lawrence's practicality in all matters sees him openly rejecting those 'psychological' possibilities, which the presentation of one actor in several guises might engage.

---

[40] Browne, *The Making of T.S. Eliot's Plays*, especially pp. 132–7. Eliot seems to have so driven himself to distraction over the problem that, by the time of that 1951 lecture, 'Poetry and Drama', he seemed to adopt the 'modern' production solution, and suggest that no Eumenides should actually appear, and that the actor playing Harry should suggest that they are figments in his mind (*OPP*, 84). Browne's discussion makes it clear, though, that, with appropriate placing on the set of the window through which the Eumenides are seen, the piece can be staged with the figures appearing to actors and audience.

(66) Eliot manifestly and repeatedly himself displayed similar resistance to 'psychological' reading, as we have seen in earlier chapters. But the potential of 'doubling' clearly struck Eliot, a writer himself drawn to a multiple and multivalent staging of personality in his critical essays, his reading of Early Modern literature, and his own multivocal poetry ('I am not all heere').[41]

Such issues had a decisive impact within Eliot's mature dramas. Most immediately, 'doubling' formed part of the stagecraft, but also the metaphysical implication, of *Murder in the Cathedral*, where the actors playing the Knights who have come to kill Thomas Becket also play the parts of the Tempters who seek to lure him from his set course towards martyrdom. Then, in what at that time would have been a radical switch at the end of the play, the same actors appear as modern-day versions of themselves, versions who address the audience directly.[42] At an ontological level, as well as a familial one, doubling hovers as a conceit to elucidate the action of *The Family Reunion*, as also Harry's (and Eliot's, as we have seen) sense that the drama which he must play out is enacted on 'several planes' simultaneously. The near-relation of doubling, the disguises adopted by so many characters that enable the plots of so many Early Modern comedies and tragedies, also proves pivotal in *The Cocktail Party*. The issue of unclear, equivocal identity or origins, familiar, engagingly, in Shakespeare's late plays, drives the revelation narrative of Eliot's *The Confidential Clerk*, as it had partially *The Rock*. Then, in Eliot's final drama, *The Elder Statesman*, issues about names, naming, and identity are worked through, as the principal dialogue and drama.

Doubling is, of course, a key potential extrapolation from that sense of artifice which is foregrounded in Early Modern drama, and which enables those characters who fascinated Eliot, from Bussy d'Ambois, Aspatia, through to Sophonisba and Othello, to conceive of themselves both as figures in a play, and as figures able to *speak about* themselves at the time of their deaths, as though they were other people, viewing figures already consigned to history. At the heart of their potential lies a crucial pressure, which Eliot carries over from Early Modern drama (Hamlet, Timon, Coriolanus, Bussy), especially after his own acceptance into the Anglo-Catholic Church: the question of the sin of pride, as it relates to the distinction of dramatic heroism. Pride, related issues about place in history, and martyrdom, form the essential temptations for Becket as Eliot's *Murder in the Cathedral* casts him; it is the 'sin' worked through most fully in the manuscripts and final rendering of *The Family Reunion*, as the next chapter shows.[43]

---

[41] The ludicrous possibilities of this are perhaps best encapsulated in Thomas Heywood's *The Wise-Woman of Hogsden*, which contains *two* characters of the same name, both in love with Young Chartley, who is himself actually in love with another woman. Eliot expressed his view that the working out of such confusion must have been 'excellent fun' in performance (*SE*, 177).

[42] E. Martin Browne discusses the 'doubling' of these characters as being true to the metaphysical idea of the play. But he also notes that, as with the 'Eumenides problem', Eliot himself became more equivocal about the same actors playing all these parts in a production. Having initially 'concurred' unequivocally, by 1956 he had become uncertain (*The Making of T.S. Eliot's Plays*, 57–8).

[43] In 1932, Eliot signalled an important shift in his evaluation of two key poets. He moved from Donne towards George Herbert, by concluding that Donne had never succeeded in overcoming his 'pride of mind', whereas Herbert had proceeded further towards the calm of humility. 'Studies in

Eliot's attention to this issue was re-concentrated, in his response, as reviewer, to critical work on the Early Modern period at the time of his Christian confirmation. Eliot responded positively to Una Ellis-Fermor's chapters on *Tamburlaine* and *Dr Faustus* in her study *Christopher Marlowe*, greeting it as the first dedicated study of that playwright (although his review lamented the book's lack of textual scholarship, and consideration of authorship and collaboration).[44] Ellis-Fermor's emphasis throughout, as acknowledged by the passages Eliot excerpted in his review, was upon the intellectual craftedness of Marlowe's writing, which was demonstrated for her in *Tamburlaine* by 'a fine instinct for the formal quality of an idea'.[45] This led, she felt, to a sculpted quality in Marlowe's drama, which 'cannot give direct utterance to an emotion'. Yet, 'it is in the world of the ideas that lie behind those outward forms that he moves familiarly'. (58) Whilst it might be tempting to consider this as a variation, translated to Eliot's terminology, of the notion of 'planes in relation' operative through drama, the posed, sculptural effects of Marlowe's 'poetry of ideas', according to Ellis-Fermor in later comments, were suggestive also of the staged tableaux through which dialogue is exchanged in Eliot's own drama.[46]

Ellis-Fermor offered the 'reiterations' and 'deliberate repetitions', exemplified by Tamburlaine's speech at the deathbed of his queen, Zenocrate, as evidence of this stasis within Marlowe's tragic actions (Part II Act II scene iv). But it is clear that she (like Eliot) considered *Tamburlaine*, with its vainglorious, imperialist, hero who readily overcomes such moments of woe as the death of his queen, to be therefore a kind of inverse of Marlowe's other masterpiece, *Dr Faustus*. In remarks praised by Eliot in his review, Ellis-Fermor read 'the central idea' of *Faustus* to be 'an idea of loss', 'the cutting off of the personality from its natural sources of inspiration and faith'. (62) Unlike the redemptive machinery of Shakespeare's late plays, to which Eliot responded so strongly in his poetry of the later 1920s and early 1930s, Ellis-Fermor's critical approach saw *Dr Faustus* as a work in which the hero's line,

Sanctity VIII: George Herbert', *The Spectator*, no. 5411, 12 March 1932, 361. Arthur Waugh's Introduction to *The Poems of George Herbert* ends with a peroration about his subject's 'well learnt' 'lesson of humility', 'the last and hardest lesson a man has to learn' (xvii). For full documentation of this refocusing of Eliot's interest towards Herbert, see Ronald Schuchard's chapter '"If I think, again, of this place": The Way to Little Gidding', *Eliot's Dark Angel: Intersections of Life and Art* (New York: Oxford University Press, 1999), 178–97.

[44] 'A Study of Marlowe', unsigned review of *Christopher Marlowe* by U.M. Ellis-Fermor, *TLS*, 3 March 1927, no. 1309, 140.

[45] U.M. Ellis-Fermor, *Christopher Marlowe* (London: Methuen, 1927), 47. Subsequent references appear in the text.

[46] This would seem to be a conclusion arrived at by Ellis-Fermor herself. In a chapter on 'Imagery in Drama' from her later book *The Frontiers of Drama*, she compared *The Family Reunion* with speeches by Chapman's Byron and Shakespeare's Ulysses in *Troilus and Cressida*: 'Mr T.S. Eliot, in *The Family Reunion*, leaves to imagery the function of revealing much of the thought or of the spiritual experience which would else prove well-nigh inexpressible within the limits of dramatic form. But the function of the imagery here is even more vital than in either of the two other cases, for these thoughts and these experiences are the main stuff of the play, sometimes the sole action' (London: Methuen, 1945, 93). David Nicholl Smith, whose work on Dryden was admired by Eliot, as is attested in 'A Dialogue on Dramatic Poetry', saw the lack of individualization of character in Dryden's plays as cause for their dramatic failure—'they were little more than talking or rhyming abstractions' (*Dryden's Poetry and Prose*, Oxford: Clarendon Press, 1925, xiii). Such is the difficulty Eliot's drama strove to avoid.

'We must sinne, and so consequently die', presents that inevitability which drives the play. Mephistophilis's variant upon the fallen-ness of the world, 'this is hell, nor am I out of it', reflects the situation of Harry, having committed his 'sin' in *The Family Reunion*, as he delineates the particular Hell of his situation.[47] This fatal consequence of loss in *Faustus*, Ellis-Fermor contested, leads to the complete terror experienced by Faustus in the final scenes. His pride, so on display early in the work, is stripped from him at the end.

Eliot quoted extensively from Ellis-Fermor's summary rendition of Faustus's situation, both in his review of her book and in his essay of the same year about Shakespeare's relation to philosophy, 'Shakespeare and the Stoicism of Seneca'. In fact, he quoted more extensively, in both cases, than is given in these lines from Ellis-Fermor's statement (*SE*, 133):

> There is no question any longer of self-reliance or of the preservation of any of the barriers that hold the personality together. For personality is dissolving under a 'touch more rare' than has ever been portrayed in art, and we have only absolute and isolated passion, unmodified and uncontaminated by the influences which must confuse all others. (86)

Unlike the consciousness that all other tragic heroes display towards their surroundings, Ellis-Fermor contended, namely the consciousness which leads them to seek to die nobly, Faustus alone displays 'the experience of a mind isolated from the past, absorbed in the realisation of its own destruction'. (87) Eliot's lengthy transcriptions of her contention, in his review and essay, do not, however, extend to the comparison that Ellis-Fermor found between the uniqueness of *Faustus*, as she conceives it, and 'Aeschylus's *Eumenides*'. In Aeschylus's play, uniquely also, 'the protagonists are man and the spiritual powers that surround him ... in the limitless regions of the mind ... upon the question of man's ultimate fate'. (87) If this is 'the greatest conflict that drama has ever undertaken to represent', as Ellis-Fermor claimed, it is also that at the centre of Eliot's *The Family Reunion*. Eliot's play stages a modern encounter between its protagonist—his mind 'upon the verge of dissolution' to the 'confusion' of his companions (as Ellis-Fermor saw Faustus's to be)—and the pursuing, vengeful, Eumenides.

Murder in the Cathedral

To this extent, certain aspects of *Murder in the Cathedral* seem to prepare for such absolute and unremitting drama. The setting of the original production of the play, the Chapter House at Canterbury Cathedral, meant that the physical conditions in which it was first performed (and for which it was written) shared many of the facets of Early Modern theatre, as Eliot would conceive it from contemporary criticism such as Symonds's and W.J. Lawrence's.[48] But the spareness of the production

---

[47] See, for the original sources, Christopher Marlowe, *Plays*, with an introduction by Edward Thomas (London: Dent, 1910), 128.

[48] E. Martin Browne has pointed to the fact that the constraints of the performance space led to the decision, with Eliot's agreement, to double the parts of the Tempters and the Knights, since otherwise there were too many people on the small platform stage at various moments in the play (*The Making of T.S. Eliot's Plays*, 57).

space surely also concentrates Eliot's conception of the play as a single completed action. Like 'The Hollow Men' and Eliot's later writing, *Murder in the Cathedral* is set in an intermediate time; the action amounts to the working out of a pre-set Fate, from the moment Becket returns to England in opposition to his king's wishes, to his death on the steps of his cathedral. Despite the attempted intervention of the Tempters, Priests, and Chorus from the Women of Canterbury, the play moves to its anticipated end with Becket's martyrdom. To that extent, the plot shares something of the determination of Marlowe's *Dr Faustus*. But, rhetorically, it comes near again to that crucial speech for Eliot, in Shakespeare's *Julius Caesar*. This is the speech that Eliot transcribed as a possible epigraph for *Sweeney Agonistes*, and which had echoed behind 'The Hollow Men':

> Between the acting of a dreadful thing
> And the first motion, all the interim is
> Like a miasma [phantasma], or a hideous dream.
> (II. i, 63–5)

In a further instance of that self-borrowing which Eliot had contemplated in Shakespeare, Becket provides a conscious echo of Eliot's earlier lyric mini-sequence through his response to Percy Allen (see Chapter Six):

> For a little time the hungry hawk
> Will only soar and hover, circling lower...
> Meanwhile the substance of our first act
> Will be shadows, and the strife with shadows.
> Heavier the interval than the consummation.[49]

As discussed in Chapter Five, Eliot's imagery here suggests that fatal shadow(s) exist in the 'interim' between thought, or the inception of action, and the act itself. Becket's use of 'consummation' is, of course, finely poised. It is Hamlet's yearned-for death ('to say we end/The heart-ache, and the thousand natural shocks/That flesh is heir to, 'tis a consummation/Devoutly to be wish'd' [III. i, 61ff]). Yet it is also a more dubious casting of the act of martyrdom as a dramatic culmination to be relished, the role Becket was born to carry through. Such role-playing might paradoxically be the means of lifting of the shadow, the achievement of the directed prayer, which is left incomplete at the end of 'The Hollow Men'.

This is the vulnerability that the Fourth Tempter of Becket plays upon, vulnerability he displays about seeing Becket's role as martyr as a later doubling of that of Christ, since, normally, 'Man's life is a cheat and disappointment'. (50) Hovering unresolvedly over the play, in other words, is the potential that Becket is guilty of the sin of pride. Pride is attributed by the First Priest to his earlier self, who rose to political power rapidly with the Chancellorship. The First Priest attributes this initially with admiration, but also with acknowledgement of the tinge of self-destructiveness involved in it: 'His pride always feeding upon his own virtues'. (28) A 'wall of pride' is seen to separate Becket, as archbishop, from King Henry, and to be the cause of their contention (and thence of Becket's death). (26) At the climax

[49] T.S. Eliot, *Murder in the Cathedral*, with an introduction and notes by Neville Coghill (London: Faber, 1965), 33. Subsequent references to this edition will be given in the text.

of the temptations the audience witnesses him confronting, Becket shows himself alert to the danger:

> Is there no way, in my soul's sickness,
> Does not lead to damnation in pride?
> I well know that these temptations
> Mean present vanity and future torment. (49)

Under the stress of recognition, Becket's sentences display that elliptical tenseness and terseness Eliot had come upon in Shakespeare's later work, and in *Pericles* particularly ('Is there…Does not'). These lines display that flexible length in terms of syllables which Eliot, in 'Poetry and Drama', claims as part of the necessary drive for the modern dramatist against strict pentameter rhythms, rhythms commonly considered to have descended from Shakespeare, as the only possible formal model for dramatic verse.[50] But, syntactically, they display something of that freedom which had been pointed to, particularly as Shakespeare's career developed, by contemporary critics, and by Eliot himself ('Poetry and Drama' cites Faulconbridge's speeches in *King John*, and the Nurse's in *Romeo and Juliet*, as important steps in this direction).[51] The crescendo within Thomas's rhetoric in his last speeches in *Murder in the Cathedral* then brings to the fore those parallelisms and repetitions that have given the play its abiding rhythm. These are parallelisms similar to those Ellis-Fermor had pointed to in *Tamburlaine*, those chant-like plays on words familiar from Shakespeare's late plays. Such repetitions do not, for all of their humility, remove the 'danger' of prideful association, dared in Thomas's acceptance of his fate:

> This is the sign of the Church always,
> The sign of blood. Blood for blood.
> His blood given to buy my life,
> My blood given to pay for his death.
> My death for His death. (80–1)

---

[50] Eliot's later comments on the drama of John Dryden suggest him as one further model for this flexible blank-verse rhythm alongside Shakespeare. In the 1921 essay 'John Dryden', Eliot had commented that it was the 'diction' of Dryden's reworking of *Antony and Cleopatra* as *All for Love* which underpinned the effective liveliness of Dryden's drama (*SE*, 313). In 1931, however, in a radio broadcast on 'Dryden the Dramatist', Eliot praised the blank verse of *All for Love*, and of Dryden's other best plays, as the 'miracle of revivification' which he effected after Shakespeare. Dryden's blank verse had been more influential, he claims, than had hitherto been noticed ('John Dryden II—Dryden the Dramatist', *The Listener*, vol. V, no. 119, 22 April 1931, 681). Paradoxically, however, Eliot feels that Dryden's plays in rhyming couplets might be closer to actual speech than his blank verse. This is a point corroborated in a further broadcast of 1943, where Eliot's emphasis had shifted again. He praised the significance of rhyme in Dryden's early tragedies as indicating his distance from the writing of the mature Shakespeare ('John Dryden's Tragedies', *The Listener*, vol. XXIX, no. 745, 22 April 1943, 487).
[51] These examples were first provided by Eliot in his series of lectures on 'The Development of Shakespeare's Verse' from 1937. A full account of the lectures is given by Charles Warren in *T.S. Eliot on Shakespeare* (Ann Arbor: UMI Research Press, 1987, 92ff.) Eliot's title for his series echoes and differs from that of his Harvard tutor George P. Baker's *The Development of Shakespeare as a Dramatist*. Baker too emphasised the need for Shakespeare to be viewed alongside his contemporaries, and promoted the idea that what made drama 'poetic' was that it should be shaped around a 'unifying idea' (New York: Macmillan, 1907, 1, 5, 308–9, 311–2). Eliot included Baker's book on his Extension list.

The circularity of this is congruent with the play's main image for Fate, an image with which Eliot was necessarily familiar colloquially, but also via such work as *King Lear*. It was an image given new currency in his thinking, perhaps, from G. Wilson Knight's discussion of it in *The Wheel of Fire*. This is the assumption of the turning imagery from *Ash-Wednesday* (and from Shakespeare's *A Winter's Tale*, 'still') into a metaphorical structure for the longer text of the play:

> for the pattern is the action
> And the suffering, that the wheel may turn and still
> Be forever still. (33, 49)

Wilson Knight sees King Lear's plight as that of man alone in a ravening natural universe, where God has become 'God', a power whose reality is gestured at, but not revealed to Lear or to the audience. Wilson Knight's image of the wheel is that of 'the fiery wheel of mortal life'.[52] Within the orbit of such ontology, Eliot's Chorus fulfils its classic function, reading the portents much as Gloucester does in *King Lear* ('These late eclipses of the sun and moon portend no good to us' [I. ii, 100])[53]:

> Ill the wind, ill the time, uncertain the profit, certain the danger.
> O late, late, late, late is the time, late too late, and rotten the year;
> Evil the wind, and bitter the sea, and grey the sky, grey grey grey. (29)

That unseasonableness, which we have remarked many times in this study as defining Eliot's paradoxical sense of modernity, here, via *King Lear*, is read as an overturning of a natural order that both predicts and mirrors a disorder overcoming the human reality.[54]

Becket's sense of a reciprocity, in the expense of his (human) 'blood' 'to pay for' Christ's blood, seems, on the surface, to re-establish a true—if extreme and suffering—ordering of humanity within the Church.[55] But, in fact, this elides the historical apocalypse that is elsewhere signalled as enacted by Becket's 'Murder', otherwise his martyrdom. Neville Coghill remarks, in his edition of *Murder in the Cathedral*, the printed text's archaic spelling of 'subtle' as 'subtile', when the Chorus responds to the charged-up rants of the Knights ('senses are quickened/By subtile forebodings'). Coghill claims that this spelling derives from John Donne's poem 'The Exstasie':

---

[52] G. Wilson Knight, *The Wheel of Fire* (London: Oxford University Press, 1930), 200.

[53] One possible source for the attitudes displayed by Eliot's Women of Canterbury, who serve as the Chorus in *Murder in the Cathedral*, might be Jonson's Chorus of the people of Rome in *Catiline his Conspiracy*. For example, 'Let us...give to every noble deed/The name it merits.//Lest we seem fallen, if this endures,/Into these times,/To love disease, and brook the cures/Worse than the crimes' (IV. vii). See *The Complete Plays*, ed, Felix Schelling (London: Dent, 1910), 161.

[54] Again, Fate is described as a 'burning wheel', normality as a 'human wheel', by Harry in *The Family Reunion* (London: Faber, 1939, 28, 94).

[55] In a draft for a speech by the Chorus, they chant that they see everything 'smeared' with blood, 'through a curtain of falling blood' (quoted by Browne, *The Making of T.S. Eliot's Plays*, 51). The drafts recall the passage in Marlowe where 'Christ's blood streams in the firmament', cited by Eliot in his essay on that playwright (*SW*, 76).

As our blood labours to beget
Spirits as like souls as it can,
Because such fingers need to knit
The subtle knot which makes us man. (73, 128–9)[56]

When treating of Donne's poem in *The Varieties of Metaphysical Poetry*, Eliot had singled it out, as exemplary of the *historical* and paradoxically 'modern' rift that had occurred between Dante's *trecento* and Donne's more psychological age. The virtual duplication of qualities as 'body' and 'soul' in 'The Exstasie' heralds that disjunction between them, which is then given apocalyptic force in English literary history (*VMP* 108–15).[57] The Women of Canterbury's intuition, hinted to readers by the archaism of the published *Murder in the Cathedral*, locates that drama at a pivotal moment in time, one at which brute physical thuggery and an Early Modern theatrical horror (the onstage killing of Thomas) threatens to impose itself upon the spiritual meditation with which the play otherwise engages. In other words, Eliot translates his by now familiar notion of historical 'dissociation', and imposes it, as the intensifier of dramatic tension, within his medieval drama.

Tonally, such pivotal historical setting for the drama is conveyed through the interjection of the prose sermon on Christ's nativity between the two Parts of *Murder in the Cathedral*. In his late self-reflection 'To Criticize the Critic', Eliot acknowledged that there might be some presence of Lancelot Andrewes' sermons behind his prose (*TCC*, 20). Becket's staged sermon was presumably eerily odd in its original performance in the Chapter House, Canterbury Cathedral. But it is reminiscent, also, of the theatrical effects Eliot had admired in Early Modern sermons in the late 1910s, effects that he would, as we shall see in the next chapter, shortly exploit himself. Becket's sermon, in this instance, captures an encompassing, undulating intention, one that seems to derive from two familiar sources in Andrewes. The instigating biblical text for his sermon, from Luke II: 14, 'Glory to God in the highest, and on earth peace to men of good will', carries desperate ironic charge within the working-out of Becket's fate being witnessed. According to the Index of the edition with which Eliot was most familiar, that Luke text is one of the most cited in Andrewes' *Seventeen Sermons on the Nativity*. It flits through most of them, always associated with singing, as in the peroration from Sermon VII on 'this day's work' 'wherein [the angels] sang aloud in the sky', and 'we have cause to make much of, and to rejoice in it; the day of the greatest "glory to God" '.[58]

---

[56] Eliot's liking of archaic spelling is evident, to less immediate effect, in his seeking to retain, through to the poem's first printing, 'aresse' as the more authentic (in many senses, since it derived from Sir Thomas Elyot's *The Governour*) spelling for 'arras' in *East Coker* I. See Helen Gardner, *The Composition of Four Quartets* (London: Faber, 1978), 96–7.

[57] Christopher Ricks locates similar troubling about 'body' and 'soul' early within Eliot's work, back to the Marvellian 'First Debate Between the Body and Soul' of 1910 (*IMH*, 228–9). In the published work, this is a 'debate' that occurs as early as 'La Figlia Che Piange', and as late as *Little Gidding*, where the two 'begin to fall asunder' (*CPP*, 194).

[58] Lancelot Andrewes, *Seventeen Sermons on the Nativity* (London: Griffith, Farran, Okeden & Welsh, n.d.), 115.

Becket's sermon memorably also takes its strain from the Ariel Poems, 'Journey of the Magi' and 'A Song for Simeon', seeing on this natal day reminder *both* of Christ's Birth and of His Death, 'as we rejoice and mourn at once, in the Birth and in the Passion of Our Lord'. (56) It is this running together of events that makes them seem to be naturally and immediately succeeded by the death of the first martyr, Stephen (and by Becket's own murder).[59] The sermon therefore takes its tone *both* from the rejoicing of the Luke II text, its subsequent resonance through the delight of Andrewes' Nativity Sermons, *and* from the 'mourning' that configures the Ash-Wednesday 1619 sermon, which had stood behind Eliot's sequence of that name. In proleptic acknowledgement of the audience's response to the portrayal of his own death, Becket's staged sermon, as rendered by Eliot, both alerts us to the 'consummation' that *Murder in the Cathedral* presents, and also to the governing tone of 'passing away' proposed by Eliot's historical understanding, which the moment of Becket's martyrdom encapsulates. Eliot's drama, with its surprising and awkward return to the modern world of its moment crucially, in the Knights' final speeches, renders the dilemmas of historical circumstance—past and present—within its ontological progression.[60]

[59] Such concatenations in Eliot's poetry, of course, look back to the early 'The Love Song of St. Sebastian' and 'The Death of Saint Narcissus'.

[60] In a later talk, *Religious Drama: Medieval and Modern*, Eliot reflected that a religious play should not seek to form a substitute for liturgy, but that it must combine the religious with 'ordinary' and 'secular' dramatic concerns (New York: House of Books Ltd, 1954 reprint, unnumbered pages).

8

'A Fusion, in Sympathy or Antipathy'
Four Quartets and the Late Plays

THE FAMILY REUNION THROUGH ITS DRAFTS

Eliot's plays after *Murder in the Cathedral* are all translations, into contemporary settings, of Greek originals. Yet they all display the impact of his extensive experience of Early Modern drama, and of its poetry.[1] Given the estranging effect of the staging of Becket's sermon in Eliot's first mature and complete drama, *Murder in the Cathedral*, it is unsurprising that his updating of the *Oresteia* as a country-house drama in his next theatre work, *The Family Reunion*, should wholeheartedly adopt familiar metaphors of theatricality. These metaphors are deployed as a means to express the play's alienating central perceptions about selfhood and destiny: the imperative 'is and seems', as received in 'Animula' (*CPP*, 108). These perceptions are then carried forward to Eliot's later plays, as well as being re-cadenced in *Four Quartets*.

In the closing chapter of this study on T.S. Eliot and his Early Modern sources, impacts and effects are picked up that have kept reiterating in different guises throughout, and which now, in his late major work, were given a final twist. For instance, selfhood and identity are embraced through theatrical metaphors with specific philosophic purpose, or become integral to the plot devices that Eliot conceived. In the process, the Early Modern work referred to often reveals a less clear, a morally troubling, resonance, which unsettles the well-made surface of the finished play. Drafts and notes become important once again in unravelling the primary motivation for Eliot's urge to remake his sources into something new and strange.

In the opening chorus of *The Family Reunion*, Ivy, Violet, Gerald, and Charles, the aunts and uncles of Harry, fret that they are 'amateur actors' who have rehearsed the wrong play, and who now have to appear in a 'different play', in different roles from those anticipated. They fear the derision of the audience.[2] By the end of the play, this fretfulness is confirmed as appropriate. After the appearance of the vengeful Eumenides, who have pursued Harry and haunted his mind since his wife's

---

[1] Euripedes' *Alcestis* is the immediate source for *The Cocktail Party*; his *Ion* for *The Confidential Clerk*. Sophocles' *Oedipus at Colonus* underwrites the final play, *The Elder Statesman*.

[2] T.S. Eliot, *The Family Reunion* (London: Faber, 1939), 21, 22. Subsequent references to this edition appear in the text.

death, and who have for the first time assumed a physical presence upon his return to the family home at Wishwood, Harry registers the 'oddity' of the situation. Like Hamlet, he had expected to find peace by returning to the place in which he grew up. Yet he has come to recognize that the 'part that had been imposed upon me', by his earlier life with the family, has become changed by his moment of extreme experience. Now, he might be forced to accept a new part, which has been 'made ready' for him, and over which he has no control. (99) That sense of actors appearing in a drama which has been authored outside themselves, so much a theme of Eliot's favourite Early Modern tragedies and Shakespearean late plays, including *The Tempest*, figures in each of Eliot's own mature plays. But it is perhaps most pronounced within the unresolved 'mystery', the literal and personal hauntedness, of *The Family Reunion*.

Within a recurring and governing metaphor of the theatre *The Family Reunion* presents the wrenching effect of Harry's 'deed', when he pushed his wife over the side of the liner on which they were travelling. Spiralling out of the sense that every character is 'acting', maintained in the latter part of the drama, there are many images centred on the broken self, or of the self that is irretrievably lost: 'I was someone else', 'I could not fit myself together', 'I not a person', 'I was not there, you were not there'. (58, 93, 101) If, in terms of the various doubling identifications of the play, Harry seems fated to repeat his father's desire to kill his wife (unsuccessfully in the father's case), he also shares the truth-telling role of the Early Modern fool. He punctures the illusions about selfhood, of the complacent survivors in the mundane world, who surround him.[3] Yet, as the recurrent images of brokenness that he uses to describe his recent situation attest, his is also the tragically 'dissolving' personality (as Una Ellis-Fermor called it)—one who, like Marlowe's Faustus, is distanced from those around him.

That the 'dissolving' of Harry's character was Eliot's primary concern in *The Family Reunion* becomes clearer from a consideration of the multiple drafts of the play. In these, from the outset, Eliot's main struggle (apart from his reconsiderations of the true relation between Harry and Mary) seems to have been with the expression of dissociation that Harry claims to have suffered through his experience, and through which he is suffering the (psychological then 'real') haunting by the Eumenides. The various typescripts of the play, held at the Houghton Library in Harvard University and in the Hayward Bequest at King's College, Cambridge, show Eliot seeking intensely and predominantly to find terms for Harry's tragic dissolution. Through this revision process Eliot comes to reconsider the established principles of what he took verse drama to be, at this late stage of his career. The drafts display Harry's speeches and character struggling to achieve 'humility' before his fate. This is a version, in Harry, of that 'aesthetic' attitude towards the awfulness

---

[3] Eliot had earlier engaged with this tradition through his response to Olive Mary Busby's *Studies in the Development of the Fool in the Elizabethan Drama*, which expands upon the 'frankness' of such figures (London: Oxford University Press, 1923, 19). S.L. Bethell, in a book endorsed with a Preface by Eliot (important, as we shall see, for his late plays), compared Sweeney in *Sweeney Agonistes* to Touchstone in *As You Like It*; the same comparison might be made of Harry. See *Shakespeare and the Popular Dramatic Tradition* (London: P.S. King and Staples, 1944), 94.

of events, which is what Eliot seems to have felt was to be the final achievement of the Early Modern tragic heroes with whom he was fascinated—Othello, Bussy d'Ambois, Coriolanus, Timon, Antony (*SE*, 130–1). The discussion here will be concerned with the traces of Harry's 'attitude' in the drafts of the play, and will observe how these travails become elided from Eliot's initial impulses—a process of suppression of original dialogue with his sources we have encountered from the outset of his career, in a consistent creative process that evolved his writings away from their initial preoccupations. As Eliot gained a clearer articulation of his under-lying 'pattern' across his drafts of *The Family Reunion*, he lost something of the immediacy with which Harry was originally treated.

In *The Family Reunion* the character of Mary is clearly created to provide a possible frisson of love interest. It remains possible that Harry's 'hell' might be redeemed through a new marriage, until he realizes that his horror at what has happened with his wife has blighted all his relationships with women. In 'Type-script A' of the play, held at the Houghton Library (which gives the play a subtitle erased in the final version: 'A Melodrama'), the interchange between Mary and Harry in Part I scene II is longer than in the final form. It includes an exchange in which Mary states her true view of Harry, one that perhaps seemed too prescriptive to Eliot on revision. Harry typically anguishes about the insubstantiality into which he seems to have lapsed ('Am I anything more/At last, than a shadow among shadows?'), to be met by rebuff:

> MARY: Is your fear not also pride? You have become the actor
> Of a single role, fearful of a new one.[4]

Mary's original comment is interesting, not just for the way it touches upon that primary sin, pride, which dogs so many tragic heroes from Marlowe onwards. It also imbues the play's recurring theatrical metaphors with an ontological truth-fulness. We are alerted to the technical difficulties of any drama, even a drama as acutely attuned to the dilemmas and dramatic possibilities of doubling, between characters and within a single character, as Eliot's. Harry himself describes this dilemma satirically but tragically, bringing that practical emphasis to the fore. In the final version of the play, when chiding the family for its conventional life and limited emotional response, Harry presents himself as, in contrast, 'awake', 'living on several planes at once', in a formula familiar from Eliot's engagement with Early Modern drama from the early 1920s onwards.

Through Harry, the inherent limitation of Eliot's version of metaphysical poetry is more starkly defined than elsewhere. Harry immediately catches himself up after his statement about the 'several planes': 'Though one cannot speak with several voices at once'. (82) The inherently dramatic quality of Eliot's poetry, its speaking in and through several voices, is hampered by its lyric past. That poetry progresses in its later phases, as we have seen, away from the multiple voicings of *The Waste Land*, towards presentation of various strains and strands within a single dominant monologue, however 'in character' or 'dramatic' that single voice is. This trend will

---

[4] Houghton Library, Harvard, MS Am. 1691.14 (37), 33.

continue in *Four Quartets*. In Eliot's actual dramas, even when presenting a distanced and reflective character like Harry, the verse cannot present the selves into which that character has become 'dissolved', simultaneously. Therefore, Harry's reflective speeches, like Sweeney's in *Sweeney Agonistes*, are markedly in contrast to the baffled banter of the other characters; we find him constantly circling back on himself (as Eliot did in his draft versions of the play) in order to express more clearly the nature and effects of the 'dissolving' of his personality, which he feels that he has undergone.

In short, Harry cannot achieve the summational final consciousness of Early Modern tragic heroes. The generic uncertainty within which he finds himself is advertised by the erasure of the generic subtitle, 'melodrama', from the various drafts of *The Family Reunion*. Yet what was first called a 'melodrama' cannot readily grow into a tragedy either. Although 'ordered' by its mythic setting, and by the dramatic unities that it derives from its Greek source, the contemporary nature of Eliot's play prevents it from establishing traditional generic coherence. We are once again within the tragicomic realm of Shakespeare's 'problem plays'; the country-house setting of *The Family Reunion* suggests light comedy: the 'dissolving' of Harry's character, something like the tragedy of Faustus or Hamlet. Eliot's many revisions to Harry's thoughts about himself across the manuscript versions only serve to suppress the extremity of his awareness of his tragically difficult situation. The drafting of Harry's long semi-soliloquy, his second speech in Part II scene II, is to the point in this regard. Harry seeks to explain his situation to the sympathetic aunt, Agatha: 'I am interested in Hell, and I must think it out' is a line crossed through in 'Typescript B', presumably because it is too 'melodramatic'.[5] Yet such deleted lines give a more directly Faustian sense to Harry's situation than the 'one hell', 'second hell' descriptions that appear in the final version of this speech. (93) The final version, in other words, is caught on the level of metaphorical description, where some of the earlier, perhaps more tonally inexpressive, versions of this, and other of Harry's speeches, provide a more exact rendition of his anguish.

The printed text of this crucial speech retains some of the 'dream' imagery that infuses the play, as Harry describes his former life as an 'old dream', which the events on the liner have distanced from his present consciousness. Life in this new interim is, once again, analogous to Brutus's 'miasma', 'phantasma', or 'hideous dream'. It is an effect augmented, in this self-consciously theatrical context, by Prospero's grandiloquent knowledge that 'we are such stuff as dreams are made on'. Yet the original typescript ending of the speech had expanded upon this brief and more obvious recurrence of one of the play's stated themes, offering a broader metaphysical and theological possibility than those available in the printed text. The final version considers that Harry's return to his home has brought to him 'The shadow of something behind our meagre childhood,/Some origin of wretchedness'. This is 'wretchedness' caused partly, of course, by his father's adultery and

---

[5] Houghton Library, Harvard, MS Am. 1691 (2) insertion.

urge to murder Amy, Harry's mother, as revealed at length in this scene by Agatha.
Yet the typescript had Harry pointing to:

> The shadow of something behind our meagre childhood,
> Some origin of evil. How far behind us?
> Perhaps the later things have only been a dream
> Dreamt through me by the minds of others. Perhaps
> I only dreamt I pushed her. Why does the reality,
> If so, seem a deeper nightmare?[6]

In the printed text, some of these later lines are redistributed to form Harry's
response to the narrative of Agatha's adultery with his father: 'Perhaps my life has
only been a dream/Dreamt through me by the minds of others. Perhaps/I only
dreamt I pushed her.' (97) Stripped of the cause and effect of such narrative explicit-
ness, however, in their original draft-form context, the lines point up the confusions
between madness, dream, shadowing, nightmare, and the loss of self that harrow
Harry throughout. The 'planes of consciousness' that Harry had earlier calmly
posited, as necessary to a wakefulness that the rest of his family could not achieve,
are here part of a nightmare that depicts maddened loss of control of the self. The
diabolical ('evil') nature of Harry's haunting (like Faustus's) is fully rendered. If
'planes of consciousness' describe the 'pattern' to be perceived in poetic drama for
Eliot, it can also, as here, describe the horrific unreality that Harry, like Brutus,
suffers in the wake of his fatal single action.

In the final version of the play, Agatha's statements about Harry's situation and
the narrative in which he finds himself make it certain that we do not miss the
Christian teleology of Eliot's analogies. This is not a tale of 'crime and punishment',
Agatha avers, but of 'sin and expiation'. Harry, in his suffering, is but the immediate 'consciousness' of this 'unhappy family'. As a result of such deliberate signalling
of the ritual pattern sustaining the play, in its final form, Harry is thereby granted
a 'different vision' of himself, one that makes him at least momentarily 'happy'. He
leaves, at the end, on his 'mission', whatever that might be. (97–8) The need to
strengthen the nature and purpose of this vision led Eliot to write additional
dialogue between Harry and his mother, Amy, in order to affirm that, as his final
(new) words put it, he is leaving 'to follow the bright angels.' (107)[7] The typescript
versions of the play do not lack this redemptive potential; in one, Agatha even talks
of 'sanctification', in thinking of Harry's future, on a note that perhaps looks
forward to Celia's fate in Eliot's next drama, *The Cocktail Party*.[8] But the drafts, in
their various revisions of Harry's statements about the dissolving of self and personality, and their lack of an articulate sense of what the 'vision' determines, do
shift the play's centre of gravity to the (Faustus- and Hamlet-like) 'hell' that the

---

[6] Houghton Library, Harvard, MS Am. 1691. 14 (39) 68. E. Martin Browne presents a redacted
version of these mss. passages in the Houghton typescripts in *The Making of T.S. Eliot's Plays* (Cambridge: Cambridge University Press, 1969), 129–36.

[7] The clearest charting of the progression of the very complicated history of the drafting of *The
Family Reunion* is to be found in an Appendix to Lyndall Gordon's *Eliot's New Life* (Oxford: Oxford
University Press, 1988), 277–8.

[8] Houghton Library, Harvard, MS Am. 1691 (2), 20.

main character is suffering. Such unease is obviously present, however altered and accommodated, in the final text, and is what makes for the play's unsettling strangeness in the theatre.

FOUR QUARTETS

Similar themes about split or dissociated selfhood figure, perhaps surprisingly, in Eliot's last major poetry. World War II, and the closing of the theatres, interrupted his development of these Marlovian themes, and led him to add three further *Quartets* to *Burnt Norton* (1935). The development of that initial work, from a discarded Chorus passage from the contemporary *Murder in the Cathedral*, deprived the passage's meditation on time, with which *Burnt Norton* now opens, of its dramatic (Greek, and Early Modern) description with the working out of Fate. This transformation reveals Eliot's interchangeable understanding that the lyric is the dramatic, but also that drama is inherently poetic. The election for the reflective, philosophical, even sermonizing speaking voice in *Four Quartets* deprives them of the scope of his plays. So, when the theatrical metaphors so pertinent to Eliot's drama recur in *Four Quartets*, they are again part of a series of renditions (equally now from *Julius Caesar* and 'The Hollow Men') about the in-between time of darkness, when we are carried behind the stage at a play as the scenery is being moved between the acts (*CPP*, 180).[9] Here, just as when an underground train is stuck between stations, is where 'terror', at emptiness and nothingness, might break through.

This 'interim', Eliot's abiding dramatic interest at this stage of his career, is further continued in the *Four Quartets*, most intensively and obviously during the staged meeting with the 'familiar compound ghost' amidst the air raid, in *Little Gidding* II. Helen Gardner's comprehensive *The Composition of Four Quartets* showed Eliot to have wrestled with the prospect of introducing the 'ghost', drawing upon a range of theatrical stage directions, directions that would all figure in the variations upon this theme in his later plays. These variations also point to the metaphysical poetic that Eliot had developed across his career. 'I assumed a double part', as it appears in the final version, relates to the core interest of Eliot's theatre. Metaphorically, it draws upon that practical facet, doubling, to which he had been alerted by the theatre historian W.J. Lawrence and, at a mythic level, by writers such as Colin Still (*CPP*, 193). Yet the earlier versions of this phrase in *Little Gidding* demonstrate how that theatrical emphasis was integrally related to Eliot's entire poetic. Such emphasis includes various dramatically rendered and juxtaposed voices in *The Waste Land*, and speakers who are formed out of many voices elsewhere.[10]

---

[9] That 'in-between time' seems particularly a facet of *The Dry Salvages* III, travelling as it does between 'the hither and the farther shore' (*CPP*, 188).

[10] In 1942, the same year *Little Gidding* was finished, Eliot presented a selection, *Introducing James Joyce*, in a note where he mentioned Joyce's own gramophone recording of *Anna Livia Plurabelle*, that many-voiced riverrun: 'the author's voice reciting it revealed at once a beauty which is disclosed only gradually by the printed page' (London: Faber), 7.

'I, becoming other and many'; 'I becoming other, so I cried'; 'I becoming also many'; 'I assumed another part'; 'I was still the same,/Knowing myself yet being someone other'; 'I was always dead,/Always revived, and always something other'.[11]

Helen Gardner found this last version 'eerie', but links it to the fact that, until the completion of the second full draft of *Little Gidding*, the 'ghost' was described as speaking in Eliot's 'own voice'. (185) The variations on this line introducing the ghost serve rather, though, to raise the question as to what an 'own' voice might be. In some of these instances of possible lines, the voice seems to slide easily into a 'many' or 'other'; in other instances, it seems to retain a sense of itself ('knowing'), but then dividing. In the last cited instance, Gardner's 'eerie' 'always dead/Always revived', we find the voice achieving a Paterian intensity again, a restlessness within, and towards, the past, which underwrites the febrile nature of Eliot's own allusive, eternally 'new', poetic.

The familiar 'ghost' (identified with Yeats and Mallarmé) in *Little Gidding* II is concerned with Lear-like old age, but also with the 'dialect of the tribe'. Debates about poetic language, which might seem remote from the immediate concerns of whatever 'self' it is that the poems contain, are repeated in each of the *Quartets* in some form. At an obvious level, however, *Four Quartets* conforms, more evidently than Eliot's previous poetry, to the prescription he drew initially from Donne, and subsequently from Dryden:

> Dryden became a great poet because he could *not* write an artificial style, because it was intolerable to him; because he had that uncorruptible sincerity of the word which at all times distinguishes the good writer from the bad, and at critical times such as his, distinguishes the great writer from the little one. What Dryden did, in fact, was to reform the language, and devise a natural, conversational style of speech in verse in place of an artificial and decadent one.[12]

Eliot's caveats were, as ever, crucial; Dryden's 'sincerity', his determination to 'reform the language', led him to 'devise' a 'style': although Dryden's style is not 'artificial', it remains a construct nonetheless.[13] The seemingly 'conversational' manner of *Four Quartets* is just such a 'style' put on. At moments, we are alerted to that possibility; intensively so, in *East Coker* II ('That was one way of putting it'). Yet, again, this part of the sequence points towards an enhanced ambition for the 'style' that has been devised throughout. Eliot discovered for *East Coker* an allusive conceit, which united the concerns of language, the educational, pedagogic, tone of the *Quartets*, together with the themes of history and inheritance that knot the sequence together. Eliot's reference to the work of his namesake and ancestor, Sir

---

[11] Helen Gardner, *The Composition of Four Quartets* (London: Faber, 1978), 174, 175, 179. Subsequent references appear in the text.

[12] T.S. Eliot, 'John Dryden I—"The Poet who Gave the English Speech"', *The Listener*, vol. V, no. 118, 15 April 1931, 621.

[13] W.P. Ker, in an essay from which Eliot quotes other passages (*UPUC*, 21–2), maintained that Dryden's Heroic Plays shared 'devotion to an ideal form' comparable to the ambitions of Epic poetry. This, he argued, was something lost in modern work ('Forms of English Poetry, *Form and Style in Poetry*, ed. R.W. Chambers, London: Macmillan, 1928, 103).

Thomas Elyot, and to his *The boke named the Governour*, confirms the Yeatsian
sense that great 'houses' successively rise and fall into decay, in *East Coker* I. Sir
Thomas Elyot had written:

> It is diligently to be noted that the associatinge of man and woman in daunsing, they
> bothe observinge one nombre and tyme in their meuyinges, was nat begonne without
> a speciall consideration, as well for the necessarye coniunction of those two persones,
> as for the intimation of sundry virtues, whiche be by them represented. And for as
> moche as by the association of a man and a woman in daunsinge may be signified
> matrimonie, I could in declarynge the dignitie and commoditie of that sacrament
> make intiere volumes, if it were nat so communely knowen to all men...[14]

Eliot's reimagining of the scene here, as happening around a bonfire in an open
field, presumably in his ancestral country in Somerset, gives Thomas Elyot's imagined sacramental event a ritualistic but also an historical resonance comparable to
that in 'The Hollow Men'. But the sense that Elyot is repeating what is the 'com-
munely knowen' in his 'diligent' noting of the 'virtues' intimated by the dance,
carries further implication within *The boke named the Governour*, as it does for T.S.
Eliot's *Four Quartets*.

Foster Watson, the contemporary editor of Sir Thomas Elyot's educational tract,
which sought to identify 'virtues' necessary to the individual ruling aristocracy,
makes much of the linguistic emphasis of Elyot's ideas. He claimed that Elyot's
book is a necessary addition to the popular series in which it appeared, Everyman's
Library, since Elyot was 'the first Englishman to feel the impulse to democratize
the knowledge of the Renascence':

> It is the distinctive feature of Elyot to have been the first to bring the Renascence spirit
> to the application of the English language.... He simply found that English could be
> used for learned purposes, for explaining difficult questions, for the uses of logic,
> rhetoric, and oratory in abstruse matters. In other words, instead of dealing with the
> philosophical and literary aspects of education, ethics, and jurisprudence in Latin, he
> found that English would do, not merely as a makeshift, but as an adequate, effective,
> and telling alternative. (xiii)

Foster Watson saw Elyot's seemingly functional work, therefore, as having a Dantean
purpose: the vernacularization of the 'new' knowledges of the Early Modern period,
through a style that can be 'adequate' but also 'effective, and telling'. This it is that
makes for the striking '"modernness"', as he calls it, of Elyot's work.[15]

---

[14] Sir Thomas Elyot, *The boke named the Governour*, Book I, XXI, introduced by Foster Watson
(London: Dent, 1907), 94. Subsequent references are given in the text.

[15] Foster Watson raises the question as to whether Elyot's 'educational endeavour' is not extremely
pertinent 'to-day'. (xviii) It is notable that T.S. Eliot began his series of lectures on *The Aims of Education*, at the University of Chicago in 1950–1, with a lecture called 'Can "Education" Be Defined?' that
reviews and celebrates the historical development of the English Language. (*TCC*, 61ff.) Eliot's adherence to the archaic form 'arresse' in the first paragraph of *East Coker*, despite protests from all readers
of the poem in typescript, is appropriate here. (Gardner, *Composition*, 97) 'Arresse' appears in Book III
of Elyot's work, associated with the false array that new riches can bring, a meaning not remote from
the emptiness conveyed by Eliot's line.

Sir Thomas Elyot's own version of the need to purify the language prefigured chords contained in *Four Quartets*:

> Wherefore they be moche abused that suppose eloquence to be only in wordes or cou-lours of Rhetoricke, for, as Tulli saith, what is so furiouse or mad a thinge as a vain sounde of wordes of the best sort and most ornate, containing neither connynge nor sentence? Undoubtedly very eloquence is in every tonge where any mater or acte done or to be done is expressed in wordes clene, propise [suited], ornate, and comely... (55)

East Coker II recasts this sentiment as a necessity to avoid a 'worn-out poetical fashion'; Eliot advertises his belatedness when he claims that the remaining 'wrestle' with words is 'intolerable' (a version of his claim that 'The Metaphysical Poets' teach the modern poet of the exaggerated need, currently, to 'dislocate' the language) (*CPP*, 179). The speaker seems to acknowledge, in *Little Gidding* II, that such demands render the modern poet a Hamlet-like figure before tradition: coming-to in the air raid, the speaker sees the 'familiar compound ghost' in the city street 'fade' 'on the blowing of the horn', or the signal for the All-Clear (*CPP*, 195).[16]

Dancing, that familiar conceit garnered by Eliot from Sir John Davies's *Orchestra*, and now from the final sections of *The boke named the Governour*, offers an instance through which 'comely' language might be structured to a different purpose. Elyot went so far as to see dance itself as a kind of language which mediates between all others. The 'confins' 'of sundry languages and maners' might be breached, he claims in a story relating to the emperor Nero, were a perfect dancer to 'expresse every thing' to be conveyed. (94) Dance is established as a paradigm, therefore, not just for the act of writing but for education as the conveyance of virtue. The pattern of the dance is conveyed most, Elyot concluded, as 'maturitie', 'the meane or medic-ritie betwene slouthe and celeritie'. (98)[17]

This set of analogies resonates across the remainder of *Four Quartets*, culminat-ing in the final section of *Little Gidding*, where the 'right' sentence is conceived of as a 'complete consort' of words, 'dancing together' (*CPP*, 197). It would seem, then, that, in writing the sequence of poems after *Burnt Norton*, which modern biographers conceive of as at least partly a disquisition upon missed or lost love, Eliot also adopted the burden towards the language that was to be found in the work of his ancestor. Or, at least, he was anxious immediately to locate those

---

[16] Marcellus says, of the ghost of Hamlet's father, 'It faded on the crowing of a cock' (I. i, 157) (*Shakespeare's Tragedy of Hamlet*, ed. Israel Gollancz, London: J.M. Dent, 1895, 8). Eliot cites this line in 'Poetry and Drama' as demonstrating the way in which the 'poetic' can emerge as part of 'conscious-ness', and as exemplary therefore of the 'musical' patterning that can be made in great plays, which are 'one' with the 'dramatic movement' (*OPP*, 76). The redemptive potential here seems captured in the reference to *Antony and Cleopatra* in the 'ghost's' final words; Antony scorns Octavius as one who, at the Battle of Philippi, 'kept/His sword e'en like a dancer' (III. xi, 35–6) (*Shakespeare's Tragedy of Antony and Cleopatra*, ed. Israel Gollancz, London: Dent, 1897, 96). The ghost's setting of the last three words as a mark of the potential for redemption emphasizes the necessity to overcome debility and cowardice within 'action'.

[17] 'Maturity' became increasingly a marker of literary greatness in Eliot's critical vocabulary, as in 'What is a Classic?': 'Virgil's maturity of mind, and the maturity of his age, are exhibited in... awareness of history' (*OPP*, 62).

themes, as they had emerged in the first of the *Quartets*, in the Early Modern paradigm established in English by Sir Thomas Elyot. Elyot saw the four elements of earth, air, fire, and water as exemplary of the 'setting in place' of everything in the universe. (3–4) To this end, *East Coker* repeats the 'whirled/world' and 'still moving' formulations from *Ash-Wednesday* (*CPP*, 179, 183).

East Coker, in opening with the image of the rise and decay of houses, suggests that it is normal, however, for 'order' to be subject to corruption and interference in this world. Any 'complete consort' is shadowed by 'fracture' and 'chaos', just as Eliot's Dantean aspiration in his later work is shadowed by his developed understanding of Early Modern 'modernity'. The other (seemingly inadvertent) direct intervention from Early Modern writing into *Four Quartets* takes hauntedness into now familiar territory. John Hayward, Eliot's friend, and a first reader of the latter three *Quartets* in draft, located in Sir Thomas Browne's work both the source for the conceit of the world as a hospital in *East Coker* IV, and the phrase suggesting the irredeemability of history, which is perceived as 'the spectre of a Rose' in *Little Gidding* III. 'Damn Sir T. Browne', Gardner reports Eliot as erupting, upon this being suggested, despite the obvious relevance of Browne to *The Waste Land*. Eliot claimed that he had never really got much from Browne's work. (202) Yet both phrases are, however subliminally, telling in relation to his wider aesthetic (as illustrated by Eliot's recouping of them for *Four Quartets*). In relation to *East Coker*, Gardner quotes the obvious phrase from Browne's *Religio Medici*, Book Two, 'For the World, I count it not an Inn, but an Hospital; and a place not to live, but to dye in.' Yet the next sentence, not cited by Gardner, takes the conceit into what becomes Eliot's metaphysics:

> The world that I regard is my self; it is the Microcosm of my own frame that I cast mine eye on; for the other, I use it but like my Globe, and turn it round sometimes for my recreation.[18]

Browne makes clear that this watchfulness occurs under the supreme watchfulness of God, who only 'can subsist by himself'. Therefore, no aloneness is possible in the world, since 'all others' (people) 'do transcend a unity, and so by consequence are many'. (82) But Browne's envisioning of the world as a hospital enforces a watchfulness over and towards the self that is also essential to John Donne's poetics and metaphysics, and to Eliot's after him. Pertinently also, Browne's conceit leads to an extended play upon living and dying as forms of sleeping and waking. Original sin ensures that 'we live a middle and moderating point between life and death', between, that is, a death-like 'life' on earth and a waking 'unto the Resurrection'. (85–6) Eliot, of course, had come to expect the interchange of such antithetical states as inevitable from the mid-1920s at least. The 'interim' situation is one that can only be redeemed by the sudden intervention of a higher purpose, those glimpsed visionary moments that his poetry can paradoxically render, precisely because they have eluded him.

---

[18] *The Religio Medici and Other Writings of Sir Thomas Browne*, ed. C.H. Herford (London: Dent, 1906), 83. Subsequent references appear in the text.

The other allusion from Sir Thomas Browne in *Four Quartets* comes with a similar force. As Gardner notes, Eliot's calling history 'the spectre of a Rose' is a rewording of Browne's original phrase 'the ghost of a rose'—Eliot had combined an unrealized reference to *The Garden of Cyrus* with a memory of the title of one of the Ballet Russe shows, *Le Spectre de la Rose*. Browne's Chapter V of *The Garden of Cyrus* had been devoted to considering 'the ancient conceit of five', the famous Quincunx that he held to have been present in Hebrew mysteries, in Cabbalism, and also in the division of the orders of the natural world, and in certain plants and creatures. Browne recognized the exhaustion that such speculation entails, however: 'We are unwilling to spin out our awaking thoughts into the phantasms of sleep, which often continueth praecogitations.' The seeming magic of the natural world is rapidly transformed into ugliness, and:

> Nor will the sweetest delight of Gardens afford much comfort in sleep; wherein the dulness of that sense shakes hands with delectable odours; and though in the Bed of *Cleopatra*, can hardly with any delight raise up the ghost of a Rose. (229)

Cleopatra, the figure who haunted Eliot's literary admiration, and was behind his urge to remake the past in his own poetry, had a bed, a note to Browne's phrase tells us, 'Strewed with roses'.[19] Such is the contemporary 'dulness' out of which *Little Gidding* is composed, compared to the phrase's implication in its original context, that 'we' are unable to 'revive' or 'restore' the past (*CPP*, 196). The 'symbol' that we acquire from history might speak to the present, but it might also be void.

The ambiguity of Eliot's position seems to be captured in the contrasting deployment that he gives to several of the parts IV of *Four Quartets*. Gardner quotes Eliot's letter to Anne Ridler of 1941, in which he claimed that in Part IV of *East Coker* he was aware of the danger of trying to repeat a religious lyric in the manner of George Herbert or Richard Crashaw—instead he opts for something in the manner of Edward Benlowes or John Cleveland, and to put to 'use this so English XVII form with a content so very un-English'. Eliot's reference to Benlowes and Cleveland signals a proper sense of the tone he was seeking for *Four Quartets*. But it might also reveal his anxiety about the meaningful ability of his technique to register content directly.

In his Introduction to Cleveland's poems in his *Minor Poets of the Caroline Period*, George Saintsbury described him as 'journalistic in verse', extremely popular in his time, but a poet who worked to 'accumulate conceits for their own sake'. Saintsbury commented on Benlowes' 'Clevelandisms' remark that he was led to 'astonishing contortions and bizarreness of thought and phrase'.[20] We are back in

---

[19] 'Seneca in Elizabethan Translation' quotes Samuel Daniel's lines from his tragedy *Cleopatra* (1081–8), which again point to the moral that all beauty fades (*SE*, 94–5). The Senecan proximity of Daniel's plays, noted both by Eliot in the essay and by his early introducer, George Saintsbury, ensures that such decay is given 'meaning' as part of a cycle of 'Nemesis'. As Cleopatra says, in words perhaps relevant to the disorderings signalled at the start of *The Waste Land* II, 'some must be the causers why/ This revolution must be wrought/As borne to bring their state to naught' (ll. 806–8). See *The Complete Works in Verse and Prose of Samuel Daniel*, ed. Alexander Grossart, vol. III (London: Hazell, Watson, and Viney, 1888), xi, 61, 71.

[20] George Saintsbury, *Minor Poets of the Caroline Period*, vol. III (Oxford: Clarendon Press, 1921, 6, 8); vol. I (1905, 312).

the territory of *The Varieties of Metaphysical Poetry*, with the sense that poetic technique in the modern age might simply display the fragmentation of its 'thought'.
This unease underlies, in *Four Quartets*, even those passages that are controlled
within traditional forms. The ABABB rhyme scheme of *East Coker* IV had been
used by such as Thomas Carew ('To my inconstant mistres'), and Richard Lovelace
('The Scrutinie'), when considering the vagaries of love and the loved one; it had
been used by Herbert himself to a variety of effects, not least when mourning the
loss of God to the world, and the loss of meaning to symbols, in 'Decay':

> I see the world grows old, when as the heat
> Of thy great love once spread, as in an urn
> Doth closet up itself, and still retreat,
> Cold sin still forcing it, till it return,
>   And calling Justice, all things burn.[21]

Eliot's deployment of the 'unEnglish' conceit of the hospital, and of Christ as a
surgeon, seems to confirm the historical point made across *Four Quartets*: that no
return can any longer be made even to this direct utterance of loss. The forms of
the 'English XVII' might remain inhabitable to the modern poet, but the content
that they might be made to contain is no longer relevant to the tradition out of
which they originally developed.

Eliot's other reference to the seventeenth century, in the drafts to *Four Quartets*,
came during his interchange with Hayward about the lyric section IV of *Little
Gidding*, to which he wished (perhaps mistakenly, he concedes) to impart 'a XVII
flavour'. (216) But here he seems to inflect that 'flavour' to positive purpose, bringing the Herculean mythography that he had deployed in 'Marina' into play once
more, to effect a Pentecostal understanding of Christian Love:

> Love is the unfamiliar Name
> Behind the hands that wove
> The intolerable shirt of flame
> Which human power cannot remove.
>   (*CPP*, 196)

Hercules' donning of the shirt of flame sent to him by his wife in revenge for his
infidelities, as reported in Act 3 of Seneca's *Hercules Oetaeus*, is re-rendered by Eliot
as an extraordinary portent of all suffering for the Word. Eliot's 'human power'
creates a nice distinction, reflecting upon the fact that Hercules alive is not to
achieve that deification promised him on completion of his Labours, whilst also
reflecting upon the strength of the Christian, over the pagan, mythological spiritu-
ality. But here, in the final *Quartet*, the Senecan reference momentarily serves to
bring the literary and theological potential of the poetry into one agonizing realization. The relationship between such moments of agony, however transfiguring and
transfigured, seems to impel Eliot's writing, once he could return to writing plays,
in the aftermath of World War II.

---

[21] *The Poems of George Herbert*, ed. Arthur Waugh, 89.

THE COCKTAIL PARTY

The assured generic status of Eliot's next drama, the 'comedy' *The Cocktail Party*, first performed in 1950, presents many issues similar to those explored in *The Family Reunion* but in a different light. The stichomythic rhythm of many of the play's opening exchanges, as the party gets under way, recalls the 'jazz' rhythms derived from Seneca, via Early Modern drama, of *Sweeney Agonistes*. Eliot rehearses at the start of the opening scene, through rapid-fire speeches, comic effects around misunderstanding, and uncertainty about names and locations, which are crucial to the issues that will be explored at greater length across the play. The guests have arrived at the cocktail party to discover that the hostess, Lavinia, has suddenly and mysteriously disappeared earlier in the day. Her husband, Edward, is holding the fort with the lame excuse that she has been called away to look after a sick aunt:

> JULIA: I feel as if I knew
>   All about that aunt in Hampshire.
> EDWARD: Hampshire?
> JULIA: Didn't you say Hampshire?
> EDWARD: No, I didn't say Hampshire.
> JULIA: Did you say Hampstead?
> EDWARD: No, I didn't say Hampstead.[22]

As though Eliot initially wished to make exchanges around mishearings, or uncertainty of location or origination, the signature for the whole play, his early drafts for *The Cocktail Party* show that, at the beginning of what he originally saw as 'Act I scene ii', some version of this stichomythic rhythm is repeated. This time, there is doubt about people's names, but also about who is calling. The whole play is a comedy about surprising entrances, and the unexpected return to the 'action' of the wrong character at the wrong point. This is advertised in the suppressed opening to this second scene. The guests have seemed to depart, and Edward is alone, when he hears:

> VOICE: Are you there Edward?
> EDWARD: Is that you, Anthony?
> VOICE: No, it's not Anthony.
> EDWARD: Is it Christopher?

And so on, until an exasperated Edward asks 'What other names are there?'[23] Here, momentarily, we return to that disembodied, unlocated, voicing from offstage that had characterized Eliot's earlier poetry, interrupted by voices or texts from elsewhere. *The Cocktail Party* transposes many related issues of identity, and its proximity to theatricality, from *The Family Reunion*. It revisits them in a space more controlled

---

[22] T.S. Eliot, *The Cocktail Party* (London: Faber, 1951), 16–17. All subsequent references to this edition are given in the text.

[23] Houghton Library, Harvard, MS Am. 1691.7 (67) Folder Four, 19. The List of Characters attached to this draft intriguingly puts 'the unidentified guest' and 'Sir Henry Harcourt-Reilly' down as though they were separate characters; the printed text's List instantly gives the game away to readers of the play.

from within, however, because the action is now overseen by 'the Unidentified Guest', later revealed to be Sir Henry Harcourt-Reilly, and his associates, who are categorized under the title of 'the guardians'.

That the guardians bear a close relation to the 'community of Christians', as conceived by Eliot in his 1939 lectures *The Idea of a Christian Society*, is something that has long been held by critics. Eliot defined this 'idea' in the lectures as being about a community 'in which there is a unified religious-social code of behaviour', one consisting of 'consciously and thoughtfully practising Christians, especially those of intellectual and spiritual superiority'.[24] In many ways the play is about the winning round of Edward and Lavinia to that 'code' by the 'guardians', who clearly retain 'superior' insight into their common condition. The 'election' of Celia to her mission suggests that Eliot viewed the 'code' as potentially boundary-less, and thought its exploration a matter of personal potential.[25]

As discussed above, that 'superiority', in Harcourt-Reilly's case, seems to derive partly from his assumption of a role like that of the Duke in Shakespeare's *Measure for Measure*, but also like that of Prospero in *The Tempest*. Quite early on, Harcourt-Reilly acts as a kind of actor-manager. When Edward exhibits a yearning to see Lavinia (despite hinted-at troubles in their marriage), 'the Unidentified Guest' assures him that 'You shall see her again—here.' (29) Yet his actual purpose, to characters in the play at least, seems clouded—and this leads to a connected series of images, across the work, suggesting that Harcourt-Reilly, and his associates, might at least be thought to have contrived the plot of the play for a darker purpose. Intriguing, in this connection, are Celia's various attempts to identify the 'Guest'. Upon hearing of this reassurance about Lavinia's return from Edward, she blurts out:

> But why should that man want to bring her back—
> Unless he is the Devil! I could believe he was. (51)

As if in a bizarre comic version of John Marston's *Sophonisba*, the intimation is that evil might lurk beneath the spiritually pure surface of the character. Celia's wild contention is immediately turned to comic effect: the audience, not knowing at this point about Edward's long-term adulterous affair with her, is bemused by Celia's assertion that 'the Unidentified Guest' must have 'bewitched' Edward into wanting Lavinia back. However, the drafts and printed text bear the teasing trace of a metaphorical continuation of this theme. Discussing the 'return' Harcourt-Reilly claims to be able to effect in bringing Lavinia back, he focuses Edward's attention by saying that 'it is a serious matter/To bring someone back from the dead'. (63) Edward emphasizes the point by observing that this is a 'dramatic' figure of speech to use, but his interlocutor notes, in his philosophical vein, that

---

[24] T.S. Eliot, *Christianity and Culture* (San Diego: Harcourt, Inc., 1976), 27–8. E. Martin Browne discusses this identification in *The Making of T.S. Eliot's Plays*, 185. As with the other plays, Browne gives substantial quotation from the draft versions in his individual chapters on each play, including much (although not all) of what is quoted here.

[25] Harry also comes to realize that he is 'elect' in his final speech in *The Family Reunion*; he seems as baffled as Celia is, as to why this is so. (107)

'we die to each other daily'. Therefore, at every new meeting, we are all 'strangers' to each other. The 'devilish' intent of Harcourt-Reilly seems in a measure to re-register that alienation within humanity which runs across Eliot's stoical works, and in which the working out of Fate simply confirms the purposelessness of character and of individuality. Lavinia at one point sees her complicity in the 'plot', the temporary leaving of her husband, as being like the setting in motion of a 'machine' that someone else controls, and which she cannot stop running to its end. (77) More than *The Family Reunion*, and than Eliot's subsequent dramas, *The Cocktail Party* seems to be less interested in 'character' than in rendering people into puppet-like entities (as we have seen, a metaphor often used by late nineteenth- and early twentieth-century critics for Early Modern plots by such as Jonson and Webster, a view followed by Eliot himself).[26]

The potential for a darker reading of the play, consonant with the bleak Early Modern work with which Eliot was so familiar, is strikingly visible in the struggle Eliot had to find the term 'guardian', which he needed to describe the group who manipulated the events of the play to a satisfactory (if, in Celia's case, horrific) conclusion. 'Guardian', E. Martin Browne tells us, was his own discovery of a *mot juste*, accepted immediately by Eliot.[27] Eliot's draft, in a speech in which Edward responds to Celia's fretful enquiry as to whether he could in fact be happy with Lavinia, uses different language to describe 'the tougher self'. This 'self' he considers to be something the normal everyday self inside a person has to come to terms with—the point being that 'the tougher self' is the one which predestines him to remain with his wife. (58) Edward draws a sharp contrast between the potential of that 'tougher self' in Eliot's first version, compared to that in the final text:

> The self that *wills*—he is a feeble creature,
> He has to come to terms in the end
> With the real, the tougher self, who does not speak,
> Who never talks, who does not argue;
> Who, in some men, may be the *daemon*, the genius,
> And in others, like myself, the dull, the implacable,
> The indomitable spirit of mediocrity.[28]

Eliot's acceptance of a change of terminology here, to 'guardians', for the (darker) internal drives beneath seeming selfhood, robs consistency from this original speech, and from that ontological understanding inherent in Harcourt-Reilly's quotation of Shelley's *Prometheus Unbound* to describe the motivation for his actions. It also denies consistency to Edward's eventual understanding about his relationship with Lavinia, which in many ways governs his acceptance of the vision of 'the guardians' at the end of the play. Gesturing again to the Faustian understanding that had so

---

[26] Puppets had a currency within 'live' drama in the Early Modern period: Jonson's *Bartholomew Fair*, on the Extension Lectures list, contains a localized puppet version of Marlowe's poem, *Hero and Leander*.

[27] Browne, *The Making of T.S. Eliot's Plays*, 184.

[28] MS 1691.7 (67), 34.

haunted Harry in *The Family Reunion*, Edward asks her, in reference to his earlier self in their marriage:

> Why could I not walk out of my prison?
> What is hell? Hell is oneself,
> Hell is alone, the other figures in it
> Merely projections. (87)

Edward's inversion of Jean-Paul Sartre's famous maxim ('Hell is other people') echoes earlier Eliot texts exploring the nature of the self, from the projecting 'magic lantern' of 'The Love Song of J. Alfred Prufrock' to the 'prison' of Part V of *The Waste Land*; Celia will in time worry that the sanatorium to which she is to be sent sounds like 'a prison'. (126) That the word 'alone' is key to Eliot's conception of *The Cocktail Party*, as it was to Faustus near his end, is clear from Harcourt-Reilly's original words to Celia as drafted—when he describes the awfulness of the ordinary world, and receives her acceptance of a spiritual mission that will lead her to escape from this world. The published text's 'the final desolation/Of solitude in the phantasmal world/Of imagination (126) was, first, 'The only final aloneness/Is to be alone in the phantasmal world/Of your own imagination.'[29] 'Phantasma': that word not forgotten perhaps, from Eliot's mistaken rendition of Brutus's lines, on the typescript of *Sweeney Agonistes*. Once again, a ghostliness infects the speech's reality; Harcourt-Reilly's original repetition of 'alone' brought a directness to the apprehension that is rather spoilt in the circumlocutory final version. Edward's dismissive phrase 'merely projections', to describe others here, looks forward to Julia's anxious enquiry about Celia's steadfastness, once she has agreed to her mission: 'Will she be frightened/By the first appearance of projected spirits?' (130) That mission, whose spiritual features remain somewhat under-articulated, is, in part, concerned with concentrating purpose upon those 'projections', which also mark the haunted existential loneliness the characters have come to realize that they (rarely) share.

As had been the case in *The Family Reunion*, the essential isolation and abandonment that is signalled by the daemonic inference releases a whole host of theatrical metaphors throughout this play, to describe the unreality of any established sense of selfhood. In 1944, in an Introduction to S.L. Bethell's *Shakespeare and the Popular Dramatic Tradition*, Eliot described the book as 'helpful' for any verse-play writer. Bethell had demonstrated definitively, Eliot argued, that the ambition of that drama was to create onstage 'the reality of a situation composed of a fusion, in sympathy or antipathy, of two or more individuals'. Once again we see Eliot reading the Early Modern through the lenses provided by fellow critics. Bethell's historical approach to the subject of his study, though, would have reminded Eliot about the rootedness of some of his favourite metaphors in and for the theatre, in the dramatic tradition. Bethell noted that Elizabethan audiences were inured to the non-naturalism of their drama, and to a 'double-consciousness of play-world and real-world', which allowed for recognition of the distance of the former from

---

[29] Houghton Library, Harvard, MS Am. 1691.7 (67), Folder Eleven, 73.

the latter. This brought about a 'critical' element in their response to the verse. But it also led, Bethell argued, to Shakespeare's adoption of techniques that might alert the audience to such distance. These included the creation of characters who tell their own story 'from a perspective outside' themselves. Bethell's example is Richard III's opening speeches—but Eliot's Edward and Harry are other such characters. Edward speaks increasingly from outside himself, as the play progresses, and he comes to understand more of his situation: the more so, in the draft versions of his speeches.

A further technique, discussed by Bethell, is the way that Shakespeare ensured audience understanding of the artifice of his play-worlds, through a 'frequent metaphorical use of play and players', a 'regression' in the play (e.g. Jacques' 'All the world's a stage'; Macbeth's 'Life's but a poor player'). Such metaphors in Shakespeare, Bethell argues, have 'philosophical significance', since they alert the audience to the differences between appearance and reality, and hence to the fragility of selfhood. As they do for Eliot, who carries those metaphors further in *The Cocktail Party* and his late plays than he had in his previous dramas.[30] The 'Unidentified Guest' begins using these metaphors, in his first conversation with Edward, once the other guests have (temporarily) departed. He describes the way in which it is possible, by such events as the withdrawal of Lavinia, to lose an assured sense of self 'with everything about you/Arranged to support you in the role you have chosen'. (26) The original version of the speech casts that settled self, however, as something much more assured of, and authoring, the contexts in which 'we' all find ourselves:

> We think of ourselves as something positive,
> Always the subject of the sentence;
> As having arranged, having been responsible
> For the part we play in the scene.[31]

While, in this early version, Harcourt-Reilly sticks to the later version's notion that the self is easily displaced into objectivity, and to passive subject-hood, the control exerted here seems true to the Duke-like nature (*Measure for Measure*) of his presence throughout. The non-'guardians' in *The Cocktail Party* seem to come to this understanding of selfhood only gradually: Edward latterly complains about the 'unreality/Of the role' that Lavinia has imposed upon him. (99)[32]

Yet, such control is integral to the insight Harcourt-Reilly claims to have about Celia's destiny, an insight that is described again as a form of doubling. Harcourt-Reilly senses that, when he first met the 'real' Celia, there was, 'standing behind her chair', an 'image' 'whose face showed the astonishment/Of the first five minutes after a violent death'. (162) It is a gruesome apparition, or revelation, of Celia's destiny. It is, again, consonant with the possibility behind the play's conception, which is partly suppressed, partly revealed, by the printed text. That there is something more horrible and traumatic underlying the 'comic' surface of the play is

---

[30] Bethell, *Shakespeare and the Popular Dramatic Tradition*, 33, 40, 65.
[31] MS Am. 1691.7 (67), Folder Three, 13.
[32] Speaking to Celia earlier in the play, Edward had acknowledged a Gerontion-like sense of the untimeliness of desire as he comes to feel old—'you have lost/The desire for all that was most desirable'. (57)

evidenced, as so often in Eliot's realizations, by the sickened perspective upon relations between the sexes in the drafts. Peter, unknowing of Edward's affair with Celia, confesses his own love for her to him. In the printed text, he is merely greeted in his proposition by a world-weary disquisition on the slackening of passion as time passes, which is appropriate to the play's themes of change and alienation ('You would have found that she was another woman/And that you were another man.') (40) In the drafts of the play, however, Peter's calm rationalization of his situation is met with a fierce denunciation, by Edward, of women and of lust:

> You have been spared the coming to awareness
> That the superficial is the substantial
> And that nothing else is left you but the yearning of the loins
> As full of lechery [concupiscence] as a weasel of eggs—
> Fry, lechery, fry! I congratulate you
> On a timely escape.[33]

Eliot's original version of the interchange in the drafts of *The Cocktail Party* repeats segments of Shakespeare's *Troilus and Cressida*, Act V scene ii. Troilus, now deserted by Cressida, secretly visits the camp where she is exchanging love vows with her new desire, Diomedes. In company with Ulysses, and Thersites, the vicious commentator on much of the play's action, Troilus watches their meeting. He retains his poise, despite witnessing a scene that tortures him. That eerie poise only the more highlights the brutality of Thersites' response to what is happening:[34]

> TROILUS: Nay, stay. I will not speak a word:
>   There is between my will and all offences
>   A guard of patience. Stay a little while.
> THERSITES: How the devil Luxury, with his fat rump and potato-finger,
>   Tickles these together! Fry, lechery, fry!
>
>   (V. ii, 59–63)[35]

Thersites' rude revelation, of what it is that weakness of the will in Troilus suppresses, points to the troubling sub-theme of *The Cocktail Party*: desire. After all, this is a play which is, like so many Early Modern works, about the consequences of the adulteries of the leading couple, Edward and Lavinia. Celia's destiny is complicit with these images in Eliot's drafts, the network of allusions to a more horrific pattern of natural drives, and of kinds of redemption, than seems obvious on the surface of Eliot's modern comedy. Her adultery, as she tells Harcourt-Reilly, has established in her 'a sense of sin'; not, she thinks, in an 'ordinary' understanding of the term. She has not felt 'immoral' in the affair, and dismisses contemporary versions of morality as precisely lacking that 'sense of sin' which has recently come to her. (119–20)

---

[33] Houghton Library, Harvard, MS Am.1691.7 (67), 25.
[34] S.L. Bethell dwells on Thersites, as the closest to a Vice figure that Shakespeare ever invented, but claims that *Troilus and Cressida* displays a Donne-like interest in philosophical abstraction—indeed, it is Shakespeare's most philosophical work (*Shakespeare and the Popular Dramatic Tradition*, 98–9).
[35] *Shakespeare's Troilus and Cressida*, ed. Israel Gollancz (London: J.M. Dent, 1896), 137.

This whole passage in *The Cocktail Party*, and the way it leads to a sense of greater purpose and understanding for Celia, is reminiscent of Eliot's attempts elsewhere to grapple into comprehensibility the historically alien morality of *The Changeling* in 'Thomas Middleton' (1927). Beatrice-Joanna, whose lust for De Flores seems to obsess her once she has slept with him, in gratitude for his having murdered her unwanted fiancée, is not 'moral' in any accepted sense, Eliot famously claims: 'she becomes moral only by becoming damned'. (*SE*, 163) In the odd, comic-spiritual world of *The Cocktail Party*, partly revelling in the horrors of Early Modern tragedy, but moving them towards a different purpose, Celia's insight, gained through sexual straying, makes her choose religious salvation, but also ironically leads to her crucifixion.[36] Harcourt-Reilly's description of the spiritual journey which she must undertake takes up, again, resonances from Andrewes' Nativity Sermons, particularly that for 1608, 'Signs never come amiss, as we cannot miss them, when we should miss without them'[37]:

> You will know very little until you get there;
> You will journey blind. But the way leads towards possession
> Of what you have sought for in the wrong place. (125)

Celia is a latter-day Magus, looking for that revelation, that sign, which she had wrongly sought previously through a human relationship with Edward. This is a human relationship that the play, as in much of Eliot's work—such is the division within the self and between selves that gives it its haunted quality—renders transitory if not impossible. It is founded, in a potentially Thersitean version of its inner momentum, upon base and hidden desires. 'This is hell, nor are we out of it', as Marlowe's Mephistophilis claims; 'Hell is oneself' is Edward's and Eliot's revision of that statement.

THE CONFIDENTIAL CLERK AND *THE ELDER STATESMAN*

Eliot's last two plays vary these themes only slightly: they are much more generically settled than *The Family Reunion* or *The Cocktail Party*, and direct in their treatment of Early Modern themes around identity and theatricality. They can therefore be treated more swiftly, as a Coda to this study of Eliot's major work. *The Confidential Clerk* sees Eliot taking on the formulas of Shakespeare's late plays, like *The Winter's Tale* or *Pericles*. It involves the discovering of parents by children and children by parents. But, along the way, there is much further

---

[36] In 1946, three years before *The Cocktail Party* was first produced, Eliot had endorsed, but extended, Dr Johnson's perception that, particularly in Shakespeare, the generic categories of tragedy and comedy provide superficial labels: 'For those who have experienced the full horror of life, tragedy is still inadequate...In the end horror and laughter may be one', when pushed to extreme circumstance. Both are 'serious'. Eliot cites as example of the proof of what he says the gravedigger scene in *Hamlet*—source for *The Rock* (*A Companion to Shakespeare Studies*, ed. Harley Granville-Barker and G.B. Harrison, Cambridge: Cambridge University Press, 1946, 244–5).

[37] Lancelot Andrewes, *Seventeen Sermons on the Nativity* (London: Griffith, Farran, Okeden & Welsh, n.d.), 195.

reflection upon divided selves, and secret potential other lives, a reflection that is related through an associated theatricality. Such reflection, in a figuration familiar from Eliot's recasting of his Early Modern sources, is linked to the difficulties in attaining a fixed sense of personhood upon which personality or character might be founded.

Both Sir Claude Mulhammer and his wife, Lady Elizabeth, have 'missing' children;[38] Sir Claude thinks he has found his child again, and taken him in, by employing the man he presumes to be his son, Colby Simpkins, as the clerk of the play's title. One thing that Sir Claude feels he shares with Colby (and which therefore makes him conclude that the young man is definitely his son) is that they are both aware they might have fulfilled, however unsuccessfully, alternative, and creative lives: Sir Claude as an artist making ceramics, Colby as a musician and organist. Both, in other words, have a developed sense of different selfhoods that might have been available to them, but also a sense of how the self changes across a lifetime. This is signalled when Colby reflects upon the self-confidence that he has not had previously:

> As if I was becoming
> A different person. Just as, I suppose,
> If you learn to speak a foreign language fluently,
> So that you can think in it—you feel yourself to be
> Rather a different person when you're talking it. (38)[39]

Sir Claude's recognition of this kind of change is what leads to the extensive swapping of stories about the potential 'other' lives that both might have led, lives in which the longed-for fulfilment is cast by Sir Claude in Paterian terms: 'There are occasions/When I am transported.../Transfigured in the vision of some marvellous creation'. (40) Notably, however, Sir Claude experiences these moments when witnessing work made by other artists. Neither he nor Colby can achieve such 'marvels' for themselves.

Hence, perhaps, the fervour of Sir Claude's quest to establish familial relations and succession. The play, in an obvious sense, is therefore about a set of actors seeking their correct roles, and so establishing their situation relative to each other. Lucasta is established from the outset as Sir Claude's illegitimate daughter (although Colby mistakenly thinks that she is Sir Claude's mistress). Her sense of the unlocated nature of her life, because her parents were not married, leads her to an exacerbated sense of the class and relational implications of the society established

---

[38] T.S. Eliot, *The Confidential Clerk* (London: Faber, 1954, 12). Subsequent references to this edition are given in the text.

[39] Colby has an extensive speech on this, in the drafts for the play. It has echoes of the opening Chorus of *The Family Reunion*, in that Colby thinks of 'difference' as being an actor who is suddenly in a 'different play' to the one he has rehearsed (quoted Browne, *The Making of T.S. Eliot's Plays*, 259). Perhaps because of Eliot's growing self-confidence as a dramatist, the drafts of *The Confidential Clerk* and of his last play, *The Elder Statesman*, do not involve the elided patterns of imagery that the drafts of the previous two plays had done. My discussion will therefore only draw upon the drafts at specific relevant moments, not without claiming they are as formative of the overall work.

around her. She chides Sir Claude's wife, Lady Elizabeth, for having typecast her fiancé the (oddly named) B. Kaghan, as lower class:

> B. knows you think him common. And so he pretends
> To be very common, because he knows you think so.
> *You* gave us our parts. And we've shown that we can play them. (100)

Eliot is at his most daring in treating of the theatre metaphors in this play in his depiction of B. Kaghan himself. Eliot creates here, strangely, a part in which stage directions are echoed by, and integrated within, Kaghan's speeches. So, upon our first meeting with him on stage:

> [*A loud knock. Enter B. Kaghan*]
> KAGHAN: Enter B. Kaghan. Hello Colby! (18)

The effect is to confirm the 'playing' of parts attributed to the younger couple by Lucasta herself, but also to underline the staged nature of the whole construction. The denouement of the drama, therefore, is achieved by the emergence of the characters from this arbitrary, artificial situation, into something that seems more natural and normal, however contrived the 'revelations' really are. B. Kaghan, at the end, has to learn a new role, when it is revealed that he is actually the son of Lady Elizabeth and a former lover of hers. The artificiality of his relationship to her across the play is, at the end, 'replaced' by a natural one. Colby achieves a whole different life, as an organist in a regional parish, once it is established that he is *neither* the child of Sir Claude nor of Lady Elizabeth. Yet, in this, he *becomes* a kind of son to the faithful company servant (and previous confidential clerk) Eggerson, whose own loved son had been killed during the war. Colby lodges in Eggerson's house from the outset of his new life. Yet, in fact, his finally following his vocation as an organist is also to the point, having learnt that his natural father was an unsuccessful organist as well. *The Confidential Clerk* is a neat reworking, therefore, of late Shakespearean paradigms, but in an un-miraculous mode. 'Correct' relations are complexly restored at the end, without any marvellous revelations, or comings-back to life, such as those that bring to conclusion Shakespeare's tragicomedies. Eliot's final play, *The Elder Statesman*, is notable therefore, in that, although it repeats many of these paradigms, it returns to some sense of the 'other world', or other plane, employing that ghostliness which had been figured within Eliot's sense of dissociated identities across his career.

For perhaps the first time, and as a reflection of Eliot's new and happy second marriage, during the time he was drafting the play, that dissociation in *The Elder Statesman* becomes positive. The mutually accepted love between the younger generation, Monica and Charles, is early advertised as creating a situation in which the loss of self might lead to a greater opening out to another—'How much of me is you?', as Monica asks; 'I'm not the same person as a moment ago', Charles varies the paean.[40] The demonstrative steadiness of their feeling for each other offsets, then, the sad centre of the drama. There, the former statesman, Lord Claverton, is

---

[40] T.S. Eliot, *The Elder Statesman* (London: Faber, 1959), 13. Subsequent references appear in the text.

hounded to the grave by his reacquaintance with two people who have been dubiously associated with divergent versions of his past self: Mrs Carghill is a former lover to whom he promised marriage (only to jilt her on his father's advice), and Federico Gomez is a former Oxford acolyte who has served time in prison, having gone to the bad under Claverton's influence, and then escaped to the colonies.

These encounters energize the by now familiar by-play in Eliot's drama with questions of identity and shifting selfhood. Much is made in the initial exchange between Claverton and Gomez about the implication of name-changes across a life. Plain Dick Ferry has become Mr Richard Claverton-Ferry after his marriage, and is now (straightforwardly or otherwise) Lord Claverton. Gomez, who has had to move countries after his criminal conviction, sees such shifts on an existential, then metaphysical, scale. Speaking words pertinent to Eliot himself, Gomez wonders at the 'meaning' of doing as he has done, taking on another language, and other behaviours, as part of the need 'to fabricate for myself another personality/ And to take another name.' (29) Striving to bring home to Claverton this 'meaning', Gomez counters Claverton's lament that he has always been 'alone' by claiming that true loneliness is only experienced by those, like himself, who have 'come to see that you have lost *yourself*'. (30) Like Lucasta from Eliot's previous play, Gomez needs to re-establish and prove the bond between him and Claverton, in order for his own 'reality' to be granted him. (31)

Claverton is, though, a flawed character. He seems to have failed in politics and sought refuge as a company director who is consulted by the political party in power. He has a dark secret in his past, which Gomez uses as leverage. Claverton it is, then, who has access to that by now achieved set of theatrical metaphors so often used in Eliot's treatment of his characters. There is a split between his public self and his private, so he has 'to make up his face before he looks in the mirror' in the morning, putting on his 'elder statesman' 'personality'. (35) When confronting him, Mrs Carghill reports a view of him as a young man given at the time by what seems her reliable friend Effie—that Claverton is not to be trusted, Effie apparently said, as he is that most Eliotic of masculine creatures, 'hollow'. (51) Mrs Carghill has herself gone through a series of name changes from her original one, Maisie Batterson, including the adoption of her stage persona in the music-halls, Maisie Montjoy. Hence her understanding of the essentially fictional nature of Claverton's current personality, 'posing', as she claims, to be an 'elder statesman'—the play's title is thence drawn into this ambit of artifice.

Claverton, though, who is Eliot's creation, writing in old age, of his final version of Gerontion, feels that he no longer has a part to play. (56) Yet, it is hard to relinquish a part that has evolved across a lifetime, particularly before close family, such as his devoted daughter, Monica:

> I've spent my life trying to forget myself,
> In trying to identify myself with the part
> I had chosen to play. And the longer we pretend
> The harder it is becomes to drop the pretence,
> Walk off the stage... (83)

Paradoxically, perhaps, because of his sense of the actorly nature of everyday being in the world, Claverton's reflective speeches show him to be the most mature of Eliot's dramatic personae, in understanding the divided nature of the self:

> What is this self inside us, this silent observer,
> Severe and speechless critic, who can terrorise us
> And urge us on to futile activity,
> And in the end, judge us still more severely
> For the errors into which his own reproaches drove us? (44)

By each of these lights, then, Claverton seems to exemplify Eliot's final version of that selfhood which he had come to understand in the later 1910s through his saturation in the work of Donne and the non-Shakespearean playwrights, a saturation that drove the distinctive nature of his modernist poetic. Here, in the masquerader Claverton (as previously in Edward), is again 'the sense of the artist as an Eye curiously, patiently watching himself as a man. "There is the Ego, the particular, the individuall, I"'.[41] Claverton is a masquerader who finds himself in a familiarly purgatorial situation once more. The nursing home to which he is translated in Act Two is also a hotel. As the matron puts it, farcically, in a moment that conjures again Sir Thomas Browne's world-as-hospital conceit, 'We don't want our guests to think of themselves as ill,/Though we never have guests who are perfectly well.' (46) The characters are also, like those in the Canterbury climate feared by the Chorus of *Murder in the Cathedral*, or those witnessing the rare moment of illumination in *Little Gidding* I, experiencing 'unseasonable' weather, spring in winter. (45, 48) Certainly, no one is meant to die at this 'hotel', although Claverton does in the final moments, having ignored the warning that the gloaming might bring with it unexpectedly freezing conditions. In the meantime, his sense that it is the divided self which characterizes personality lends him a sense of his own insubstantiality. Initially he flippantly resists the notion that he might return to the City. 'They don't want my ghost . . ./And I, who recognise myself as a ghost/ Shan't want to be seen there.' (22)

Latterly, however, Claverton seems to be increasingly taken over by the voices that have always come to him 'between waking and sleeping'. (88) He seems increasingly to dwell in that time and mental space which is always, with Eliot, when the most terrifying and vivid rendition of the 'planes' of reality, 'between two worlds', recurs. Claverton dismisses the notion of Mrs Carghill and Gomez; 'they are not real', they are 'spectres' who have 'always been with me'; yet now, paradoxically, nearing death:

> I see myself emerging
> From the spectral existence into something like reality. (85)

He reconciles himself with his feckless son, Michael, who is to be whisked away to Gomez's dubious colonial business world, and affirms his father's love once more to Monica, and gives it more truly, having stepped out of his role at last. Eliot had great difficulty in conveying Claverton's death, which, according to the Greek

---

[41] Eliot, 'The Preacher as Artist', *The Athenaeum*, no. 4674, 28 November 1919, 1252.

convention, was to occur offstage. Before settling for implying it, as now happens in the brief final exchange between Charles and Monica in the printed text, one earlier version had tried out a reimagining of the Voice that the messenger in Eliot's main source, *Oedipus at Colonus*, reports hearing at the hero's death. In that previous version, impractical in the theatre and, so, rejected, the Voice gives a statement which seems true of Eliot's haunted poetic across his life, animated as it is by the selves and strains from the past, and which lays it to temporary rest:

> I am alone at last, yet always with you.
> I have found the place of my destiny and purpose
> To die in.[42]

This study has followed the changes and renegotiations in Eliot's engagement across his writing career with his favourite earlier literary period, the Early Modern. By comprehensively analyzing the poems and plays that fascinated him, in the editions through which he knew them, and by considering the critical commentaries from nineteenth to early twentieth-century writers and poets he himself read and responded to in print, this book has uncovered a more nuanced version of the Early Modern in his work than has hitherto been possible. The book has illuminated some of the familiar metaphors from the earlier period commonly derived from, and applied to, Eliot's work, such as 'metaphysical', 'wit', and 'planes in relation'. It has also revealed lesser known terms, such as 'cryptogram', the form of decoding that might unlock the connections between allusions and Early Modern textual contexts, from which Eliot created his ever surprising, self-consciously modern poetry.

Out of this discussion has evolved a broader sense of the distinctive nature and parameters of the Early Modern as Eliot conceived it. The Eliot who has emerged is a less clinical, impersonal, or classical writer than he is usually presumed to have been. Common themes have surfaced: about loss and mourning; untimeliness and unseasonableness; the intimate alliance of the moral and virtuous with the sinful, or with hell or damnation. Eliot's need for historical understanding in his thought and practice is enlivened, through his engagement with the Early Modern, by a perhaps surprising attention to the historical abuse of women, and the figuring of historical suffering through those means. Eliot's concerted attention to technique became a form of imaginative possibilities, enabling him to echo and create new voices. His perception of the alliance between Early Modern dramatic speech and *vers libre* was part of that amalgamation of the lyric and the dramatic, otherwise understood through Eliot's knowledge of the work of John Donne, and of the critical tradition surrounding him. This study has also broadened that sense of the dissociated (or 'dissolving') self radiating from Eliot's poems and plays, by revealing that his sources projected that version of the self also as a means to vigilance, greater philosophical awareness, but primarily as the basis for imaginative scope. We have observed that doubling has a practical application, as have the theatrical metaphors applied to the performance of the self; yet doubling also has an ontological

---

[42] Cited by Browne, *The Making of T.S. Eliot's Plays*, 336.

purpose, which can work, for instance, to dramatize the historical moment at which the movement from Stoicism to Christianity affected particular lives and inflected the voices of specific characters.

Eliot's own work, his essays and poetry, acted as a bridge between the Early Modern and the modern age; they opened that period up for other modernist writers to exploit. Primarily, Eliot established a definitive version of the Early Modern as a lens through which the devastated world of the 1920s to 1940s, and the alienation felt in later periods, might be read. Because of the lack of rigidity, the constant re-readings and re-nuancings, in his account, and the exciting mediation performed by his poetry and drama, the Early Modern, in his wake, became a constant recourse for educators, but, thrillingly and unarguably, for subsequent male and female playwrights, novelists, and poets.

Bibliography

ARCHIVES

'Ash-Wednesday' materials, Hayward Bequest, King's College, Cambridge, MS V6.

Letter to G. Wilson Knight, of 30 December 1930, Brotherton Library, Leeds, MS 20c Knight 2(K).

'Marina' materials, Bodleian Library, Oxford, MS don C 23/1–3 (x. ii, 100).

Materials for *The Rock*, Bodleian Library, Oxford, MS don d. 44, 99.

Materials relating to *The Cocktail Party*, Houghton Library, Harvard, MS Am. 1691.7 (67), Folder Three and Folder Four.

Notes from broadcast on 18 December 1957 at the BBC Written Archives Centre, Caversham, file 48114.

Partial inventory by Vivien Eliot of Eliot's library (information about), Bodleian Library, Oxford, MS Eng. Lett B 20.

'Typescript A' of *The Family Reunion*, Houghton Library, Harvard, MS Am. 1691.14 (37), 33.

'Typescript B' of *The Family Reunion*, Houghton Library, Harvard, MS Am. 1691. 14 (39) 68.

Typescript of *Sweeney Agonistes*, Hayward Bequest, King's College, Cambridge, Hb/V/7A.

PRINTED WORKS BY T.S. ELIOT, IN CHRONOLOGICAL ORDER

'Eeldrop and Appleplex', *The Little Review*, vol. IV, no. 1, May 1917, 7–11, Tunbridge Wells: The Foundling Press, 1992.

'The Noh and the Image', *The Egoist*, vol. IV, no. 7, August 1917, 102–3.

'Reflections on Contemporary Poetry I', *The Egoist*, vol. IV, no. 8, September 1917, 118–9.

'Studies in Contemporary Criticism', *The Egoist*, vol. V, no. 10, November–December 1918, 131–3.

'The New Elizabethans and the Old', *The Athenaeum*, no. 4640, 4 April 1919, 134–6.

'Beyle and Balzac', *The Athenaeum*, no. 464, 30 May 1919, 392–3.

'Reflections on Contemporary Poetry', *The Egoist*, vol. VI, no. 3, July 1919, 39–40.

'Hamlet and his Problems', *The Nation and Athenaeum*, no. 4665, 26 September 1919, 940–1.

'The Preacher as Artist', *The Athenaeum*, no. 4674, 28 November 1919, 1,252–3.

'The Old Comedy', *Athenaeum*, no. 4702, 11 June 1920, 760–1.

'Andrew Marvell', *TLS*, no. 1002, 31 March 1921, 201–2.

'John Dryden', *TLS* no. 1012, 9 June 1921, 361–2.

'Dramatis Personae', *The Criterion*, vol. I, no. 3, April 1923, 303–6.

'John Donne', *The Nation and Athenaeum*, no. XXXIII, 10 June 1923, 331–2.

'Andrew Marvell', *The Nation and Athenaeum*, vol. xxxiii, no. 26, 29 September 1923, 809.

'The Beating of a Drum', *The Nation and Athenaeum*, vol. XXXIV, no. 1, 6 October 1923, 11–12.

Homage to John Dryden: Three Essays on Poetry of the Seventeenth Century, London: Hogarth Press, 1924.

'Introduction', *Le Serpent par Paul Valéry*, trans. Mark Wardle, published for the *Criterion*, London: R. Cobden-Sanderson, 1924.

'A Popular Shakespeare', *TLS*, no. 1255, 4 February 1925, 76.

'An Italian Critic on Donne and Crashaw', *TLS*, no. 1248, 17 December 1925, 878.

'Shakespeare and Montaigne', *TLS*, no. 1249, 24 December 1925, 895.

'Wanley and Chapman', *TLS*, no. 1250, 31 December 1925, 907.

'Introduction', Charlotte Eliot, *Savonarola: A Dramatic Poem*, London: R. Cobden-Sanderson, 1926.

'Philip Massinger', *TLS*, no. 958, 27 May 1926, 325–6.

'The Author of the "Burning Babe"', *TLS*, no. 1278, 29 July 1926, 508.

'Plague Pamphlets', *TLS*, no. 1279, 5 August 1926, 522.

'Hooker, Hobbes and Others', *TLS*, no. 1293, 11 November 1926, 789.

'Massinger', *TLS*, 18 November 1926, 1,294.

'Sir John Davies', *TLS*, no. 1297, 9 December 1926, 906.

'The Sources of Chapman', *TLS*, no. 1306, 10 February 1927, 88.

'The Problems of the Shakespeare Sonnets', *The Nation and Athenaeum*, vol. XL, no. 19, 12 February 1927, 664–6.

'A Study of Marlowe', *TLS*, no. 1309, 3 March 1927, 140.

'Plays of Ben Jonson', *TLS*, no. 1329, 21 July 1927, 500.

'The Silurist', *The Dial*, September 1927, 259–63.

'Stage Studies', *TLS*, no. 1349, 8 December 1927, 927.

'Introduction', *Seneca His Tenne Tragedies Translated into English Edited by Thomas Newton Anno 1581*, London: Constable 1927.

The Sacred Wood: Essays on Poetry and Criticism, London: Faber, 1928 edition with Preface; 1997.

For Lancelot Andrewes, London: Faber, 1928; 1970 edition.

Not in Gallup, Preface of 1928 to Charles Claye's 'The Merry Masque of Our Lady in London Town' 'produced by Perpetua Press, Oxford to accompany the exhibition of Stanley Revell's Eliot collection in the University Church of St. Mary the Virgin in May 1988'.

'John Webster', *TLS*, no. 1356, 26 January 1928, 136.

'Poet's Borrowings', *TLS*, no. 1366, 5 April 1928, 255.

'*The Complete Works of John Webster*, ed. F.L. Lucas', *The Criterion*, vol. VII, no. IV, June 1928, 155–8.

'Elizabeth and Essex', *TLS*, no. 1401, 6 December 1928, 959.

'Introduction to Ezra Pound', *Selected Poems*, London: Faber and Gwyer, 1928.

Of Dramatick Poesie An Essay 1668 by John Dryden. Preceded by a Dialogue on Poetic Drama by T.S. Eliot, London: Frederick Etchells and Hugh MacDonald, 1928.

'The Genesis of Philosophic Prose. Bacon and Hooker', *The Listener*, no. 4674, 26 June 1929, 907–8.

'The Prose of the Preacher: The Sermons of Donne', *The Listener*, vol. II, no. 25, 3 July 1929, 22–3.

'A Game at Chesse', *TLS*, no 1460, 23 January 1930, 56.

'Thinking in Verse: A Survey of Early Seventeenth-Century Poetry', *The Listener*, vol. III, no. 61, 12 March 1930, 441–3.

'Rhyme and Reason: The Poetry of John Donne', *The Listener*, vol. III, no. 62, 19 March 1930, 502–3.

'The Devotional Poets of the Seventeenth Century: Donne, Herbert, Crashaw', *The Listener*, vol. III, no. 63, 26 March 1930, 552–3.

'Mystic and Politician as Poet: Vaughan, Traherne, Marvell, Milton', *The Listener*, vol. III, no. 64, 2 April 1930, 590–1.

'The Minor Metaphysicals: From Cowley to Dryden', *The Listener*, vol. III, no. 65, 9 April 1930, 641–2.

'Preface', *Anabasis*, London: Faber, 1931; 1959 edition.

John Dryden I, 'The Poet who Gave the English Speech', *The Listener*, vol. V, no. 118, 15 April 1931, 621–2.

John Dryden II, 'Dryden the Dramatist', *Listener*, vol. V, no. 119, 22 April 1931, 681–2.

John Dryden III, 'Dryden the Critic, Defender of Sanity', *Listener*, vol. V, no. 120, 29 April 1931, 724–5.

'Donne in our Time', *A Garland for John Donne 1631–1931*, ed. Theodore Spencer, Cambridge, MA: Harvard University Press, 1931.

'George Herbert', *The Spectator*, no. 5, 411, 12 March 1932, 360–1.

The Use of Poetry and the Use of Criticism, London: Faber, 1933; 1967 edition.

Selected Essays, London: Faber, 1934; 1972 edition.

The Rock: Book of Words, New York: Harcourt Brace and Company, 1934.

'The Need for Poetic Drama: A Schools Broadcast to Sixth Forms …', *The Listener*, vol. XVI, no. 411, 25 November 1936, 1–6.

Religious Drama: Medieval and Modern, New York: House of Books Ltd, 1937; 1954 reprint.

'The Lion and the Fox', *Twentieth-Century Verse*, 6–7 November/December 1937, 6–9.

'A Note on Two Odes of Cowley', *Seventeenth-Century Studies Presented to Sir Herbert Grierson*, ed. John Dover Wilson, Oxford: Clarendon Press, 1938.

The Family Reunion, London: Faber, 1939.

'Introduction', *A Choice of Kipling's Verse*, London: Faber, 1941.

'The Duchess of Malfy', *The Listener*, vol. XXVI, no. 675, 18 December 1941, 825–6.

'Introduction', *Introducing James Joyce*, London: Faber, 1942.

'John Dryden's Tragedies', *The Listener*, vol. XXIX, no. 745, 22 April 1943, 486–7.

'Introduction', *Shakespeare and the Popular Dramatic Tradition*, by S.L. Bethell, London: P.S. King and Staples, 1944.

'Shakespearean Criticism I From Dryden to Coleridge', *A Companion to Shakespeare Studies*, ed. Harley Granville-Barker and G.B. Harrison, Cambridge: Cambridge University Press, 1946.

The Cocktail Party, London: Faber, 1950.

'Foreword', *Shakespeare and the Elizabethans* by Henri Fluchere, New York: Hill and Wang, Inc., 1953; 1959 edition.

The Confidential Clerk, London: Faber, 1954.

'Introduction', *Literary Essays of Ezra Pound*, London: Faber, 1954.

On Poetry and Poets, London: Faber, 1957.

George Herbert, Plymouth: Northcote House, 1962; 1992 edition.

Murder in the Cathedral, with an introduction and notes by Neville Coghill, London: Faber, 1965.

To Criticize the Critic and other writings, London: Faber, 1965; 1988 edition.

The Complete Poems and Plays of T.S. Eliot, London: Faber, 1969; 1978 edition.

The Waste Land: a facsimile and transcript, ed. Valerie Eliot, London: Faber, 1971.

The Selected Prose of T.S. Eliot, ed. Frank Kermode, London: Faber, 1975.

The Varieties of Metaphysical Poetry, ed. and intro. Ronald Schuchard, London: Faber, 1993.

Inventions of the March Hare: Poems 1909–1917, ed. Christopher Ricks, London: Faber, 1996.

The Letters of T.S. Eliot, Volume I, 1898–1922 Revised Edition, ed. Valerie Eliot and Hugh Haughton, London: Faber, 2009.

The Letters of T.S. Eliot, Volume II, 1923–1925, ed. Valerie Eliot and Hugh Haughton, London: Faber, 2009.

PRINTED WORKS BY OTHERS

Ackroyd, Peter, *T.S. Eliot*, London: Abacus, 1985.

Aitken, G.A., ed., *The Poems of Andrew Marvell, Sometime Member of Parliament for Hull*, London: Lawrence & Bullen: New York: Charles Scribner's Sons, 1892.

Allen, Percy, *Shakespeare, Jonson, and Wilkins as Borrowers: A Study in Elizabethan Dramatic Origins and Imitations*, London: Cecil Palmer, 1928.

Andrewes, Lancelot, *Selected Writings*, ed. P.E. Hewison, Manchester: Carcanet, 1995.

—— *Seventeen Sermons on the Nativity*, London: Griffith, Farran, Okeden & Welsh, n.d.

Archer, William, *The Old Drama and the New: A Re-Valuation*, London: William Heinemann, 1923.

Badenhausen, Richard, *T.S. Eliot and the Art of Collaboration*, Cambridge: Cambridge University Press, 2004.

Baker, George P., ed., *Select Plays by Beaumont and Fletcher*, London: Dent, 1907.

—— *The Development of Shakespeare as a Dramatist*, New York: Macmillan, 1907.

Banks, Joanne Trautmann, ed., 'Some New Woolf Letters', *Modern Fiction Studies*, vol. 30, no. 2, Summer 1984, 154–8.

Beeching, Canon, *The Poems of Henry Vaughan, Silurist*, 2 vols., London: George Routledge, 1905.

—— ed., *Sermons by Hugh Latimer Sometime Bishop of Worcester*, London: J.M. Dent, 1906.

Bergonzi, Bernard, *T.S. Eliot*, New York: Macmillan, 1972.

Bethell, S.L., *Shakespeare and the Popular Dramatic Tradition*, London: P.S. King and Staples, 1944.

Boas, Frederick S., ed., *Bussy d'Ambois and the Revenge*, Boston: D.C. Heath, 1905.

Bradley, A.C., *Shakespearean Tragedy: Lectures on Hamlet, Othello, King Lear, Macbeth*, London: Macmillan, 1904.

Bradley, F.H., *Appearance and Reality: A Metaphysical Essay*, London: George Unwin, 1916.

Brightman, F.E., ed., *The Preces Privatae of Lancelot Andrewes*, London: Methuen, 1903.

Brooke, C.F. Tucker, ed., *The Shakespeare Apocrypha*, Oxford: Clarendon Press, 1908.

Brooke, Rupert, *John Webster and the Elizabethan Drama*, London: Sidgwick and Jackson, 1916.

Brooker, Jewel Spears, *Mastery and Escape: T.S. Eliot and the Dialectic of Modernism*, Amherst, MA: University of Massachusetts Press, 1994.

—— ed., *T.S. Eliot and Our Turning World*, Basingstoke: Macmillan, 2001.

Brooks, Cleanth, *Modern Poetry and the Tradition*, Chapel Hill: University of North Carolina Press, 1939.

Browne, E. Martin, *The Making of T.S. Eliot's Plays*, Cambridge: Cambridge University Press, 1969.

Bullen, J.B., *The Myth of the Renaissance in Nineteenth-Century Writing*, Oxford: Clarendon Press, 1994.

Burrage, Champlin, *The True Story of Robert Browne (1550?–1633) Father of Congregationalism*, London: Henry Froude, 1906.

Busby, Olive Mary, *Studies in the Development of the Fool in the Elizabethan Drama*, London: Oxford University Press, 1923.

Bush, Ronald, *T.S. Eliot: A Study in Character and Style*, New York: Oxford University Press, 1983.

—— ed., *T.S. Eliot: The Modernist in History*, Cambridge: Cambridge University Press, 1991.

Chambers, E.K., ed., *Poems of John Donne*, New York: Charles Scribners' Sons, 1896.

Chelli, Maurice, *Etude sur la Collaboration de Massinger avec Fletcher et son Groupe*, Paris: Les Presses Universitaires de France, 1926.

Childs, Donald J., *T.S. Eliot: Mystic, Son and Lover*, London: Athlone Press, 1997.

Chinitz, David, *T.S. Eliot and the Cultural Divide*, Chicago: University of Chicago Press, 2003.

Clark, Arthur Melville, *Thomas Heywood: Playwright and Miscellanist*, Oxford: Basil Blackwell, 1931.

Coleridge, Samuel Taylor, *Essays and Lectures on Shakespeare and Some Other Old Dramatists*, London: Dent, 1907.

Corcoran, Neil, *Shakespeare and the Modern Poet*, Cambridge: Cambridge University Press, 2010.

Crashaw, Richard, *The Poems English Latin and Greek*, ed. L.C. Martin, Oxford: Clarendon Press, 1927.

Crawford, Robert, *The Savage and the City in the Work of T.S. Eliot*, Oxford: Clarendon Press, 1987.

Cruickshank, A.H., *Philip Massinger*, Oxford: Basil Blackwell, 1920.

Cunliffe, John W., *The Influence of Seneca on Elizabethan Tragedy: An Essay*, New York: G.E. Stechert & Co., 1925.

Davies, Rupert Brookes, ed., *Silver Poems of the Sixteenth Century*, London: Dent, 1992.

Dekkers, Odin, *J.M. Robertson: Rationalist and Literary Critic*, Aldershot: Ashgate, 1998.

Donne, John, *Devotions Upon Emergent Occasions, together with Death's Duell*, Ann Arbor, MI: University of Michigan Press, 1959.

Donoghue, Denis, 'Eliot's "Marina" and Closure', *The Hudson Review*, vol. 49, no. 3, Autumn 1996, 367–8.

—— *Walter Pater*, New York: Alfred. A. Knopf, 1995.

Eliot, George, *Romola*, Harmondsworth: Penguin, 1996.

Ellis, Havelock, ed., *Christopher Marlowe*, London: Vizetelly, 1887.

—— ed., *John Ford*, London: Vizetelly, 1888.

—— ed., *Thomas Middleton*, 2 vols., London: Vizetelly, 1887.

Ellis-Fermor, U.M., *Christopher Marlowe*, London: Methuen, 1927.

—— *The Frontiers of Drama*, London: Methuen, 1945.

Ellmann, Maud, *The Poetics of Impersonality: T.S. Eliot and Ezra Pound*, Brighton: Harvester, 1987.

Elyot, Sir Thomas, *The boke named the Governour*, intro. Foster Watson, London: Dent, 1907.

Fox, Alice, *Virginia Woolf and the Literature of the English Renaissance*, Oxford: Clarendon Press, 1990.

Freed, Lewis, *T.S. Eliot: The Critic as Philosopher*, West Lafayette, IN: Purdue University Press, 1979.

Froude, James Anthony, *The Reign of Elizabeth* (1858), London: J.M. Dent, Everyman Edition, 1912.

Frye, Northrop, *T.S. Eliot*, Edinburgh: Oliver and Boyd, 1963.

Gardner, Helen, *The Art of T.S. Eliot*, London: Faber, 1949; 1968 edition.

—— *The Composition of Four Quartets*, London: Faber, 1978.

Goldie, David, *A Critical Difference: T.S. Eliot and John Middleton Murry in English Literary Criticism 1919–1928*, Oxford: Clarendon Press, 1998.

Golding, Arthur, trans., *Ovid's Metamorphoses*, ed. Madeleine Forey, Penguin: Harmondsworth, 2002.

Gollancz, Israel, ed., *Shakespeare's Comedy of A Winter's Tale*, London: J.M. Dent, Temple Edition, 1894.

—— ed., *Shakespeare's Comedy of Measure for Measure*, London: J.M. Dent, Temple Edition, 1894.

—— ed., *Shakespeare's Comedy of The Tempest*, London: J.M. Dent, 1894.

—— ed., *Shakespeare's Tragedy of Hamlet*, London: J.M. Dent, 1895.

—— ed., *Shakespeare's Tragedy of Coriolanus*, London: J.M. Dent, 1896.

—— ed., *Shakespeare's Tragedy of Pericles*, London: J.M. Dent, 1896.

—— ed., *Shakespeare's Troilus and Cressida*, London: J.M. Dent, 1896.

—— ed., *Shakespeare's Tragedy of Antony and Cleopatra*, London: J.M. Dent, 1897.

Gordon, Lyndall, *Eliot's New Life*, Oxford: Oxford University Press, 1988.

—— *T.S. Eliot: An Imperfect Life*, New York: W.W. Norton, 1998.

Gosse, Edmund, *The Jacobean Poets*, London: John Murray, 1894.

—— *The Life and Letters of John Donne*, 2 vols., London: William Heinemann, 1899.

Grady, Hugh, *The Modernist Shakespeare*, Oxford: Clarendon Press, 1991.

Gray, Piers, *T.S. Eliot's Intellectual and Poetic Development 1909–1922*, Brighton: Harvester, 1982.

Green, Edward J.H., *T.S. Eliot et la France*, Paris: Editions Contemporains, 1951.

Grierson, Herbert J.C., ed., *Metaphysical Lyrics and Poems of the Seventeenth Century*, Oxford: Clarendon Press, 1921.

—— ed., *The Poems of John Donne*, 2 vols., Oxford: Oxford University Press, 1912.

Grosskurth, Phyllis, *Havelock Ellis: A Biography*, London: Quartet Books, 1980.

Haffenden, John, 'Vivien Eliot and *The Waste Land*: The Forgotten Fragments', *PN Review*, 175, vol. 33, no. 5, May–June 2007, 18–23.

Halpern, Richard, 'Shakespeare in the Tropics: From High Modernism to New Historicism', *Representations*, 45, Winter 1994, 1–25.

Harding, Jason, ed., *T.S. Eliot in Context*, Cambridge: Cambridge University Press, 2011.

Haskin, Dayton, *John Donne in the Nineteenth Century*, Oxford: Oxford University Press, 2007.

Hawkes, Terence, *Meaning By Shakespeare*, London: Routledge, 1992.

Hay, Eloise Knapp, *T.S. Eliot's Negative Way*, Cambridge, MA: Harvard University Press, 1982.

Hearnshaw, F.J.C., ed., *Social and Political Ideas of the Sixteenth and Seventeenth Centuries*, London: George Harrap, 1926.

Herford, C.H., ed., *The Religio Medici and Other Writings of Sir Thomas Browne*, London: Dent, 1912.

Hood, Christobel M., *The Book of Robert Southwell, Priest, Poet, Prisoner*, Oxford: Basil Blackwell, 1926.

Hooker, Richard, *Of the Laws of Ecclesiastical Polity*, Book V, ed. Ronald Boyce, London: J.M. Dent, 1907.

Howarth, Herbert, *Notes on Some Figures Behind T.S. Eliot*, London: Chatto and Windus, 1965.

Hudson, W.H., ed., *John Dryden: Essays*, London: Dent, 1912.

Hudston, Jonathan, ed., *George Chapman: Plays and Poems*. Harmondsworth: Penguin, 1998.

Hunter, G.K., *Dramatic Identities and Cultural Tradition: Studies in Shakespeare and his Contemporaries*, Liverpool: Liverpool University Press, 1978.

Johnson, Samuel, *Lives of the Most Eminent English Poets*, London: Frederick Warne & Co.: New York: Scribner, Welford and Armstrong, 1872.

Kenner, Hugh, *The Invisible Poet: T.S. Eliot*, London: Methuen, 1960.

Ker, W.P., *Form and Style in Poetry*, ed. R.W. Chambers, London: Macmillan, 1928.

Knight, G. Wilson, *The Imperial Theme: Further Interpretations of Shakespeare's Tragedies including the Roman Plays*, London: Oxford University Press, 1931.

—— *The Shakespearean Tempest*: London: Oxford University Press, 1932.

—— *The Wheel of Fire*, London: Oxford University Press, 1930.

Laity, Cassandra and Gish, Nancy K., eds., *Gender, Desire, and Sexuality in T.S. Eliot*, Cambridge: Cambridge University Press, 2004.

Lamb, Charles, *Specimens of English Dramatic Poets*, London: Routledge, 1927.

Lawrence, W.J., *Pre-Restoration Stage Studies*, Cambridge, MA: Harvard University Press, 1927.

—— *The Physical Conditions of the Elizabethan Public Playhouse*, Cambridge, MA: Harvard University Press, 1927.

Lewis, Wyndham, *The Lion and the Fox: The Role of the Hero in the Plays of Shakespeare*, London: Grant Richards, 1927.

Lucas, F.L., *Seneca and Elizabethan Tragedy*, Cambridge: Cambridge University Press, 1922.

—— *The Complete Works of John Webster*, London: Chatto and Windus, 1928.

Lynch, Kathleen M., *The Social Mode of Restoration Comedy*, London: Macmillan, 1926.

Manganiello, Dominic, *T.S. Eliot and Dante*, Basingstoke: Houndmills, 1989.

Marston, John, *The Works of John Marston*, 2 vols., ed. A.H. Bullen, London: John C. Nimmo, 1887.

Martin, Graham, ed., *Eliot in Perspective: A Symposium*, London: Macmillan, 1970.

Mathiessen, F.O., *The Achievement of T.S. Eliot: An Essay on the Nature of Poetry*, New York: Oxford University Press, Third Edition, 1959.

Mayer, John T., *T.S. Eliot's Silent Voices*, New York: Oxford University Press, 1989.

McGrath, F.C., *The Sensible Spirit: Walter Pater and the Modernist Paradigm*, Tampa: University of Southern Florida Press, 1986.

McIntire, Gabrielle, *Modernism, Memory, and Desire: T.S. Eliot and Virginia Woolf*, Cambridge: Cambridge University Press, 2008.

Menand, Louis, *Discovering Modernism: T.S. Eliot and His Context*, New York: Oxford University Press, Second Edition, 1987.

Miller, James E., *T.S. Eliot: The Making of an American Poet 1888–1922*, Pennsylvania: University of Pennsylvania Press, 2005.

Moody, A. David, *Ezra Pound: Poet. A Portrait of the Man and his Work. The Young Genius 1885–1920*, Oxford: Oxford University Press, 2007.

—— *Thomas Stearns Eliot: Poet*, Cambridge: Cambridge University Press, Second Edition, 1994.

Murry, John Middleton, *Countries of the Mind: Essays in Literary Criticism*, London: Collins, 1922.

—— *Discoveries: Essays in Literary Criticism*, London: Collins, 1924.

—— 'Our Inaccessible Heritage', *The Nation and Athenaeum*, no. 4654, 11 July 1919, 581–2.

Nicholson, Brinsley, ed., *Ben Jonson*, London: T. Fisher Unwin, 1893.

Pater, Walter, *Appreciations: With an Essay on Style*, London: Macmillan, 1910.

—— *Marius the Epicurean: His Sensations and Ideas*, vol. II, London: Macmillan, 1910.

—— *Studies in the History of the Renaissance*, London: Macmillan, 1873.

Patterson, Gertrude, *T.S. Eliot: Poems in the Making*, Manchester: Manchester University Press, 1971.

Perl, Jeffrey M., *Skepticism and Modern Enmity: Before and After Eliot*, Baltimore: Johns Hopkins University Press, 1989.

Phelps, William Lyon, ed., *The Plays of George Chapman*, New York: Charles Scribner's Sons, 1895.

Pietro, Carly di, *Shakespeare and Modernism*, Cambridge: Cambridge University Press, 2006.

Poe, Edgar Allan, *The Complete Tales and Poems of Edgar Allan Poe*, Harmondsworth: Penguin, 1965.

Poel, William, *Shakespeare in the Theatre*, London: Sidgwick and Jackson, 1913.

—— *What is Wrong with the Stage*, London: George Allen, 1920.

Potter, George R., and Simpson, Evelyn M., eds., *The Sermons of John Donne*, Berkeley: University of California Press, 1957.

Pound, Ezra, *ABC of Reading*, London: Faber, 1951.

—— *A Memoir of Gaudier-Brzeska*, New York: New Directions, 1970.

—— *Selected Prose 1909–1965*, ed. William Cookson, London: Faber, 1973.

—— *The Translations of Ezra Pound*, London: Faber, 1943.

Praz, Mario, *The Flaming Heart*, New York: Norton, 1958.

Pritchard, William H., 'Reading *The Waste Land* Today', *Essays in Criticism*, vol. XIX, no. 2, April 1969, 176–92.

Rainey, Lawrence, *Revisiting The Waste Land*, New Haven and London: Yale University Press, 2005.

Ramsay, Mary Paton, *Les Doctrines médiévales chez Donne, le poète metaphysicien de l'Angleterre (1573–1631)*, London: Oxford University Press, 1917; 1924 second edition.

Read, Herbert, *Reason and Romanticism: Essays in Literary Criticism*, London: Faber and Gwyer, 1926.

—— *T.S.E.: A Memoir*, Middletown, CT: Wesleyan University Press, 1971.

Rhys, Ernest, ed., *Everyman and Other Interludes*, London: Dent, 1909.

Ricks, Christopher, *The Force of Poetry*, Oxford: Oxford University Press, 1984.

Robertson, J.M., *Elizabethan Literature*, London: Williams and Norgate, 1914.

—— *'Hamlet' Once More*, London: Richard Cobden-Sanderson, 1922.

—— *Shakespeare and Chapman: A Thesis of Chapman's Authorship of 'A Lover's Complaint' and his Origination of 'Timon of Athens' with indications of further problems*, London: T. Fisher Unwin, 1917.

—— 'The Evolution of Blank Verse', *The Criterion*, vol. II, no. 6, February 1924, 176–88.

—— *The Problem of 'Hamlet'*, London: George Allen & Unwin, 1919.

—— *The Problems of the Shakespeare Sonnets*, London: Routledge, 1926.

—— 'The Scansion of Shakespeare', *The Criterion*, vol. VIII, no. xxxiii, July 1929, 638–54.

Saintsbury, George, *A History of Elizabethan Literature*, London: Macmillan, 1907.

Schelling, Felix E., ed., Ben Jonson, *Complete Plays*, 2 vols., London: Dent, 1910.

—— *Elizabethan Drama 1558–1642*, 2 vols., Boston: Houghton, Mifflin, and Co., 1908.

Schoell, Franck L., *Études sur l'Humanisme Continental en Angleterre à la Fin de la Renaissance*, Paris: Librarie Ancienne Honoré Champion, 1926.

Schofield, Martin, 'Poetry's Sea-Changes: T.S. Eliot and *The Tempest*', *Shakespeare Survey*, 43, ed. Stanley Wells, 1990, 37–42.

Schuchard, Ronald, *Eliot's Dark Angel: Intersections of Life and Art*, New York: Oxford University Press, 1999.

Seccombe, Thomas, and Allen, J.W., *The Age of Shakespeare (1579–1631)*, 3 vols., London: G. Bell & Sons 1903; 1914 edition.

Sencourt, Robert, *T.S. Eliot: A Memoir*, ed. Donald Adamson, London: Garnstone Press, 1971.

Sidnell, Michael J., *Dances of Death: The Group Theatre of London in the Thirties*, London: Faber, 1984.

Sigg, Eric, *The American T.S. Eliot*, Cambridge: Cambridge University Press, 1989.

Smith, Carol H., *T.S. Eliot's Dramatic Theory and Practice*, Princeton: Princeton University Press, 1963.

Smith, David Nicholl, *Dryden's Poetry and Prose*, Oxford: Clarendon Press, 1925.

Smith, G. Gregory, *Ben Jonson*, London: Macmillan, 1919.

Smith, Grover, *T.S. Eliot's Poetry and Plays: A Study in Sources and Meaning*, Chicago: University of Chicago Press, Second Edition, 1974.

Smith, Logan Pearsall, *Donne's Sermons: Selected Passages*, Oxford: Oxford University Press, 1919.

Soldo, John J., *The Tempering of T.S. Eliot*, Epping: Bowker, 1983.

Southam, B.C., *A Student's Guide to the Selected Poems of T.S. Eliot*, London: Faber, 1994.

Sparrow-Simpson, W.J., *Archbishop Bramhall*, London: Society for Promoting Christian Knowledge, 1927.

Spencer, Theodore, 'John Marston', *The Criterion*, vol. III, no. LIII, July 1934, 582–93.

Spender, Stephen, *Eliot*, London: Fontana, 1975.

Spens, Janet, 'Chapman's Ethical Thought', *Essays and Studies by Members of the English Association*, vol. XI, ed. Oliver Elton, Oxford: Clarendon Press, 1925.

Spingarn, J.E., *A History of Literary Criticism in the Renaissance*, London: Macmillan 1899; 1908 Second Edition.

Spurr, David, *Conflicts in Consciousness: T.S. Eliot's Poetry and Criticism*, Chicago: University of Illinois Press, 1994.

Still, Colin, *Shakespeare's Mystery Play: A Study of The Tempest*, London: Cecil Palmer, 1921.

Stoll, E.E., *Hamlet: An Historical and Comparative Study*, Minneapolis: University of Minneapolis Press, 1919.

Strachey, J. St. Loe, ed., *The Best Plays of Beaumont and Fletcher*, 2 vols., London: T. Fisher Unwin, 1893.

Strachey, Lytton, *Elizabeth and Essex: A Tragic History*, Harmondsworth: Penguin, 1971.

Stubbs, John, *Donne*, London: Viking, 2006.

Swinburne, A.C., *Contemporaries of Shakespeare*, ed. Edmund Gosse and Thomas James Wise, London: Heinemann, 1919.

—— *Prose Works*, vol. II, ed. Edmund Gosse and Thomas James Wise, London: Heinemann, 1926.

—— *The Age of Shakespeare*, London: Chatto and Windus, 1908.

Sykes, Norman Dugdale, *Sidelights on Shakespeare: Studies of Two Noble Kinsmen and Other Plays*, Stratford-upon-Avon: The Shakespeare Head Press, 1919.

Symonds, John Addington, *Shakespere's Predecessors in the English Drama*, London: Smith Elder, 1884, reprinted 1920.

—— ed., *Webster and Tourneur*, London: Vizetelly, 1888.

Tate, Allen, ed., *T.S. Eliot: The Man and his Work*, London: Penguin, 1971.

Taylor, Gary, 'Lives and Afterlives', in Thomas Middleton, *The Collected Works*, Oxford: Clarendon Press, 2007.

—— *Reinventing Shakespeare: A Cultural History from the Restoration to the Present*, London: Vintage, 1988.

Thomas, Edward, ed., *Christopher Marlowe: Plays*, London: Dent, 1909.

Thorndike, Ashley, ed., *The Minor Elizabethan Drama*, 2 vols., London: J.M. Dent, 1910.

Van Doren, Mark, *John Dryden: A Study of His Poetry*, New York: Harcourt, Brace and Howe, 1920.

Verity, A. Wilson, *Thomas Heywood*, London: T. Fisher Unwin, 1888.

Waddington, Raymond B., *The Mind's Empire: Myth and Form in George Chapman's Narrative Poems*, Baltimore: Johns Hopkins University Press, 1974.

Waugh, Arthur, ed., *The Poems of George Herbert*, London: Oxford University Press, 1907.

Williamson, George, *The Donne Tradition: A Study in English Poetry from Donne to the Death of Cowley*, Cambridge, MA: Harvard University Press, 1930.

Williamson, Hugh Ross, *The Poetry of T.S. Eliot*, London: Hodder and Stoughton, 1932.

Wood, H. Harvey, ed., *The Plays of John Marston in Three Volumes*, vol. I, Edinburgh: Oliver and Boyd, 1934.

Yeats, W.B., *Essays and Introductions*, London: Macmillan, 1989.

Index